True Stories of Crime in Modern Mexico

Other titles on Latin America available from the University of New Mexico Press:

Independence in Spanish America: Civil Wars, Revolutions, and Underdevelopment (revised edition)
—Jay Kinsbruner

Heroes on Horseback: A Life and Times of the Last Gaucho Caudillos
—John Charles Chasteen

The Life and Death of Carolina Maria de Jesus
—Robert M. Levine and José Carlos Sebe Bom Meihy

¡Que vivan los tamales! Food and the Making of Mexican Identity
—Jeffrey M. Pilcher

The Faces of Honor: Sex, Shame, and Violence in Colonial Latin America
—Edited by Lyman L. Johnson and Sonya Lipsett-Rivera

The Century of U.S. Capitalism in Latin America
—Thomas F. O'Brien

Tangled Destinies: Latin America and the United States
—Don Coerver and Linda Hall

Everyday Life and Politics in Nineteenth Century Mexico: Men, Women, and War
—Mark Wasserman

Lives of the Bigamists: Marriage, Family, and Community in Colonial Mexico
—Richard Boyer

Andean Worlds: Indigenous History, Culture, and Consciousness Under Spanish Rule, 1532–1825
—Kenneth J. Andrien

The Mexican Revolution, 1910–1940
—Michael J. Gonzales

Quito 1599: City and Colony in Transition
—Kris Lane

Argentina on the Couch: Psychiatry, State, and Society, 1880 to the Present
—Edited by Mariano Plotkin

A Pest in the Land: New World Epidemics in a Global Perspective
—Suzanne Austin Alchon

The Silver King: The Remarkable Life of the Count of Regla in Colonial Mexico
—Edith Boorstein Couturier

National Rhythms, African Roots: The Deep History of Latin American Popular Dance
—John Charles Chasteen

The Great Festivals of Colonial Mexico City: Performing Power and Identity
—Linda A. Curcio-Nagy

*The Souls of Purgatory:
The Spiritual Diary of a Seventeenth-Century Afro-Peruvian Mystic, Ursula de Jesús*
—Nancy E. van Deusen

Dutra's World: Wealth and Family in Nineteenth-Century Rio de Janeiro
—Zephyr L. Frank

Death, Dismemberment, and Memory: Body Politics in Latin America
—Edited by Lyman L. Johnson

Plaza of Sacrifices: Gender, Power, and Terror in 1968 Mexico
—Elaine Carey

*Women in the Crucible of Conquest:
The Gendered Genesis of Spanish American Society, 1500–1600*
—Karen Vieira Powers

Beyond Black and Red: African-Native Relations in Colonial Latin America
—Edited by Matthew Restall

Mexico OtherWise: Modern Mexico in the Eyes of Foreign Observers
—Edited and translated by Jürgen Buchenau

Local Religion in Colonial Mexico
—Edited by Martin Austin Nesvig

Malintzin's Choices: An Indian Woman in the Conquest of Mexico
—Camilla Townsend

From Slavery to Freedom in Brazil: Bahia, 1835–1900
—Dale Torston Graden

Slaves, Subjects, and Subversives: Blacks in Colonial Latin America
—Edited by Jane G. Landers and Barry M. Robinson

Private Passions and Public Sins: Men and Women in Seventeenth-Century Lima
—María Emma Mannarelli

*Making the Americas: The United States and Latin America
from the Age of Revolutions to the Era of Globalization*
—Thomas F. O'Brien

*Remembering a Massacre in El Salvador: The Insurrection of 1932,
Roque Dalton, and the Politics of Historical Memory*
—Héctor Lindo-Fuentes, Erik Ching, and Rafael A. Lara-Martínez

Raising an Empire: Children in Early Modern Iberia and Colonial Latin America
—Ondina E. González and Bianca Premo

*Christians, Blasphemers, and Witches:
Afro-Mexican Rituals in the Seventeenth Century*
—Joan Cameron Bristol

Art and Architecture of Viceregal Latin America, 1521–1821
—Kelly Donahue-Wallace

Rethinking Jewish-Latin Americans
—Edited by Jeffrey Lesser and Raanan Rein

**Series advisory editor: Lyman L. Johnson,
University of North Carolina at Charlotte**

True Stories of Crime in Modern Mexico

Robert Buffington
Pablo Piccato

UNIVERSITY OF NEW MEXICO PRESS | ALBUQUERQUE

© 2009 by the University of New Mexico Press
All rights reserved. Published 2009
Printed in the United States of America

14 13 12 11 10 09   1 2 3 4 5 6

Library of Congress Cataloging-in-Publication Data

True stories of crime in modern Mexico /
[compiled by] Robert Buffington, Pablo Piccato.
p. cm.
Includes index.
ISBN 978-0-8263-4529-5 (pbk. : alk. paper)
1. Detective and mystery stories, Mexican—History and criticism.
I. Buffington, Robert.
II. Piccato, Pablo.

PQ7207.D48T76 2009
863´.087209972—dc22
2008043155

Book design and type composition by Melissa Tandysh
Composed in 10.5/14 Minion Pro
Display type is Scala Sans OT

CONTENTS

LIST OF ILLUSTRATIONS

ix

ACKNOWLEDGMENTS

xi

INTRODUCTION
Crime Stories
Robert Buffington and Pablo Piccato

1

CHAPTER ONE
Tales of Two Women:
The Narrative Construction of Porfirian Reality
Robert Buffington and Pablo Piccato

25

· CHAPTER TWO
I Was a Man of Pleasure, I Can't Deny It:
Histories of José de Jesús Negrete, a.k.a. "The Tiger of Santa Julia"
Elisa Speckman Guerra

57

CHAPTER THREE
A Sense of the Tragic in Life:
Text and Context in Mexico City's General Insane Asylum
Cristina Rivera-Garza

106

CHAPTER FOUR
The Girl Who Killed a Senator:
Femininity and the Public Sphere in Postrevolutionary Mexico
Pablo Piccato

128

CHAPTER FIVE
Who Killed Roberto González?:
Murder, Radicalism, and Catholic Nationalism
in Postrevolutionary Michoacán
Christopher R. Boyer
154

CHAPTER SIX
Of Intersections and Parallel Lives:
José de León Toral and David Alfaro Siqueiros
Renato González Mello
179

CHAPTER SEVEN
The Case of the Murdering Beauty:
Narrative Construction, Beauty Pageants, and the
Postrevolutionary Mexican National Myth, 1921–1931
Víctor M. Macías-González
215

CHAPTER EIGHT
Mothers of Invention:
Narratives of Maternity, Paternity,
and Modernity in Early Twentieth-Century Mexico
Katherine Elaine Bliss
248

INDEX
265

LIST OF ILLUSTRATIONS

1.1. José Guadalupe Posada, *Drama sangriento en la Plazuela de Tarasquillo: Asesinato de la Malagueña*, 1897 — 34
1.2. José Guadalupe Posada, *Lágrimas y sollozos en la cárcel de Belén*, 1897 — 36
1.3. María Villa from Carlos Roumagnac's *Los criminales en México* — 38
1.4. Caricature of Federico Gamboa from *Frivolidades*, 1910 — 47
2.1. José Guadalupe Posada, *La vida de un bandolero. Los crímenes más notables de Jesús Negrete (a) "El tigre de Santa Julia." Aprehensión de sus cómplices* — 61
2.2. José Guadalupe Posada, *Jesús Negrete (a) "El tigre de Santa Julia,"* 1909 — 73
2.3. *El Tigre de Santa Julia*, 1908 — 74
2.4. *En la barra de la defensa*, 1908 — 77
2.5. *El Tigre Declaring*, 1908 — 79
2.6. *Jesús Negrete in the Chapel*, 1910 — 87
2.7. *El fusilamiento de Jesús Negrete (a) "El tigre de Santa Julia." El 22 de diciembre de 1910 a las 6 y 25 de la mañana. En el patio del Jardín de la Cárcel de Belem. Últimos detalles*, 1910 — 87
2.8. *El fusilamiento de Jesús Negrete o sea "El tigre de Santa Julia,"* 1910 — 90
2.9. *Jesús Negrete (a) "El tigre de Santa Julia." Fusilado en la Cárcel de Belem. El 22 de diciembre de 1910* — 91
6.1. José de León Toral, *El Oro, Mex*, 1924 — 189
6.2. Anonymous, *Matrimonio de José de León Toral* — 191
6.3. José de León Toral, *IGLES/XICO*, 1928 — 193
6.4. José de León Toral, *San Humberto*, ca. 1928 — 194
6.5. Anonymous, *José de León Toral haciendo ejercicio*, 1923 — 195
6.6. José de León Toral, *Toral y el Sagrado Corazón de Jesús*, 1928 — 197
6.7. David Alfaro Siqueiros, *Cristo de Pueblo*, 1963 — 199
6.8. José de León Toral, *Mi martirio*, 1928 — 200
6.9. David Alfaro Siqueiros, *El tormento (El castigo del preso)*, 1930 — 201
6.10. David Alfaro Siqueiros, *Confinamiento solitario* — 205
6.11. David Alfaro Siqueiros, *Víctima proletaria (también en la China contemporánea)*, 1933 — 207

ACKNOWLEDGMENTS

Despite our best intentions, this project has taken several years to complete. Along the way we have incurred many debts.

By way of acknowledgment, we would like to thank the following:

Our authors for their intellectual insights, for their hard work through several rounds of revisions, and, not least, for their patience.

General editor for the Diálogos series, Lyman Johnson, for his enthusiasm, thoughtful critique, and uncompromising standards.

The staff at the University of New Mexico Press for their encouragement, timely responses, and unfailing good cheer.

Nora Jaffary for providing crucial insights into the long history of crime stories in Mexico.

Eugenia Lean and Eithne Luibhéid for their thoughtful critiques.

Ann Gresko and Shannon Proctor for their help copyediting the manuscript.

The Institute of Latin American Studies at Columbia University and the College of Arts and Sciences at the University of Colorado at Boulder for logistical and financial support.

Thank you all!

INTRODUCTION

Crime Stories

Robert Buffington and Pablo Piccato

Two hundred thousand people march through the streets of Mexico City to protest widespread public insecurity. The organizers and most marchers are respectable citizens who have suffered either directly or indirectly from crime. Strongly supported and extensively covered by the media, the demonstration conveys the indignation of Mexican society in the face of growing crime rates and several well-publicized instances of violence. "A bunch of guys kidnapped my cousin and the bastards killed him," one participant bitterly complains. "Now what I'm asking for is the death penalty against them and if no one does anything we're going to take justice into our own hands." Another warns that "from this mobilization onward, the ones that ought to be scared are the politicians, because they will see the power that civil society has when it demands attention to its problems." Just as the dust begins to settle, however, a strange dissonance regarding the meaning of the march emerges. Andrés Manuel López Obrador, Mexico City mayor, complains that the whole demonstration had been manufactured to undermine the mayor's popularity. For the organizers, the mere suggestion is offensive. They all have strong personal reasons to demand that federal and local authorities do more to combat crime. (Among other things, kidnappers had cut four fingers from the hand of the husband of María Elena Morera, one of the march's main organizers.) Days later, President Vicente Fox meets with the organizers and promises ten crime-fighting measures. Most are already in place, and none is really new. Gradually things seem to go back to the way they were.[1]

The June 27, 2004, Mexico City march against crime was an example of the growing tendency to politicize crime and punishment taking place in many societies since the last decades of the twentieth century. In Mexico, which is plagued by rapidly increasing crime rates, public fears of violence and corruption were expressed in opinion polls, which in turn influenced political discourse and, to a lesser degree, actual policies.[2] Around the world, city dwellers and governments have embraced retributive punishment as the best way to prevent crime, endorsing harsh sentences against minors and nonviolent drug offenders and reviving criminological discourses that depict "criminals" as unworthy, even incapable of citizenship—as subhumans who are easily distinguished from the law-abiding population and who deserve nothing but isolation.[3] Despite the tough talk, in actual practice law enforcement in most cases has merely sought to keep crime within acceptable levels (the goal of rehabilitation having long been abandoned), while citizens resort to private security (closing up streets and hiring security companies) to allay their fears. The result of this contradiction between practices and normative discourses is the increasing marginalization of the urban poor in dangerous "high crime" areas, and use of the language of fear to justify discrimination against immigrants and ethnic minorities.[4] In contemporary Mexico, perceptions of police ineptitude and corruption in the face of a boom in drug trafficking have further concentrated the political implications of public demonstrations against crime.

The political manipulation of fear, needless to say, is hardly conducive to rational and objective inquiry. Yet, by putting crime at the center of the public debate, the marchers unwittingly revealed major inconsistencies in contemporary knowledge of the problem. One frequent and dissonant aspect of this knowledge is the use of quantitative data to either criticize authorities or celebrate their accomplishments. The publication of crime rates, victimization surveys, and other crime indicators are now common newspaper fare; authorities routinely report monthly and even weekly numbers for crime-related incidents; and researchers crave more numbers to buttress their ideas about the best crime-prevention strategies. The premise is that either numbers do not lie, or they only show the tip of an iceberg of illegality and are therefore unreliable indices of the problem. At the same time, the irrefutable character of numbers implies that the modern data-gathering state is the only actor capable of solving the problem. Even though most crime statistics are produced by the state itself, the trends reflected in those numbers are read as the best indicator of the state's efficacy—as if crime responded only to policy and policing without consideration of social, economic, and cultural factors. Conversely, measuring crime with numbers better fits the administrative questions posed by the state because it establishes correlations between resources invested, suspects imprisoned, and crime rates. In this sense, statistics are the state's preferred narrative genre: omniscient and therefore objective, taxonomic and therefore analytical, "scientific" and therefore not open to debate by the general public. Few state-endorsed treatments of statistical data begin with a careful consideration of how that data is produced, nor do they examine crime as the product of political, economic, social, and cultural forces.[5]

Although doubtlessly aware of statistical evidence suggesting a serious crime wave in Mexico City, marchers did not need to refer to figures to justify their indignation. The mutilated hands of Morera's husband, Pedro Galindo, became a prominent image in a series of televised spots produced in mid-2005 by her organization, México Unido Contra la Delincuencia (Mexico United Against Delinquency), and aired with the support of the main television networks. Both analysts and politicians understand that "perceptions" of insecurity (as opposed to its "reality") are a more influential indicator of the general public's knowledge about crime than statistics are. The mass media is the usual suspect here, with its relentless reports on crimes, great and small, typically conveyed in a graphic style intended to elicit emotional responses of fear and outrage rather than rational debate.[6] Conversations among citizens in the street tend to reproduce those feelings. In her work on crime in São Paulo, Brazil, anthropologist Teresa Caldeira has labeled these everyday narratives "talk of crime"—the informal conversation elicited by the victimization process. According to Caldeira, talk of crime gives structure to the general public's fragmented experience of social change by creating a simplistic world of before and after (the crime) and of good versus evil (usually expressed in terms of race or class), and by connecting the social with the personal. She argues that these narratives are antidemocratic because they justify the privatization of public space and the public use of retaliation by making simultaneous appeals for the stigmatization of "criminals" en masse and for the death penalty.[7]

As is the case with talk of crime, television and newspaper reports rely on implicit premises that few challenge. One premise is that most victims are ordinary people, members of a general public that can identify with them and relive the experience of crime through their stories. This creates a coherent public for crime news and debates: everyone knows about crime and is strongly invested in it, whether through direct or indirect experience. Another premise is that a single crime holds the key to understanding all other crimes and, more specifically, that one criminal can explain all other criminals. Both premises were clearly at work in June 2004 when marchers obsessed about a number of well-known kidnappings (*secuestros*). The crime was not among those most frequently committed, but kidnapping cases had been prominent in the media, and several organizers of the march had been victims of *secuestradores*.

Although most secuestros never reach the public eye because they are resolved by paying the ransom without police involvement, a few are publicized, and these combine narrative ingredients that have a powerful effect on public opinion. A kidnapping is often a developing story, a crime taking place in real time, which gives it a dramatic impact. This impact is absent in reports of a murder that happened the previous night and appeared in newspapers as a fait accompli.[8] Information reaches the public gradually and makes visible the suffering of the victim's loved ones. Since the arrest of a few notorious gangs of kidnappers, secuestro has also become associated with a particular kind of sadistic criminal who likes to cut off victims' ears or fingers and send them as proof of identity to their relatives. At the same time, suspicion often extends to relatives or even to the employees of the victim, thereby reinforcing traditional views of domestic workers' inherent criminality.[9]

In the state of Morelos, Governor Jorge Carrillo Olea was forced to resign when he was indicted for his involvement with drug trafficking and kidnapping rings. The suspected complicity of policemen and politicians in high-profile kidnapping cases further supports most kidnapping victims' reluctance to press charges.[10] These well-known stories have everyday echoes: although most kidnapping victims in Mexico are wealthy, many Mexico City inhabitants have suffered what have come to be called *secuestros express*, in which a small ransom is demanded from relatives while the victim is driven around. Anyone can identify with a kidnapping victim, making secuestro the perfect narrative model for contemporary crime in Mexico City. It mobilizes emotions in the service of political demands, provides an explanation for crime in general, and constitutes the publics that have brought crime to the center of popular consciousness in recent years.

Except for one chapter, this book is not about contemporary crime or even kidnapping. Our goal as historians is to examine how crime stories have shaped the way Mexican society thinks about criminals and about itself. We argue first that public narratives focused on the transgression of societal norms are key to understanding the politicalization of fear; and second, and more important from the perspective of our discipline, that these narratives have profoundly shaped the way historians write about society. The chapters that follow show how stories about murders, religious heterodoxy, insanity, infanticide, and kidnapping can become narratives that purport to make sense of Mexican society and politics at different periods in the country's history. In so doing, these stories illuminate aspects of life that more conventional accounts have slighted, misunderstood, or ignored altogether. To prepare the reader for this unorthodox approach, this introduction advances some ideas about the ways crime stories have shaped our own perceptions about society and history, much as they influenced the Mexico City marchers—and not always in the direction of a more objective understanding of the past.[11]

The notion that crime has played a historically important if unsavory role in human social relations should seem obvious enough. The nature of that role, however, is more complicated than it might appear at first glance. Over a century ago, in his influential *The Rules of Sociological Method* (1893), French social theorist Emile Durkheim made a series of provocative claims about the importance of crime to human societies. These claims turned conventional wisdom on its head. Durkheim noted that by most statistical measures, late nineteenth-century Europe and the rest of the developed world had suffered dramatic increases in criminal activity—crime was up 300 percent in France, for example—despite a century of social advancement and relative political stability.[12] For most observers, this crime wave was incontrovertible evidence of individual depravity and social dissolution. Durkheim disagreed. Deplorable though it might be, in his view, crime was both "normal" and "necessary" to society's well-being. "Let us make no mistake," he insisted, "to classify *crime* among the phenomena of normal sociology is not merely to declare that it is an inevitable though regrettable phenomenon arising from the incorrigible wickedness of men; it is to assert that it is . . . an integrative element in any healthy society."[13]

Durkheim based his counterintuitive argument on three central ideas. The first is that *crime is normal* because it is present in all societies: "[T]here is not one [society] in which criminality does not exist, although it changes form and the actions which are termed criminal are not everywhere the same."[14] The second is that *crime is necessary* because it represents the unavoidable "dark side" of the creative processes essential to any social progress: "[F]or [moral consciousness] to evolve, individual originality must be allowed to manifest itself. But so that the originality of the idealist who dreams of transcending his era must display itself; that of the criminal, which falls short of the age, must also be possible. One does not go without the other."[15] The third is that *crime strengthens group identity* because it prompts the otherwise self-interested members of a given society to close ranks in response to a threat: "[C]rime brings together upright consciences and concentrates them."[16] Seen in this light, the identification and punishment of crime is essential to the development and maintenance of what Durkheim calls the *conscience collective*—"the totality of beliefs and sentiments common to average citizens of the same society"—necessary to social solidarity.[17] This makes even better sense if, as one critic sensibly suggests, rather than understanding "the conscience collective as an emergent property of 'society-as-a-whole,' we ... conceive of a dominant moral order which is historically established by particular social forces."[18]

Intended as a set of general principles applicable to all human societies, Durkheim's ideas about crime are a bit abstract. There is, however, considerable historical evidence to support them. For instance, in the Salem witch trials, local leaders used the allegations of impressionable teenage girls to justify the community-building punitive ritual they hoped would bring social cohesion to a village stressed by internal divisions and inassimilable outsiders.[19] Mexican history too includes numerous cases of lynching and other forms of public punishment that served to strengthen community ties—even when those communities broke the law in the process. For example, writing about the 1998 public lynching of two alleged child abductors by residents of the town of Huejutla, journalist Sam Quinones comments that the rash of *linchamientos* that occurred throughout Mexico during the final decade of the twentieth century was not a sign of racial prejudice or Wild West–style lawlessness but "a bellow of rage by the powerless majority against corrupt cops and politicians, protected criminals—against a justice system that people know to be unfair."[20] These collective bellows of rage were often moments of intense community solidarity as well.

These historical examples may support Durkheim's theories about crime and the conscience collective; they also reveal one of their weaknesses. While the notion of conscience collective makes sense for relatively small communities like Salem or Huejutla, where most of the parties involved were personally known to each other, it does not work quite as well for larger urban populations like Mexico City, where the moral outrage provoked by crime is experienced largely by and among strangers. Folks in a small town might, as Durkheim observes, "stop each other on the street ... visit each other ... seek to come together to talk of the event and to wax indignant in common," but the common indignation even of close-knit urban neighborhoods can hardly be said to represent the "public temper" in any comprehensive way—although local responses still figure into the equation (as we will see in several of the chapters in this book).[21]

Despite these limitations, Durkheim's ideas do—with some strategic tweaking—tell us a great deal about how crime and punishment (and the stories they generate) function to promote common moral codes in modern societies. In *Punishment and Modern Society*, sociologist David Garland notes that Durkheim's seminal work underscores the importance of collective emotions in a society's response to crime, that "the criminal act violates sentiments and emotions which are deeply ingrained in most members of society . . . [and] provokes a sense of outrage, anger, indignation, and passionate desire for revenge."[22] In a modern, impersonal society, however, this sense of collective outrage is heavily mediated by the criminal justice system with its elaborate network of laws, courts, penal institutions, and so forth. As a result, the criminal justice system takes on much of the expressive and pedagogical burden of punishment formerly assumed by local communities and religious institutions. "For Durkheim," Garland argues, "the rituals of criminal justice—the court-room trial, the passing of sentence, the execution of punishment—are, in effect, the formalized embodiment and enactment of the *conscience collective*. In doing justice, and in processing criminals, these procedures are also giving formal expression to the feelings of the community—and by being expressed in this way those feelings are both strengthened and gratified."[23] Indeed, the theatricality of the courtroom and the aura of collective performance it sometimes engenders are clearly demonstrated in several of the chapters that follow.

The power of crime and punishment to shape perceptions extends far beyond the courtroom, however. In this broader sense, Garland's analysis of their didactic power in modern societies is extremely useful and merits quoting at some length:

> Penal signs and symbols . . . provide a continuous, repetitive set of instructions as to how we should think about good and evil, normal and pathological, legitimate and illegitimate, order and disorder. Through their judgments, condemnations, and classifications they teach us (and persuade us) how to judge, what to condemn, and how to classify, and they supply a set of languages, idioms, and vocabularies with which to do so. These signifying practices also tell us where to locate social authority, how to preserve order and community, where to look for social dangers, and how to feel about these matters, while the evocative effect of penal symbols sets off chains of reference and associations in our minds . . .[24]

Although focused more on state-centered penal practices than on crime stories per se, Garland's recognition of the central role of "penal signs and symbols" is amply supported by the chapters in this volume that deal directly or indirectly with the criminal justice system.

As the chapters in this book that focus on mass media demonstrate, we can see similar, if less deliberate, expressive and pedagogical processes at work in press coverage of criminal causes célèbres. In these sensational accounts, newsworthy instances of social transgression generate compelling public narratives with boldly delineated "stock" characters—the deviant aggressor, the naïve victim, the righteous prosecutor, the implacable judge—whose reassuring presence serves to draw in the general public. According to historian Joy Wiltenburg, "the discourses of sensationalism . . . mark a unique point of intersection between structures of power and normative emotional demands—between public order and the interior life of the individual . . . [that] presumes a like-minded community, a group responding to a common appeal."[25] Along with their pure (and often prurient) entertainment value, these public narratives also include "lessons" about the moral and social implications of crime. Like the institutional discourses identified by Garland, these media lessons appeal to a general public whose sense of shared identity—despite the lack of personal connections—stems in no small part from its collective response to media-generated crime stories.

Acknowledging the centrality of crime stories to the development and maintenance of a modern conscience collective complicates the sociological insights of Durkheim and Garland. As scientific crime stories, case studies have been important in delineating the boundaries of the disciplines and narrative genres that deal with deviance in individual and social behaviors. From detective novels onward, the melding of scientific evidence and narrative coherence in the case study has come to define modern understandings of deviance and normalcy. Arthur Conan Doyle's stories, for example, usually start with Watson reporting on a memorable Sherlock Holmes case. Readers are surprised as much by the intricacies of the criminal mind as they are by the detective's uncanny ability to gather evidence and draw irrefutable conclusions from small details that escape normal perception. Conan Doyle's sequential laying out of the "facts" prepares the ground for the reader's surprise yet preserves the scientific prestige of Holmes's "analytical" method. In this way, according to Rosemary Jann, the detective is able to "reassure readers of the reliability of [legal] codes and to render logical the social order that they imply." Interpreting the unremarkable signs exhibited by suspects' bodies, Holmes claims to be applying common sense, but he is in fact constructing social typologies that serve to reinforce common sense about crime.[26]

Holmes's extraordinary capacity for scientific analysis was explained in part by the social and racial distance Conan Doyle established between his detective and offenders in general—a clearly identifiable breed of humans labeled "criminals." Yet Holmes had "amazing powers in the use of disguises," turning himself, in "A Scandal in Bohemia," into "a drunken-looking goon" identical to the kind of criminals supposed to be his moral and social opposites.[27] Conan Doyle's readers could see these disguises as a hint that all signs of social identity were ultimately roles in a narrative. Just as distance lent Holmes scientific authority, his dangerous proximity to crime and criminals gave his voice a dramatic strength it would otherwise lack, which happened, in deliberate parody, in the cases of Isidro Parodi, the detective who solved mysteries without leaving his Buenos Aires cell.[28]

Complete objectivity, the premise of Holmes's ability to cross the borders of appearance, was harder to claim, however, when criminals produced stories of their own—an infrequent occurrence in Conan Doyle's writings. Pierre Rivière, a French peasant, wrote just such an account as he attempted to justify the murder of his family in 1853 by connecting his mother's tyranny with social oppression at large. More than a hundred years later, Michel Foucault coordinated an effort to examine Rivière's story and to untangle the scientific and legal explanations that made the case a battlefield for competing disciplines, each testing its claims about causes of deviance and notions of legal responsibility. For example, medical diagnosis prefigured Holmes's methods by pointing to details in the patient's "symptoms," thus dwelling on an inductive reasoning that could safely ignore social causes of disease or, in Holmes's cases, crime. On the issue of legal responsibility, Foucault used Rivière's case to probe the law's ambiguities regarding homicide, an act judged differently according to the social status of the actor and deemed acceptable if committed in self-defense or in war. "Murder," for Foucault, "is where history and crime intersect."[29]

By anchoring multiple observations, a single case can reinforce the authority and coherence of scientific disciplines and concurrently link them to everyday preoccupations about crime. Carlo Ginzburg notes the risks that historians face when working from the apparently objective facts that emerge in and around dramatic acts such as murder: like doctors and detectives, they look for clues that would reveal causal connections; like lawyers and other masters of rhetoric, they try to present convincing explanations to support their judgments. At the same time, however, Ginzburg deplores recent historical literatures that dismiss the historian's affinity with the judge and the need for proof in favor of an exclusive emphasis on "representations"—in other words, writing a history about the texts themselves, rather than the realities to which those texts refer.[30] We contend that analysis of case studies as historically grounded narratives can help historians and readers alike establish critical distance from the competing explanations that made criminals like Pierre Rivière objects of study in authoritative texts and take into account his attempt to tell his own story. As Foucault notes in the case of Rivière, "[t]he murder and the narrative of the murder were consubstantial." His extensive written confession, like those that appeared in the era's popular broadsheets, put everyday, small events in a perspective that made them meaningful even if the author produced "a history below the level of power, one which clashed with the law."[31] By proposing his own version of the meaning of his crime, Rivière was reminding future readers of the always specific, seemingly idiosyncratic connections between transgression and the social realities that scientific perspectives of his time often neglected as trivial.

We can, however, take some leads from the specialists on crime who, by producing their own scientific texts and by letting criminals talk and write, leave for us valuable sources of data. As historians, we should hear critical criminologists' warnings that academic knowledge about crime has always been torn between the purely scientific pursuit of explanations and the urgent demands of politics—the latter articulated not only as crime control, but also as the expression of popular views about justice.[32] Analyzing transgression means engaging diverse speakers and discourses, from the ideally detached academic inquiry to the queries of judges, politicians, and administrators who respond to political pressures, and from the testimonies of prisoners to the "respectable" audience of newspaper readers. Case studies connect these often contradictory voices by combining the deductive and inductive logic of scientific research (the featured criminal is an example of a larger species but is also a source of evidence about it), the common-sense reasoning of cops, and the drama of biographical narratives crowned by transgression and punishment.

In Mexico, this complex approach to case studies found its best representative in popular criminologist Carlos Roumagnac, who interviewed Mexico City prisoners and published three books between 1906 and 1912 based on those interviews. From the position of power conferred by his proximity to prison authorities, Roumagnac questioned inmates about the various aspects of their lives; these facts, according to the criminological theories of the day, revealed the causes of their deviance: alcoholic parents, precocious sexual experiences, living in the dangerous areas of the city, and learning about crime in prison. Roumagnac also noted the physiognomic traits of the prisoners—indicators of criminal tendencies, according to criminal anthropologists like Cesare Lombroso and fictional detectives like Sherlock Holmes—and provided visual confirmation in the form of mug shots. Like other criminologists, Roumagnac considered prisons "laboratories" that could provide everything from the crania of dead criminals to an endless supply of informants whose life stories could serve to advance knowledge and to satisfy the curiosity of their readers.

But Roumagnac's observations did not stop there: he prompted prisoners to express their innermost thoughts, and he used their voices (through interviews and fragments of their writings) to construct compelling stories that, unlike those of Conan Doyle, did not obscure their meaning, and implied Roumagnac's sympathy for their fates.[33] A journalist as much as a criminologist, Roumagnac was undoubtedly influenced by the "aesthetic rewriting of crime" during his time, when criminals and their deeds acquired a larger cultural meaning beyond the "everyday epic of illegalities" that, according to Foucault, had characterized earlier popular pamphlets about executions.[34] In Porfirian Mexico, the public sphere contained diverse examples of that rewriting, including José Guadalupe Posada's prints in broadsheets, published by the Vanegas Arroyo shop, about "terrible events" such as the daughter who killed her mother, and Federico Gamboa's obsession with prostitution and prisoners in *Santa* and *La llaga*.[35]

Perhaps because of the hybrid character of their work, early twentieth-century criminologists had a profound impact on subsequent developments in the Mexican social sciences. Roumagnac's contemporary, Julio Guerrero, another social commentator cum criminologist, had made the city, especially Mexico City, the privileged site for exploring the highs and the lows of Mexican society. In doing so, he contributed tropes and explanations that other writers about *lo mexicano* would exploit later in the twentieth century.[36] Anthropologists, also decisive in shaping ideas about the nature of the Mexican people, followed the same interest in narratives produced by otherwise silent subjects. Such was the case, to cite a famous example, of Oscar Lewis's *Children of Sánchez*, an influential case study centered on an urban family whose members (no strangers to illegality, by their own reckoning) seemed to have the main voice, with the anthropologist's role limited to that of editor. Thus conveyed, evidence about marginality and violence was more much dramatic and politically charged than detached academic analysis—in similar fashion to today's growing genre of *narco* narratives.[37] Highbrow literature also borrowed from this combination of voices and perspectives. The idea of *el mexicano*, a central theme in mid-twentieth-century literature, was based on the notion that there were individuals, real or composite, who embodied national traits. Thus, in their attempts to explain the Mexican essence, influential thinkers (*pensadores*) such as Samuel Ramos and Octavio Paz explored distinctive, quasi-criminal types as emblematic of the Mexican community, including *el pelado* and *el pachuco* (one the lowly urban rascal, the other the Americanized tough guy), which they used to produce influential descriptions of national culture.[38] Mexican anthropologists have since advanced beyond nationalism and the overwhelming influence of the pensadores, yet the case studies and first-person accounts continue to be effective narrative devices when experts seek to reach beyond the limited realm of specialized readers while claiming the authority of scientific methods.[39]

Crime stories, especially media-driven causes célèbres, have another important function that we might miss if we only look at their textual record and forget about the circumstances under which they were produced: their ability to create publics. Publics are not merely audiences that passively consume newspaper articles or criminological reports. They are collectives that acquire their cohesion, sometimes fleeting but often politically influential, when they are addressed as "the public" by discourses and debates in the public sphere. Roumagnac's readers, for example, included police officers, criminal anthropologists, novelists, and a good number of general readers. Such disparate company shared the explanations and narratives about Mexican criminals put forth by medical and legal experts, criminal anthropologists, police reporters, and naturalist novelists such as Gamboa. Later in the twentieth century, photojournalists including the Casasolas, the brothers Mayo, and Nacho López used the visual impact of photography to enhance the public appeal of criminological knowledge. As important contributors to the public sphere, these authors claimed the voice of public opinion and thus the "right" to address authorities with advice, demands, or criticism. In doing so, they expanded the cast of actors entitled to intervene in debates that in the nineteenth century would have been monopolized by educated politicians and a few well-respected journalists. As the public sphere expanded, journalists, victims, and even suspects began to talk and write about everyday problems such as the threats to personal safety and quotidian abuses that affected people from all walks of life. Yet this did not mean that the circulation of popular crime stories made the public sphere more open and democratic. Stories and explanations imbued with the class and ethnic prejudices of criminologists, police reporters, and detective story writers continued to have great influence on the public. As we can see in debates and in the "talk of crime" in contemporary Mexico, the organizing principle of the public brought into being by notorious secuestro cases and other famous crimes is a shared sense of indignation on the part of actual or potential victims. The mass media, particularly television, fosters indignation through an odd combination of "scientific" truisms about criminals and melodramatic depictions of victimization. The result has been a considerable expansion of the publics invested in crime stories.[40]

Publics are not brought together by learned discussions, but by emotional responses that give them coherence as conscience collectives and thus political influences.[41] The cases examined in the following pages provoked diverse emotions, from outrage that led to political violence to professions of love for women suspects. Although emotion often drives contemporary perceptions of crime, we argue that emotional responses are not the defining feature of publics so much as the vocabulary through which members of the public articulate their understanding of and concerns about deviance and morality. But we should not forget that other languages have been relevant in the past. The following chapters also show how psychiatric discourse made possible the construction of mental patients as objects of clinical intervention, how individual women's health became a way to talk about disease and reproduction, and how allegations of violence against children justified the persecution of political opponents as criminals. In all these instances, the authority of the human sciences (from theology to legal medicine and criminology) and the power of narrative to make sense out of complex events were available for different actors to use in different ways.

Today the talk of crime and crime stories is unrivaled in its ability to constitute publics. While national and ethnic identities come to be increasingly challenged as virtual or contingent by the circulation of peoples and information, the narrative power of crime stories, the authority of explanation by example, and the self-identification of citizens with transgressors or victims make public discourse about crime an especially important source for social values, enabling the mutual recognition of participants who, according to Michael Warner, "do not commonly recognize themselves as virtual projections" but as members of a real public.[42] Ultimately what the following chapters show is that, through crime stories, even the authoritative discourses of scientific elites contributed to the formation of publics capable of exerting influence and, when necessary, taking action in pursuit of their perceived interests.

Each chapter in this volume deals with a different crime story, and each author takes care to situate his or her "story" in a specific place and time. Nevertheless, we can discern three levels of analysis at work in each chapter. The first level takes the story itself as the object of study—its principal actors, its ins and outs, and its denouement—as represented in the contemporary narratives it generates. Here, the focus is on texts directly related to the case: on a "dossier" of sorts composed of documents, news stories, bureaucratic reports, and court records considered both as archival traces of real events and as symbolic acts with real consequences. The second level situates the story in the larger discourses on crime, punishment, honor, and family that determined its resonance. At this level, questions of audience and reception by the legal and medical communities, government policy makers, journalists, and the general public take center stage. The third level engages with the story's larger significance in the material world of labor and other economic exchanges, and with the inevitable political, economic, and social disruptions that result from long-term structural "adjustments." Seen from this vantage point, the power of crime stories to reflect and especially to constitute social realities in periods of wrenching change emerges as a significant formative influence in Mexican history.

In *The Political Unconscious: Narrative as a Socially Symbolic Act*, cultural theorist Fredric Jameson insists that "the conventional sociology of literature or culture, which modestly limits itself to the identification of class motifs or values in a given text, and feels that its work is done when it shows how a given artifact 'reflects' its social background, is utterly unacceptable."[43] Although we might question Jameson's insistence on grounding all textual analysis in class struggle (as important as class undoubtedly is), we certainly share his critique of "conventional" analysis, whether sociological or historical. Thus, each chapter in this volume seeks not only to show how individual cases reflected social realities, but also to expose what Jameson calls the "determinate contradictions" embedded in each case. These contradictions emerge from the inevitable and irreconcilable differences produced by persistent social inequalities that the case narratives tended to gloss over (sometimes intentionally, sometimes not), resolve without confrontation, or deny altogether. Jameson argues that the conscientious analyst must take into account that "real social contradictions, insurmountable in their own terms, find a purely formal resolution in the aesthetic realm."[44] The process through which crime stories seek to formally resolve real social contradictions is clearly evidenced in the chapters that follow.

Jameson makes another point about modern master narratives such as class struggle, liberal progress, the cold war, and the global struggle against violent extremism that has interesting implications for stories about crime. These master narratives, he argues, with their collective heroes and villains—proletarians, peasants, bourgeoisie, totalitarians, authoritarians, free marketers, freedom fighters, terrorists, and so on—carry an "immense charge of anxiety and libidinal investment . . . which necessarily informs all of our cultural artifacts."[45] Jameson is referring here to master narratives that explain global processes; we argue that crime stories do much the same work on the national, regional, or local level. In other words, like global master narratives, crime stories spark and shape our anxieties and fears, inform our cultural artifacts, and help to construct our social reality. Moreover, they speak to the everyday concerns of ordinary people in ways that global struggles cannot, save perhaps when global struggle is translated into the local vernacular of the crime story. Thus, everything from interpersonal relations to home architecture, urban planning, and artistic production references the "immense charge of anxiety and libidinal investment" provoked and sustained by crime stories.

Unlike the apparently seamless global master narratives and modernist novels Jameson analyzes in *The Political Unconscious*, and perhaps more than any other narrative genre, crime stories struggle more or less openly with their determinate contradictions, especially when they become public narratives developed by disparate and sometimes contradictory sources. In this sense, they take on some of the attributes of a classic public sphere in which competing visions of society are freely discussed and evaluated, although without the pretensions to rational-critical debate that characterized the Enlightenment-era ideal described by Jürgen Habermas. Crime stories often bring to light important issues of persistent social inequalities, the privileges of wealth and influence, and the coercive power of state institutions—not so much to engage in a dispassionate public debate over social justice as to play off the hopes, desires, and fears of the publics they address and constitute.

Unable to suppress social contradictions or reconcile us to the social order (although they often attempt to do both), crime stories are the preferred genre of cultural revolutions, those times when society's determinate contradictions can no longer be effectively managed by the master narratives of God, empire, nation, progress, or democracy. In Mexico, as the chapters in this volume demonstrate, these moments of cultural revolution coincided with the irruption of "modern" notions of social organization (linked to the expansion of capitalist modes of production) into elite culture in the late colonial period and into popular culture in the late nineteenth and early twentieth centuries.

In "Tales of Two Women: The Narrative Construction of Porfirian Reality," the editors explore the second great irruption of modernity in Mexico through a case involving two women rivals. One of the first great causes célèbres of the Porfiriato (1876–1910), the 1897 Tarasquillo Street murder of Esperanza Gutiérrez by María Villa—prostitutes by profession and rivals in love—produced a gamut of often contradictory accounts that ran from newspaper articles and trial transcripts to popular broadsheets, criminological case studies, and published memoirs. This chapter uses these very different sources to expose the "determinate contradictions" of a cultural epoch and a political regime committed to bringing "order and progress" to a country ravaged by years of internecine strife, economic uncertainty, and social dislocation. Of special note here is the analysis of something that cultural theorist Rita Felski calls the "gender of modernity," and especially "the images of femininity [that] play a central role in prevailing anxieties, fears, and hopeful imaginings about the distinctive features of the 'modern age.'"[46] Prominent among these images in the Tarasquillo Street murder case was a symbolic linkage between femininity and death that posed in its various guises a potent challenge to prevailing optimism about Mexico's social evolution, the onset of modernity, and the mastery of elite men.

Elisa Speckman Guerra's "I Was a Man of Pleasure, I Can't Deny It: The Histories of José de Jesús Negrete, a.k.a. 'The Tiger of Santa Julia'" analyzes the different news stories surrounding the crimes, captures, escapes, and eventual execution of notorious bandit Jesús Negrete. Her analysis reveals the cacophonous and sometimes contradictory voices at work in the construction of public narratives. Her careful comparison of sources ranging from the *Gaceta de Policía* to mass dailies of various political persuasions and popular broadsheets illustrated by master engraver José Guadalupe Posada clearly demonstrates the ambivalent nature of crime stories even in the hands of the writers and editors of a newspaper like *El Imparcial*, whose claims to impartiality were sullied by government subsidies. Jesús Negrete, for example, was represented variously as a common criminal with no redeeming features (by the mainstream press), as a common criminal who was nevertheless brave, honorable, and respectful of women (by the popular press), and as a social bandit/protorevolutionary who fought against an inequitable system the only way he knew how (in later revolutionary mythology). These different interpretive possibilities weakened whatever moral or ideological message writers and editors might have hoped to convey to their readers. In her work on sensationalism in early modern Germany, historian Joy Wiltenburg emphasizes the political effects of crime stories and argues that sensationalism enhances those effects. Speckman Guerra's analysis supports both points (as do most of the chapters in this volume), but at the same time it insists on the unstable nature of crime narratives—an instability that complicates their role in the reinforcement of social norms.[47]

Taking up the radical implications of Michel Foucault's work on Pierre Rivière noted above, Cristina Rivera-Garza's "A Sense of the Tragic in Life: Text and Context in Mexico's General Insane Asylum" fractures a classic case study into its constituent components to reveal the determinate and tragic contradictions at work in the perplexing documentary fragments that tell the story of Marino García, a "beggar" committed to the General Insane Asylum, La Castañeda, in 1919 for punching one General Tejada in the face in Amecameca, a small town outside Mexico City. Rivera-Garza not only deconstructs the narrative fragments found in García's institutional dossier; she also critiques the historian's understandable desire to make sense of the past through narration. To this end, she highlights the similarities between the historian's narrative compulsion and that of the asylum's medical and bureaucratic personnel. They sought to impose on Marino García's life their narrative in a form appropriate to the medical knowledge that structured their authoritative understanding of mental illness, even as they insisted that he tell his story in his own words—if only to hear his "confession" and thus confirm their diagnosis. At the same time, Rivera-Garza allows for an "uneven yet dynamic" dialogue between doctor/historian and patient/historical subject that allows an attentive listener to hear the textual echoes of the patient's voice. Rivera-Garza insists on the virtues of a "fractal" history that eschews narrative's temporal sequencing and a dominant interpretation. She nonetheless carefully connects the resulting fragments to their larger historical context: the disruptive impact of modernity on everyday life (in this case through the discourses and practices of medicine and psychiatry), revolutionary violence (as exemplified in García's assault on the general and his nightmares of political persecution), and the social reform agenda of the postrevolutionary state, which made possible García's final testimonial. More than any of the others, this chapter explores the violence—categorical, conceptual, psychological, physical, and structural—that narratives, including the historical narratives in this collection, often obscure or explain away as they attempt to make meaning out of the impossible complexities of people's lived experiences.

Pablo Piccato's chapter, "The Girl Who Killed a Senator: Femininity and the Public Sphere in Postrevolutionary Mexico City," looks at a cause célèbre of postrevolutionary Mexico—the 1922 murder of Senator Francisco Tejeda Llorca by the fourteen-year-old daughter of a politician he had killed. The media frenzy that surrounded Tejeda Llorca's murder revealed competing views about proper age and gender roles during a moment of great political stress. The case generated extensive press coverage, inspired the accused María del Pilar Moreno to write her memoir, and attracted large audiences to her jury trial. The public narrative of the case, brought to rhetorical perfection by her defense lawyer, Querido Moheno, emphasized the tragic filial piety that moved Moreno to commit a justifiable homicide and eventually led to her acquittal. Yet even as violence remained a routine component of politics, and many men and women expressed their support for the young assassin, the case raised many questions that prefigured changes in society's view of women and children in postrevolutionary Mexico. Were women supposed to be knowledgeable in the use of firearms? Was it legitimate to mix family and public life? Were María del Pilar's intellectual ambitions, nurtured by her loving father, the cause of her ill-fated intervention in public life? Although she avoided punishment, the tragic tone of the story stressed the need to understand her case as an exception that would encourage, by contrary example, other families to maintain a strict divide between domesticity and public life.

In "Who Killed Roberto González?: Murder, Radicalism, and Catholic Nationalism in Postrevolutionary Michoacán," Christopher R. Boyer exposes the complex political machinations that surrounded the 1923 kidnapping and murder of Roberto González, the ten-year-old son of a prominent conservative landowner. Michoacán, at the time of the kidnapping, was an on-again, off-again hotbed of postrevolutionary reform. The state had just undergone yet another political upheaval as conservative elites and small-scale landowners (rancheros) joined forces to oust radical governor Francisco J. Múgica in response to his efforts to undermine the still powerful Catholic Church and initiate agrarian reforms. In this context, the González kidnapping became a national cause célèbre and a rallying point for conservative forces in Michoacán (including the local Catholic newspaper, *El Cruzado*) and elsewhere in Mexico as these forces sought to discredit the radical revolutionary project. The subsequent arrest and execution of Ramón Ascencio, a prominent local *agrarista* (land reformer), provided both sides in the dispute with martyrs in what would soon blossom into the armed rebellions, known collectively as the Cristero rebellion, waged by conservative pro-Catholic forces against a postrevolutionary central government, slowly but surely consolidating its control of national politics. Boyer carefully analyzes the various narratives generated by the González case to reveal the political agendas at work and to examine the evidence for and against Ascencio. The executed man's guilt or innocence, he confesses, is impossible to ascertain. However, the sordid details of the case—congressmen as intermediaries, allegations of planted evidence and coerced witnesses, pistolero henchmen—will seem depressingly familiar to observers of contemporary secuestros.

Renato González Mello's "Of Intersections and Parallel Lives: José de León Toral and David Alfaro Siqueiros" uses the case against José de León Toral, who assassinated president-elect Álvaro Obregón in 1928, to weave together the parallel lives of Toral (Catholic zealot, soccer player, and aspiring artist) and David Alfaro Siqueiros (Stalinist revolutionary and world-renowned muralist). Beyond the use of violence in the pursuit of higher political and spiritual goals, both men tried to develop a plastic language that would express the centrality of their own bodies to their public personas. In the case of Toral, the narrative context was provided by the judicial case brought against him for the assassination of Obregón. His drawings told the story of an athletic body subjected to torture. Thus, rather than the production of truth expected from the judicial procedures, whose results were all but predetermined, Toral transformed his case into a narrative of mystical sacrifice. Siqueiros also used his prison stays (some of them caused by his own assassination attempts on political opponents such as Leon Trotsky) to fully develop a rhetoric of violence and a critique of punishment in which the painter's own powerful body became a sign of his personal and ideological power. Both men's visual productions reveal, better than a purely verbal narrative ever could, the tensions between the different notions of truth—the "determinate contradictions"—at play in art, justice, and historical writing.

Víctor M. Macías-González's "The Case of the Murdering Beauty: Narrative Construction, Beauty Pageants, and the Postrevolutionary Mexican National Myth, 1921–1931" builds a rich discussion of gender, race, violence, and the media around a cause célèbre that shocked and titillated the country at a crucial juncture in its history: the consolidation of postrevolutionary power by the new Sonoran dynasty of Álvaro Obregón and Plutarco Elías Calles. The 1929 murder of a bigamist husband, General Moisés Vidal Corro, by his new bride, María Teresa de Landa, Miss Mexico 1928, and her public trial by jury garnered a huge audience with as many as four hundred thousand tuned in to a twelve-hour radio broadcast of the trial's final day. In addition to its inherent fascination, the case demonstrates the tremendous social tensions that accompanied the emergence of modern notions of femininity in 1920s Mexico. As in the case studied by Piccato, the embrace of violence by the postrevolutionary political elite—wife-beating in this instance—impeded the professional development of an ambitious young woman who sought to be defined not only by her beauty, but also by her strong desire for a professional career. At the same time, in her trial defense, de Landa and her lawyers played to conventional middle-class notions of domesticity, femininity, and racial purity to portray her as the innocent female victim of the cruel macho arriviste general Vidal Corro—a defense that resonated with bourgeois concerns about postrevolutionary political corruption and violence.

In "Mothers of Invention: Narratives of Maternity, Paternity, and Modernity in Early Twentieth-Century Mexico," Katherine Elaine Bliss uses a 1937 case of infanticide to examine competing ideas about motherhood in circulation during the 1930s, as Mexican policymakers contemplated the demographic losses of the Revolution (before the accelerated population growth of the 1940s complicated the issue). From the judge's perspective in the infanticide trial, harsh punishment was not the best way to address the deep-seated social inequalities that had led to Soledad Romero Padilla's decision to abandon her child. During this same period, the government was actively engaged in pronatalist campaigns and in the production of books, pamphlets, and other texts intended to teach Mexican women how to be productive, hygienic mothers. As the judge's ruling in the infanticide case makes clear, the uplifting narratives contained in these didactic campaigns and texts were set against the backdrop of serious endemic health problems among the poor. Although the attempt to introduce contraception on a broad scale during the 1930s came decades before its time (at least in the eyes of progressive policymakers), it nevertheless exposed the same persistent connections between work, domesticity, sexuality, and motherhood that emerged so eloquently in the story of Soledad Romero Padilla—despite her own reluctance to speak out at the trial. Bliss's examination of the convergence of multiple fictions about motherhood highlights the need to understand the determinate contradictions at work in public discourse, even as we try to understand conceptions and policies grounded in "hard" social facts such as public health and demographic change.

The 2004 Mexico City marchers expressed their indignation in a common language derived from notorious crime stories and spread in the public sphere through different media: newspapers, radio, television, and informal conversations among neighbors and people on the street. Yet the stories and languages they deployed were part of a narrative tradition that owed much to the marginal actors and penal institutions that marchers were so eager to blame. Although we would be tempted to argue that an expansion of the public sphere always benefits democracy, a critical stance is necessary if we hope to understand the specific ways in which certain themes and narrative forms shape debates therein. In other words, it is good that more voices are engaged in public debate about crime, but not so good that the debate is shaped almost exclusively by fear or anger.

A few themes connect the explosive debates about crime taking place in contemporary Mexico with the cases examined in this book. Among them is the notion that individual cases explain larger social problems. In 2004 this meant that certain areas of Mexico City, such as Colonia Buenos Aires and barrio Tepito, were understood to be the source of all criminal activity. Rather than examining the role of these areas in the illegal economy of the city, it was easier for the general public to connect place and personality, the faces of suspects on television and a broader sociological "truth" about dangerous urban spaces. As historians, however, we face the added challenge of examining crimes and the stories they generate not only as direct sources of evidence or important pieces of a historical puzzle, but also as narratives that need to be deconstructed to reveal the logics they impose on public debates. This historical critique involves an examination of the scientific and legal languages that shape the records we use to document our accounts. It also requires that we place those narratives in the historical contexts that give them political and cultural meaning. We invite you to read the following pages with the same critical spirit, engaging these crime stories and their authors in all their dramatic appeal and empirical richness.

Notes

1. For a chronicle, see *La Jornada*, 28 June 2004; on López Obrador's reactions, see *La Jornada*, 26 June 2004; on the use of kidnappings as part of political disputes between the federal and city governments, see *La Jornada*, 24 June 2004, and *Reforma*, 26 June 2004; on diverse interpretations of the march and Fox's ten promises, see *La Jornada*, 2 July 2004.
2. Jesús Ramírez Cuevas, "Los rostros del miedo," Masiosare section of *La Jornada*, 14 December 2003. For a political interpretation of crime, see Rafael Ruiz Harrell, "Democracia y delincuencia," *Reforma*, 17 July 2004.
3. Robert Buffington, *Criminal and Citizen in Modern Mexico* (Lincoln: University of Nebraska Press, 2000); David Garland, *The Culture of Control: Crime and Social Order in Contemporary Society* (Oxford: Oxford University Press, 2001).
4. David Garland, "The Limits of the Sovereign State: Strategies of Crime Control in Contemporary Society," *British Journal of Criminology* 36, no. 4 (1996): 445–71; Garland, *Culture of Control*; John Braithwaite, *Crime, Shame and Reintegration* (New York: Cambridge University Press, 1989); Teresa P. R. Caldeira, *City of Walls: Crime, Segregation, and Citizenship in São Paulo* (Berkeley: University of California Press, 2000).
5. For the use of statistics as part of political debates leading to the June 2004 march, see *La Jornada*, 26 June 2004; also see Rafael Ruiz Harrell, *Criminalidad y mal gobierno* (Mexico City: Sansores y Aljure, 1998). A diagnostic of available statistics is available in Arturo Arango, "Indicadores de Seguridad Pública en México: La Construcción de un Sistema de Estadísticas Delictivas" (15 May 2003) in Center for U.S.-Mexican Studies, Project on Reforming the Administration of Justice in Mexico, http://repositories.cdlib.org/usmex/prajm/arango. For critical views, see Pierre Bourdieu, Jean-Claude Chamboredon, and Jean-Claude Passeron, *El oficio de sociólogo: Presupuestos epistemológicos*, trans. Fernando Hugo Azcurra and José Sazbón (Mexico City: Siglo Veintiuno, 1975), 23; Mike Maguire, "Crime Statistics, Patterns, and Trends: Changing Perceptions and their Implications," in *The Oxford Handbook of Criminology*, ed. Mike Maguire, Rod Morgan, and Robert Reiner (New York: Clarendon Press, 1994). Also see Ira Beltrán and Pablo Piccato, "Crimen en el siglo XX: Fragmentos de análisis sobre la evidencia cuantitativa," in *Los últimos cien años, los próximos cien años*, ed. Ariel Rodríguez Kuri and Sergio Tamayo (Mexico City: Universidad Autónoma Metropolitana, 2004), 13–44. A historical perspective is offered in Silvana Patriarca, *Numbers and Nationhood: Writing Statistics in Nineteenth-Century Italy* (New York: Cambridge University Press, 1996); and Mauricio Tenorio-Trillo, *Mexico at the World's Fairs: Crafting a Modern Nation* (Berkeley: University of California Press, 1996).
6. See the spots, several referring to *la ciudad del miedo* ("city of fear," implicitly, Mexico City) at http://www.mexicounido.org/. Also see *La Jornada*, 29 July 2005.

7. Caldeira, *City of Walls*, 2, 20, 27, 30, 35. On stigmatization, see Braithwaite, *Crime, Shame and Reintegration*.
8. See Lila Caimari, "El caso Ayerza. Historia de una pasión punitive" (paper presented at "La Ley de los Profanos. Nociones Populares de Crimen, Castigo y Justicia en la Argentina, 1880–1955," Universidad de San Andrés Interdisciplinary Symposium, Buenos Aires, 2004).
9. See Pablo Piccato, *City of Suspects: Crime in Mexico City, 1900–1931* (Durham, NC: Duke University Press, 2001), chapter 3. Increasing penalties were proposed for relatives and employees involved in kidnapping. *La Jornada de Oriente*, 22 June 2005.
10. Daniel Arizmendi, "El Mochaorejas," was sentenced to thirty-eight years in prison. He cut off his victims' ears to coerce relatives into paying the ransom. *La Jornada*, 2 February 2003. On accusations against Carrillo Olea regarding kidnapping and narcotrafficking, and his resignation, see *New York Times*, 23 February 1997; *New York Times*, 10 February 1998; and *New York Times*, 13 May 1998.
11. Historians have reflected on the use of transgression cases to illuminate broader patterns. For Mexican examples, see Kevin Terraciano, "Crime and Culture in Colonial Mexico: The Case of the Mixtec Murder Note," *Ethnohistory* 45, no. 4 (1998); Paul J. Vanderwood, *Juan Soldado: Rapist, Murderer, Martyr, Saint* (Durham, NC: Duke University Press, 2004). Carlo Ginzburg, for example, stresses the dialogical character of inquisition and ethnographic narratives in *The Judge and the Historian: Marginal Notes on a Late-Twentieth-Century Miscarriage of Justice*, trans. Antony Shugaar (London: Verso, 1999).
12. Emile Durkheim, *The Rules of Sociological Method*, ed. Steven Lukes, trans. W. D. Halls (New York: The Free Press, 1982), 98.
13. Ibid.
14. Ibid.
15. Ibid., 101.
16. Cited in David Garland, *Punishment and Modern Society: A Study in Social Theory* (Chicago: University of Chicago Press, 1990), 33.
17. Cited in Garland, *Punishment and Modern Society*, 79.
18. Garland, *Punishment and Modern Society*, 53.
19. Kai T. Erikson, *Wayward Puritans: A Study in the Sociology of Deviance* (New York: John Wiley, 1966). Also see Richard J. Evans, *Rituals of Retribution: Capital Punishment in Germany, 1600–1987* (New York: Oxford University Press, 1996).
20. Sam Quinones, *True Tales from Another Mexico: The Lynch Mob, the Popsicle Kings, Chalino, and the Bronx* (Albuquerque: University of New Mexico Press, 2001), 42–43.
21. Cited in Garland, *Punishment and Modern Society*, 53.
22. Garland, *Punishment and Modern Society*, 30.
23. Ibid., 67.
24. Ibid., 252.
25. Joy Wiltenburg, "True Crime: The Origins of Modern Sensationalism," *American Historical Review* 109, no. 5 (December 2004): 1380.
26. Rosemary Jann, "Sherlock Holmes Codes the Social Body," *Journal of English Literary History* 57, no. 3 (Autumn 1990): 685–708, citation p. 685.

27. Arthur Conan Doyle, *The Complete Adventures and Memoirs of Sherlock Holmes* (New York: Bramhall House, 1975), 6.
28. Jorge Luis Borges and Adolfo Bioy Casares, *Seis problemas para don Isidro Parodi* (Buenos Aires: Sur, 1942).
29. Michel Foucault, ed., *I, Pierre Rivière, Having Slaughtered my Mother, my Sister, and my Brother . . . : A Case of Parricide in the 19th Century*, 1st American ed. (New York: Pantheon Books, 1975), xi, 191, 205–6. On prisoners' narratives, see Pablo Piccato, "Interpretations of Sexuality in Mexico City Prisons: A Critical Version of Roumagnac," in *The Famous 41: Sexuality and Social Control in Mexico, 1901*, ed. Robert McKee Irwin, Edward J. McCaughan, and Michelle Rocío Nasser (New York: Palgrave, 2003). On interviews as underused resources, see Richard Wright and Trevor Bennett, "Exploring the Offender's Perspective: Observing and Interviewing Criminals," in *Measurement Issues in Criminology*, ed. Kimberly Kempf Leonard (New York: Springer-Verlag, 1990), 138. The differences of power expressed by interviewees (Mexican female prisoners) are explored in Mauricio Nelligan, *Mujeres que matan: Prostitución y homicidio femenil en México* (Mexico City: Edamex, 1988), 7, 49.
30. Ginzburg, *The Judge and the Historian*, 12, 14, 16.
31. Foucault, ed., *I, Pierre Rivière*, 204–5.
32. David Garland, "Of Crimes and Criminals: The Development of Criminology in Britain," in *The Oxford Handbook of Criminology*; and Ian Taylor, "The Political Economy of Crime," in *The Oxford Handbook of Criminology*.
33. Carlos Roumagnac, *Los criminales en México. Ensayo de psicología criminal. Seguido de dos casos de hermafrodismo observado por los señores doctores Ricardo Egea . . . Ignacio Ocampo* (Mexico City: N.p., 1904). Roumagnac had been a young prisoner himself because of his journalistic work in the 1890s. See Martín Gabriel Barrón Cruz, "Bosquejo histórico. La cárcel de Belén y el sistema carcelario" (Mexico City: unpublished manuscript, 2001); Buffington, *Criminal and Citizen*; Piccato, "Interpretations of Sexuality." On prisons as laboratories, see Francisco Martinez Baca and Vergara Manuel, *Estudios de Antropología Criminal: Memoria que por disposición del Superior gobierno del Estado de Puebla presentan* (Puebla: Benjamín Lara, 1892). An excellent study of the genre is in Lila M. Caimari, "Remembering Freedom: Life as Seen from the Prison Cell (Buenos Aires Province, 1930–1950)," in *Crime and Punishment in Latin America: Law and Society since Late Colonial Times*, ed. Ricardo Donato Salvatore, Carlos Aguirre, and Gilbert M. Joseph (Durham, NC: Duke University Press, 2001). Also see Philippe Artières, ed., *Le Livre des Vies Coupables: Autobiographies de Criminels (1896–1909)* (Paris: Albin Michel, 2000).
34. Michel Foucault, *Discipline and Punish: The Birth of the Prison* (New York: Vintage, 1979), 68. Also see Peter Linebaugh, *The London Hanged: Crime and Civil Society in the Eighteenth Century* (New York: The Penguin Press, 1991).
35. See José Guadalupe Posada, *Una niña que mata a su anciana madre*, metal type print, n.d., in *Posada's Popular Mexican Prints*, ed. Roberto Berdecio and Stanley Appelbaum (New York: Dover, 1972). Also see Federico Gamboa, *La llaga* (Mexico City: Eusebio Gómez de la Puente, 1922); Federico Gamboa, *Santa* (Mexico City: Eusebio Gómez de la Puente, 1927).

36. Julio Guerrero, *La génesis del crimen en México: Estudio de psiquiatría social* (Paris: Viuda de Charles Bouret, 1901). See Ariel Rodríguez Kuri, "Julio Guerrero," in *Ciencia, filosofía y sociedad en cinco intelectuales del México liberal*, ed. Carlos Illades and Ariel Rodríguez Kuri (Mexico City: Universidad Autónoma Metropolitana, 2001).
37. Oscar Lewis, *The Children of Sánchez: Autobiography of a Mexican Family* (New York: Random House, 1961). Lewis edited the testimonies with his own literary and theoretical agenda in mind. Also see Matthew C. Gutmann, "Los hijos de Lewis: La sensibilidad antropológica y el caso de los pobres machos," *Alteridades* 4, no. 7 (1994). The book caused a storm when the Fondo de Cultura Económica published it in Spanish, leading to President Gustavo Díaz Ordaz firing the press's director, Arnaldo Orfila Reynal. For an example of the narrative devices of the growing literature in novels and reportage on narcos, see Darío Fritz and María Idalia Gómez, *Con la muerte en el bolsillo* (Mexico City: Planeta, 2005).
38. Octavio Paz, *El laberinto de la soledad*, 3rd ed. (Mexico City: Fondo de Cultura Económica, 1963); and Samuel Ramos, *El perfil del hombre y la cultura en México*, 2nd ed. (Mexico City: P. Robredo, 1938).
39. See, for example, Larisa y Marisol Pérez Lizaur Adler Lomnitz, *Una familia de la élite mexicana, 1820–1980: Parentesco, clase y cultura* (Mexico City: Alianza, 1993). See the critique of pensadores in Claudio Lomnitz-Adler, *Exits from the Labyrinth: Culture and Ideology in the Mexican National Space* (Berkeley: University of California Press, 1992). On Mexican anthropology, see Buffington, *Criminal and Citizen*, chapter 7; and Matthew Gutmann, *The Meanings of Macho: Being a Man in Mexico City* (Los Angeles: University of California Press, 1996).
40. See Michael Warner, *Publics and Counterpublics* (New York: Zone Books, 2002), 67–68. Publics are distinguished from audiences in that they are the points of reference for discourses, but also in that they do not require the physical proximity of members. More important, in Warner's view, are the cultural forms that mediate their coming together (p. 72). On photographers and justice, see John Mraz, *Nacho López, Mexican Photographer*, vol. 14 (Minneapolis: University of Minnesota Press, 2003).
41. Eugenia Lean, *Public Passions: The Trial of Shi Jianqiao and the Rise of Popular Sympathy in Republican China* (Berkeley: University of California Press, 2007). On police chronicles, see Carlos Monsiváis, *A ustedes les consta: Antología de la crónica en México* (Mexico City: ERA, 1980); and Eduardo Téllez Vargas and José Ramón Garmabella, *¡Reportero de policía!: El Güero Téllez* (Mexico City: Ediciones Océano, 1982).
42. Warner, *Publics and Counterpublics*, 114.
43. Fredric Jameson, *The Political Unconscious: Narrative as a Socially Symbolic Act* (Ithaca: Cornell University Press, 1981), 80–81.
44. Ibid., 79.
45. Ibid., 80.
46. Rita Felski, *The Gender of Modernity* (Cambridge: Harvard University Press, 1995), 19.
47. Wiltenburg, "True Crime," 1403.

CHAPTER ONE

Tales of Two Women
The Narrative Construction of Porfirian Reality

~≈~ Robert Buffington and Pablo Piccato ~≈~

It was the perfect murder, really. Illicit passions: two beautiful women of the night feuding over a dashing young rake, a masked ball, casual taunts, thwarted assaults, escalating threats. Heinous crime: the lover's borrowed gun, a midnight bordello visit, fighting words, a gunshot, a maid's scream, a young woman's tragic death. Cruel punishment: suicidal remorse (by some accounts), humiliating public trial, twenty lost years (the maximum sentence for a woman) in Mexico City's squalid Belén jail. The Tarasquillo Street murder had it all!

And so it happened that, in an era enamored of all things French, Mexico City had its very own cause célèbre. A scant twelve years earlier, professional Francophile and amateur criminologist Rafael Zayas de Enríquez had devoted an entire volume of his *Fisiología del crimen* to notorious foreign criminals such as Alfonse Dupont, the hunchbacked wife killer, and Charles Guiteau, the deranged anarchist assassin of President Garfield.[1] Now, Mexico too could claim a prominent place in the international annals of infamous crime.

Infamous *modern* crimes, that is. In the tales of the Tarasquillo Street murder, there would be no scowling highwaymen to intimidate travelers and choke off commerce: perpetrator María Villa (a.k.a. "La Chiquita"), victim Esperanza Gutiérrez (a.k.a. "La Malagueña"), and faithless lover Salvador Ortigoza were thoroughly modern characters. In theses tales—even as Mexico's "indispensable caudillo" Porfirio Díaz presided over the birth of a new century—degenerate urban sophisticates had supplanted, at least in "our cultured capital," the romantic rural bandits of Mexico's formative, not to say, distressingly crude nineteenth century.[2] In these tales, the setting could just as well have been Paris.

A modern murder for a modern age! It couldn't help but capture the popular imagination. Mexico City's thriving (if increasingly persecuted) press certainly had a field day: respectable dailies, tabloids, and court reporters were irresistibly drawn to the Tarasquillo Street murder like moths—the classic harbingers of death—to the city's new electric lights.[3] So were two of Porfirian Mexico's leading artistic lights: popular engraver José Guadalupe Posada, illustrator of numerous broadsides and mainstay of the capital's prolific penny press, and his elite counterpart, novelist Federico Gamboa, whose Zolaesque *Santa* (based as we will see on considerable personal experience) would soon titillate an international audience with its provocative glimpses of Mexico City's underworld.[4] Nor did Esperanza's murder suffer the usual quick fade from the fickle public's collective consciousness. Seven years later (perhaps not coincidentally the year following the publication of Gamboa's *Santa*), another criminologist, Carlos Roumagnac, in his *Los criminales en México,* gave pride of place to extensive interviews with the still incarcerated María.

So much ado about nothing—after all, Mexico City's murder rate was more than twelve times higher than Madrid's during this period—compels the historian's gaze.[5] Why all the fuss? Who did the fussing? What does it mean? On the surface, the answer to the first question is fairly straightforward. Sociologists have long insisted that the apparently universal fascination with crime reflects its crucial boundary-delimiting function in human societies. Moreover, from a historical perspective, the crimes that most fascinate are those, like Mexico City's Tarasquillo Street murder, through which societies explore the impact of changing economic and social relations on behavioral norms. In this light, an argument can (and will) be made for often-analyzed late nineteenth-century phenomena such as urbanization, industrialization, modernization, as well as less concrete (if ultimately more illuminating) explanations like the onset of modernity. The answer to the second question is even more obvious: all the tales surrounding the Tarasquillo Street murder are told by and mostly for men, albeit men of different classes and interests.

The question of meaning is more difficult, however, because it hinges on the recovery of individual perceptions, collective mentalities, and their complex dialectical interaction. Truth be told, historians' efforts to psychoanalyze the past often encounter insurmountable obstacles (inadequate sources in particular) or drift into unsupportable conjecture (the analyst-patient relationship is slippery enough with both parties present). In the introduction to *The Bourgeois Experience: Victoria to Freud,* Peter Gay makes a spirited defense of "history informed by psychoanalysis," concluding that "[psychoanalytic] theories and . . . techniques, can build the very bridge between individual and collective experience that most historians, deeply uneasy with the Freudian dispensation, have persisted in treating as problematic."[6] Gay's recognition of the need to connect individual and collective experiences is certainly still germane. Nonetheless, the psychoanalytic turn in cultural studies, which uses post-Freudian insights into the construction of the "self" to probe past perceptions of everything from gender and the body to sexuality and death, has many historians more deeply uneasy than ever.[7] And indeed the attempt to recover experiences and perceptions is, at its best, wonderfully insightful, but as historical practice it is uncomfortably presumptuous—at least from the perspective of a profession that, by and large, still clings to positivist notions of objectivity.

Recent work in cultural psychology, however, especially Jerome Bruner's explorations into "the narrative construal of reality," suggests an intriguing alternative to the pitfalls of earlier psychohistory.[8] In *Acts of Meaning*, Bruner claims that "one of the most ubiquitous and powerful discourse forms in human communication is *narrative*," the act of meaning through which humans individually and collectively make sense of their world and thereby "ensure the achievement of civility" needed for the construction and maintenance of a "cultural community." But if narratives ensure civility, Bruner is not suggesting that they serve a directly ideological function because their purpose "is not to reconcile, not to legitimize, not even to excuse, but rather to explicate."[9]

For the prospective psychohistorian, Bruner's shift of focus from the psychoanalysis of individual subjects and collective actors to an exploration of narratives and their role in the construction of culture promises a more manageable approach, one better able to explain the complex, contentious, even contradictory aspects of past "acts of meaning." Thus, this chapter makes no claims to have heard past voices (whether of elite narrators or subaltern subjects), to have understood how our narrators (never mind their subjects) really felt about things, to have tapped into the Porfirian zeitgeist, or even to have uncovered the objective truth about the murder. Instead, taking its cue from Bruner, it analyzes the different tales told about the Tarasquillo Street murder for what these "narrative construals" of Porfirian reality can tell us about the "cultural community," turn-of-the-century Mexico City, that found them so irresistible.

Public Narrative and the "Truth" about Tarasquillo Street

Any cause célèbre is by definition a public narrative. It is public in the sense that it is constructed by multiple narrators (newspaper reporters, witnesses, participants, lawyers, the judge) in public spaces (police stations, courtrooms, newspapers). It is also, for that reason, highly unstable. Ambiguity of reference and inherent negotiability (two of Bruner's "universals of narrative reality") are especially true of publicly constructed narratives, and they are especially true of the newspaper reports generated by the Tarasquillo Street murder and María's subsequent trial. By the trial's end, a dominant construal—reflected in the guilty verdict and harsh sentence—had indeed emerged, but not without challenges. According to this dominant construal, María's crime breached "the ordinariness of life"; her trial explored and defined the nature of that breach, and her punishment repaired it. But how effectively? And for how long?[10]

The contested public narrative of the Tarasquillo Street murder went something like this: María Villa and Esperanza Gutiérrez had worked together in the elegant brothels of the capital, but they had become rivals for the love of Salvador Ortigoza, the son of a respected lawyer. The father's money allowed Salvador to dress well and spend lavishly at Mexico City's many night clubs and restaurants.[11] Salvador was María's lover and visited her almost every day, but he had also been seen with Esperanza. This triggered María's jealousy and led to Esperanza's public defiance. A verbal confrontation in a restaurant escalated when Esperanza pushed María, who spat on her. Esperanza then hit María and even tore her dress. People intervened to prevent further fighting but María refused to let it drop. The dispute might have seemed trivial, given that both women were prostitutes and Salvador was not willing to "rescue" María from her job; but María's previous experience with an earlier lover, who had set up an apartment for her, suggested that close friendship with a male protector could become important in the future.[12] Her reputation was at stake.

In María's eyes, the dispute concerned her honor, which was undermined by Esperanza's ongoing affair with her lover.[13] Earlier, when Salvador had appeared unwilling to decide between them, the two women had agreed on a duel. The duel was to occur in a neutral place and both women would be armed because María was physically stronger. These arrangements respected the equal conditions and public setting expected of a proper duel—even though duels, especially with guns or swords, were considered the exclusive provenance of upper-class men.[14] Other prostitutes intervened before the encounter could take place and the rivals were dissuaded from pursuing the matter further. But the issue was not resolved: María became obsessed by hatred of Esperanza and love for Salvador. During the trial María testified that, at her request, Salvador had stopped seeing Esperanza three months before the murder; Esperanza nonetheless continued to humiliate María in public by claiming that she still owned Salvador's affection.[15]

Instead of a duel, as María had hoped, the murder was a relatively simple event, taking place in the intimacy of Esperanza's bedroom with only the victim's maid as unwilling witness. Esperanza had publicly mocked María at a masquerade ball during the early morning hours of March 8, 1897. On the taxi ride home, María borrowed Salvador's gun, ostensibly to prevent a "mishap" in view of his recent fight with a former friend. Salvador gave her the gun, expecting to recover it the following day.[16] A few hours later, María went to Esperanza's bordello, expecting to find Salvador with her. She was let in because they knew her at the house. Once inside, she walked directly to Esperanza's bedroom and knocked. The door was closed, so María knocked again. Esperanza, who was about to go to sleep, opened the door. According to trial records, their conversation went something like this:

María: Why are you mocking me?
Esperanza: Because I want to (followed by more insults).
María: Well, you shouldn't do it.
Esperanza: I'll mock you if I please.

A short struggle ensued and María shot Esperanza in her left eye with Salvador's gun.[17]

For the public, the gun added a surprising twist (it occupies center frame in Posada's broadside; see fig. 1.1). Women, even prostitutes, did not commonly carry guns. But in using a gun against Esperanza, María was only doing what any man would do. Physical punishment for adultery and other circumstances in which a male offender was expected to defend "his honor" were accepted as mitigating circumstances by the penal code.[18] María's case was extraordinary only because she was a woman.

According to the traditional view, women could lose honor but depended on men to recover it. They were thus categorically excluded from traditional dueling.[19] Nonetheless, there is ample evidence that women engaged in duel-like confrontations to defend their reputations.[20] Like their male counterparts, lower-class women were sometimes prompted by their peers to use violence to repair damage to their public honor. In a 1904 case, for example, alleged assailant María Rojas insisted that María Cleofas Pérez had addressed her with "grave insults" because of "previous quarrels having to do with jealousy." As in a duel, both women were accompanied by other women who served as informal seconds. One of Rojas's friends told her, "Don't hold back girl, hit her" and handed her a knife with which Rojas wounded Pérez in the face.[21] And although duels, regardless of class, usually involved parties of the same sex, in rare cases women even defended their reputations by attacking men.[22]

María apparently felt a similar sense of justification: she had committed a crime but in the defense of her personal honor. After Esperanza fell to the floor, mortally wounded, María placed the gun on the victim's nightstand, sat on a chair, and waited for the police to come and arrest her. She was unwilling to run away from an act intended to vindicate her public persona. Even after the initial shock had worn off and the enormity of her deed became apparent, María acknowledged her responsibility for what was the restoration of her reputation. She told the first policeman to arrive that she had killed Esperanza. She then proceeded to threaten Esperanza's maid, María Torices, with the reminder that one day she would return from the Belén jail.

At the police station, María confessed to the crime, carefully maintaining her dignity. She explained the enmity between herself and the victim, and detailed the events of the preceding night. She stated that she had not wanted to respond to Esperanza's mockery at the dance because that would have caused a confrontation between Salvador, who was dancing with María, and Esperanza's male companion. María was careful to take all the blame on herself and protect Salvador. She also declared her lack of remorse: "If Esperanza had ten lives," she swore, "ten times I would have killed her, one by one."[23] But subsequent events changed her attitude. María soon realized that she faced severe punishment, and during the trial she would contradict these earlier statements.

The September trial was well attended with an audience that included glamorous "women of the street," famous bullfighters, and other exotic (and erotic) figures from Mexico City's nightlife.[24] Although María, like most lower-class defendants, stood little chance of acquittal, this aura of glamour and tragedy kept the public's rapt attention throughout the trial.

The trial itself was something of a farce. Judge Manuel F. de la Hoz and the public prosecutor, José Peón del Valle, both questioned María about the crime. The judge, as in most Mexican jury trials, functioned as the principal prosecutor, grilling María mercilessly to extract the open and complete confession that would ensure a guilty verdict. In this particular case, the judge and prosecutor stood to gain considerable reputation with a conviction.[25] Moreover, María lacked proper legal representation. During the proceedings that followed her arrest, no defense lawyer assisted her. When the case reached the pretrial stage at which the defense attorney was to present María's case to the judge and refute the prosecution's conclusions, nothing was done. The judge assigned two public defense lawyers, José María Pavón and Rafael Rodríguez Talavera, to her case only on the final day of the jury hearing.[26]

Frustrated by her lack of legal counsel, María attempted to defend herself against the judge's relentless questions. Trial records show that in court María contradicted her earlier statements to police—denying her ongoing dispute with Esperanza and claiming that the gun had gone off accidentally during a struggle—in an effort to reduce her legal responsibility. The obvious contradictions were not her principal concern; María was appealing to the jury's mercy by manipulating prevalent images of women as victims rather than as perpetrators of violence. Crimes of passion allowed women in late nineteenth-century France, for example, to construct exculpatory narratives based on the premise of mental feebleness that allowed them to escape punishment for attacking their lovers or husbands. In Mexico, similar cases would become the focus of press attention a few years after María's trial. In these self-serving narratives, later elaborated by journalists and consumed by voracious readers, the defense of honor was not the principal argument. Rather, narrators (including the defendants themselves) used notions of "insanity" and "blind passion" to emphasize the tragic (as opposed to criminal) elements of their stories.[27] These cases, however, typically involved upper-class women and their lovers. As a lower-class prostitute, despite her upscale clientele, María would not be so lucky.

In an effort to suggest that she had committed the crime in a moment of "blind passion," María said that her memory of the murder was hazy. Asked to visualize the crime, she declared that the gun had gone off accidentally as suggested by the gunpowder burns inside her coat. The judge rejected that claim, noting that the bullet had entered the left eye and followed a downward trajectory, even though Esperanza was much taller than María.[28] Then María insisted that she barely knew Esperanza: she had seen her but never talked to her. The judge pressed her, noting that she had previously confessed to a dispute with Esperanza. Other prostitutes had heard María say that, despite Esperanza's beauty, she did not like her. But María continued her denials.[29] Finally, after focused questioning, María acknowledged that on one occasion Esperanza had "offended" her and that they exchanged blows and spat on each other.[30] María struggled in the face of the judge's relentless questioning. When she declared that the gun had "fired itself" in the struggle with Esperanza, the judge accused her of lying because that contradicted her previous statements to police. She replied that her recollection was not clear.[31] The judge asked María to reproduce the "bad words" (*malas palabras*) that Esperanza addressed to María moments before the crime; María refused to repeat them. When the judge asked her why the police found her at the scene with a piece of Esperanza's robe in her hand, María remained silent.[32]

While María tried to maintain her dignity, the judge sought to prove her immorality and "shady past" (*malos antecedentes*). He insisted that the origin of the fatal dispute was trivial because the suspect had no honor to defend.

Questioned by the judge, Salvador acknowledged that María was a prostitute and that he never intended "to make her his mistress ... [or] separate her from her current lifestyle." The judge asked him if he was aware that both María and Esperanza "had relations with other men since they were women who sold their bodies to whoever could afford them." Salvador did not reply.[33] And, to undermine María's defense, the judge sought to prove that she had.

María's advocate, Rodríguez Talavera, supplied some final oratorical flourishes in support of María's arguments even though he had played no part during previous interrogations. He presented himself as a humble law student but then vigorously defended the accused, who he described in emotional terms as a persecuted victim, an approach that earned him public applause and prompted the judge to empty the courtroom of most spectators. Rodríguez Talavera argued that María was not a criminal but a victim of unfortunate circumstance, the product of seduction and exploitation, which had pushed her to prostitution "not through badness but through the workings of fate."[34] He failed, however, to obtain an acquittal or a more lenient sentence for the defendant.[35]

Not surprisingly, the judge's interpretation of events—designed to appeal to a class-conscious society that conceded honor solely to upper-class female offenders in crimes of passion—proved decisive. The jury found María guilty of murder. The judge sentenced her to twenty years in prison, the harshest punishment she could receive since the penal code excluded women from the death penalty.[36]

In this reconstruction of the Tarasquillo Street murder and María Villa's trial, cobbled together from various news reports, all the ambiguities and negotiations typical of public narrative take center stage. To be sure, the judge's interpretation of events, backed by the considerable power of the state, became the official story. But the alternative narratives still played a prominent and subversive role in the story's trajectory.

The court's reading of the Tarasquillo Street murder proved definitive only in a legal sense. The public narrative was more complicated. The court may have rejected María's and her lawyer's attempts to present alternate readings, but, as the audience's noisy agreement with the defense's closing argument indicates, not everyone was convinced by the official version, which explains the judge's reaction. For example, in her interview with Roumagnac, which we will examine later, María pointed out the double standard embedded in the Mexican criminal justice system, noting that when a jealous former lover had used a gun against her, the jury chose not to punish him. He had not killed her, of course, but in her case the jury had rejected jealousy as a mitigating circumstance because "for women like me, they judge us heartless, incapable of feeling true affection."[37]

The coexistence of these different constructions of reality raises some interesting questions about the nature of cultural hegemony. If Bruner is right and the cultural function of narratives (in the anthropological sense) is "not to reconcile, not to legitimize, not even to excuse, but rather to explicate," then public narratives, like the case of Tarasquillo Street, can both support and subvert that hegemony. The court's attempt to impose its highly ideological interpretation of a widely shared story is thus only a temporary and inherently unstable negotiation—a plea for, rather than an assertion of, public legitimation. The nominally liberal Mexican judicial system might abjure exemplary public punishment for women, but open courtrooms and even the government-subsidized mass press provided spaces for alternative readings of a woman's criminal actions. Stories of violence and uncontrolled sexuality thus proved dangerous vehicles for the promulgation of elite ideologies. And for Porfirian elites the need for ideological consensus had become something of an obsession.

The Tarasquillo Street murder occurred during a period of rapid development in Mexico City. As capitalism expanded under the watchful eyes of Porfirio Díaz's *científico* advisors (including criminologists like Carlos Roumagnac), class, ethnic, and gender roles became increasingly unsettled: immigration swelled the city's population; women in ever-greater numbers abandoned the family hearth for salaried jobs in the public sphere; and streets, restaurants, dance halls, bars, and brothels took on an aura of uncontrolled and thus dangerous popular sociability. The Díaz regime, firmly committed to both "order and progress," responded with a series of "scientific" (if still authoritarian) gestures: modernizing the police, building new prisons, and revising the penal code.[38] But these gestures were often limited and sometimes merely cosmetic; broad areas of marginality, squalor, and danger surrounded the capital's well-policed central spaces. According to the regime's own statistics, crime actually increased during the last decades of the nineteenth century despite corrective measures. In this context, crime stories helped depict and make sense of the contradictions and conflicts associated with urbanization, industrialization, and the new culture of modernity that accompanied them.[39]

Not surprisingly, then, those who produced the public narratives of the Tarasquillo Street murder both reflected and attempted to alleviate the many anxieties of a society under stress, a "cultural community" fearful of changing class and gender relations. But just how reassuring was it? In *The Consequences of Modernity*, Anthony Giddens notes that modernity (as a mode of perception) promises a stability that its inherent reflexivity (the constant revision of knowledge essential to the notion of advancement) constantly undermines.[40] Seen in this light, the Porfirian motto seems fundamentally paradoxical: progress might promise reassurance and stability but could only bring anxiety and disorder. The unsettling "truth" of increasing crime, verified by "scientific" statistics (the quintessence of reflexivity), suggests that this was indeed the case in turn-of-the-century Mexico City. So does the court's extremely harsh punishment of María. The tale of Tarasquillo Street, as public narrative, likely raised more questions than the court's best efforts could ever hope to resolve.

The Popular Take on Tarasquillo Street: Murder as Melodrama

If the public narrative remained open to multiple readings, not all of those readings represented a direct threat to public order. In fact, the best publicized popular response—José Guadalupe Posada's broadside, *Bloody Drama in Tarasquillo Square: Assassination of La Malagueña*—ignored the murder's political and social implications altogether (see fig. 1.1). Instead it played off the alternate readings best suited to attract a popular audience: defense of honor and blind passion. Murder as melodrama was the popular order of the day.⁴¹

Posada's print depicts the actual moment of the murder: the discharging gun occupies center frame and Esperanza falls backward, presumably shot through

1.1. José Guadalupe Posada, *Drama sangriento en la Plazuela de Tarasquillo: Asesinato de la Malagueña* (Mexico City: Imprenta de Antonio Vanegas Arroyo, 1897), engraving.

the left eye. The setting (possibly the hall outside Esperanza's bedroom) includes the overstuffed velvet sofa and elegant armchairs of a turn-of-the-century upper-class parlor. María is fashionably dressed in black and carefully coiffed in somewhat matronly bourgeois style for an evening out; Esperanza, having just gotten ready for bed, is in a white slip and stockings with her hair hanging loose. The colors are ambiguous: black as evil or respectability, white as innocence or immodesty. But everything in the print—furnishings, clothes, hairstyles, and especially the gun—is unequivocally modern, stylish, and even glamorous.

Only María's posture disturbs. Left arm akimbo, right arm outstretched, right leg forward, head high, she demonstrates the classic form of the upper-class male duelist. If narratives seek novelty "by making the ordinary strange again," then Posada's print succeeds wonderfully.[42] A similar scene between two armed men in a public space would have been mildly interesting but hardly remarkable. This "duel," fought by women in a private space, could not help but shock its intended audience. Another possibility—María as cuckolded spouse (hence her hyper-respectable dress and coiffure) taking revenge on her rival (in immodest underwear and free-flowing hair)—is more shocking still.

Another Posada broadside, *Tears and Sighs in Belén Jail*, tells a much different, even contradictory, tale—one that stresses María's suffering as she struggles with remorse, shame, and the hardships of prison (see fig. 1.2).[43] Two images, one of María crying and the other confronting Esperanza's ghost, accompanied by their respective texts, convey the consequences of transgression. The prose text expresses her "very sad and terrible situation . . . the palpable and true result of a woman who sunk herself in the mire of life." And although it recognizes that "she adopted this career almost through necessity," it nevertheless insists that "had this poor woman dedicated herself to honest work, she wouldn't be lamenting such a dismal deed today." As in a classic fable, the lesson is self-evident: "This shameful event serves as a real and positive example for young women who find themselves in the beginning of life in the situation of this unfortunate woman." The poems (and the accompanying image) expand the theme by dwelling on the cruel torment produced by the evil deed on both the perpetrator and the victim's mother. The first poem is remarkable for its repentant tone.

> Me parece que ya miro
> a mi víctima de frente
> Con el rostro ensangrentado,
> Y la mirada ferviente
>   Si! Si! aquí estás, Esperanza,
> Perdona mi alevosía!

No me atormentes ya más,
Será eterna mi agonía.
    Perdóname, Dios bendito!
Mi crimen es muy inmenso,
Y cada vez crece más
En mi alma el remordimiento!
    Día ocho del mes de Marzo
Del año noventa y siete!
Cometí este horrible crimen
Fecha fatal . . . indeleble!
    Ay, Dios, quítame la vida
Que ya no puedo vivir,
Que ya es preferible la muerte
A este incesante sufrir![44]

In this poem, María is said to feel a remorse for which there is little actual evidence (at least until her interview with Roumagnac seven years later). Her initial statement—"If Esperanza had ten lives, ten times I would have killed her, one by one"—suggests that she felt quite justified; nor does her courtroom

1.2. José Guadalupe Posada, *Lágrimas y sollozos en la cárcel de Belén* (Imprenta de Antonio Vanegas Arroyo, 1897), leaflet.

testimony echo the near suicidal tone of the broadside verses. While the print in which she murders Esperanza seems to capture her defiant attitude quite well, the poem cries out, "Oh, God, take my life . . . death is preferable to this incessant suffering," a woman's classic lament for her lost innocence. The poet most likely ignored the facts, instead borrowing a timeworn trope from the cultural stock of famous last words—murder leads to damnation—to provide a proper lesson that would offset the shocking callousness of the cold-blooded murder depicted in Posada's print. And what more appropriate torment for a selfish, heartless woman than ghostly apparitions and eternal self-recrimination?

Taken together—prints, poems, and prose—Posada's broadside tale put a sensationalistic, sentimental, moralistic, even traditional spin on the Tarasquillo Street murder. Emotional rather than legalistic, this reading threatened social order only in the sense that it glamorized the breach in the ordinariness of life that the official story sought to close. The purpose here was heightened sensation—to reduce narrative to its two most melodramatic moments: Esperanza's murder and María's remorse. According to Bruner, another universal of narrative reality is *generic particularity*. "Narratives deal with (or are "realized" in) particulars," he notes, "but particularity seems only to be the vehicle of narrative realization. For particular stories are construed as falling into genres or types."[45] This is especially apparent in Posada's broadsides, which rely heavily on the reader's ability to supply the proper genre to the particulars it sets forth. The technique is remarkably efficient but necessarily dependent on deeply embedded tropes and traditions, in part because it leaves no space to develop a complex narrative. Deprived of historical context and unconcerned about the known facts of the case, the author of *Bloody Drama in Tarasquillo Square* and *Tears and Sighs in Belén Jail* had little inclination or opportunity to explore the larger political and social implications of the murder; the guilt and remorse are María's alone—a threat perhaps to what Giddens calls "ontological security" but hardly an immediate danger to Porfirian social structures.[46] Instead, like the larger public narrative of which it was a part, it served to explicate social change to its popular audience. The broadside's immediacy likely reflects the greater intensity with which the lower classes experienced that change. It did not, however, suggest remedial action.

Lingering Concerns: Criminology as Ideological Narrative

The public narrative of the Tarasquillo Street murder, generated by both the respectable and tabloid presses, was highly ambiguous and much negotiated. These characteristics were much less prominent in the criminological narrative of María's life published seven years after the fact by científico, journalist, litterateur, criminologist, and sometime police inspector Carlos Roumagnac.[47] Instead, in Roumagnac's tale, yet another of Bruner's narrative universals, *actions have reasons*, takes center stage. "What people do in narratives," Bruner argues, "is never by chance, nor is it strictly determined by cause and effect; it is motivated by beliefs, desires, theories, values, or other 'intentional' states."[48] Roumagnac's study, *Los criminales en México*, was all about getting to the bottom of the intentional states that produced criminal behavior and, for that purpose, María's case was perfect. The public exploration of the immediate events leading up to and including Esperanza's murder continued through the trial. Roumagnac's in-depth investigation of intentional states would require considerably more context.

As Roumagnac tells the story, María Villa was born, probably in 1875, in San Pedro, Jalisco, to lower-class but respectable parents (see fig. 1.3). Her father was gainfully employed (*empleado particular*) and lived a healthy, well-ordered life until his death from pneumonia at age seventy-five. Her mother died of tuberculosis (like her mother before her) when she was twenty-nine and her youngest child, María, was nine. The two older siblings were still alive and in good health in 1903, the year of Roumagnac's interview.

His obsession with medical histories reflected Roumagnac's professional agenda. María's background was fairly wholesome; most of his other female

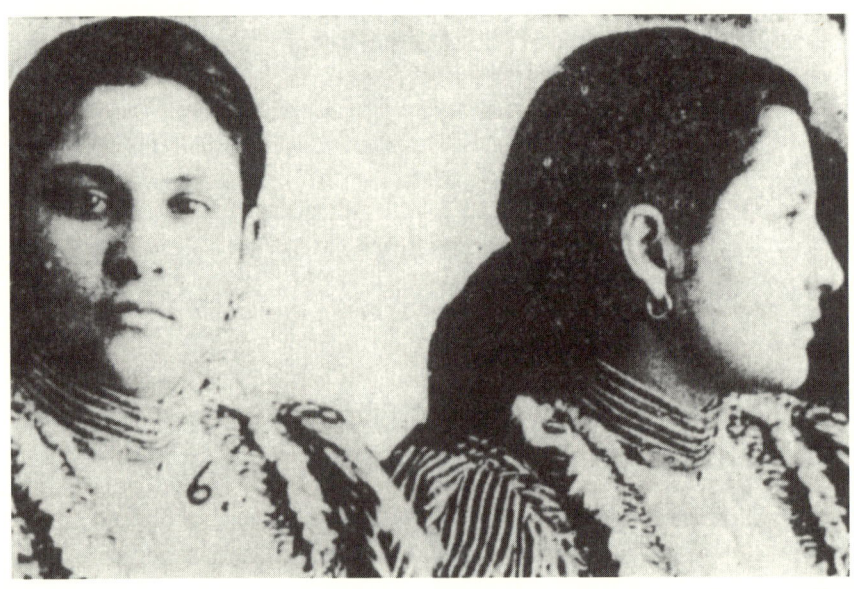

1.3. María Villa from Carlos Roumagnac's *Los criminales en México*, 104.

inmate interviewees had family histories of alcoholism and epilepsy, which criminologists considered potent indicators—environmental, genetic, or some combination—of physical degeneracy and potential criminality. Tuberculosis, a killer especially of malnourished, overworked lower-class women, carried more ambiguous but still negative connotations of physical weakness and endemic poverty. The implied link to María's maternal line is hardly coincidental. And other details from María's medical history—smallpox at age six or seven, yellow fever two years later, chronic headaches since childhood, bed wetting until age eight, a spastic upper colon as an adult—reinforced this impression of debility by insinuating a connection between various physical maladies and later criminal behavior.[49]

In Roumagnac's construction (and he was typical of his profession), the roots of criminality lurked somewhere in each criminal's shady past, awaiting only the focused gaze of the scientist/criminologist to expose them. Again, however, María's case was far from clear cut. At age five, she was sent to a Catholic girls' boarding school in Guadalajara where she received "some instruction and good examples." In the interview, she assured Roumagnac that each girl kept to her own bed at night and that they entertained no "clear notion of vice." In liberal Mexico, many intellectuals regarded the Catholic Church as a reactionary, even decadent presence in civil society that frightened superstitious peasants into obedience (and out of their meager earnings) rather than inculcating proper moral values. Women were considered especially susceptible to its pernicious influence. If Roumagnac shared these views, he does not say; the liberal reader, however, was free to draw the "obvious" conclusion.[50]

Another of Roumagnac's concerns was María's love life. It began at age thirteen when the twenty-one-year-old son of her patrons fell in love with her, took her out of school, and kept her as his mistress for a year and nine months. During this time he "enjoyed" her only three times because, according to María, "she suffered a lot in the first encounter and remained terrorized by those that followed." She further assured Roumagnac that "she experienced no pleasure in her cohabitations." In an aside, he noted that up to this point "she had yet to embark on the road she was soon to follow," adding approvingly that "she didn't get drunk and, as for her health, it was good and she slept normally without dreams or nightmares."[51] A victim of male perfidy perhaps, but still with a clear conscience.

That conscience would quickly become clouded. Obviously unhappy and feeling trapped, the fifteen-year-old María "fell into the clutches" of a "trafficker in human flesh" on a routine recruiting trip to Guadalajara who had heard about her plight from two friends.[52] The desperate María signed "the infamous contract" and was taken to a Mexico City bordello. In Roumagnac's narrative, this is the turning point in her tale. Under male protection in Guadalajara (never mind that she may have had little choice in the matter) and careful to preserve what was left of her virtue, María could sleep without dreams or nightmares. Without that protection and with her virtue for sale, María's fall—as Roumagnac tells it—was inexorable.

After María arrived in Mexico City, things went slowly from bad to worse. She worked for only three months in the bordello before leaving as the mistress of a German patron. She stayed with him for three years. During this time she began to drink but just "to make herself happy nothing more." She also took a lover. When the German discovered them together, he pulled out a revolver and shot María in the knee and side. He was set free on appeal for "reasons [María] could not explain" but that were doubtless related to the circumstances of the attempted murder (*homicidio frustrado*) and her dubious reputation. She rejected a second older male protector, who responded with physical attacks for which he paid no apparent price at all.

Again, the intended lesson as narrated by Roumagnac was hard to miss. The second overt rejection of patriarchal authority marked the beginning of a precipitous moral decline. At age eighteen, María was back in the "public house" where she remained until her arrest for Esperanza's murder. In the bordello, the vices of underworld life began to take their toll. Here, one of her customers ("lovers" for Roumagnac) introduced her to morphine, which made her feel "very content and sleepy" at first, although after she fell asleep it gave her "visions" and "horrible dreams in which cadavers appeared and chased after her with daggers in their hands." She managed to quit for a while until her tempestuous affair with the man Roumagnac calls simply X. (no doubt to protect Salvador Ortigoza's reputation) prompted a relapse and even an increase in dosage.[53] Roumagnac's depiction of María's growing substance abuse underscored his warning to Mexican women about the dangers of resisting patriarchy; it also served as a likely indicator of her inherent criminality.

Her sexuality provided still more clues. During this same period, two Spanish colleagues introduced María to the pleasures of *safismo* (female homosexuality), which they argued was "better than loving a man."[54] After three tries, she gave it up because of her intense love for X., the man she told Roumagnac was the "first and only love of my life."[55] These incidents, which María dismissed as transient, signified much more to her interviewer (and probably his readers). Criminologists of the period generally conflated all socially stigmatized behavior, effectively linking sexual and criminal deviance in a single all-embracing category. Thus María's sexual experiments provided yet another indicator (along with her physical maladies, rejection of patriarchal authority, and substance abuse) of a fundamentally deviant personality.

Further, by reading her life backward, Roumagnac established a likely predisposition to crime that made both María's criminality and Esperanza's murder seem inevitable. The crime, in Roumagnac's narrative, defines the subject. María, of course, might have told her story much differently, but this loss of control would become even more acute once her crime propelled her into the limelight. Not surprisingly, then, the murder itself provided Roumagnac with his dramatic climax. And while it added little to the public narrative's account (and is omitted here for that reason), his retelling reminded his readers that María's past was, in essence, defined by that single act. So too was her future.

Once in jail, as Roumagnac tells it, María's perspective about her crime changed. Despite her initial bitterness, María found a way to recover in jail some of the respect she had lost on the outside. As a prisoner in Mexico City's infamous Belén jail, she came to grips with her disgrace. In her prison diary, excerpted by Roumagnac, she presented herself as a victim of fate and complained about the unfair severity of her sentence:

> How hard and severe justice is when it castigates criminals, but I'm not a criminal at heart because I didn't know what I was doing; it happened suddenly without my realizing it, but the world doesn't judge me like that, but just the opposite.[56]

The style of these passages is sentimental and melodramatic, much like the Posada broadside, but intended more to elicit sympathy than to express remorse.

During the trial, María found herself alone. "Friends have come to visit me in jail," she wrote, "but I understand that it is only out of curiosity; I understand that if they sentence me to a long term, they will flee from me scared, like one flees from a leper or a disease that they might get and they will forget me like the dead." Ortigoza also abandoned her, only after being sure that she would not implicate him in the crime. His letters came less frequently and finally stopped altogether.

After the sentence was handed down, María attempted suicide. The day-to-day grind in Belén was too hard even for her, although she had worked in several whorehouses. Overcrowding, disease, and violence characterized life in the Belén jail (a former women's convent) as they would the new penitentiary, which was inaugurated in 1900.[57] Solitude added to her suffering because she was segregated from the other prisoners and received better treatment than most. Immediately upon her arrival, someone recommended her to the warden, who placed her in a separate room with the company of "only one maid" to protect her from the violence and squalor of the collective dormitories. She saw herself above the rest of the inmates, preferring to read novels than to mingle with the riffraff. To Roumagnac, she stressed her initial distance from other female prisoners: "[T]hey do not understand me and I do not understand them."[58]

With time, however, María slowly overcame her prejudices and was integrated into prison society, establishing successful relationships with fellow inmates and even some prisoners from the men's section. In 1900, prison authorities permitted her to acquire a guitar and mandolin. These were technically illegal, but she, like many other inmates, was allowed to improve her life with a few possessions. Many drank alcohol and some even had dogs; she only wanted to sing. Gradually she began to feel a little better; "it seems that God has sent me consolation," she wrote.[59] On May 5, 1900, the other prisoners "gave [her] a ball with music."[60]

Increasingly integrated into prison life, María soon reached positions of influence in the jail. First, she made money by selling cigarettes.[61] Then she became *mayora*, the prisoner of authority in the women's section.[62] Later, María was separated from her duty because authorities discovered that a male prisoner had visited her. Her removal prompted a rebellion among the female inmates, but the measure was sustained, and María Trinidad T., who had been in charge of the production of atole (a corn beverage served as breakfast), and mayora in other sections, replaced her.[63]

María also managed to preserve an active sex life and enjoy the advantages of a close relationship with male inmates. While in prison she met two men, first Arnulfo P. and then Francisco R., who both managed to enter the women's department to see her by using bribes or disguises. Francisco R. sent her clothes, shoes, and messages through another female prisoner. At first, María rejected him with the argument that "his social sphere is too low for me," but finally gave in to his desires because she felt gratitude for his protection.[64] María hoped to establish marital life with Arnulfo P. after they left prison, but she broke off the relationship when she discovered that he had married another woman inside the prison. She maintained her decision even though he tried to change her mind with promises and threats.

Despite María's longing for the respectability of marital life, she also had close relationships with female inmates. It is difficult to separate intimacy related with mutual protection from the common allegations of homosexuality. Some female inmates established stable relationships that linked love and mutual protection by placing themselves under the shelter of a religious image.

These alliances were formalized through the practice of *madrinazgo*. The *madrina* (godmother) would sponsor another inmate by placing a scapular of the Virgen de la Soledad or a *medida*, a ribbon the size of a saint's face, around her neck, and then praying the "Our Father" three times. This ceremony symbolized protection before the sponsored *ahijada* (godchild) was to appear in court. Although the sources are mute on this point, María may well have participated in just such a relationship.

Homosexual relations were another matter. María acknowledged to Roumagnac that she had homosexual relations when she was a prostitute, but she denied continuing them in Belén. Roumagnac asserted that María's claim was known to be false.[65] In his view, prisoners usually denied their own homosexuality while acknowledging that the practice was common among the rest of the prison population. Homosexual practices were common in both sections of the jail, but male homosexuality concerned authorities more because it often involved violence and was judged more dangerous for the health of society.[66] Here too, Roumagnac's aspersions aside, the extent of María's involvement is far from clear and, indeed, his narrative seems to vacillate on the issue of her redemption, noting both her normal and deviant tendencies.

On the question of remorse, Roumagnac is equally vague. He ends the narrative appropriately enough with María's pledge "to completely rehabilitate herself, lead an ordered life and if God permits her to leave prison alive, to give up vice and dedicate herself to work."[67] The concerns of the criminologist (rehabilitation), policeman (ordered life), moralist (give up vice), and social reformer (dedication to work) were all deliberately addressed in this brief statement. After a few years in the Mexican criminal justice system, María had clearly mastered, if not internalized, criminological discourse. In Roumagnac's jaded estimation, however, these promises (like her denials of safismo) were either duplicitous or naïve and, in several other biographies in *Los criminales en México*, he juxtaposed inmates' pledges with footnotes documenting subsequent arrests. Fittingly enough, on this ambiguous note, his narrative closes. Roumagnac returned to María several years later. In a series of articles published in 1933 he remembered the case and provided additional details of her life in prison. A picture of her aged face in particular suggests a deeper appreciation of her role as a teacher and protector of other inmates in the years preceding her release. The ideological impact of the great 1910 social revolution may well have changed the criminologist's view on criminals like María, who were clearly victims of class exploitation.[68]

Throughout his narrative, Roumagnac expresses a certain ambivalence about María's criminality, but that is not the case with the overall thrust of the narrative itself. On the contrary, her apparently innate gift for dissimulation, for seeming normal while exhibiting hints of degeneracy, reinforces his authority as narrator. For example, in a strategy designed to draw in the reader, Roumagnac stresses María's "feminine coquetry": "In our first interview, [María] presented herself to me as she doubtlessly was in her cell, unkempt and without decoration; while in subsequent [interviews] she dressed as best she could, putting a red ribbon in her hair, and on her hands and ears, the few and humble jewels she still possessed." As in other parts of the narrative, he toys with the reader's expectations: it is never clear if what he describes is "typical" female behavior or the clever machinations of a born criminal. In the final analysis, only an expert criminologist was observant enough to catch the whiff of sulfur behind María's charming facade. Thus, Roumagnac, with considerable literary skill, turns the ambivalent public narrative on its head. In his tale, there is still ambiguity of reference and inherent negotiability, but both signify a hidden danger to Porfirian society. Only the expertise of a well-trained technocrat could guarantee public safety in an ever more confusing world.

The warning—to Mexican women about the fatal price of eschewing male protection, to Mexican men about the criminality lurking behind feminine wiles—was thus loud and clear. And for a científico such as Roumagnac the stakes were high indeed. The accelerated modernization efforts of the Díaz regime had intensified elite anxieties about female criminality. Like their predecessors, Porfirian elites saw modern families anchored by morally irreproachable mothers, wives, and daughters as crucial support systems for productive male workers and citizens. They also readily acknowledged that delinquent women undermined national progress. The social Darwinian subtext of the regime's dominant positivist discourse exacerbated these concerns. Women, especially mothers, symbolized national fertility. And, as women performed vital reproductive and civilizing functions in Porfirian social engineering, their transgressions threatened Mexico's biological and moral survival in the international "struggle for life."[69] In this technocratic vision, María Villa and her ilk were not just criminals but traitors as well, hence the compelling need for the scientific gaze and the opportunity to sound a timely warning.

Esperanza Gutiérrez: Eros and Thantos in Porfirian Mexico

If Roumagnac's narrative history of María Villa's life was objective in style and ideological in content, the same could not be said for the diary entry recording renowned Porfirian novelist Federico Gamboa's visit to view the corpse of Esperanza Gutiérrez. Gamboa's tale is intensely, even self-consciously, personal.

Told in the naturalist style pioneered by Émile Zola (*Nana*, his daring novel about a French prostitute, inspired Gamboa's own *Santa*), this tale plumbed the psychological depths of Porfirian masculinity, revealing (again quite self-consciously) the anxieties around which elite Mexican men constructed their private selves (see fig. 1.4). Women endangered not just the national project but identity itself.

The entry dated March 8, 1897, in Gamboa's diary begins when the author is awakened by his friend and cohort, Jesús Contreras:

> Once in my room, Jesús deciphers the enigma for me: Esperanza Gutiérrez, a pretty young woman of the night, native of Málaga, and with whom we conversed last night at the public costume party, was murdered this morning by María Villa of Guadalajara and also an unredeemed sinner.
>
> At first, the news makes little impression on me; but after analyzing it in the cab in which Jesús took me to the Ministry, I become alarmed at the prospect of being called into court, and with it, and with my name appearing in daily papers and tabloids, the *people of good conscience* will raise a hue and cry and put me on probation, which precedes complete dismissal. The case is grave.
>
> And my fear, bearable at first, turns to panic as I see myself caught up in a prying and implacable criminal investigation, as a witness, no doubt, but as a witness to things not necessarily false but badly done. Taking the bull by the horns, to the court to see the judge, who is a person I regard highly and an acquaintance....
>
> —Relax, the crime is already solved and your name was never mentioned. And between a smile and sermon, he added:—But let this embarrassing incident serve as a warning, use better judgment, man, use better judgment....
>
> [The two friends attend an elegant lunch.]
>
> Why on rising from the table, content, did it occur to Jesús that we should go to the morgue of the Juárez Hospital to see the murdered women on the "slab"?
>
> The upshot is that we went, that the employee who allowed us access to the sinister locale, did it because he was a friend of Jesús's and because he had read one of my books....
>
> Two corpses could be seen in the autopsy room, or "depository," as the "mortician" who escorted us explained; a woman of the people, already sewed up and of a lamentable anatomy, dead of tuberculosis; on the other slab, with forced posture, *reposed* the "Malagueña," in

a nudity totally without temptations, a cadaver's nudity, the bloodless feet, resembling old marble, the exuberant flesh stained with blood; the face with a horrible wound, under the left eye, the imprint of the bullet that ended her suffering; the lips, half open, with the rictus of those that are truly departed, and that can be construed as either a smile or a grimace, depending on how we glimpse it in the final hour. . . .

As moved as I was, Jesús began to draw a pencil sketch of the dead woman.

And while Jesús drew, I never took my eyes off the "Malagueña," seeing how the flies, oh! but hundreds of flies persistent and half drunk from the setting sun, the suspicious odors and the aged and redried blood, hovered and fluttered over the nude and defenseless corpse; gazing at the flesh, yesterday so pleasing and silky, and today rigid, in palpable decomposition, on the way to the worms that devour us all when our time comes. . . . I was drawn, prophetically, to the scar of her wounded eye, a diminutive scar over which fell, tangled, the blond strands of her magnificent hair, uncombed, and dirty. . . .

A very disagreeable detail: the employee that let us in and acted as host in the morgue, while Jesús drew and I pondered a world of thoughts, spoke to me, [. . .] all the while smoking a thick cigar that finally went out between his yellowed fingers. And with a frightful but sincere oath, he threw the slobbered butt into a big puddle of semi-coagulated blood in the floor drain, under the "slab" of marble mottled by previous bloods, that corresponded to metal head rests in which lay the head, the back destroyed, of the "Malagueña," and from which it still dripped, stubbornly . . .

This, and the orgy of flies, propel me from that sinister place, riveting me to the pitiful garden, where I wait for Jesús to put the final touches to his funereal sketch.

We return on foot, in the afternoon, through the sad and populous streets of the Buena Muerte—what horror, *the good death!*—We separate on the corner of San Miguel and Aduana Vieja, dumbfounded, each thinking perhaps in our own way an appropriate thought.[70]

Gamboa's narrative reveals much about Porfirian upper-class masculine anxieties. His precious tone, his questionable concern about the murdered prostitute, and even his peculiarly overwrought romantic/naturalistic style betray the complacency of a self-absorbed cosmopolitan aesthete; but behind the smug veneer lurks "the good death" that leaves him "dumbfounded."[71] The juxtaposition of death and sexuality mirrored in the decomposing corpse of a once desirable prostitute was a common late nineteenth-century bourgeois trope.[72] And Gamboa deploys it without much variation: signs of physical attraction—"nude and defenseless . . . flesh, yesterday so pleasing and silky . . . blond strands of her magnificent hair"—set against signs of bodily degeneration—"horrible wound . . . hundreds of flies . . . palpable decomposition, on the way to the worms that devour us all when the time comes"—seek to reproduce in

1.4. Caricature of Federico Gamboa from *Frivolidades*, 10 October 1910. The poem translates roughly as "What times those were! The bird it sings, / what times those were, of carousals, of 'Santa.' / Today what a difference, so many gold-braided generals, / a thousand ambassadors, a thousand delegates / and a plucked fowl, (he lost his hair) / the bird it says: what times those were!"

TALES OF TWO WOMEN

the reader the narrator's horror, disgust, and fear. Even his inability to avert his eyes from the horror of Esperanza's corpse was standard naturalist fare.[73] So was the belief, only implicit in this excerpt, in a determining environment and the impotence of individual will in the face of "nature."

Typically Porfirian was Gamboa's strongly ingrained sense of class that persisted in spite (and probably also because) of a long-standing history of carnal relations between upper-class men and lower-class women. His diary entry also reveals an abiding interest in and anxiety about the linkages between sexuality and criminality that had by the Porfirian era penetrated deep into literate Mexican society: an interest that bordered on voyeurism and an anxiety perilously close to titillation.

The connections to the public narrative and Roumagnac's more "scientific" project are obvious, although both those sources allowed María at least some opportunity for rebuttal. Gamboa's considerable craft and the personal nature of his chosen genre effectively precluded other voices. This tale is decidedly not about Esperanza herself. Aside from a few physical details—that "magnificent" blond hair—Esperanza is entirely absent from Gamboa's account. Other sources provide only a few clues. The newspaper accounts relate that she was taller than María at 1.506 meters (four feet eleven inches) and a Spanish immigrant (from Málaga, according to Gamboa) come to *hacer la América*. María testified that she had known Esperanza for two or three years from places such as the cantina El Congreso Americano—where they had one of the public fights that preceded the murder—but that they were not close friends.[74] Esperanza's personality, however, emerges only in her fights with María: an offensive gesture that causes María to spit in her face, a retaliatory shove that tore María's dress, her comment "I don't want to be alone" (that María thought was directed at Salvador Ortigoza) the night of the masked ball, and, right before she was killed, "I'll mock you if I like" to María.[75] A proud, tough, even fearless woman comes through these fragmented impressions but nothing else, only "the lips, half open, with the rictus of those that are truly departed, and that can be construed as either a smile or a grimace."[76] Or perhaps in Gamboa's vivid image of the morgue attendant throwing a cigar butt into Esperanza's "semi-coagulated blood . . . that still dripped, stubbornly" from the back of her head into the floor drain. In an essay on subaltern studies, Gayatri Spivak argues that as women are inserted into the historical record they are unavoidably "drained of proper identity."[77] In this tale, the violence of that process strikes forcibly home.

According to Bram Dijkstra, nineteenth-century novelists and artists such as Gamboa and his friend Jesús Contreras typically represented women as "idols of perversity." Moreover, by the turn of the century, these representations had taken a masochistic turn in which "the image of woman as an all-destroying, rampaging animal . . . [expressed the artist's] attempt to come to terms with the implications of his own marginalization."[78] The physicality of Gamboa's description (and presumably Contreras's drawing) certainly suggests a hint of the slaughterhouse, possibly even a touch of relief in a "nudity totally without temptations." If Esperanza in all her glory represents an "all-destroying, rampaging animal," then perhaps her decomposing corpse signifies the defeat of a dangerous creature, the reassertion of an insecure male authority. And Gamboa's narrative reinforces his own marginalization, beginning with his fear of exposure and ostracism by "people of good conscience" and proceeding to a humbling encounter with a prominent judge who advises him to "use better judgment, man, use better judgment." Dijkstra's reading is certainly plausible, even likely. It is not, however, sufficient.

If ambiguity of reference is present in all narratives, it infuses every line of Gamboa's tale. At one level this may be nothing more than the narrator's ironic gift and the carefully composed nature of the text (despite the illusion of spontaneity implied by the diary as a genre). However, in *Over Her Dead Body*, Elisabeth Bronfen insists that "femininity and death serve as western culture's privileged topoi and tropes for what is superlatively enigmatic."[79] Gamboa's final paragraph—"what horror, the good death" followed by the parting of friends "each thinking . . . an appropriate thought"—self-consciously supports her analysis. Gamboa begins his tale with a picaresque scramble to safeguard his reputation and then Jesús's cavalier decision to visit the morgue. The final tone is still ironic but manages nonetheless to subtly mock its own facetiousness. Experiencing Esperanza's corpse might well have signified his own survival (the Other's death confronted and conquered), perhaps even a triumph over dangerous women, but the confrontation with death still left Gamboa "dumbfounded." As with Roumagnac, the ambiguities and negotiations are heavily mediated by a skillful narrator, but whereas criminological narrative demonstrated a certain mastery of the subject, here that mastery dissolves into impotence—the master of language is unable finally to speak.

Conclusion

The principal difficulty of narrative psychohistory is precisely the historian/analyst's compulsion to construct a coherent narrative, to reach clear-cut conclusions in the face of so many ambiguities and negotiations. We intend to resist that compulsion since the often contradictory interpretations appropriate to each narrative cannot easily be applied to all. Bruner's first universal of narrative reality is *a structure of committed time*, and the "humanly relevant actions that occur within its limits."[80] But perhaps human relevancy is not so easily bounded after all, hence the multiplicity of narratives that surround the Tarasquillo Street murder. And the interpretive possibilities seem to grow exponentially with each narrative. Favoring narrative interpretation over psychoanalysis may remove some of the presumption from historical inquiry into past mentalities; it is no less troublesome for all that.

There is, however, a common thread that binds the Tarasquillo Street tales together. In all these narratives, the threat posed to "ontological security" (whether of the individual, class, gender, nation, or cultural community) by the potent combination of femininity and death is always already present. Bronfen argues that

> [f]emininity and death cause a disorder to stability, mark moments of ambivalence, disruption or duplicity and their eradication produces a recuperation of order, a return to stability. The threat that death and femininity pose is recuperated by representation . . . And yet . . . the recuperation is imperfect, the regained stability not safe, the urge for order inhabited by a fascination with disruption and split, and certainty emerging over and out of uncertainty.[81]

The conflicted, contested narratives that emerge under these circumstances do indeed "recuperate" but they do not necessarily reassure. Insecurity rather than confidence permeates the Tarasquillo Street narratives in their construal of Porfirian reality. "Order and progress" or "disorder and degeneration"—the two constructions appear inextricably intertwined. Even Roumagnac, the technocratic ideologue, cannot seem to decide on the true nature of María's criminality. In an era characterized by dramatic social changes, things just were not what they seemed. Bruner reminds us that "the coherence of culture is the existence of interpretive procedures for adjudicating the different construals of reality that are inevitable in any diverse society." Historical analysis of the Tarasquillo Street tales can only hope to illuminate those inevitable differences.

Notes

This chapter was first published in *The Americas* 55, no. 3 (January 1999): 391–424, and is reprinted by permission.

1. Rafael Zayas de Enríquez, *Fisiología del crimen: estudio jurídico-sociológico*, 2 vols. (Veracruz: Imprenta de R. de Zayas, 1885).

2. Ramón Corral quoted in Javier Piña y Palacios, ed. "Las Islas Marías a principios de este Siglo," *Criminalia* 36, no. 5 (May 1970): 216.
3. On the Mexico City press during the Porfiriato, see Florence Toussaint Alcaraez, *Escenario de la porfiriato* (Mexico City: Fundación Manuel Buendía, 1989); and Phyllis Lynn Smith, "Contentious Voices Amid the Order: The Porfirian Press in Mexico City 1876–1911" (PhD diss., University of Arizona, 1996).
4. Federico Gamboa, *Santa* (1903; repr., Mexico City: Eusebio Gómez de la Puente, 1922).
5. Miguel Macedo, *La criminalidad en México: medios de combatirla* (Mexico City: Oficina Tip. de la Secretaría de Fomento, 1897), 5–6. Late nineteenth-century statistics suggested that "the Mexican people were the most criminal in the world." Carlos Roumagnac, *La estadística criminal en México* (Mexico City: Imp. de Arturo García Cubas Sucesores Hermanos, 1907), 10, 27. Roumagnac considered these statistics very unreliable and Mexico's unsavory reputation undeserved.
6. Peter Gay, *The Bourgeois Experience: Victoria to Freud*, vol. 1, *The Education of the Senses* (New York: Oxford University Press, 1984), 8, 16.
7. This literature is extensive. For an overview and critique, see Diana Fuss, *Essentially Speaking: Feminism, Nature and Difference* (New York: Routledge, 1989). A thoughtful and provocative example that explores the connection between "self" construction, sexuality, and death is Elisabeth Bronfen's *Over Her Dead Body: Death, Femininity and the Aesthetic* (New York: Routledge, 1992).
8. See especially Jerome Bruner, *Acts of Meaning* (Cambridge: Harvard University Press, 1990) and *The Culture of Education* (Cambridge: Harvard University Press, 1996). To be fair, Peter Gay resists the term *psychohistory* and insists that his own work (as previously noted) is "history informed by psychoanalysis."
9. Bruner, *Acts of Meaning*, 77 (his emphasis), 95.
10. Bruner discusses "the narrative construal of reality" in chapter 7 of *The Culture of Education*, 130–49.
11. Hernán Robleto, *Crímenes célebres desde el Chalequero hasta Gallegos: La delincuencia en México* (Mexico City: El Gráfico, 1932), 199.
12. *El Foro* 50, no. 63 (6 April 1898), p. 251.
13. On Mexican notions of honor, see Steve J. Stern, *The Secret History of Gender: Women, Men, and Power in Late Colonial Mexico* (Chapel Hill: The University of North Carolina Press, 1995); and Patricia Seed, *To Love, Honor, and Obey in Colonial Mexico: Conflicts over Marriage Choice, 1574–1821* (Stanford: Stanford University Press, 1988).
14. Antonio Martínez de Castro, principal author of the 1871 Penal Code, acknowledged that dueling, although undesirable, was still commonly practiced by the Mexican upper classes and had the support of public opinion; thus, he explained, legislators had decided not to classify it as homicide or battery. Antonio Martínez de Castro, *Código Penal para el Distrito Federal y Territorio de Baja California* [1871] (Veracruz and Puebla: La Ilustración, 1891, hereafter cited as CP 1871), 53.
15. *El Foro* 50, no. 63 (6 April 1898), p. 251.
16. *El Foro* 50, no. 70 (20 April 1898), p. 283.

17. The newspaper report indicated that the bullet hit the right eye, but at the trial the left eye was mentioned. *El Diario del Hogar*, 10 March 1897, p. 2; *El Foro* 50, no. 66 (13 April 1898), p. 263; the dialogue appears in *El Foro*, p. 259.
18. See an example of a husband killing his wife in *El Imparcial*, 13 August 1897. Honor was explicitly acknowledged as an attenuating circumstance. Article 34 of the 1871 Penal Code established that the accused who acted "in defense of their person, honor, property or the person, honor, or property of others" were exempted from penal responsibility (CP 1871, p. 34). The husband who found his partner committing adultery, or his daughter "in the carnal act," and then committed battery would receive a reduced sentence (CP 1871, pp. 534–35). In the case of homicide, articles 554 and 555 of the 1871 Penal Code gave shorter sentences for offenses committed in similar circumstances.
19. See Robert A. Nye, *Masculinity and Codes of Honor in Modern France* (New York: Oxford University Press, 1993). On honor, see Julian Pitt-Rivers, "Honour and Social Status," in *Honour and Shame: The Values of Mediterranean Society*, ed. Jean Peristiany (London: Weinfeld, 1965), 21, 29.
20. In January 1906, *El Imparcial* reported a similar case between women of even lower status. Two women, forty and sixty years of age, engaged in a knife duel to end a protracted dispute over some chickens. They followed the dictates of the "code of honor," meeting with witnesses (also women) in a neutral place, the road of La Piedad, and using the same weapons. One died, and the other was arrested shortly afterward. The newspaper depicted the setup of the duel in an ironic tone but described the fight itself as a "quarrel." *El Imparcial*, 12 January 1906, p. 4, col. 1–2.
21. Archivo del Tribunal Superior de Justicia del Distrito Federal, Reclusorio Sur (hereafter cited as AJ-RS), 430156, Lesiones, 1904. In front of the judge, Rojas recanted this last detail: she declared that none of her friends had participated in the fight, thus protecting them from criminal charges.
22. See, for example, the case of María del Refugio Dorantes, who was seated on a bench waiting for a tram when Modesto Díaz accosted her, thinking she was a prostitute, and offered her one peso. Dorantes did not reply; instead she hit him with a jar she carried in her hand. She explained that she had "a husband and couldn't accept the gift and was so insulted by his presumption" that she had to hit him. The judge did not accept the explanation and Dorantes was sentenced to two months and eight days of arrest. AJ-RS, 4301160, Lesiones, 1904.
23. For María's account to Roumagnac, see Roumagnac, *Los criminales en México*, 108–11. For reports of the crime, see *El Diario del Hogar*, 10 March 1897, p. 2.
24. *Crímenes célebres*, 207. This is one of the most famous jury trials in Mexican history. The use of popular juries in common criminal cases was abolished in 1929. *Excélsior*, 8 October 1929, 2nd sec., p. 1.
25. For the aggressive role of judges in jury trials, and the lack of counsel for defendants, see Demetrio Sodi, *El jurado en México: Estudios sobre el jurado popular* (Mexico City: Secretaría de Fomento, 1909), 144–47, 315–19. In the Mexican judicial system, as in most of Latin America, the judge was also the head investigator, which encouraged a more active role in the trial.

26. *El Foro* 50, no. 62 (5 April 1898), p. 247.
27. See, for example, *El Imparcial*, 23 January 1906, p. 1; *El Imparcial*, 16 August 1912, p. 1; *El Imparcial*, 10 September 1913, p. 1. See the chapters by Víctor Macías-González and Pablo Piccato below.
28. *El Foro* 50, no. 66 (13 April 1898), p. 263.
29. *El Foro* 50, no. 63 (6 April 1898), p. 251.
30. Ibid.
31. *El Foro* 50, no. 62 (5 April 1898), p. 247.
32. *El Foro* 50, no. 65 (12 April 1898), p. 259.
33. *El Foro* 50, no. 70 (19 April 1898), p. 279.
34. *El Imparcial*, 19 September 1897, p. 3.
35. For an incomplete account of the trial, see *El Foro*, April 1898.
36. *El Foro* 49, no. 100 (23 November 1897), p. 3. María attempted an appeal in the supreme court without success. *El Foro* 50, no. 29 (15 February 1898), p. 1. The death penalty was abrogated for most crimes by 1900. Antonio Ramos Pedraza, *La ley penal en México de 1810 a 1910* (Mexico City: Díaz de León, 1911), 14.
37. Roumagnac, *Los criminales en México*, 111–12.
38. On these efforts, see Pablo Piccato, "El Paso de Venus por el disco del Sol: Criminality and Alcoholism in the Late Porfiriato," *Mexican Studies/Estudios Mexicanos* 11, no. 2 (Summer 1995): 203–24; Robert Buffington, "Revolutionary Reform: Modernization, Prison Reform, and Executive Power," in *The Birth of the Penitentiary in Latin America: Essays on Criminology, Prison Reform, and Social Control, 1830–1940*, ed. Ricardo D. Salvatore and Carlos Aguirre (Austin: University of Texas Press, 1996), 169–93; and Laurence J. Rohlfes, "Police and Penal Correction in Mexico City, 1876–1911: A Study of Order and Progress" (PhD diss., Tulane University, 1983).
39. Sociologist Anthony Giddens, for example, argues for a "transformation of intimacy" as modern societies abandon localized kinship networks, which encourage gender segregation for spatially "liberated" nuclear families, with the personal relationship of the married couple as their core. It is the latter version of intimacy with its stress on interpersonal relationships that is transgressed by the illicit doings of María, Esperanza, and Salvador. See Giddens's *The Transformation of Intimacy: Sexuality, Love, and Eroticism in Modern Societies* (Stanford: Stanford University Press, 1992).
40. Anthony Giddens, *The Consequences of Modernity* (Stanford: Stanford University Press, 1990), 36–45. Giddens claims that "the reflexivity of modernity actually subverts reason. [W]e are abroad in a world which is thoroughly constituted through reflexively applied knowledge, but where at the same time we can never be sure that any given element of that knowledge will not be revised" (p. 39).
41. On Posada's crime broadsheets, see Patrick Frank, *Posada's Broadsheets: Mexican Popular Imagery, 1890–1910* (Albuquerque: University of New Mexico Press, 1998), chapter 1.
42. Bruner, *The Culture of Education*, 139–40.
43. Jaime Soler and Lorenzo Avila, eds., *Posada y la prensa ilustrada: signos de modernización y resistencias* (Mexico City: Instituto Nacional de Belles Artes, 1996), 214.

44. The poem translates loosely as "It seems to me that I still see / my victim in front of me / with bloodied face / and fervent look // Yes, yes, there you are Esperanza / pardon my treachery / torment me no more / my agony will be eternal // Forgive me, blessed God! / my crime is very immense / and each time [I see you] / the remorse grows in my soul // On the eighth day of March / of the year 1897 / I committed this horrible crime / fatal day . . . indelible // Oh, God, take my life / because now I can no longer live / because now death is preferable / to this incessant suffering." The second poem purports to be written by Esperanza's mother and laments her daughter's decision to go to Mexico.
45. Bruner, *The Culture of Education*, 133.
46. Giddens, *The Consequences of Modernity*, 92. He defines *ontological security* as "the confidence most human beings have in the continuity of their self-identity and in the constancy of the surrounding social and material environments of action."
47. Roumagnac's narrative technique is explored in much more detail in Robert Buffington, *Criminal and Citizen in Modern Mexico* (Lincoln: University of Nebraska Press, 2000), chapter 3.
48. Bruner, *The Culture of Education*, 136.
49. Roumagnac, *Los criminales en México*, 105. Roumagnac also provides physical data on María, including various measurements and descriptive features. This data was collected using the French "Bertillon" method designed ostensibly to facilitate identification. Much of the data also carried racial (nose width, for example) and cultural indicators such as tattoos. Because María was "white" (*pigmentado pequeño*) and without tattoos, this data too was ambiguous in her particular case (pp. 114–15).
50. Roumagnac, *Los criminales en México*, 105–6.
51. Ibid., 106.
52. Ibid. According to Lara y Pardo's classic work on Mexican prostitution, women from Guadalajara were considered especially desirable (probably because they were "whiter" than most Mexican women) by Mexico City bordello owners. Luis Lara y Pardo, *La prostitución en México* (Mexico City: Librería de la Viuda de Charles Bouret, 1908).
53. Roumagnac, *Los criminales en México*, 106–7. Trial records give his name as Salvador Ortigoza.
54. Although Roumagnac ignores the connection, Esperanza (La Malagueña) was Spanish too. Another reading, not highlighted in the sources but possibly implied in Posada's print of her murder, is Mexican María defending the national honor against the decadent *gachupina*.
55. Roumagnac, *Los criminales en México*, 107–8.
56. Ibid., 117.
57. For a description of conditions in late nineteenth-century Mexico City, see Miguel Macedo, "El Municipio. Los establecimientos penales. La asistencia pública," in *México, su evolución social*, vol. 1, ed. Justo Sierra (Mexico City: Ballescá, 1900), 698–99; Joaquin García Icazbalceta, *Informe sobre los establecimientos de beneficencia y corrección de esta capital . . .* (Mexico City: Moderna Librería Religiosa, 1907), 65–66; and José Ceballos, *Memoria presentada al C. Lic. Manuel Romero*

Rubio Secretario de Estado y del Despacho de Gobernación por el . . . Gobernador del Distrito Federal y que comprende los años de 1886 y 1887 (Mexico City: Eduardo Dublán, 1888), 140.

58. Roumagnac, *Los criminales en México*, 113.
59. Ibid., 123.
60. Ibid., 122–23.
61. Ibid.
62. Prison officials often rewarded certain prisoners by promoting them to positions of authority in which they assisted in the vigilance of their fellow inmates. *Presidentas* or *mayores* could enforce order with a club and had *cabos* at their orders. The use of violence was clearer in the men's section, but the women's section was organized along similar lines. For the organization of prisons, see Roumagnac, *Los criminales en México*, 215–16; Ceballos, *Memoria presentada*, 147; and Manuel González de Cosío, *Memoria que presenta al Congreso de la Unión el General . . . Secretario de Estado y del Despacho de Gobernación* (Mexico City: Imprenta del Gobierno Federal, 1900), 886.
63. Roumagnac, *Los criminales en México*, 131. In other cases, holding a charge was related with economic activities. Emilia M. was the presidenta of the kitchen with fifty-two female inmates under her orders, a salary of ten pesos a month, and the responsibility for the daily meals of all prisoners (p. 127).
64. Roumagnac, *Los criminales en México*, 113, 121–23.
65. Emilia M. also recognized the option but favored heterosexuality: "[E]ven if I desired a man," she declared, "I would not be so dirty [*tan puerca*] as to mingle with a woman like me." Roumagnac, *Los criminales en México*, 107–8, 112, 127.
66. See, for example, Dr. González Enríquez, "La visita conyugal y otras consideraciones," in *Memoria del Primer Congreso Nacional Penitenciario celebrado en la Ciudad de México del 24 de noviembre al 3 de diciembre de 1932* (Mexico City: Talleres Gráficos de la Nación, 1935), 124; and Pablo Piccato, "'Such a Strong Need': Sexuality and Violence in Belem Prison," in *Gender, Sexuality, and Power in Latin America since Independence*, ed. Katherine Elaine Bliss and William E. French (Wilmington: Scholarly Resources, 2007), 87–108.
67. Roumagnac, *Los criminales en México*, 113.
68. Carlos Roumagnac, "Recuerdos de Belem," *El Nacional*, 23 July 1933, 2nd sec., p. 2. According to another account, she served for a long time and lived an "exemplary life" in prison as a teacher of her fellow inmates, helping them learn to write and sew. She finally left prison with her hair gray (*Crímenes célebres*, 207). She may well have been released earlier than her scheduled date (1917) but no reference has been found in the judicial archives of the Federal District.
69. The most prominent expression of this concern for Mexico's national survival is in Justo Sierra's classic history, *The Political Evolution of the Mexican People*, trans. Charles Ramsdell (Austin: University of Texas Press, 1969).
70. Federico Gamboa, *Mi diario*, primera serie, vol. 2 (Mexico City: Eusebio Gómez de la Puente, 1910), 13–17. The ellipses, quotation marks, and italics are all Gamboa's.

71. Many of Gamboa's works, however, including his most famous novel *Santa*, which some biographers suggest was inspired by this incident, exhibit considerable insight into Mexico's social problems.
72. This theme is dealt with extensively in Sander L. Gilman, "Black Bodies, White Bodies: Towards an Iconography of Female Sexuality in Late Nineteenth-Century Art, Medicine, and Literature," in *"Race," Writing, and Difference*, ed. Henry Louis Gates Jr. (Chicago: University of Chicago Press, 1986), 223–61; and in chapter 7 of Charles Bernheimer, *Figures of Ill Repute: Representing Prostitution in Nineteenth-Century France* (Cambridge: Harvard University Press, 1989), 200–233. Gamboa's attitudes toward sexuality (including references to this diary excerpt) are discussed in Franco, *Plotting Women*, 95–98. Sigmund Freud in *Beyond the Pleasure Principle*, vol. 18, *Standard Edition* (London: The Hogarth Press, 1920) argues that sexuality (eros) and death (thanatos) are inextricably intertwined in the human psyche.
73. Bernheimer, *Figures of Ill Repute*, 221.
74. *El Foro* 50, no. 62 (5 April 1898), p. 247.
75. *El Foro* 50, no. 63 (6 April 1898), p. 251; Roumagnac, *Los criminales en México*, 110; *El Foro* 50, no. 65 (12 April 1898), p. 259.
76. Gamboa, *Mi diario*, 16.
77. Gayatri Chakravorty Spivak, "Subaltern Studies: Deconstructing Historiography," in *In Other Worlds: Essays in Cultural Politics* (New York: Routledge, 1988), 220. She makes a similar point in "The Rani of Sirmur: An Essay in Reading the Archives," *History and Theory* 24, no. 3 (1985): 247–72.
78. Bram Dijkstra, *Idols of Perversity: Fantasies of Feminine Evil in Fin-de-Siècle Culture* (New York: Oxford University Press, 1986), 374.
79. Bronfen, *Over Her Dead Body*, xiii.
80. Bruner, *The Culture of Education*, 133.
81. Bronfen, *Over Her Dead Body*, xii.

CHAPTER TWO

I Was a Man of Pleasure, I Can't Deny It
Histories of José de Jesús Negrete, a.k.a. "The Tiger of Santa Julia"

~ Elisa Speckman Guerra ~

Francisco Chávez was more devious or more astute than The Tiger, which is not to say that Jesús Negrete did not have his strong points. His alias alludes to his fierceness and his ability to evade capture. In an article published before the soon-to-be notorious bandit had committed his first crime, Mexico City's principal daily newspaper, *El Imparcial*, maintained that the "most dangerous and repulsive" lawbreakers were "born criminals" who carried in their organism "the virus of crime." They were "beasts with human form" who committed acts of unusual cruelty, who, carried away by the "instinct of certain ferocious animals," acted with the sole purpose of calming their "red, raging blood." Born criminals could only be identified as "monsters" or "tigers," which was, according to the article, what they were commonly called.[1] This might be one explanation for Negrete's nickname, "The Tiger," but there is another. According to *El Imparcial*'s competitor, *El País*, Chief of the Federal District Secret Police Francisco Chávez gave Negrete the moniker in acknowledgment of Negrete's ability to escape from danger and elude his pursuers.[2]

Jesús Negrete was indeed as slippery as a feline. Beginning in May 1906, the Mexico City police spent six straight months pursuing him, and that is only if we count the time that transpired after his last prison escape (which he managed with considerable dexterity), because, truth be told, the bandit had held the authorities at bay for more than six years.

Faced with the near impossibility of capturing Negrete, Chávez came up with a plan. Although the fugitive was extremely careful, he often visited his lovers. He never stayed more than twenty-four hours with any of them, however, which meant that the police never had time to discover his hiding place. Nevertheless, his weakness for one woman, Guadalupe Guerrero, was well known, and Chávez figured out how to take advantage of it. As *El Imparcial* told the story, he assigned one of his agents the task of seducing her and "arousing the jealousy of the beast." The agent complied and Jesús Negrete, "consumed with jealousy, forgot his meticulous precautions and began to make very frequent and very long visits to the Tacubaya house [where she lived]."[3] Blinded perhaps by passion, by the desire to win back his lover, or with the intention of keeping an eye on her, the criminal spent more time with Guadalupe than usual—enough time for the police to prepare an ambush. They surrounded the house, waiting for the just the right moment to nab the fugitive. In the end, they surprised him while he was defecating behind a cactus bush. The Tiger could do nothing; when he looked up, four men had pointed rifles straight at his head. He could only say, "I give up! Don't tie me up!"[4]

Thus ended the career of one of the most celebrated criminals of the Porfiriato (1876–1911), an era presided over by longtime president Porfirio Díaz and characterized by his often-voiced obsession with "order and progress." Among Negrete's notable deeds would have to figure the escape from the Belén jail and the robberies at the Aragón hacienda, the Molino de Valdéz, the artillery barracks, and the post office. In addition, he was responsible for a series of homicides resulting from bar fights and his many confrontations with the police.

Starting early in his criminal career, Jesús Negrete began to attract the attention of journalists and the public, and his fame spread throughout Mexican society. As a result, rumors and anecdotes about his deeds gave rise to carefully constructed, if often inconsistent, histories as his life's diverse episodes and events took on narrative form. Not just his major crimes but also his minor run-ins with the police, his escapes, his trial, and his execution all received intense coverage in mainstream newspapers and became the subjects of numerous pamphlets and broadsheets. Moreover, these events were interpreted, explained, judged, and related in diverse ways by each source. These interpretive differences, with their many convergences and contradictions, produced various portraits of the criminal, his feats, and his punishment.

To reconstruct the multiple histories of Jesús Negrete, I relied on three sources: the mainstream press, police magazines, and broadsheets. The richest of these sources is the mainstream press. These newspapers were edited by members of the elite and middle classes, who were also their principal readership. Nonetheless, the most popular newspapers also found an audience among the lower classes, including the illiterate, because they were often read aloud in groups. At the same time, the newspapers presented different ideas, points of view, objectives, and editorial intentions. For that reason, I reviewed several: *El Imparcial*, *El Diario del Hogar*, *El País*, and *El Popular*.

Under the directorship of ambitious empresario Rafael Reyes Spíndola, *El Imparcial* became the unofficial mouthpiece of the Porfirian regime. Thanks to sizable government subsidies and technological innovations in the printing process, the newspaper managed to both increase its production and lower its cost to consumers. In addition, by shifting focus from editorials and opinion pieces to news and photojournalism, it revolutionized the Mexican press. Because of its low cost and innovative approach, *El Imparcial* was the most likely of all the mainstream newspapers to attract a sizable lower-class readership. *El Imparcial*'s major competitor was *El País*, a pro-Catholic paper directed by Trinidad Sánchez Santos. *El País* was sympathetic to the Díaz regime's modernization program, the socially progressive Catholicism of Pope Leo XIII (1878–1903), and the middle-class values of its readership. Much less important, at least in terms of the Negrete story, were newspapers such as *El Diario del Hogar*, a liberal daily founded by prominent opposition journalist Filomeno Mata that agitated against electoral fraud and perpetual reelection (especially of eight-term president Porfirio Díaz), and otherwise represented the doctrinaire or "Jacobin" liberalism associated with former president Benito Juárez and the Reform movement of the 1860s and 1870s. Less prominent too in the Negrete story was the role played by *El Popular*, the independent daily directed by Francisco Montes de Oca, which featured political coverage with a humorous twist.[5] *El Imparcial* and *El País* provided extensive coverage of newsworthy events for a broad readership, although the former made more of an effort to cater to lower-class readers (and listeners); *El Diario del Hogar* and *El Popular* published mostly opinion pieces generally directed at the educated middle and upper classes.

The principal police magazine in those days was the *Gaceta de Policía*. In keeping with its quasi-official status, this publication reflected the police perspective on police matters and alerted the public to the accomplishments of officers. Along with its propagandistic functions, the *Gaceta* also attempted to aid in the capture of delinquents by broadcasting their modi operandi and mug shots.

Crucial to the development and propagation of Negrete's legend were the broadsheets (*impresos sueltos*) produced by the publishing house of Antonio Vanegas Arroyo. These single sheets, which were often printed with colored ink or on colored paper, sold for an affordable price at newsstands, markets, and town squares throughout Mexico. Most broadsheets featured news bulletins, poems, or songs usually in the form of corridos (story ballads) intended to be recited and sung in public venues. They also featured eye-catching, sensationalistic headlines coupled with riveting illustrations by well-known printmakers such as Manuel Manilla and José Guadalupe Posada. Unlike the prominent journalists who wrote for the mainstream newspapers, broadsheet editors did not generally come from the privileged sectors of Mexican society, although like their mainstream press counterparts they were often from the middle classes—less well-off than their more respectable colleagues perhaps but from the *gente decente* (decent folk) all the same. The fundamental difference between the two genres derives not from the class origins of their producers but from their respective publics. Broadsheet writers and illustrators produced mostly for the lower classes, especially the working class, and took great care to use language and images that appealed to their intended readership. But here again the class line is far from clear because broadsheets, like the mainstream dailies, were popular with all readers regardless of their social position or political inclinations.[6]

Even if it is impossible to determine with any precision who read what, a close reading of the sources has allowed me to reconstruct the viewpoints of their producers—mainstream newspapermen, police reporters, broadsheet editors—and the messages they sought to convey to their audiences. Through the pages of these different sources, I have also been able to discern the perspective of the principal actors in the drama, including the public prosecutor, the defense attorney, and the accused himself. Taken together, these different perspectives comprise the complex history with its competing versions, value judgments, and descriptions of the life, exploits, trial, and execution of Jesús Negrete, The Tiger of Santa Julia.

Amid these differences, the compelling need to make sense of the criminal and his acts emerged as a central theme. This need ultimately transformed Negrete's many histories into legend, and finally, emptied of its contingent, contradictory historical content, into myth. According to Roland Barthes, myth "abolishes the complexity of human acts, it gives them the simplicity of essences, it does away with all dialectics, with any going back beyond what is immediately visible, it organizes a world which is without contradictions because it is without depth, a world wide open and wallowing in the evident, it establishes a blissful clarity: things appear to mean something by themselves."[7] Such was the fate of The Tiger.

All the sources agree that Negrete did not act alone, but instead headed a gang of criminals. His band was composed of José y Agustín Cisneros, Marciano Cornejo, José Galván, Pedro Herrera, José Guadalupe Martínez, Fortino Mora, Tranquilino Peña, Heraclio Rodríguez, Apolunio Ruíz, and Pedro Soria, among

2.1. José Guadalupe Posada, *La vida de un bandolero. Los crímenes más notables de Jesús Negrete (a) "El tigre de Santa Julia." Aprehensión de sus cómplices* (Mexico City: Imprenta de Antonio Vanegas Arroyo, n.d.).

others. Negrete's band also included a woman, María Inés Escogido. She was the only woman put on trial, but Negrete relied on the complicity of several lovers, including Simona Morales and Ramona Cabrera, and, to a lesser extent, Manuela Álvarez, Ubelia Cisneros, Engracia Herrera, and Mariana Torres, just to mention those who appeared at his trial.[8]

Nevertheless, Negrete was variously depicted as being responsible for a "long string of crimes"; an "interminable" series of robberies, killings, fights, and other offenses; or as the author of "numerous crimes: robberies, assaults, homicides, armed attacks on policemen on night patrol almost always in a deserted area."[9] Others described him as the "head of a gang of bandits that wandered around the Federal District committing all manner of depredations and defying the police" or as an "audacious, terrible, and bloody bandit who has demonstrated a savage courage in all the bloody encounters that he has had with representatives of the law."[10] Thus, for some writers, Negrete was a common criminal, and for others he was a social bandit.

A common criminal was someone who acted in his own interest and as neither a revolutionary nor a reformer, he shared his booty only with his crew. In contrast, the term *social bandit* refers to a criminal with a social conscience who confronts the rich and powerful by avenging injustices and outrages against himself and others, who mocks authorities and becomes a popular hero, who represents the social aspirations and defends the ideals and cherished values of his peers, who kills only in self-defense or for revenge, who shares the bounty (whether symbolic or economic) among the common people, and who counts on the sympathy and support of the community.[11] It is important to note here that the criminal is given over to punishment and oblivion, while the social bandit is transformed into a legendary hero.

I conclude that, although he shared certain traits with the prototype, Jesús Negrete was not a social bandit or even a rural bandit. And he was not treated as either by his contemporaries, although at times the sympathy he generated within the community was similar to that generated by seekers of social justice. Still, the stories that circulated around his actions lent themselves easily to myth. Moreover, I argue that the process of transforming Negrete's story into myth began in earnest with his death. In life, the mainstream press generally depicted The Tiger as a common criminal whose delinquency derived primarily from a mix of environmental and organic causes, although some dailies allowed for social causes. It also portrayed him with attributes the community despised: ignorance, crudeness, cowardliness, betrayal, and disloyalty. In contrast, the broadsheets generally imbued him with positive qualities such as daring, courage, respect for women, honor, and a high degree of heroism. This divergence has its roots in the sociocultural origins of the authors and audiences of the different publications, but also in the editorial intentions of each source. Taken together, these differences provided the slippage—the overdetermined images, the ideological contradictions, the permutations of meaning—essential to the emergence of a myth. The cultural resonance of myth, after all, does not depend on getting the facts straight because in myth the complexities of history are replaced by a mythological concept that is "a formless, unstable, nebulous condensation, whose unity and coherence are above all due to its function."[12] Thus Negrete came to signify the Mexican Revolution, which incarnates the innate desire of all men for social justice. This, then, is the real story behind the various histories of José de Jesús Negrete, The Tiger of Santa Julia.

As stated earlier, his death by firing squad, coupled with the advent of the Revolution, lent Negrete the traits of the social rebel and even the political opponent, the avenger of injustice, and the defender of the weak, the poor, and the oppressed. I believe this construction was encouraged willingly—although not necessarily consciously—by the criminal himself, his attorneys, and the authors of broadsheets and corridos. Moreover, this process was encouraged unwillingly—or even unconsciously—by the authorities and the police. Of course the emergence of the black legend surrounding Porfirio Díaz and his regime, along with the simultaneous exaltation of the rebellious revolutionary and armed insurrection, played roles as well.

That said, I now move on to the competing histories of Negrete's career: the origins of his life of crime, his exploits, his captures, his trial, and his execution.

"It All Happened Because I Couldn't Read"

José de Jesús Negrete was born in 1874.[13] His family was originally from Cuerándaro, a rural town in the state of Guanajuato that, according to the bandit himself, had no more than two thousand inhabitants.[14] In those days, the application of liberal land laws, designed to break up the communal landholdings of civil corporations, especially the Catholic Church and the Indian village, initiated an avalanche of land seizures by surveying companies. This process began to concentrate agricultural lands in large estates or haciendas. As a result, many dispossessed and impoverished campesinos (peasants or field workers) were forced to work for the hacienda owners. This apparently was the case with Negrete's father, who was a hacienda peon, according to *El País* (perhaps a reflection of its commitment to Catholic social justice).[15]

The education campaign sponsored by presidents Benito Juárez, Sebastián Lerdo de Tejada, and Porfirio Díaz had also begun to bear fruit. Nevertheless, its effects had yet to reach Cuerándaro, which, also according to *El País*, lacked schools.¹⁶ Thus The Tiger passed his first years working in the field rather than learning to read or write. Consequently, like his father and—according to *El Popular*—in accordance with his father's wishes, Jesús too was expected to seek employment at the hacienda.¹⁷

Despite his illiteracy, Negrete had greater ambitions than a life of peonage, so he took up arms. *El Imparcial* maintained that "when a fleeting glimmer of aspiration caused him to think about a broader field of endeavor, his rough brain could suggest no better solution than to enroll in the army."¹⁸ *El País* took up this version of Negrete's story and expanded on it, affirming that he did not become a soldier out of a need to better himself, but from a desire "to serve his country." According to this daily (and from this point on we will follow its narrative) the idea came to him at seventeen when he saw a group of soldiers pass by. He then walked to Mexico City to enlist in the national army because he did not have money for transportation. When he arrived at the Tacubaya artillery barracks, he asked for the officer in charge and was taken to see a colonel. The officer was impressed with the new arrival's attitude and helped him enlist as an artilleryman. In the barracks,

> [n]otwithstanding the fact that he had come from a remote state and a distant population, without connections of any kind, Jesús Negrete demonstrated from the beginning considerable aptitude for his new profession. He understood orders and carried them out with energy and intelligence.¹⁹

Negrete was promoted from private to corporal to sergeant to staff sergeant, and, finally, to master sergeant. But his promotions ended there because master sergeant was the highest rank to which an illiterate could aspire. As a consequence,

> Negrete felt deceived by his military career, because in his fervid imagination, it had seemed like an extraordinary thing to do, full of struggles and battles, of doubts and emotions.²⁰

In sum, Negrete—in the eyes of *El País*—appeared to be a young man enthusiastic about having taken up arms but disillusioned by the obstacles in his path.²¹

This image differs from that presented by *El Imparcial*, which, along with doubting the young man's patriotism, favored the prosecutor's version that

Negrete had not voluntarily enlisted in the army but had been compelled to do so as punishment for some infraction. To this accusation The Tiger responded, "That's not true; in my previous life there was no disreputable act. I was a soldier not out of perversity but by choice."[22] It is not clear, then, whether the army encouraged Jesús Negrete's later criminal behavior. According to *El Imparcial*, however, the army at least reinforced that behavior in the barracks because the soldiers "talked only of crime," admiring those who "were really men and didn't fear the law," "those for whom life has no more value than the [bullet] . . . that is needed to end it."[23] What is clear, as Negrete himself admitted, is that he recruited his henchmen in the army.[24] Among them was Heraclio Rodríguez, a former railroad worker who trained the regiment's horses.[25] Having decided on a life of crime, the two scaled the armory wall and, without being discovered, helped themselves to mounts, pistols, and machetes.[26]

"He loved crime; he loved it without thinking, as if it were his first love." With this statement, *El Imparcial* signaled the commencement of Negrete's true criminal career.[27] In 1900, leading a group of men (one disguised as a woman), Negrete assaulted the Hacienda de Aragón, a rural estate located next to the Villa de Guadalupe highway. During the ensuing skirmish, the hacienda's administrator and mayordomo were injured.[28] The event provoked indignation among the authorities, prompted a police investigation, and caused The Tiger to flee the capital district.

He returned to the area two years later. Drunk and fighting with his mistress, Negrete fired a shot in the air. Although the police surrounded the house, the delinquent managed to escape. Policemen pursued Negrete for several hours and apprehended him with the help of neighbors.[29] The apprehension proved temporary. His lover, Ramona Cabrera, gave him a serape in which she had hidden a pistol. Once armed, The Tiger took flight, killing Arnulfo Sánchez, one of the policemen who pursued him.[30] Antonio Vanegas Arroyo recorded these deeds in a broadsheet that narrated Negrete's most notorious crimes:

> After just a short time
> Here in the capital
> He shot a policeman
> With singular malice.
>
> His accomplice in crime
> Was his sweetheart Ramona
> The policeman was taking him away
> For the disturbances he had caused.

The criminals fled
Without being caught
And so it went unpunished
This ferocious crime.

[Después de esto al poco tiempo
Aquí ya en la capital
A un gendarme dio un balazo
Con vileza singular.

Su cómplice fue en este crimen
Su querida la "Cabrera"
El gendarme lo llevaba
Por escándalos que alteran.

Huyeron los criminales
Sin que pudieran prenderlos
Y al pronto quedando impune
Ese delito tan fiero.]

The image popular illustrator José Guadalupe Posada produced reinforces the written text and graphically renders the malice and ferocity of the crime. Posada portrays Negrete larger than his victim, thus emphasizing his physical superiority. Furthermore, he represents Negrete as the obvious aggressor by having him shoot from a standing position and face-to-face—rather than over his shoulder in the act of flight—at the unarmed policeman (see fig 2.1).[31]

Only a few months would pass without further news of Jesús Negrete. On the outskirts of Mexico City, his gang robbed and killed two mule skinners. Later, he broke into and robbed the Molino de Valdez. Without a doubt, his best year was 1904, when the gang assaulted and robbed the artillery barracks and the post office. For the most part, Negrete targeted military and government buildings. These crimes against important government institutions appeared to challenge and mock the authorities and thus threatened to undermine the political legitimacy of the Porfirio Díaz regime, whose official slogan, "order and progress," committed it to maintaining public security.

Besides dealing these blows to Porfirian pretensions, The Tiger participated in several robberies and minor squabbles including these two examples from 1904. The scene: two cantinas in Tacubaya, the first located in the barrio of Puerto Pinto, the second in Santa Julia. The actors: on the first occasion, the bandit was accompanied by two men (José Cisneros and Marciano Cornejo) and two women (Guadalupe Martínez and María Inés Escogido); on the second, by five men (Marciano Cornejo, Pedro Herrera, José Galvan, Lauro Frías, and Vicente Godínez). The antecedents (similar in both cases): on the first occasion, Negrete got Marcelino Molina drunk and stole his poncho, and as a consequence the aggrieved party left in search of a firearm; on the second, he picked a fight with Godínez and Frías, who were not part of his gang and, because they were unarmed, they went off to their houses to retrieve their guns. The facts (even more similar): on both occasions, it took Negrete's rivals longer to return than to lose their lives; as soon as The Tiger saw them, he shot them. The outcome (different in each case): in the first encounter, Molina died and his killer escaped, but the police apprehended Ubelia Cisneros after the crime and she denounced her lover; in the second, Frías was killed and Godínez was wounded, but despite his wounds he made it to the police station and alerted the *rurales* (rural police), who took off in search of Negrete.

The incident in the Santa Julia cantina and the subsequent pursuit gave The Tiger the second part of his alias. Thirteen men on horseback and five on foot pursued the remaining delinquents until they reached the edge of a cliff. In the ensuing exchange, Regino Aguilar, one of the rurales, was killed and the other, José Álvarez, was wounded. The fugitives escaped but were cornered again near the Hacienda de los Morales, where in another skirmish, Leonardo Enríquez, a "countryman" who accompanied one of the rurales, was slain along with José Galván, one of Negrete's followers. Negrete was also wounded. According to *El Imparcial*, after the shootout, the rurales and the fugitives fought hand to hand, and The Tiger received two machete blows to the head. The rurales thought he was dead and threw him in a wagon, but when they arrived at Tacuba one of the guards noticed him moving and took him to the hospital and, later, to jail.[32] A Vanegas Arroyo broadsheet offered a similar version of events but omitted the details about the machete wounds and the trip in the meat wagon.[33] Notwithstanding these minor differences, the press made clear that the bandit had been apprehended like a brave man, fighting with no thought of surrender until overcome by his wounds.

Jesús Negrete was locked in one of the Belén jail's securest cells. Nonetheless, he escaped with four other inmates before his trial had even begun. The versions of these events published in *El Imparcial* and *El País* are practically identical. The prisoners asked a jailor to let them assemble in cell 68 to play cards, which was a common practice in the prison. Inexplicably—or perhaps bribed by the inmates—the jailor agreed. Cell 68 was near a staircase to the jail roof. The delinquents broke through the cell wall and ascended to the rooftop where they used a drainpipe and a rope to climb down.[34] The first Vanegas Arroyo broadside supports this version of the escape.³⁵ A later broadside, however, showed the fugitives breaking through the bars of the cell window, jumping to a thick wall, and then onto the street.³⁶

"They're going to nab you guys right away, me, I'm going home." These were the words Negrete used to say good-bye to his companions.³⁷ As he predicted, police quickly rounded up his accomplices in the days that followed the escape, but six months passed before the police again apprehended The Tiger. It was just as the newspapers had foreseen. *El País* had insisted all along that it would be difficult to find Negrete and imagined him hidden in "the house of some comrade in crime," while *El Imparcial* had glimpsed him in a lover's lair because, it reminded its readers, he was "a sultan with regard to women, always keeping three or four in their respective houses."³⁸

For its part, the *Gaceta de Policía* insisted that Negrete had formed a gang and, in the company of José Bonilla, "The Terror of Ajusco," and José Albear, "The Herbalist," he was terrorizing the travelers and hacienda owners of the Chalco region a few miles east of Mexico City. The editors argued that, faced with the pressing need to capture the bandits, Mexico City police chief (and nephew of the president) "Colonel Félix Díaz, with the perspicacity for which he is known," not only maintained constant communication with local authorities but had infiltrated agents into the region disguised as civilians. The police kept their disguises on even when they consulted with the presiding magistrate (*juez conciliador*) because they knew he was a Negrete sympathizer. The ruse worked. The police uncovered the delinquents' hideout, but they managed to apprehend only Bonilla.³⁹ The *Gaceta de Policía* is the only source for news of Negrete's crimes after the escape from Belén; no other source accuses him of the crimes in Chalco, not even the prosecutor. It seems that when he fled from jail, The Tiger obtained his liberty but never recovered his freedom of action. He thought only about hiding from the police until he was apprehended for the third and last time in March 1906.

As we have seen, the crimes and captures of The Tiger of Santa Julia were reported in several sources, and each produced narratives of varied length and tone in addition to painting diverse portraits of the man and his criminal tendencies. It is worth noting, first of all, that the *Gaceta de Policía* and the Vanegas Arroyo broadsheets offered more complete coverage of Negrete's crimes than did the dailies, which reported them piecemeal. In fact, both sources credited him with more crimes than he committed, or at least more than the prosecutor formally accused him of committing. Among other things, the *Gaceta* blamed him for the crimes in Chalco, and the broadsheet corridos provided detailed accounts of his actions:

Everyone listen carefully
To the principal crimes
That will bring to the gallows
"The Tiger" for his misdeeds

His deeds began
In nineteen-hundred and three
When he took with cruel fury
The lives of two mule skinners

Only a short time later
A loyal policeman
He rewarded with a bullet
Fired with evil intent

The next year another death
In Tacubaya it happened
Through betrayal and treachery
That he took another man's life

And another horrible murder
He committed beside a maguey [cactus]
There from hiding, he shot
A poor man and robbed him

Later he killed another policeman
With two well-placed bullets
But they couldn't capture him
Negrete was too smart for that

Finally, the worst
Of his crimes against the law
Took place in Santa Julia
At six o'clock in the morning

"The Tiger of Santa Julia"
They called him after that
It happened in a cantina
With cruel ferocity[40]

[Escuchen todos atentos
Los crímenes principales
Que llevarán al cadalso
Al "tigre" por sus maldades

Comenzaron sus hazañas
En mil novecientos tres
Que a dos arrieros la vida
Les quitó con furia cruel

Después y muy poco tiempo
A un gendarme por ser fiel,
Le soltó muy buen balazo
Con bastante avilantez

Al siguiente año otra muerte
En Tacubaya fue a hacer
Con traición y alevosía
A otro hombre quitóle el ser

Y otro asesinato horrible
Cometió junto a un maguey
Allí oculto dio un balazo
A un pobre que robó él

Después mató a otro gendarme
Con dos balazos muy bien
Pero no podían cogerlo
Negrete muy listo fue

Y por último el más grande
De sus delitos por ley
Aconteció en Santa Julia
Una mañana a las seis

El "Tigre de Santa Julia"
Le pusieron aquí bien,
Fue el caso en una cantina
Con ferocidad muy cruel]

Journalists mostly focused on particular fights and robberies, that is to say, on everyday urban criminality, and, with the exception of the escape, accorded little space to spectacular feats or the big assaults on government institutions. Moreover, *El País* insisted that neighbors had helped the police apprehend Negrete the first time.[41] Thus, journalists worked to ensure that the authorities would not look ridiculous and that Negrete would not be seen as a defender of the weak and oppressed, or as an avenger of social injustice.

Toward the same end—lauding the authorities and denigrating the delinquent—the dailies covered Negrete's captures in detail. Regarding his second capture after Santa Julia, mainstream journalists praised the courage and strength of the rurales. *El Imparcial* mentioned The Tiger's wounds to demonstrate his tolerance for pain, a tolerance that, according to the editor, distanced him from humans and linked him to wild beasts rather than showing, as the Vanegas Arroyo broadside had done, that Negrete only surrendered after being severely wounded. In contrast, regarding the third capture, journalists reveled in Negrete's vulnerable position. This was especially true of *El Imparcial*. While the more restrained *El País*, with its insistence on Catholic family values, noted only that the delinquent was taken "unarmed" and in a "difficult situation," the regime's unofficial mouthpiece omitted none of the embarrassing details.[42] The *Gaceta de Policía* took the same line and emphasized the merits of the police. It credited the chief's "tact and caution" for having captured the celebrated criminal without bloodshed, and extolled the police in general by acknowledging their preparations and actions. In the *Gaceta* account, police chief Francisco Chávez and eleven agents, employing "the necessary precautions," surrounded the Puerto Pinto house and, "in a rash and audacious gesture" but without showing "the least faintheartedness," entered the house and checked the rooms. When the intrepid officers failed to find the criminal inside, they went outside to the patio where they discovered him defecating behind a cactus.[43] The broadsheet editor for Vanegas Arroyo took a different tack, relating simply that Negrete's "capture took place in a Tacubaya hideout five months after the flight from Belén."[44] In this way, he referenced the circumstances of the surrender while reminding readers—as his mainstream rivals had not—that the delinquent had escaped after his second arrest and mocked the police for months.

The desire to diminish or enhance the Negrete's stature also colored the press's approach to his love life. As Alberto del Castillo has noted, *El País* systematically avoided mentioning his lovers.[45] For example, the newspaper recalled Negrete's flight in the company of his henchmen but ignored the presence of his women. Instead it described him as "ugly and repugnant" and thus lacking the physical attributes of a Don Juan.[46] This position, hardly surprising given the newspaper's espousal of Catholic morality, contrasts with that of *El Imparcial*, and even more with that of the Vanegas Arroyo broadsheets, whose editors maintained that several women had aided him and that women were the only ones who served as "accomplices in his robberies."[47]

Beyond noting the differences, it is worth considering whether the press's descriptions of Negrete's love affairs detracted from or added to his reputation as The Tiger. Again I agree with Castillo, who affirms that it might have enhanced Negrete's reputation in the eyes of the lower classes but not with the middle class or the elite, who likely considered his amorous relations as yet another indicator of his amorality (even as they vicariously enjoyed press accounts of his romantic exploits). Mainstream newspapers directed their accounts primarily to the latter groups. Thus, *El País*'s omission subtracted nothing from Negrete's reputation, while *El Imparcial* both celebrated and condemned his love affairs. On the other hand, broadsheets targeted the popular sectors whose members, it was assumed, took unabashed pleasure in Negrete's success with women, a success that reaffirmed his manhood and strengthened his image as a macho.

As far as image went, this aspect of his reputation mattered a great deal to all concerned, including Negrete himself, the media, and the general public. Thus José Guadalupe Posada reinforced the text that accompanied his illustrations by basing his drawing of The Tiger on a photograph by Agustín Casasola, the most prominent photojournalist of the era. Negrete is depicted as full-bodied, gallant, haughty, and dressed like a charro (Mexican cowboy; see fig. 2.2). In contrast, the only photograph published in *El Imparcial* showed Negrete's face on the last day of his trial looking bloated, tired, and defeated (see fig. 2.3).

The explanations of Negrete's criminal tendencies were as dissimilar as the descriptions of the delinquent and his deeds. On the question of criminal tendencies, it is instructive to compare the opinions of the prosecutor, the defense attorney, *El Imparcial*, and *El País*, which oscillated between biological and social determinism. Biological determinism was derived from the ideas of the positivist school of penal law. One of its branches, criminal anthropology, founded by Italian criminologist Cesare Lombroso, saw crime as the result of anomalies in the delinquent's organism. This extreme version of biological determinism was modified somewhat by another Italian criminologist, Enrico Ferri, who argued that not all delinquents demonstrated the same inclinations, because for "born" criminals the organic element was predominate and beyond treatment, but for "occasional" or "passional" criminals physical predisposition was minimal and they committed crimes only if the circumstances were favorable or if they were impelled by passion. In contrast, social determinism

2.2. José Guadalupe Posada, *Jesús Negrete (a) "El tigre de Santa Julia." Nuevo corrido*, in *El Cancionero Popular* 2 (Mexico City: Imprenta de Antonio Vanegas Arroyo, 1909).

2.3. *El Tigre de Santa Julia*, in "'El Tigre de Santa Julia' fue sentenciado a la pena capital," *El Imparcial*, 14 June 1908. Hemeroteca Nacional, Universidad Nacional Autónoma de México.

attributed most criminality to social factors. Here we encounter the second branch of the positivist school, criminal sociology (associated with French criminologists such as Gabriel Tarde), which emphasized external factors from climate to education.[48] Criminal sociologists sometimes extended these environmentalist arguments to include issues of poverty and lack of opportunity, explanations that would find favor after the Revolution.[49]

These explanations for criminality compete in most popular accounts. For example, a note from El País categorized Negrete as one of "the bandits of old-time novels that are these days known as born criminals" (alluding to Enrico Ferri's classification and the school of criminal anthropology), while other accounts in El País and elsewhere explained the delinquent's criminal tendencies as deriving from misery and ignorance.[50] Thus, on more than one occasion, the press mentioned the impact of Negrete's illiteracy on his life which, among other things, forced him to give up his stalled military career.[51] This interpretation coincided with the explanations of the defense attorney and Negrete himself, who lamented during his trial that "if I get out of this [situation] I'm not going to get mixed up in another! It all happened because I couldn't read."[52]

The prosecutor, supported in the press by El Imparcial, rejected this line of argumentation. The former denied that illiteracy had helped push Negrete into a life of crime and asserted that even if he had known how to read he would have been a criminal—an even more dangerous criminal. This conviction was based on the prosecutor's certainty that Negrete was a born criminal as identified by the biological determinists.[53] El Imparcial agreed with this interpretation, systematically discussing Negrete's "criminal and bloody instincts."[54] For example, the paper maintained that he had abandoned his daughter because he "fatally" pursued a destiny of "long nights of watching out for some defenseless owner or his property, and long stays in jails or hospitals, sometimes wounded, other times as a captive."[55] And he did it because his organic structure and his "moral physiognomy" dated from "the troglodyte era of cavemen." According to the editor, this was reflected in "his jutting jaw, his broad nose, distended nostrils, thick lips, and his attitude when he was interrogated, when he displayed all the contortions of a four-legged beast."[56] In this way, the daily compared the delinquent with prehistoric men, just as criminal anthropologists commonly did.

Again, the Vanegas Arroyo press, more closely attuned to popular tastes and aspirations, played up the bandit's criminal trajectory and acknowledged the factors that enhanced his stature (manliness, valor, fierceness, audacity, astuteness, and intelligence), while refraining from anthropological explanations of his criminal tendencies. In contrast, the mainstream press, closer to the interests of the political and economic elite, and worried about preserving the status quo and the social order, lumped him in with common criminals, minimized his feats, and lauded the police. Nevertheless, while *El Imparcial* (as a good defender of the regime and its economic and political institutions) chose to conceive of criminality as an individual problem unrelated to the state, *El País* (alert to social problems thanks to its Catholic "socialism") revealed a tendency that would predominate in the twentieth century, which supposed that the authorities and society had a certain responsibility toward criminals. Finally, the *Gaceta de Policía* also built up the criminal but for opposite reasons than the Vanegas Arroyo press: by exaggerating the dangerousness of the already captured and subdued Negrete, the *Gaceta de Policía* exalted the successful work of the police.

"Five Death Sentences! Not Even if I Was a Cat!"

After his final capture, Jesús Negrete was taken to Lecumberri Penitentiary, which had opened six years earlier and offered more security that the dilapidated Belén jail.[57] He was there for two years. Then in May 1908, on board a paddy wagon named El Diablo (The Devil), he returned to Belén to stand trial.[58]

The trial consumed the first thirteen days of June. Judge Telésforo A. Ocampo presided. As Presidente de Debates (Presiding Judge), his job was to run the hearings, instruct the jurors, and, after receiving their verdict, determine the sentence. The nine members of the jury were to decide on the nature of the crime, establish Negrete's guilt or innocence, and determine any aggravating or mitigating circumstances.[59] Given the importance of the case, the attorney general himself, José María Lozano, served as prosecutor.

Negrete's defense attorneys—Carlos Belina, and, later, Justo San Pedro—appeared in the press as unidentified sketches and lacked Lozano's stature (see fig. 2.4). Both men were most likely novices because five years earlier they were not listed among the lawyers practicing in the Federal District; certainly at the time of the trial, neither figured among the prominent attorneys in the capital.[60] One of the defense attorneys, assuming that the case's notoriety would attract professional attention, even asked his client, "Hasn't someone eminent offered to defend you?"[61] And it is certain that no "eminence" is listed among the ranks of the defenders of record, and none seemed interested in representing him since to do so would have meant being publicly censured by the press for "taking the side of iniquity."[62]

Negrete rounded out the cast of characters. His demeanor and dress were described in meticulous detail by a press obsessed with finding out the thoughts and sentiments that drove the criminal. The detailed descriptions began as soon as the accused arrived at the Belén jail. *El País* reported that

2.4. *En la barra de la defensa*, El Imparcial, 12 June 1908. Hemeroteca Nacional, Universidad Nacional Autónoma de México.

> [t]his fearsome defendant feigns a frightful tranquility, and no trace of suffering is discernible in his countenance. The Penitentiary cell, like the Belén cage, hasn't had the least effect on him; on the contrary, he's put on a bit of weight.[63]

At the same time, *El Imparcial* noted that

> J. Jesús Negrete, like all criminals who have gained a reputation as brave men or take pride in having one [such a reputation], put on for the benefit of their future and past prison companions a disdainful air, haughty look, bullying posture. Their eyes shoot out weird gleams and the thick lips of their big mouths show traces of a deprecating sneer directed at all that surrounds them.[64]

Moreover, according to the daily, Negrete was growing more belligerent by the hour:

> He begins to clearly manifest a zeal to distinguish himself. Yesterday as soon as he returned to his cell he wanted to talk to the warden, who he asked to transfer him to another cell, better than the one he was in. Later, he again called for [the warden] and requested that three

blankets that he had in the Penitentiary be sent over, and that he be given special food.[65]

According to both newspapers, he exhibited the same attitude at the beginning of his trial, and his dress reflected it. He showed up in court wearing a new charro outfit given him by his defense attorney, Carlos Belina, that *El País* described as "yellow with black trim, reddish brown shoes, wide sombrero, decorated hatband and pant seams," and in more detail by *El Imparcial* as fitted trousers with a vest and jacket of the same style and color, a white shirt with flared collar, a red tie, reddish brown shoes with stitching, and a wide beaver hat "trimmed with silver and a bit more subdued in color than the suit."[66] In other words, Negrete wore a charro suit like the one in the Casasola photograph and the Posada illustration, an outfit that lent him not only glamour and presence, but also imbued him with important attributes (valor, dexterity, and elegance) that linked him to rural life and banditry and distanced him from the drab, sketchy figure of the urban criminal.

Nevertheless, both dailies also registered an attitude change in the accused with the passing of the hours and especially of the days. *El Imparcial* noted that when the accusations were read, Negrete lost his haughty look and listened "tranquil and still" to the list of his crimes as if "caught up in vague and terrible longings."[67] *El País* commented on Negrete's loss of "bluster" and found him sad, weak, and depressed.[68] With this, the editors showed that Negrete had given himself over to justice and the authorities, but they attempted to avoid awakening readers' compassion by associating his tranquility with the absence of remorse and moral sentiments. Thus they insisted that his "coldness and tranquility" contrasted with the "horror" his crimes generated among the jury members and the general public.[69]

It is worth noting that the illustrations *El Imparcial* published did not always coincide with the textual descriptions: the illustrators showed not a haughtiness that diminished day by day, but one that grew over the course of the trial. On the first day, June 3, the defendant was shown from behind, symbolizing perhaps his refusal to look readers in the face (see fig. 2.5). The image for the second day, June 7, was much richer: a large color illustration in *El Mundo Ilustrado* showed the accused's face in an inset medallion, while the principal image depicted the full-bodied bandit in profile with a tranquil, serene demeanor and his arms crossed behind his back. On the last day, June 12, he was shown seated among his henchmen; his head was held high and he faced the reader head on with a haughtiness that stood in sharp contrast to the demeanor of his companions, who crossed their arms and bowed their heads.

2.5. ⚘ *El Tigre Declaring, El Imparcial*, 3 June 1908.
Hemeroteca Nacional, Universidad Nacional Autónoma de México.

This brings us to the principal actors in the drama. Each presented different arguments, opinions, and values. Over the course of the trial there is a notable contrast between and among the expressions and decisions of the judge, prosecutor, jury members, defense attorneys, accused, witnesses, reporters, and attending public.

The "instructing" judge, who was not the same as the presiding judge, and the prosecutor agreed that there was sufficient evidence to accuse Jesús Negrete of five murders: the two policemen (Arnulfo Sánchez during his first arrest and Regino Aguilar in the Santa Julia skirmish), and three civilians (Marcelino Molina in the Puerto Pinto cantina, Lauro Frías in the Santa Julia cantina, and Leonardo Enríquez in the Santa Julia skirmish). In addition, he was accused of wounding two policemen (Rafael Bejarano during the Adams robbery and José Álvarez in the Santa Julia skirmish) and committing four robberies (the assaults on the Hacienda de Aragón, the artillery barracks, and the Molino de Valdez, and planning the robberies of the bakery and Irene Pacheco de Adams's house).

As *El Imparcial* pointed out, the sentences for each of these crimes added up to twenty years and six months in prison, plus five death sentences.[70] The Tiger retorted, "Five death sentences? Why? I don't deserve them. And then... five death sentences? Not even if I was a cat! How can I pay up? Only they [cats] have seven lives.[71]

And he was no cat, even if during the trial he defended himself like "a cat with his claws out." Over the course of the trial, the defense attorneys and the accused questioned the veracity of the witnesses, justified the minor and uncontestable infractions, and denied the gravest, indeed all, the crimes.

El País and *El Popular*, which both focused on the position of the accused while *El Imparcial* focused on that of the prosecutor, alleged that during the proceedings there had been irregularities or violations of legal procedures. They emphasized that the authorities had threatened some witnesses and had bribed others. One example was Ubelia Cisneros, who, according to *El País*, after she had been converted into "an instrument of the police," had played a "repugnant role."[72] *El Popular* described her this way:

> She appeared simply but decently dressed like a woman of the middle class, and it was apparent that her statements were memorized and that she recited them like a parrot [. . .] There were moments, above all when she was questioned by the defense, in which Cisneros, ashamed of her conduct, blushed up to her eyeballs, and it seemed as though she would confess that she was bought off, but then someone would glare at her from the jury box and let her continue with the work of destruction she had begun.[73]

In the opinion of *El País* and *El Popular*, the bought witnesses not only lied, but also were not credible in the first place. The two papers rejected the testimony of some witnesses, especially the women, because most had been lovers of the accused, and that was enough to invalidate their statements.

El País maintained that Cisneros was angry with Negrete and that her resentment was evident.[74] Negrete himself said as much when his attorney questioned him about her motives for accusing him: "I already said that it was because I spurned her love."[75] He said the same thing about Manuela Torres: "What aren't women capable of? Their words just aren't trustworthy and that's especially true of Torres who accuses me without motive, out of spite."[76] On the other hand, regarding María Inés Escogido, he maintained that his lovers had no ground for accusing him because they were not party to his plans and that he "was not accustomed to confiding his business to women."[77]

In similar fashion, Negrete and his defenders denied and/or justified his crimes. For example, they insisted that he was not the only one who had shot at Marcelino Molina and that he had done it in self-defense.[78] They also claimed Negrete was drunk when he killed Lauro Frías, so the defendant argued that "the guilty one was Eufemio Martínez [the cantina owner] for selling us so much liquor."[79] Moreover, he had not killed policeman Arnulfo Sánchez because the other policemen had wounded him accidentally during the getaway.[80] Then he asked to confront his accusers face-to-face "in order to expose their lies to the jury and the public," declaring that "I am innocent and if they accuse me it's because some have been paid to do it and others enjoy slandering honorable people." He reiterated that "my words aren't considered credible because of the bad impression that people have of me, but I frankly declare to you that I am innocent."[81]

Beyond these legal strategies, Negrete could appeal to popular attitudes to dispute the prosecutor's accusations. One example involved the treatment of women. For the bandit, as for many men (even of the privileged classes), having various women was a sign of manliness, even if maltreating them was not. Thus he freely admitted his love affairs but emphatically denied having "molested a woman" and having abandoned his daughter.[82] Another example involves Negrete's crimes being assigned different rankings of seriousness: the accusers emphasized the gravity of the murders and the major assaults while bringing to light acts of petty thievery, some committed by Negrete against his own henchmen, probably with the intention of discrediting the delinquent. Perhaps they were the first to be shocked when the accused exclaimed, "I have killed, but not robbed. I am a man, not a petty thief [*ratero*]."[83]

Negrete admitted to the crimes most severely punished by law, and he did it because, as the presiding judge rightly pointed out, he was defending "his reputation as a brave man." In other words, he admitted to the crimes that did no damage to his honor but put his life in danger, and he denied those that sullied his honor. On this point, I agree with Pablo Piccato that despite the discourse of elites, which considered popular groups to be without honor and thus incapable of fighting to defend it, honor played an important role among the masses and revolved around a set of values (trustworthiness, honesty, manliness, etc.) and a willingness to defend that honor when it was threatened, which required manliness and courage. In addition, like duels, popular quarrels (*riñas*) followed a series of rules known and respected by the opponents.[84] In this sense, confrontations were justified if opponents fought fairly and respected the unwritten rules in defense of their honor.

That was how The Tiger saw it, thus the two elements of the declaration, "I am a man; I have killed." He could accept having killed because like all "real" men he had reacted violently against his rivals, and he had done it as it should be done—face-to-face and without unfair advantage. On this point the defense and the accused agreed. The former affirmed, using legal terminology, that the homicides had been committed in self-defense and that the accused had only "mixed it up" with armed opponents.[85] The latter, referring to the murder of Lauro Frías, maintained that "I never attacked without provocation, much less from behind," and "I always wound from the front as my friends can attest."[86] The alternative—to wound an unarmed man from behind—would have been a cowardly act, just as it would have been cowardly to steal from friends, as his reference to petty thefts (*robos rateros*) suggests.

It seems that members of the public who attended the trial shared these values and codes of conduct and delighted in a man who questioned or mocked the authorities. Or perhaps many of them simply felt sympathy for the bandit, but it is certain that they were on Negrete's side. They whistled derisively every time the prosecutor intervened and applauded each time the defense spoke. In fact, the community apparently supported the defendant, a fact that the press could not manage to grasp. Instead journalists lamented that misguided individuals, in the name of friendship, were willing to help criminals escape justice, and those same individuals were nonetheless integrated into Mexican society.[87]

In the final analysis, a notable opposition of ideas, values, prejudices, fears, and sympathies is revealed in the different attitudes of the judge, prosecutor, and popular supporters. It is worth recalling that in the beginning Negrete was accused of five homicides, wounding two men, and four robberies. At the trial's conclusion, the prosecutor sustained those accusations with the exception of one civilian death (Leonardo Enríquez) and the robbery of Mrs. Adams's house. That left four first-degree homicides, two wounded policemen, and three robberies.

The presiding judge developed an extensive questionnaire to help the jury vote because, according to law, the questions had to include the conclusions or essential points of the allegations as presented by the defense attorney and the representative of the Public Ministry. The questionnaire also served to establish the participation or guilt of each accomplice in each crime, the antecedents of all the accused, which were taken into account in determining the aggravating and mitigating circumstances, and the conditions under which the crimes were committed (to properly classify them and, again, to establish the circumstances).

The jury found Jesús Negrete guilty of three homicides, wounding one policeman, and two robberies. Only one of the three was considered first-degree murder. So, after six hours of deliberation, the jurors found him not guilty of the murder of Arnulfo Sánchez, of wounding José Álvarez, and of the artillery barracks robbery. They also reduced the charges to second-degree murder for the homicides of Marcelino Molina and rural policeman Regino Aguilar because they occurred during scuffles and were not premeditated.[88]

The jury's conclusions resulted not in five death sentences but in one. Still, all that was needed for the death penalty was a conviction for the first-degree murder of Lauro Frías. On this subject there were different opinions. The accused did not think he deserved death: "Let them impose the prison term that my judges asked for but not that! I understand that I shouldn't be on the street because what I've done is no laughing matter; but I don't deserve the death penalty."[89] The defense attorney appealed, alleging contradictions in three of the 234 pages included in the questionnaire that the judge had presented to the jury.[90] Nevertheless, between May and August 1909, the district superior court confirmed the court's decision and rejected the appeal, and the supreme court denied judicial review (*amparo*).[91]

To persuade the authorities and avoid execution, Jesús Negrete resorted to institutional language, arguing that "they shouldn't shoot me because I can rehabilitate myself."[92] The reference was to the underlying spirit of the 1871 Penal Code which, in accordance with the ideas of the liberal school of penal law, insisted on the possibility of correction, vested its aspirations in the corrective power of the prison, and contemplated the abolition of the death penalty once the penitentiary system was established (which had happened in 1900 with the founding of Lecumberri).[93] To further convince the authorities, Negrete demonstrated his capacity for regeneration with deeds: in prison he not only lived an exemplary life, he also—as *El Imparcial* and *El País* revealed— learned to read and write.[94] His writings show disillusionment, pain, and even repentance, an essential element in regeneration, as he admitted his guilt and sought oblivion and anonymity:

I was a man of pleasure, I can't deny it
And all alone I suffered from my passions
This thankless world that has controlled me
Made me understand its illusions

I only ask of all my friends
That they remember not what I was before
Because the deceptions of this sad world
Reveal to me that all good times come to an end.

All the world is false and deceitful
Youth, strength, vigor
Hope, dreams, everything passes
And the eternal truth is pain

I beg you, overlook my stupidity
Because in the end I was no more than a pleasure seeker
But tomorrow, if God grants me life
My craziness will pass on to a better state.[95]

[Fui hombre de gusto, no puedo negarlo
Y solito sufrí todas mis pasiones
Este mundo ingrato que me ha dirigido
Me hizo comprender de sus ilusiones

Sólo les encargo a todos mis amigos
Que no hagan recuerdo de lo que antes fui
Por que el desengaño de este triste mundo
Me vino a decir que todos los tiempos llegan a su fin.

Todo el mundo es falso y engañoso
La juventud, las fuerzas, el vigor
La esperanza, los sueños, todo pasa
Y la eterna verdad es el dolor

Yo les suplico, disimulen mi torpeza
Por al fin no fui más que un aficionado
Pero mañana si Dios la vida me presta
Mi ciencia loca pasará á mejor estado.]

Moreover, according to newspaperman Guillermo Mellado, he was accorded "a certain affection" by the other prisoners:

> When money came into his hands, he was accustomed to helping those who needed it most, and often the food that was sent from his house or through his friends was shared with those who were too sick to eat the "slop" that they were given. The last act of this bandit's life, when he realized that his request for a pardon had been denied and that he would be shot, was to give everything in his cell to the neediest elderly prisoner.[96]

Negrete also enjoyed the respect of prison authorities. Mellado recounts that he intervened in defense of an old man who was being beaten for no reason by the *presidente* (prisoner in charge) of the cell block.[97] And, after learning of the event, the warden deposed the section head and named Negrete in his place.[98]

Despite all this, Porfirio Díaz refused to pardon him. Perhaps it was because an armed uprising called by Francisco Madero had begun one month earlier and Díaz needed to show his strength, impose respect for the authorities, and discourage the insurgents. On receiving the news, Negrete was "calm" and "serene, at once proud but not haughty." Nevertheless, with the words "I won't sign. No sir, I won't sign off on my death!" he refused to sign the official papers, taking leave by saying, "Well, if those are your orders, just do it."[99]

"I Have to Die Like a Man; the One Thing I Regret Is Not Having Killed Pancho Chávez"

On December 20, 1910, Jesús Negrete was transferred again to the Belén jail, this time to be executed on its patio. Only one phrase, written on the wall of his cell, records his stay in Lecumberri Penitentiary: "I have to die like a man; the only thing I regret is not having killed Pancho Chávez. If only he hadn't nabbed me...."[100]

Again the dailies strained to guess the condemned man's ideas and feelings. According to *El País*, not even in these last moments did he lose his composure, and he left the penitentiary dressed in the charro suit Belina had given him. But, according to *El Imparcial*, he was decked out in red pants, shirt, and serape, and in place of his old swagger, he entered with "an uncertain step."[101] The official daily went out of its way to show him as a defeated man.

The next day he was put *encapillado*, or "on notice." For a *capilla* (chapel), the jailor's room was outfitted with an altar to the Virgin of Guadalupe. Inside were two beds, one for the bandit and another for the priest, Julián Villalain, who was to accompany him until the final moment (see figs. 2.6 and 2.7). The condemned man's last hours fueled the cupidity of reporters who, with shocking headlines, fought to attract readers. For example, *El Imparcial* announced, "'The Tiger of Santa Julia' heads to the gallows. Today he will enter the chapel and in this antechamber of death he will pass the twenty-four most anguished hours of his life."[102] *El País* reported that "Jesús Negrete awaits with resignation the instant in which he will be shot."[103] A Vanegas Arroyo broadside promised that its public would know "the final words of Jesús Negrete (a.k.a.) 'El Tigre de Santa Julia.'"

The details of the execution and its preparations were repeated in all the daily newspapers. We know that the condemned man dined on a slice of meat and a large cup of coffee with milk, and that, unable to sleep, he spent the night writing verses that he dedicated to Justo San Pedro and letters either to his daughter or to make arrangements for her. In this final note he wrote, "I am very close to death, and not even in this state do I feel any fear. I lament my failings and trust that God will pardon me."[104] He did not believe that this pardon required his confession, and in the face of the priest's insistence, he answered, "For what? If God chooses to pardon me, he will pardon me with my confession or without my confession." Nevertheless, he agreed to hear Mass "with sincere devotion" and prayed "fervently and from the heart."[105]

The accounts of *El Imparcial*, *El País*, and the Vanegas Arroyo press coincide here for the first time—with one important exception. The broadside editors showed compassion for the condemned man and imagined him repentant, exclaiming phrases like the following:

They are finally going to kill me,
I will pay with my life
When I think of this fate
I want to weep...[106]

[Me van, al fin, a matar,
Voy a pagar con la muerte
Cuando pienso en esta suerte
Me dan ganas de llorar...]

Or, in another broadsheet:

2.6. ❦ *Jesús Negrete in the Chapel*, El Imparcial, 22 December 1910. Hemeroteca Nacional, Universidad Nacional Autónoma de México.

2.7. ❦ *El fusilamiento de Jesús Negrete (a) "El tigre de Santa Julia." El 22 de diciembre de 1910 a las 6 y 25 de la mañana. En el patio del Jardín de la Cárcel de Belem. Últimos detalles* (Mexico City: Imprenta de Antonio Vanegas Arroyo, 1910).

My rages I deplore
I repent although it's too late
My remorse is great
I can do nothing more and I weep

And that proud, fierce man
Raised his hand to his face
To hide it [his weeping] in vain
He controlled it firm and calm

Then with muffled voice
Continued in this manner
Very softly for those who could hear
A futile request

Goodbye cruel and thankless world
Goodbye sad and evil life
I go to a world in which all are equal
The vilest and greatest of beings

There I go to rest
With all that I've suffered here
To weep repentant
So much guilt to weep [for].[107]

[Mis arrebatos deploro,
Me arrepiento aunque ya tarde,
Mi remordimiento es grande
Yo no puedo más y lloro

Y aquel hombre altivo y fiero
Llevó a su rostro la mano
Para ocultar lo que en vano
Contenía firme y sereno

Después con voz apagada
Continuó de esta manera
Muy quedo cual si le oyera
Una exigencia ignorada

Adiós mundo cruel e ingrato
Adiós vida triste y mala
Voy a un mundo en que se iguala
El ser más vil y el más alto

Allá voy a descansar
Tanto como aquí he sufrido
A llorar arrepentido
Tantas culpas a llorar.]

These broadsheet descriptions surely stirred the sympathy of readers. In order to avoid awakening similar sentiments in its public or to appear to be questioning the resolve of Porfirio Díaz, *El Imparcial* warned that "[i]t was the same Tiger, he of Santa Julia, he of the frightful and bloody deeds, only a bit fatter. His same attitude, the same half scornful smile that always sprang to his lips as soon as he found himself face to face with the majesty of the Law, the same charro suit that he wore during the trial."[108] Perhaps the delinquent was the same, but his suit was not—The Tiger had requested a new suit and the warden at Belén had granted his request. The Vanegas Arroyo editor reports that Negrete received it gratefully and "in order to celebrate the debut of his apparel he toasted with a cup of cognac, demonstrating the true serenity of all valiant men."[109]

On the question of his serenity, all the newspaper sources again agreed. The reporter for *El País* wrote, "Jesús Negrete in the final moments of his existence found himself calm and completely resolved to ascend the scaffold without fear of death."[110] For its part, *El Imparcial* affirmed that "he lit his last cigar with a notable steadiness of hand, as the light of the match shook not at all, and after he was handcuffed the cigar remained between his teeth and he arrived at the wall."[111] Once in front of the wall, he refused the blindfold because "I want to look death in the face."[112] Then, with "a strong voice and resolved attitude," he positioned himself to receive the shots of the firing squad, "sticking out his chest and throwing his head back so as to avoid being shot in the face."[113] That is how he appeared in the only images of execution, those realized by José Guadalupe Posada for the Vanegas Arroyo press (see figs. 2.8 and 2.9). As Guillermo Mellado concluded, and as the condemned man had foretold, Negrete "died like a man, with tranquility, without moving a muscle, not even when placed against the 'wall,' not even when staring down the mouths of five carbines, poised to send him the message of death."[114]

The sources also agree on the tone of his last words. Perhaps this agreement is a matter of faithful reconstruction, but not necessarily because his last

2.8. ~ *El fusilamiento de Jesús Negrete o sea "El tigre de Santa Julia"*
(Mexico City: Imprenta de Antonio Vanegas Arroyo, 1910).

2.9. Jesús Negrete (a) "El tigre de Santa Julia." Fusilado en la Cárcel de Belem. El 22 de diciembre de 1910 (Mexico City: Imprenta de Antonio Vanegas Arroyo, 1910).

words correspond to a much-repeated formula that traditionally touches on two points: pardon for the executioner and exaltation of the condemned man's cause (often with a dose of nationalism). For the leaders of political or social movements, cause and nationalism unite; they die for the cause, the nation, and their comrades' well-being. In the case of Negrete, the exaltation of country is less prominent. His example shows a condemned man who loves his country, although he rejects its authorities and has broken its laws, and who acknowledges the bonds of his people and his community. Moreover, an appeal to nationalism never fails to move the reader. Negrete's last words, therefore, as imagined by the Vanegas Arroyo editor were

> Soldiers, your duty
> Moves me and I pardon you
> You needn't fear my curse
> This had to be[115]

> [Soldados, vuestro deber,
> Me conmueve y los perdono;
> No temais sufrir mi encono
> Esto así tiene que ser]

According to *El País*, Negrete's parting words were "Goodbye everyone"; according to *El Imparcial* and Vanegas Arroyo, "Goodbye everyone, forgive me gentlemen. Long live Mexico!"[116]

Final Considerations

Jesús Negrete was neither a common criminal nor a social bandit. He did not act to avenge social injustices, he did not share his triumphs or his booty, he did not question the justness of the law or other institutions, and he did not pretend to reform or revolutionize the political and social order. Nevertheless, he did exact revenge for his exclusion from social and economic opportunities, and this exclusion was clearly revealed in his institutional experience: school was closed to him and the army was restricted. Only jail was left, and he took advantage of its educational benefits and learned how to use institutional language, as evidenced by his supposed regeneration. Thus he was socially marginalized and he punished the society that excluded him. By confronting the rich and powerful rather than submitting to them, he represented the social aspirations of ordinary folk, and thus transformed himself into an instrument of vengeance and justice. For these reasons, Negrete received the support and sympathy of the popular classes.

The figure of The Tiger of Santa Julia brought together various elements to effect Negrete's transformation into a popular hero and eventually a myth. First, from his humble, illiterate, rural origins, he managed not only to get to Mexico City, but also to transcend it, stand out in the crowd, and impose himself on society. He confronted the authorities, humiliated the rural and urban police, and appeared to mock the system of power imposed by Porfirio Díaz. Second, even if Negrete did not rob from the rich to give to the poor, he did challenge the powerful and rob them of their weapons and money; with this, he did avenge social injustice. Third, he was astute, and this intelligence helped him plan his attacks, escape, and fool his pursuers. He also spoke the same language as the authorities, played the game of regeneration or the role of the loving father, and even wrote in the language of the poets. Finally, he answered to the image of the brave man, the macho Mexican. He had multiple lovers willing to lay down their lives for him. And he was frightened of nothing, always responding manfully to provocations and imposing his will on his rivals. Like Juan Charrasqueado, protagonist of the famous corrido, "he was rancher, lover, drunk, brawler, and gambler" and like all "good roosters" they could only kill him (or in this case capture him the second time) by jumping him all at once. Or, like a good lover and again like Juan, he was only captured on the third attempt when he lost the love of a woman and she betrayed him to Francisco Chávez.

Various sources contributed to the myth's creation, as the scriptwriter of the most recent films dedicated to The Tiger of Santa Julia understood. To create a legend, the man and his deeds are not enough; propagandists and apologists are also necessary, and Negrete has certainly had his share. Some have contributed in spite of themselves, and others with pleasure. Among the unwilling contributors were policemen and journalists who sought to promote the bandit in order to promote the police who captured him, but the bandit kept the glory nonetheless. On the other hand, as *El Popular* rightly pointed out, by deploying "such a security apparatus in order to guard him and transport him to his trial," the police revealed their own fear and supported the image of "a man gifted with supernatural powers." The editor concluded that

> [a]ll these precautions, all this apparatus, all this excessive force prove counterproductive, because the ignorant multitude doesn't take these concerns for what they are, guarantees of security, but sees them as fear of the prisoner, for which he himself feels a secret satisfaction, and in this way the authorities embellish the wretched fame of men whose

deeds, far from provoking some noble sentiment, awaken nothing more than repugnance, scorn, and indignation.[117]

The newspapers also helped embellish the bandit's fame, again despite their intentions. In their articles and in spite of their differences, *El Imparcial* and *El País* systematically dedicated themselves to diminishing and criticizing the delinquent. They omitted things that showed him in a good light, warned of the danger he represented to society, to men of his class, and even to his henchmen and lovers, and showed his repudiation of the community. Still, they provided publicity. This was pointed out by *El Popular* and *El Diario del Hogar*, who accused reporters of "glorifying crime" in their desire to get sensational stories and expand their public.[118] And in fact, even when they criticized bandits, according to *El Popular*, they found themselves addressing a public that "because of its background" had a propensity "to cultivate these legends of great criminals," to see "a hero in each delinquent," and a martyr "in each convicted man."[119] The glorification of the criminal was further abetted by the Vanegas Arroyo press, which had fewer compunctions about fomenting the myth and, in consideration of its public, exalted Negrete and his deeds.

Abetted in greater or lesser measure by all these sources, Negrete awoke the admiration or at least the interest of Mexico City society. Thus *El Imparcial* admitted that "the bandit's fame arouses great interest for being widely known" and "has managed to attract public attention in a powerful way."[120] This explains why people formed long lines in the patio of the judicial palace to obtain tickets to attend the trial. Those who remained outside crowded around the building and the surrounding streets, seeking to at least be the first to get the news. And those who managed to get seats in the courtroom did not limit themselves to listening; they applauded the accused and hoisted the defense attorney on their shoulders as if they were at a bullfight.[121]

The "public" was faithful to The Tiger until the end. They bought the broadsides that recounted his deeds, as evidenced in the repeated versions the Vanegas Arroyo press produced and sold. Along with these popular testimonials to Negrete's manly heroism, the public collected less flattering memorabilia including clay figures that showed him defecating, just as he was doing when he was captured.[122] Either way, they remembered him. The day of his execution, people crowded the environs of the Belén jail and authorities had to wait several hours for the streets to clear before the coffin could be moved to the Dolores cemetery—at least according to *El Imparcial* (*El País* minimized the presence of spectators at the execution).[123]

The public remained faithful to Negrete's memory after his death too. The legend has survived more than a hundred years and become myth. During his life, Negrete's image vacillated between common criminal and social bandit, and after his death he was transformed into a champion of justice, a social rebel, and a protorevolutionary. Exemplary visions from the twentieth century include a corrido from the 1920s, a novel by Carlos Isla published in 1999, and two films (the first was filmed in 1973 under the direction of Arturo Martínez, and the second was filmed in 2001 under the direction of Alejandro Gamboa). These popular visions have produced a new incarnation of The Tiger, whose name has been adopted by sports teams and bars. As if to ensure that Negrete's nickname would be passed from generation to generation, the Mexican Academy of Science used it for the Science in the Schools program. In a mathematics exercise, teachers asked primary school students to solve the following problem: "In Santa Julia there are approximately three thousand residents, and one hour after the capture of the Tiger everyone knew about it. Without writing down numbers, but based on your best guess, say how long each resident waited before informing three others."

It remains to be shown how the current myth deals with the traits of the bandit turned popular hero. First, his reputation as a womanizer has grown and he is now considered a gallant ladies' man, respectful and a defender of women, which can be seen in the following corrido:

> Jesús was his first name
> Negrete was his last
> His symbols were bullets
> His name-saint was Cupid
>
> They say he had a thousand loves
> In the barrio of Santa Julia;
> Like the mountain lion
> He counted them by colors.[124]
>
> [Jesús por nombre tenía
> Negrete por apellido
> Sus señas eran las balas
> Su santo el mismo cupido
>
> Le decían el mil amores
> Del barrio de Santa Julia;
> Como el tigre de la sierra
> Las contaba por colores.]

In these new sources, then, many women follow him, and their role in the events surrounding his life has taken on greater significance. This is especially apparent in the second film in which women are not only part of the gang but practically run it. Thus, in the current versions of Negrete's myth, women are a source of his strength and also of his weakness, since he was apprehended through the betrayal of a spurned woman.

Second, the novel, like the 2001 film, imagines a painful childhood full of violence and abandonment, and a difficult youth full of injustices and abuses committed by the rich and powerful, to which Negrete responds in kind. In the first film, as a child Negrete witnesses his sister's rape and his father's murder, and takes his revenge on legal systems and authorities who protect only the powerful. Personal troubles make him aware of the suffering of the weak and less fortunate, and he dedicates himself to defending and helping them. And from these notions comes the third aspect of the new legend: he robs from the rich to help the poor, and he attacks the strong to protect the weak, especially targeting corrupt and unjust authorities. Thus the criminal Negrete passes over to the side of the righteous. This is evident in the corrido, which not only compares him to Chucho el Roto (another Porfirian-era bandit), but also to Christ the King himself:

> He stole from the rich
> A bloody jackal
> Avenger of the poor
> And feared by all
>
> He robbed dandies and haciendas
> He killed a lot of cops
> And he didn't spare the shops
> Where he made a ruckus
>
> From Tacuba to Tacubaya
> From Guerrero to La Piedad
> He was a scourge to government
> And to all society
>
> He was like Chucho el Roto
> And like Christ the King himself
> José de Jesús Negrete
> As he was known by the law.[125]

[Ladrón fue de los ricos
Y un chacal sanguinario
Vengador de los pobres
Y entre todos temerario

Robó catrines y haciendas
Mató muchos tecolotes
Y no le faltaron tiendas
Donde hiciera borlote

De Tacuba a Tacubaya
De Guerrero a La Piedad
Fue al azote del gobierno
Y de toda la sociedad

Fue como Chucho el Roto
Y como el mismo Cristo Rey,
José de Jesús Negrete
Por nombre de buena ley.]

This comparison is apparent in the second film as well, in which, according to its critics, Negrete is represented as a "doer of good deeds in the community" and a "Mexican Robin Hood."[126] On the silver screen, The Tiger is not exactly a hero, but he is a good man. And he is good for two reasons: first because he confronts evil in the form of the policeman and the soldier who maltreated him when he was in the army and murdered his best friend and tortured to death one of his women; and second because he confronts perpetrators of evil. The evildoers—just as in the first film—are villains of Mexican history, including Porfirio Díaz and his minions. Both cinematic histories situate Negrete even closer to the Revolution than he was—not on the eve of revolution, but within its context. In this way, he goes from participation in the generalized struggle of an oppressed people against the rich and powerful to active participation in a social revolution.

In sum, the Revolution has helped shape the current image of the bandit. We cannot help but think that if The Tiger had operated closer to the outbreak of the armed insurrection, or if the authorities had lagged a few years in capturing him, he might have passed into history—not just into myth—as a true social bandit or even as a revolutionary leader. Negrete suggested as much; when an *El Imparcial* reporter asked his opinion of the growing sedition, he responded, "What a pity I was locked up! Free I might have had my own party and a lot of followers; knowing that I was going to be their chief they would have fought with spirit."[127]

Notes

1. "Los delincuentes más peligrosos, criminales natos," *El Imparcial*, 25 August 1898.
2. "Continúa el jurado del tigre de Santa Julia y socios," *El País*, 3 June 1908. According to other sources, Chávez was security prefect.
3. "'El Tigre de Santa Julia.' Espléndido triunfo de la policía," *El Imparcial*, 28 May 1906; "El Tigre de Santa Julia," *El Imparcial*, 29 May 1906; and "El bandido Negrete en la penitenciaría," *El Imparcial*, 31 May 1906.
4. "El Tigre de Santa Julia," *El Imparcial*, 29 May 1906.
5. For an overview of the press during the Porfiriato and for more on *El Diario del Hogar, El Imparcial, El País,* and *El Popular*, see Blanca Aguilar Plata, "El Imparcial. Su oficio y su negocio," *Revista Mexicana de Ciencias Políticas* 28 (July–September 1982), 77–102; Cano Andaluz Aurora, ed. *Las publicaciones periódicas y la historia de México (Ciclo de conferencias)* (Mexico City: Instituto de Investigaciones Bibliográficas UNAM, 1995); Alberto del Castillo, "El surgimiento del reportaje policiaco en México. Los inicios de un nuevo lenguaje gráfico (1888–1910)," *Cuicuilco* 5, no. 13 (May–August 1998): 163–94; and "Entre la moralización y el sensacionalismo. Prensa, poder y criminalidad a fines del siglo XIX en la ciudad de México," in *Hábitos, normas y escándalo. Prensa, criminalidad y drogas en el porfiriato tardío*, eds. Ricardo Perez Montfort, et al. (Mexico City: CIESAS—Plaza y Valdés Editores, 1997), 17–73; Irma Lombardo, *De la opinión a la noticia. El surgimiento de los géneros informativos en México* (Mexico City: Kiosco, 1992); Laura Navarrete Maya and Blanca Aguilar Plata, eds., *La prensa en México. Momentos y figuras relevantes (1810–1915)* (Mexico City: Addison Wesley Longman, 1998); Erica Pani, "Democracia y representación política. La visión de dos periódicos católicos de fin de siglo. 1880–1910," in *Tradición, modernidad y alteridad. La ciudad de México al cambio de siglo (XIX–XX)*, ed. Claudia Agostini and Elisa Speckman Guerra (Mexico City: Instituto de Investigaciones Históricas UNAM, 2001), 143–60; Nora Pérez Rayón, *México 1900. Percepciones y valores en la gran prensa capitalina* (Mexico City: Universidad Autónoma Metropolitana Azcapotzalco—Grupo Editorial Miguel Ángel Porrúa, 2001); and Florence Toussaint, *Escenario de la prensa en el Porfiriato* (Mexico City: Universidad de Colima—Fundación Manuel Buendía, 1989).
6. On broadsheets, see Enrique Flores, *Unipersonal del arcabuceado* (Mexico City: Instituto Nacional de Belles Artes UNAM, 1988); Elisa Speckman Guerra, "De amor y desamor: ideas, imágenes, recetas y códigos en los impresos de Antonio Vanegas Arroyo," *Literaturas populares* 1, no. 2 (July–December 2001): 68–101; "Pautas de conducta y código de valores en los impresos de Vanegas Arroyo," in *Literatura mexicana del otro fin de siglo*, ed. Rafael Olea Franco (Mexico City: El Colegio de México, 2001), 425–48; and Elisa Speckman Guerra, "Cuadernillos, pliegos y hojas

sueltas de la casa de Antonio Vanegas Arroyo," in *La república de las letras. Asomos a la cultura escrita en el México decimonónico*, vol. 2, *Publicaciones. Periódicos y otros impresos* (Mexico City: Universidad Nacional Autónoma de México, 2005), 391–414. For an analysis of the corridos, also see Vicente T. Mendoza, *El corrido mexicano* (Mexico City: Fondo de Cultura Económica, 1954); María del Carmen Garza de Koniecki, *El corrido mexicano como narración literaria* (PhD diss., El Colegio de México, n.d.); and Merle E. Simmons, *The Mexican Corrido as a Source for Interpretive Study of Modern Mexico (1870–1950)* (Bloomington: Indiana University Press, 1957).

7. Roland Barthes, *Mythologies*, trans. Annette Lavers (New York: The Noonday Press, 1957), 143.
8. "El sensacional jurado del tigre de Santa Julia," *El País*, 2 June 1908.
9. *Jesús Negrete (a) "El tigre de Santa Julia" fusilado en la Cárcel de Belem. El 22 de diciembre de 1910* (Mexico City: Imprenta de Antonio Vanegas Arroyo, 1910) (impreso suelto); "Si tuviera cinco vidas, cinco vidas le quitarían," *El Imparcial*, 31 May 1908.
10. "La evasión de criminales," *El País*, 2 December 1905; and "Un jurado sensacional. Las hazañas del "Tigre de Santa Julia" y socios," *El País*, 1 June 1908.
11. On the figure of the European social bandit, see Eric Hobsbawm, *Rebeldes primitivos. Estudios sobre las formas arcaicas de los movimientos sociales en los siglos XIX y XX*, trans. Joaquín Romero Maura (Barcelona: Ediciones Ariel, 1968), 27–47. On the applicability of Hobsbawm's model for Mexican bandits, see Paul Vanderwood, *Desorden y progreso. Bandidos, policías y desarrollo mexicano* (Mexico City: Siglo Veintiuno, 1986), 11, 130–31, 139.
12. Barthes, *Mythologies*, 119.
13. Fragment of a declaration of Jesús Negrete in "Las últimas horas de vida de un gran culpable," *El Imparcial*, 22 December 1910.
14. "Continúa el jurado del tigre de Santa Julia y socios," *El País*, 3 June 1908.
15. "Un jurado sensacional. Las hazañas de 'El Tigre de Santa Julia' y socios," *El País*, 1 June 1908.
16. Ibid.
17. "Hoy se efectuará el jurado de Jesús Negrete," *El Popular*, 1 June 1908.
18. "Los defensores de Negrete y las palomas viajeras . . . o los globos dirigibles," *El Imparcial*, 3 June 1908.
19. "Un jurado sensacional. Las hazañas de 'El Tigre de Santa Julia' y socios," *El País*, 1 June 1908.
20. Ibid.
21. "Un jurado sensacional. Las hazañas de 'El Tigre de Santa Julia' y socios," *El País*, 1 June 1908; "El sensacional jurado del tigre de Santa Julia y socios," *El País*, 2 June 1908; and "Continúa el jurado del tigre de Santa Julia y socios," *El País*, 3 June 1908.
22. "Los defensores de Negrete y las palomas viajeras . . . o los globos dirigibles," *El Imparcial*, 3 June 1908.
23. Ibid.

24. "Los defensores de Negrete y las palomas viajeras . . . o los globos dirigibles," *El Imparcial*, 3 June 1908; and "El sensacional jurado del tigre de Santa Julia," *El País*, 2 June 1908.
25. "Un jurado sensacional. Las hazañas de 'El Tigre de Santa Julia' y socios," *El País*, 1 June 1908; and "Hoy se efectuará el jurado de Jesús Negrete," *El Popular*, 1 June 1908.
26. "Hoy se efectuará el jurado de Jesús Negrete," *El Popular*, 1 June 1908.
27. "Los defensores de Negrete y las palomas viajeras . . . o los globos dirigibles," *El Imparcial*, 3 June 1908.
28. "El asalto a la hacienda de Aragón," *El País*, 18 August 1900; "Más sobre la agresión del administrador en Aragón," *El País*, 16 October 1900; "Tragedia en Aragón," *El Popular*, 17 August 1900; and "La tragedia en la Hacienda de Aragón," *El Popular*, 18 August 1900.
29. "Un jurado sensacional," *El País*, 1 June 1908.
30. "Un jurado sensacional," *El País*, 1 June 1908; and *El fusilamiento de Jesús Negrete o sea "El tigre de Santa Julia"* (Mexico City: Imprenta de Antonio Vanegas Arroyo, 1910) (impreso suelto).
31. *La vida de un bandolero. Los crímenes más notables de Jesús Negrete (a) "El tigre de Santa Julia." Aprehensión de sus cómplices* (Mexico City: Imprenta de Antonio Vanegas Arroyo, n.d.) (impreso suelto).
32. "La fuga sensacional," *El Imparcial*, 1 December 1905.
33. *El fusilamiento de Jesús Negrete o sea "El tigre de Santa Julia"* (impreso suelto).
34. "Sensacional fuga de cinco presos," *El Imparcial*, 30 November 1905; "La fuga sensacional," *El Imparcial*, 1 December 1905; "Escandalosa fuga de presos de la cárcel de Belén," *El País*, 30 November 1905; "La evasión de presos de la cárcel de Belén," *El País*, 1 December 1905; and "La evasión de criminales," *El País*, 2 December 1905.
35. *La sensacional fuga de cinco presos de la Cárcel de Belén. El día 29 de noviembre del presente año* (Mexico City: Imprenta de Antonio Vanegas Arroyo, 1910) (impreso suelto).
36. *El fusilamiento de Jesús Negrete o sea "El Tigre de Santa Julia"* (impreso suelto).
37. "La fuga sensacional," *El Imparcial*, 1 December 1905.
38. "La evasión de criminales," *El País*, 2 December 1905; and "La fuga sensacional," *El Imparcial*, 1 December 1905.
39. *Gaceta de Policía*, 1 April 1906, pp. 13–14.
40. *Jesús Negrete (a) "El tigre de Santa Julia." Nuevo corrido*, in *El Cancionero Popular* 2 (Mexico City: Imprenta de Antonio Vanegas Arroyo, 1909) (impreso suelto).
41. "Un jurado sensacional," *El País*, 1 June 1908.
42. "Aprehensión de Jesús Negrete, 'El tigre de Santa Julia,'" *El Imparcial*, 29 May 1906; and "Hazañas del 'Tigre de Santa Julia,'" *El Imparcial*, 30 May 1906.
43. *Gaceta de Policía*, 3 June 1906, p. 14.
44. *El fusilamiento de Jesús Negrete o sea "El tigre de Santa Julia"* (impreso suelto).
45. Castillo, "Entre la moralización y el sensacionalismo," 44.
46. "Hazañas del 'Tigre de Santa Julia,'" *El País*, 30 May 1906.
47. *El fusilamiento de Jesús Negrete o sea "El tigre de Santa Julia"* (impreso suelto).

48. On the ideas of the positivist school of penal law, see Alessandro Baratta, *Criminología crítica y crítica del derecho penal* (Mexico City: Siglo Veintiuno, 1991); Rosa del Olmo, *América Latina y su criminología* (Mexico City: Siglo Veintiuno, 1981); Massimo Pavarini, *Control y dominación. Teorías criminológicas burguesas y proyecto hegemónico* (Mexico City: Siglo Veintiuno, 1983); and León Radzinowicz, *En busca de la criminología* (Caracas: Universidad Central de Venezuela, 1970). On the positivist school's adoption or adaptation in Mexico, see Robert Buffington, *Criminales y ciudadanos en el México Moderno* (Mexico City: Siglo Veintiuno, 2001), 61–100; Antonio Padilla Arroyo, *De Belem a Lecumberri. Pensamiento social y penal en el México decimonónico* (Mexico City: Archivo General de la Nación, 2001), 97–144; Pablo Piccato, "El discurso sobre la criminalidad y el alcoholismo hacia el fin del porfiriato," in *Hábitos, normas y escándalo. Prensa, criminalidad y drogas en el porfiriato tardío*, eds. Ricardo Pérez Montfort, et al. (Mexico City: CIESAS—Plaza y Valdés Editores, 1997), 63–71; Elisa Speckman Guerra, *Crimen y castigo. Legislación penal, interpretaciones de la criminalidad y administración de justicia (Ciudad de México, 1871–1910)* (Mexico City: El Colegio de México—Instituto de Investigaciones Históricas UNAM, 2002), 93–110; and Beatriz Urías Horcaditas, *Indígena y criminal. Interpretaciones del derecho y la antropología en México 1871–1921* (Mexico City: Universidad Iberoamericana, 2000), 145–66.
49. On this important shift, see the essential works of José Ángel Ceniceros and Luis Garrido, many of which are published in the journal *Criminalia*.
50. "Aprehensión de Jesús Negrete, el 'Tigre de Santa Julia,'" *El País*, 29 May 1906.
51. "Un jurado sensacional. Las hazañas de 'El Tigre de Santa Julia' y socios," *El País*, 1 June 1908.
52. "Las últimas horas de la vida de un gran culpable," *El Imparcial*, 22 December 1910.
53. "El jurado del tigre de Santa Julia," *El País*, 12 June 1908.
54. "Llegamos al último acto del sensacional jurado," *El Imparcial*, 13 June 1908.
55. Ibid.
56. Ibid.
57. The quotation in the heading comes from a fragment of a declaration of Jesús Negrete in "Ya se que acabaré en el jardín, dijo 'El Tigre de Santa Julia,'" *El Imparcial*, 2 June 1908.
58. "Si tuviera cinco vidas, cinco vidas le quitarían," *El Imparcial*, 31 May 1908; and "Insaculación de jurados," *El País*, 30 May 1908.
59. On the procedures for jury trials, see *Código de procedimientos penales de 1894*, Art. 39; *Ley de organización judicial para el Distrito Federal y territorios federales*, 9 September 1903; *Ley que reforma la de organización judicial en el Distrito y Territorios Federales*, 28 December 1907; and *Ley de jurados en materia criminal*, 24 June 1891. For a study of the popular jury (*jurado popular*), see Elisa Speckman Guerra, "El jurado popular para delitos comunes: Leyes, ideas y prácticas (Distrito Federal, 1869–1929)," in *Historia de la justicia en México (siglos XIX y XX)*, ed. Salvador Cárdenas Aguirre (Mexico City: Suprema Corte de la Justicia de la Nación, 2005).

60. On the procedures for sentencing in jury trials, see *Código de procedimientos penales de 1894*, Art. 39; *Ley de organización judicial para el Distrito Federal y territorios federales*, 9 September 1903; *Ley que reforma la de organización judicial en el Distrito y Territorios Federales*, 28 December 1907; and *Ley de jurados en materia criminal*, 24 June 1891.
61. "Continúa el jurado de 'El tigre de Santa Julia' y socios," *El País*, 4 June 1908.
62. Ibid.
63. "Traslación de Negrete a Belén. 'El Tigre de Santa Julia' vestido de charro," *El País*, 31 May 1908.
64. "Si tuviera cinco vidas, cinco vidas le quitarían," *El Imparcial*, 31 May 1908.
65. Ibid.
66. "Traslación de Negrete a Belén. 'El Tigre de Santa Julia' vestido de charro," *El País*, 31 May 1908; "Si tuviera cinco vidas, cinco vidas la quitarían," *El Imparcial*, 31 May 1908.
67. "Ya se que acabaré en el jardín, dijo 'El tigre de Santa Julia,'" *El Imparcial*, 2 June 1908.
68. "Continúa el jurado de 'El tigre de Santa Julia' y socios," *El País*, 4 June 1908.
69. "Los defensores de Negrete y las palomas viajeras . . . o los globos dirigibles," *El Imparcial*, 3 June 1908.
70. "El Tigre de Santa Julia fue sentenciado a la pena capital," *El Imparcial*, 14 June 1908. The sum was calculated by adding up the penalties established by the penal code for each alleged crime: capital punishment for each aggravated homicide (committed with treachery, unfair advantage, or betrayal), and the median punishment for each attack and assault, punishments that could be increased or reduced by up to a third by factoring in aggravating or attenuating circumstances (1871 Penal Code).
71. "Ya se que acabaré en el jardín, dijo 'El tigre de Santa Julia,'" *El Imparcial*, 2 June 1908.
72. "Declaraciones de Ubelia Cisneros. Dice que tiene mala voluntad y odio al tigre," *El País*, 11 June 1908.
73. "Ayer declaró la mujer Judas," *El Popular*, 11 June 1908.
74. "Declaraciones de Ubelia Cisneros. Dice que tiene mala voluntad y odio al tigre," *El País*, 11 June 1908.
75. "El defensa Serrano pide para Negrete las rosas del suplicio," *El Imparcial*, 4 June 1908.
76. "El sensacional jurado de 'El Tigre de Santa Julia' y socios," *El País*, 2 June 1908.
77. Ibid.
78. Ibid.
79. "Los defensores de Negrete y las palomas viajeras . . . o los globos dirigibles," *El Imparcial*, 3 June 1908.
80. "El sensacional jurado del 'Tigre de Santa Julia,'" *El País*, 2 June 1908.
81. Ibid.
82. "Continúa el jurado del 'Tigre de Santa Julia' y socios," *El País*, 3 June 1908; and "Los defensores de Negrete y las palomas viajeras . . . o los globos dirigibles," *El Imparcial*, 3 June 1908.

83. "Los defensores de Negrete y las palomas viajeras . . . o los globos dirigibles," *El Imparcial*, 3 June 1908.
84. Piccato, "El discurso sobre la criminalidad y el alcoholismo," 77–102.
85. "El sensacional jurado del 'Tigre de Santa Julia,'" *El País*, 2 June 1908.
86. "Continúa el jurado del 'Tigre de Santa Julia' y socios," *El País*, 3 June 1908; and "Los defensores de Negrete y las palomas viajeras . . . o los globos dirigibles," *El Imparcial*, 3 June 1908.
87. "Nuestros íntimos y el 'Tigre de Santa Julia,' la amistad es un sentimiento purísimo por encima de las leyes y preceptos sociales," *El Imparcial*, 14 May 1908.
88. "La última audiencia del jurado del 'Tigre de Santa Julia,'" *El País*, 14 June 1908.
89. "Continúa el jurado del 'Tigre de Santa Julia' y socios," *El País*, 4 June 1908.
90. "Comienzan a pesar en la balanza algunas pruebas favorables a Negrete," *El Imparcial*, 10 June 1908.
91. "Si así está mandado que se haga . . . 'El Tigre de Santa Julia' va camino al patíbulo," *El Imparcial*, 21 December 1910.
92. "El jurado del 'Tigre de Santa Julia,'" *El País*, 13 June 1908.
93. On the ideas of the liberal school of penal law, see Baratta, *Criminología crítica y crítica del derecho penal*; Olmo, *América Latina y su criminología*; Pavarini, *Control y dominación*; and Radzinowicz, *En busca de la criminología*. On its adoption or adaptation in Mexico, see Buffington, *Criminales y ciudadanos*, 21–60; Padilla Arroyo, *De Belem a Lecumberri*, 97–144; Piccato, "El discurso sobre la criminalidad y el alcoholismo"; and Speckman Guerra, *Crimen y castigo*, 83–92.
94. "Fue negado el indulto al 'Tigre de Santa Julia,'" *El Imparcial*, 20 December 1910; and "Encapillarán hoy a las seis de la mañana al 'Tigre de Santa Julia,'" *El País*, 21 December 1910.
95. Verses of Jesús Negrete in *El fusilamiento de Jesús Negrete (a) "El tigre de Santa Julia." El 22 de diciembre de 1910 a las 6 y 25 de la mañana. En el patio del Jardín de la Cárcel de Belén. Últimos detalles* (Mexico City: Imprenta de Antonio Vanegas Arroyo, 1910) (impreso suelto); and "Las últimas horas de vida de un gran culpable," *El Imparcial*, 22 December 1910.
96. Guillermo Mellado, *Belem por dentro y por fuera* (Mexico City: Criminalia, 1959), 148–49.
97. It was the custom in Lecumberri to name as presidente or *mayor* one of the prisoners—usually the fiercest and most hardened criminal—and charge him with controlling their companions, although that usually involved extortion and brutal treatment. See Mellado, *Belem por dentro y por fuera*, 36–39; and Aldo Coletti, *La negra historia de Lecumberri* (Mexico City: Editorial Universo México, 1981), 66–67.
98. Mellado, *Belem por dentro y por fuero*, 148–49.
99. "Fue negado el indulto al 'Tigre de Santa Julia,'" *El Imparcial*, 20 December 1910; "Si así está mandado que se haga . . . 'El tigre de Santa Julia' va camino al patíbulo," *El Imparcial*, 21 December 1910; "Las últimas horas de vida de un gran culpable," *El Imparcial*, 22 December 1910; and *El País*, "Encapillarán hoy a las seis de la mañana al 'Tigre de Santa Julia,'" 21 December 1910.

100. Words recorded by Guillermo Mellado, who omitted the final comments because he considered them crude. Mellado, *Belem por dentro y por fuera*, 90.
101. "Encapillarán hoy a las seis de la mañana al 'Tigre de Santa Julia,'" *El País*, 21 December 1910; and "Si así está mandado que se haga . . . 'El tigre de Santa Julia' va camino al patíbulo," *El Imparcial*, 21 December 1910.
102. *El Imparcial*, 21 December 1910.
103. *El País*, 22 December 1910.
104. Ibid.
105. All the sources agree on this description. "Si así está mandado que se haga . . . 'El tigre de Santa Julia' va camino al patíbulo," *El Imparcial*, 21 December 1910; "Las últimas horas de vida de un gran culpable," *El Imparcial*, 22 December 1910; "'El Tigre de Santa Julia' fue fusilado ayer," *El País*, 23 December 1910; and *El fusilamiento de Jesús Negrete (a) "El tigre de Santa Julia." El 22 de diciembre de 1910 a las 6 y 25 de la mañana* (impreso suelto).
106. *El fusilamiento de Jesús Negrete (a) "El tigre de Santa Julia." El 22 de diciembre de 1910 a las 6 y 25 de la mañana* (impreso suelto).
107. *Últimas palabras de Jesús Negrete (a) "El tigre de Santa Julia"* (Mexico City: Imprenta de Antonio Vanegas Arroyo, 1910) (impreso suelto).
108. "Las últimas horas de vida de un gran culpable," *El Imparcial*, 22 December 1910.
109. *El fusilamiento de Jesús Negrete (a) "El tigre de Santa Julia." El 22 de diciembre de 1910 a las 6 y 25 de la mañana* (impreso suelto).
110. "J. Jesús Negrete espera resignado el instante en que morirá fusilado," *El País*, 22 December 1910.
111. "A las seis y veintisiete de la mañana Jesús Negrete pagó en el patíbulo todos sus crímenes," *El Imparcial*, 22 December 1910.
112. "'El Tigre de Santa Julia' fue fusilado ayer," *El País*, 23 December 1910.
113. "A las seis y veintisiete de la mañana Jesús Negrete pagó en el patíbulo todos sus crímenes," *El Imparcial*, 22 December 1910.
114. Mellado, *Belem por dentro y por fuera*, 90.
115. *Últimas palabras de Jesús Negrete (a) "El tigre de Santa Julia"* (impreso suelto).
116. "'El Tigre de Santa Julia' fue fusilado ayer," *El País*, 23 December 1910; "A las seis y veintisiete de la mañana Jesús Negrete pagó en el patíbulo todos sus crímenes," *El Imparcial*, 22 December 1910; and *El fusilamiento de Jesús Negrete (a) "El tigre de Santa Julia." El 22 de diciembre de 1910 a las 6 y 25 de la mañana* (impreso suelto).
117. "La custodia del 'Tigre de Santa Julia,' ¿Porqué tanto lujo de fuerza?" *El Popular*, 6 June 1908.
118. "Negrete y la prensa de escándalo," *El Diario del Hogar*, 10 June 1908; and "Horror al crimen pero compasión al delincuente," *El Popular*, 4 June 1908.
119. "A propósito del sensacional jurado de 'El Tigre de Santa Julia,'" *El Popular*, 5 June 1908; and "Horror al crimen, pero compasión al delincuente," *El Popular*, 4 June 1908.
120. "Ya se que acabaré en el jardín, dijo 'El tigre de Santa Julia,'" *El Imparcial*, 2 June 1908.
121. "El jurado del 'Tigre de Santa Julia,'" *El Imparcial*, 7 June 1908; "Si tuviera cinco vidas, cinco vidas le quitarían," *El Imparcial*, 31 May 1908; "Llegamos al último acto

del sensacional jurado," *El Imparcial*, 13 June 1908; and "Continúa el jurado del 'Tigre de Santa Julia' y socios," *El País*, 4 June 1908.

122. Press notice cited in Castillo, "Entre la moralización y el sensacionalismo," 47.

123. "'El Tigre de Santa Julia' fue fusilado ayer," *El País*, 23 December 1910; and "A las seis y veintisiete de la mañana Jesús Negrete pagó en el patíbulo todos sus crímenes," *El Imparcial*, 22 December 1910.

124. Antonio Avitia Hernández, *Corrido histórico mexicano. Voy a cantarles la historia*, vol. 2, *1910–1916* (Mexico City: Porrúa, 1997), 7–8.

125. Ibid.

126. See Montgomery Guillaume Frankenheimer van der Beck, *Revista Cinefagia*; Pablo y José Martín Sulaimán, *CinEncanto*; and the anonymous critics in *Revista Vértigo o Cinemanía*.

127. "Las últimas horas de vida de un gran culpable," *El Imparcial*, 21 December 1910.

CHAPTER THREE

A Sense of the Tragic in Life
Text and Context in Mexico City's General Insane Asylum

≫ Cristina Rivera-Garza ≪

Since universal *world time* is gearing up to outstrip the time of erstwhile localities in historical importance, it is now a matter of urgency that we reform the "whole" dimension of general history so as to make way to the "fractal" history of the limited but precisely located event.
        Paul Virilio, "Calling Card" in *A Landscape of Events*

The Text (Documents from the Institutional Dossier of Marino García)

No. 6002
October 25th, 1919.
Marino García, Polotitlán, Mexico, 1857. Tinsmith. Married. Resides in Amecameca. Catholic. Robust constitution. Normal development during childhood.

The person who accompanies him says that, this morning, Mr. García punched General Tejada in the face, in Amecameca. This person does not believe he is insane. García says that he talks with the King of the Heavens and that he only receives orders from Him (this is the reason why he has not allowed any examination to take place). He claims that he needs to be immediately released. When he speaks with God he kneels down. Delusions of grandeur, absurd, paradoxical, and incoherent. His memory is normal; his affect appears diminished. It is not possible to examine him because of his irascible temper. When he talks, his lips and eyelids tremble. General Progressive Paralysis.

At the General Insane Asylum, at 10:00 am on the 10th day of November, 1931. Gathered in the Administration building are Rogelio Garmendia, Chief Administrator; Simón López Muñoz, superintendent; Fidencio Rodríguez, Head of Nurses; and Ricardo Reyes, nurse on the neuro-syphilis ward. The former [Chief Administrator Garmendia] informed us that he had discovered that in the ward mentioned above, a patient named Marino García kept, in the room where he slept, several boxes with iron tools, which constituted a risk for the inmate and other ward patients. For this reason, he [Garmendia] ordered the superintendent and the head nurse, together with the nurse in charge of the patient, to pick up whatever the above-mentioned patient had in his possession, informing him [Garmendia] in an expedient manner of the findings resulting from this search. Having carried out this mission, we [López Muñoz, Rodríguez, and Reyes] proceeded to inspect the room of Marino García. We picked up four boxes of different sizes which contained, among other things, two big razor blades, about 50 used pages for typewriter "Guillet" style, a pair of tin snips, a hammer, and a great many iron tools of different sizes. We [López Muñoz, Rodríguez] interrogated the charge nurse, Mr. Reyes, about why the patient was allowed to have all those objects around, and about why he was able to have a room all to himself, to which the nurse answered that since he had been working at the ward only for a few days, because he was only replacing Mr. Santillán who was discharged from his position, he had not had time to check the room. He [Reyes] also said that the patient, judging by what he [Reyes] knew, had received no treatment whatsoever in the last four years. Having heard this, we called in the patient, who confirmed what Mr. Reyes had said, and he added that he had been at the insane asylum for the last 12 years; that he was brought to this institution because he was a beggar; and that he, although it was clear that he was not insane, was placed on the neuro-syphilis ward. He also said that, since he had never felt ill, he had not allowed anyone to administer any treatment to him in the last four years, and that the iron trinkets he had collected himself, little by little. Since the Chief Administrator believed that Mr. García's declaration was quite abnormal, he asked the medical intern, Dr. Luis Vargas, to perform a brief examination, just to find out whether or not he [García] was affected by mental perturbations. The medical intern, Dr. Vargas, stated in writing that "the patient was altogether ready to go back to his family and society, and, for that reason, he authorized his discharge." According to this report it is obvious that this individual has been unduly confined to this hospital for a long period of time. With this, I conclude the present report. Signatures at the margin.

※ ※

October 15th, 1941.
Male. 74 years old. Single. Polotitlán, Jalisco. Peasant. With a memo from the 10th Police Precinct. It is not known why he was led there. A policeman accompanies him.

An old man of ascetic aspect who had been confined years ago in this establishment. He remembers all that [his previous internment] quite well, including names. He says that he was a guard (?) back then and that he is not crazy. He opposes his internment, although he agrees to stay on as gardener. He relates that, recently, people have bothered him at the movie theaters. He says that, there, they shoot bullets, and that several of them had touched him. He tries to point out the place, uncovering his back and showing his bald head. "But he had not died because His Father has told him that he is Eternal God." He says that at this moment His Father is saying to him "that if I inject him, He will send lighting upon the person who dares to inject him." That he has not touched woman and will not do it until the timing is right, without giving further details in this regard. That in the place he works there was war and that both Villistas and Carrancistas chased him, without cause, [an event] which he refers to as recent. These could be the mere pseudo-memories of a senile man or confabulations [babbling]. In summary, there are elements of a paranoid psychosis. There are discrepant diagnoses in his file. Dr. Miranda diagnosed him with progressive general paralysis, and Dr. Salazar diagnosed him with cataphrenia, terminology of Magnan. Probably we should revise this diagnosis with a diagnosis of Paranoid Psychosis, now with discrete senile elements. His mental state is, on the other hand, in a relatively good shape, and his reasoning is clear. Physically, there is nothing of interest. Diagnosis: Paranoid Psychosis. Dr. M. Fuentes.

Clinical History of Inmate
Marino García Martínez
File Number 6002
Observation Ward.

Antecedents.
This is a re-admission. The first time he [García] was at the Insane Asylum was from October 19th through November 31st. Diagnoses of PGP [General Progressive Paralysis] by Dr. Miranda, and positive reaction in the lab tests carried out by Dr. Andrés Martínez Solís, who also diagnosed him with PGP. Another one [diagnosis] done by Dr. Samuel Ramírez Moreno, signed by his own hand. Dr. Salazar Viniegra did not agree with the preceding diagnoses and describes episodes of delirium, at times with manic excitation, [typical] of a cataphrenic. Dr. Vargas discharged the patient because he was able to live in society. Now, sent by the 10th police demarcation, he is received by Dr. Mario Fuentes, who in addition to noting his symptoms (hallucinations, interpretations, confabulations) diagnoses him with Paranoid Psychosis.

Current state.
We transcribe his discourse: "I was wandering on the streets, bullets from the Indians who are playing up there in outer space fall upon me, but they do not shoot at me on purpose. I started noticing this since we have attended the cinematographer [sic], but My Father God is the one who speaks to me. It has been a long time since He speaks to me. That is the reason I came here the first time; that is precisely my story, for the last fifteen years. From here (from the earth) I own nothing; from above, I have the sun, the earth, the air, I have it all, because He gave it all to me. You do not believe me. Among those who are playing and shooting bullets there are Christians and Mexicans. Yesterday, I saw an Arab up in the air, up in the sky, where the bombs explode. I have not died because of the bullets because my Father, who is Eternal, told me that I am going to be eternal too. I am 98 years old now, and my Father tells me that, by now, I have been reincarnating in my body for the last 15 years. My Father has told me that, in a year, I will be ready to take the body of a woman, body to body, now I console myself just as San José did. There

is one air which is as an injection, which cleanses it all, not only the body of the woman. Here you have me" (he rolls his shoulders saying that this is "the air that cleanses").

We have no knowledge of his evolution over the last 10 years outside of this asylum. It would seem that the stages of hypo-maniac agitation have diminished or, even, disappeared. But his delirious state itself does not seem to have evolved in the form of episodes, because the patient himself claims that that condition has been continuous. Judging from all this data, we consider this to be a case of paraphrenia. The lab tests of the spinal fluid show a mild reaction from the meninges [perhaps indicative of meningitis], but it is not significant from the point of view of infection. Dr. Edmundo Buentello.[1]

Quotable Past

I took the preceding text from a file I found at the Archive of Public Health—one of the seventy-five thousand dossiers that comprise the documentary legacy of Mexico City's General Insane Asylum, La Castañeda. Founded in 1910, only a couple of months before the beginning of the Revolution, La Castañeda was the largest state mental health institution for men, women, and children in Mexico. By the time I came upon Marino García's case, I had read about a hundred files; afterward I would read about two hundred more. For reasons that I hope to explain in this chapter, this text remained in my memory—haunting and hunting me while I wrote my doctoral dissertation and, even later, in the process of writing a novel about the medical institution—in a manner that I imagine similar to determined informants who, by virtue of tenacity or cleverness, choose their own anthropologists as recipients, recorders, and translators of their stories.[2] Very much like writers of fiction, historians tend to believe that both the subject matter and the documents with which we substantiate such subject matter choose us. This is something that we rarely admit in public because it imbues the process of historical reconstruction with an otherworldliness our profession has long disavowed. Those historians open to the human, political, and even redemptive aspects of the writing of stories (with a lowercase *s* at the beginning and a plural *s* at the end) are often referred to as storytellers—an absorbing crowd indeed, but not necessarily "professional"—or as academic radicals whose dubious methods threaten professional standards. Aspiring to the status of the former, although unfortunately lacking the stamina for the latter, but always as a historian, I now present the text through which Marino García turned his life—as minuscule as the lowercase *s* that precedes the word "story" in the previous sentence, peripheral if you like, marginal certainly—into a quotable past. Even though his case was never a cause célèbre, he nonetheless managed to insert himself, whether consciously or not, into the historical record of early twentieth-century Mexico City during a turbulent era that witnessed the downfall of the authoritarian regime of longtime president Porfirio Díaz, and the emergence of postrevolutionary regimes committed to modernizing the nation once and for all.[3]

In his "Theses on the Philosophy of History," Walter Benjamin argued that only a redeemed humanity has a past that is quotable at every moment.[4] If this is the case, then García's reluctant telling of the story of his life with illness, of his life in and around the General Insane Asylum, is hardly a trivial matter. Developed within the ominous shadows of progress and modernity, punctuated by suffering and decay, this life story constitutes one of those *ruins* so dear to the theoretical imagination of the German thinker—a ruin that contains, whether cut short or undeveloped, an alternative past and, consequently, an alternative present.

In this article I quote profusely from the texts authored by Marino García, his doctors and nurses, as well as the administrators of the General Insane Asylum, first and foremost to make those texts *present* or, in other words, to help them fulfill their own trajectory and find their right addressees.[5] But I also quote from them to counteract the derealization of the Other—the violent process through which some lives become unreal, remaining "neither alive nor dead, but interminably spectral" and, for that reason, beyond intelligibility.[6] Beyond humanity. In many ways, this article is a long-overdue obituary for what Judith Butler calls a *grievable* life. A life lived. A life that counts in its own right. Last, I quote from Marino García's text because the tragic elements of this life—its emphasis on suffering and the limits of human experience, its stress on the encounter of antagonistic forces able to disturb the hierarchies that hold them in place—might contribute to a revision of our contemporary notions of what history is and who makes it.

Pure Illumination

It is not at all uncommon for us as historians to concern ourselves primarily with placing the text (facts, events, documents, stories) within the context we strive to illuminate. Like a ventriloquist's dummy, the historical text is expected to speak for something larger than itself, such as family, city, gender, society, or nation—things that talk to us in a voice made soft, almost inaudible, by the passage of time and the noise of contemporary life. It is the task of the historian—as the ventriloquist—to attune the ears to the dynamic range of distant voices, from the loudest to the quietest, identifying (or more to the point producing) the significant while discarding the trivial in the process. Some, the empiricists among the ventriloquists, seek to rescue pieces of information, elements of the story, in which they believe the bond between text and context is most apparent. Others, those drawn to the linguistic turn and charmed by the intricacies of human meaning, try to rescue story lines, the narrative strategies through which the long-vanished voice lived, interpreted, and produced that context.[7] In both cases, however distinct they may be from one another, the emphasis falls on the illuminated context—the outcome, so often taken for "natural," of historical research and argumentation: knowledge.

I am writing this "history" to present what I perceive to be an alternative, yet not completely opposed, view of this process of knowledge formation—a view deeply influenced by my activities as a writer of fiction (as they call *escritores* in the United States) and a poet. Simply put, I am siding with the aspect of the story that we call text—the sentences and paragraphs, the anecdotes and characters, the one-word lines, the atmosphere, the descriptions, the sense or lack of sense, the format and its constraints, the syntax, the blank spaces, the opening line and the chosen ending and their relation to other textual elements—the text we read as if it were a voice. I believe, with experimental writer Gertrude Stein, that a "contemporary" text, a text dense with its own sense of presentness, is one that embodies, in its grammar and syntax, its very own context.[8] From this perspective, the text is not a reflection, a metaphor, or a repository of the real, but one of its incarnations. The text does not stand for, but is (at least one version of the) real. The text *is*. The text does not illuminate its context; the text is pure illumination.

I am convinced that in the plenitude of the *is* that characterizes the text lies the historical, mutable, fleeting "I," which historians, at least those committed to the recovery of meaning, aspire to get hold of and to be moved by.[9] Neither buried nor on the surface of the text, but in it as its very marrow, the plural and often contested experiences contained and expressed by the historical subjects we study are able to confer humanness, that shared sense of the personal, which lies both within and beyond the subject, to the stories we write. This then is a reading of the text in and through which Marino García's experiences and perceptions, his alternative story of the rapid modernization of life in Mexico, traversed time. It is a reading that explores the ways in which texts embody their contexts. Thus I will search for the ways in which context lives and breathes through García's text in the here and now, producing a shared sense of meaning rather than a scientific knowledge in the service of power.

This process of temporal translation is, in my opinion, what modern societies have entrusted historians to do. As keepers of the convention we call "the anecdote," I do believe that historians and the disturbing stories they sometimes tell belong around the bonfire where community finds its most meaningful core.

A Punch in the Face

For us, it all started on October 25, 1919, the date on which Marino García, wearing a straw hat and sporting a big moustache, first entered the General Insane Asylum as a free and indigent inmate diagnosed with progressive general paralysis by a medical intern whose signature remains illegible at the end of the official questionnaire, the first of the documents through which his story—the story of his life with illness—remains accessible to us.[10] For Marino García, who claimed to be ninety-eight years old in 1941, the story began much earlier, in Polotitlán, a town in the state of Jalisco. Yet he said very little, or else the medical intern wrote down very little, about the years of his life spent outside asylum grounds. García claimed he had brothers but said he did not remember any of them. He once mentioned a daughter but neglected to mention her ever again. He said he had suffered from an ulcer, only adding that it developed in his scrotum. He said he neither ingested alcohol nor smoked. And, before passing to the section describing his current state (the document that begins the chapter), the medical intern noted that Marino García claimed he was not insane.

We know this information, rather than something else, because Marino García, or his anonymous companion of 1919, was answering fixed questions from the institution's medical questionnaire—a document that included his picture on the left side of the page as well as the heading "General Asylum" and the subheading "Interrogatory" in bold print. The questionnaire displayed information about his personal background to the right of his image and, in six different sections, gathered data about his health and the health of his family, from the remote past to the present. It ended with the doctor's diagnosis. The terminology of each section, which included headings such as "Family antecedents, direct, atavistic or collateral," and questions such as "Are there or have there ever been in your family any nervous, epileptic, crazy, hysterical, alcoholic, syphilitic, suicidal or vicious individuals?" clearly betrayed the pervasive influence of nineteenth-century psychiatry on the official medical and social views of state asylum personnel.[11]

So, when Marino García met the unnamed medical intern at the observation ward of the institution he was not really telling the story of his life as he saw it but, limited by the general format of the interrogatory and the unwritten yet established ritual of the first examination, he was conforming "his" story to the interests and concerns of the physicians, nurses, and authorities of the asylum. He was thus telling the story of his life with illness; more precisely, he was constructing the narrative of his life up to this point as a preamble to his history as a patient in the General Insane Asylum. He was also, in many ways, translating himself, first to himself (if we accept that remembering is a process that involves situating the past in the context of the present) and, more fundamentally, to the medical intern, on whose expert judgment his future depended.

It was this unnamed physician who first recorded—not quoting García's speech directly but referring to it indirectly through the use of "he said"—that the prospective inmate spoke with the King of the Heavens and that he only received commands from Him.[12] Referring to information offered by the anonymous man who accompanied García, the medical intern briefly acknowledged that García had punched the face of a certain General Tejada in Amecameca, the town in the state of Mexico in which García resided. In his description of the interview, the medical intern noted that Marino García knelt down when speaking with God. Writing as a medical expert, he observed the interviewee's delusions of grandeur, which he qualified as absurd, contradictory, and incoherent. While the intern acknowledged that he had not been able to physically examine the patient because of his irascible temper, the intern nevertheless diagnosed him with progressive general paralysis—a conclusion that was at times disputed, and at times confirmed, by the various doctors who examined Marino García in later years.

From this exchange of information and especially from the structure of that exchange, we learn that the General Insane Asylum, as we might expect, was organized according to an internal hierarchy that placed greater relevance on and gave more power to the words and conclusions of physicians than those of patients.[13] As in all state mental health institutions, for example, it was inconsequential that the patient might have argued, or even proved, that he or she was not ill. Institutional protocol nonetheless required (in order to substantiate the diagnosis) the incorporation of inmates' views, preferably in their own words. This institutional use of García's words alerts me to the potential for complicity that can develop between an intern seeking to become a professional psychiatrist and a patient vehemently insisting on his or her mental sanity or explaining the reasons for the emergence of the illness.[14] Unequal yet dynamic, the relationship between the unnamed medical intern and Marino García was also based on a crucial yet partial void—the silence that surrounds the incident in Amecameca, an alleged punch to the face of one General Tejada after which

Marino García was sent, accompanied by yet another unnamed source, to the General Insane Asylum on the outskirts of Mexico City.

This eliding of the context, quite clear in the text, signals the irruption into our story of Marino García and the anonymous intern's presentness. Absent because it was everywhere, unremarkable because it was ever present, the reality of the 1910 Mexican Revolution, whose armed phase remained unfinished in 1919, enters the text surreptitiously and inadvertently like an unwelcome but unavoidable guest. Marino García's file, which held a medical version of his life, was all about this unavoidable but unspoken presence. His illness, whether real or imputed, embodied the abnormality of the punch that struck General Tejada's face, for, without that gesture, Marino García would not have been led by that unnamed companion to the asylum. His confinement thus constitutes the "in which," as we often refer to the larger place, or larger narrative, that allegedly contains the event or story we are recounting.

As things stood in 1919, Marino García suffered from progressive general paralysis, a condition more commonly associated with men than with women and one of the most common diagnostic classifications at the institution. Accordingly, he was placed in the ward for neuro-syphilitic patients—one of six wards that comprised the institution.[15]

Unduly Confined

Perhaps we would not have heard of Marino García again had it not been for the concern of the asylum's chief administrator, Rogelio Garmendia, who became alarmed when he learned that one of the inmates appeared to have a great many iron tools in his room. And so, thanks to the investigative team promptly organized by Simón López Muñoz, superintendent of the institution, we gained access to Marino García's life with illness and at the General Insane Asylum twelve years later, after the postrevolutionary presidencies of *norteño* generals Álvaro Obregón and Plutarco Elías Calles had come to an end and the country found itself in the midst of the so-called Maximato, a period dominated by the behind-the-curtains political maneuverings of General Calles.[16] In a rapidly growing metropolis and receiving renewed attention from social welfare bureaucracies keen to offer revolutionary regimes the material and ideological means to reform Mexican citizens and thus to contribute to the creation of the New Man, the General Insane Asylum experienced a period of unexpected (and brief) prosperity.[17] After years of near total neglect, a group of physicians vigorously led by psychiatrists Samuel Ramírez Moreno and Guevara Oropeza had initiated the first administrative and medical reform of La Castañeda in 1929, implementing standard scientific nomenclature in wards, paying greater attention to the medical objectives of the state institution, and, above all, emphasizing work therapy as the main treatment offered by the establishment.[18] Rogelio Garmendia's alarm and López's prompt response would have been impossible prior to these transformations.

Based on answers from the male nurse, Ricardo Reyes, who had had direct contact with Marino García, Garmendia came to know not only that the patient had the privilege of sleeping in a room of his own—a rare case in a very crowded institution, especially for a patient admitted with the status of free and indigent—but also that García had indeed collected a great many objects, some of them iron tools, which he kept in his room, possibly jeopardizing his own as well as other patients' safety. Again according to Reyes, Marino García had not received any medical treatment during his previous four years of confinement.

When interrogated, Marino García briefly confirmed Reyes's version of events. He had been at the institution for twelve years, specifically on the neuro-syphilis ward, even though he was not insane. He had collected the iron tools little by little and had not allowed the medical personnel to examine him because he did not feel ill. Interestingly enough, at this point, the assault on General Tejada, which had first brought him from Amecameca to the asylum, had disappeared. This time Marino García had come to the state institution because he was a beggar, a term duly underlined by a research team undoubtedly aware of the ongoing efforts of the public welfare bureaucracy to differentiate between the deserving and the undeserving poor in its social assistance programs.[19]

Structured as an official report and typed for the first time (rather than written out in long hand), the information about Marino García's life collected in 1931 did not come as a result of a direct exchange between doctor and patient. Instead it originated from a long and increasingly hierarchical line of asylum players, starting, in descending order, with the alarmed chief administrator, followed by the diligent superintendent, the attentive head nurse, the succinct ward nurse, only to end, once again, with the patient himself. In this more bureaucratic milieu, the participation of García, who was consulted last, became less relevant. The report failed to include direct quotes from his speech and allotted him only five to six lines in a text of forty—and this merely to confirm what had been said by others and already recorded in the report. It did not mention either the delirious ideas that the unnamed medical intern had found so absurd, incoherent, and paradoxical in 1919, nor did it make any mention of his life in the asylum. How was he able to get a room of his own? How did he acquire the objects he collected inside and outside the asylum? How did he use the iron tools in his possession? Neither the chief administrator nor the superintendent attempted to address, and much less to answer, these questions, at least not in the written report. Marino García's situation, however, was so uncommon at La Castañeda that the chief administrator did not hesitate to describe it as abnormal, calling almost immediately for the expert advice of one of the physicians.

Written in the impersonal third-person singular, as was all official correspondence, the report refers indirectly (in the "he said" mode) to all the information generated by the implicated actors with the sole exception of the lines written by physician Luis Vargas, who swiftly examined the patient, found him in good health (without resorting to lab tests), and authorized his release. In the physician's words, García was fit to return to a family the patient did not in fact have and a society he had not seen or been part for twelve years. In a laconic and objective tone, the report merely notes that the findings of the investigation reveal that "this individual was unduly confined for a long period of time."

Marino García's file does not include information about his release. We do not know whether he was relieved or apprehensive about such a radical change so late in his life. We do not know whether he interpreted such a quick change of affairs as a miracle worked by the King of the Heavens or as punishment from the very earthbound authorities of the institution. All we know is that he left the asylum in 1931, only to return ten years later.

Which Is Precisely My Story

In 1941 Dr. Mario Fuentes typed updated information about Marino García on a simplified entry form with the heading "Public Welfare of the Federal District" followed by "General Asylum" and an even smaller, centered subheading of "Entry Form." García appeared as an elderly man with a white beard and swollen cheeks who nonetheless stared intently into the lenses of the camera that photographed him. That time had passed became strikingly clear not only in Marino García's face but also in the structure and language of the new, streamlined entry form. The official format no longer included questions addressing the "atavistic" family antecedents of the patient, nor did it ask in an explicit way about his sexual or drinking habits. Instead, it divided incoming data into four different and neutral-sounding sections: previous confinement; antecedents prior to enrollment (referring parties, certificates presented, accompanying parties); condition of the incoming patient (aspect, attitude, expression, clothing, etc.); evolution of the affliction (according to informants). If slippery modernity had once meant the triumph of science over popular belief, the victory of cutting-edge science over outmoded tradition, these apparently value-free headings showed that even the most peripheral institution of the public welfare system was prepared to leave behind its obscure and rather infamous past.[20]

When Marino García came back to the asylum—just one year after General Lázaro Cárdenas left the presidency, just as an era of (allegedly) serious social reforms in land, labor, and education was coming to an end, just when the country was headed toward a period of increased cooperation with international capital—more than just the entry form had changed.[21] According to the final documents, García was no longer married, but single; he was no longer a tinsmith, but a peasant. Furthermore, he arrived this time in the company of a policeman. Although he was referred by the Tenth Police Precinct of Mexico City, the attending physician, Dr. Mario Fuentes, attested that no information about the reasons for García's return was available from that source. It is clear, however, that Dr. Fuentes took his own job as a psychiatrist at the mental health institution very seriously. He described the patient's condition in great detail and allowed the patient's speech to enter, rather freely, into his own narrative, mediated only by the use of quotation marks. That doctor Edmundo Buentello did the same a bit later only confirmed his status as one of the most prolific and well-regarded psychiatrists of the mid-twentieth century in Mexico City.[22] It is thus thanks to the increasing professionalism of psychiatry, embedded in the entry form and manifested in the doctors' careful rendering of facts, that we now have access to Marino García's own version of his past and his present as an inmate at the state asylum. It is because of this professionalism, and not despite it, that Marino García's words finally came to occupy a relevant space both on the page now simply called "Entry Form" and in the semiotic interaction, the production and interpretation of "signs," that lies at the core of all medical diagnoses.[23]

Just as he had done ten years earlier, García argued once again that he was not crazy, adding that indeed he had been at the institution before, for twelve years, although not as an inmate but as a guard.[24] This time he agreed to remain at the institution as a gardener. Once this was decided, Marino García proceeded to talk while Dr. Mario Fuentes, and later Dr. Edmundo Buentello, transcribed his speech—an apparently long and convoluted discourse about aspects of life that we usually compartmentalize under such rubrics as religion, history, nature, medicine, and sex. We do not know how long the session lasted or whether the doctors gathered all the information in one session or in several. What we do know is that Marino García took advantage of the attentive audience before him. We know that he spoke

On religion: My Father, God, is the one who speaks to me. It has been a long time since he talks with me. That is the reason why I came here the first time, precisely that is my story . . . I have not died because my Father is Eternal and he told me that I, too, shall be eternal. I am 98 years old, and my Father tells me that I have been reincarnating in my body for the last 15 years.

On nature: From here (from the earth), I own nothing; from above, I own the sun, the earth, the air. I own everything. Since he gave it all to me . . . There is a kind of air which is like an injection—it cleanses everything . . . It is the air that cleanses.

On history: Where I worked, there was war and the Villistas and the Carrancistas chased me, without cause.

On medicine: At this very moment, my Father is telling me that if you inject me, he will send lighting upon the person who injects me.

On sex: My Father has told me that, in a year, I will be ready to take the body of a woman, body to body. For now I console myself just as San José used to console himself.

So this is what we have of Marino García some fifty years later: a collection of quotes from his quotable past; a set of fragmented maxims of his life; a dossier of intimate fractals; the ABCs of an alphabet unknown to us. Marino García, in other words, did not prepare a narrative of his life—the unfolding of meaning over time, the mechanism that "resolves a fundamental antagonism by reorganizing its terms in a temporal succession."[25] Perhaps, given the opportunity, he could have done it. But, at least at the asylum and in the presence of psychiatrists, he did not. He was not required to. Or he did not want to. Or he did not know how to. Perhaps this was not the way in which he would have organized the story of his life. He gave the psychiatrists, however, the crucial pieces of information they needed to arrive at a scientific diagnosis. He also gave them the limited but precisely located interpretative events that opened windows into themselves—that is, into the meanings of his life refracted through their eyes. And that is how, further in time and farther from place than the patient and his doctors, we came to know about Marino García's life.

Through these alephs of sorts we know that Marino García was a deeply religious and physically strong man who since 1919 had been able to endure twelve years inside an institution famous for its neglect and overcrowding.[26] We know that his faith kept him alive outside the asylum for the next ten years after his release, of which the only certain fact is that he went to movie theaters. We know that his Catholicism was rather flexible and heterodox, including direct contact with a masculine and paternal God, acceptance of the miraculous power of saints, and the concept of reincarnation.[27] We know that although poor, for he clearly said he owned nothing from earth, he remained proud of his natural and divinely given possessions—the air, sky, fields and landscape. We know that he associated the female body with spiritual pollution and that, although about to take the body of a woman himself, he did not have sexual contact with women, resorting instead to celibacy in the manner of Saint Joseph, Mary's husband.[28] We know that he recognized and clearly differentiated between Indians, Mexicans, Christians, and Arabs in his social milieu—a classification that follows a standard reminiscent of Borges's mappings of the world.[29] He was familiar too with the violence of bullets and the existence of armies of Villistas and Carrancistas, both of whom, without motive, had once chased him. All this he had overcome, not with the help of Western medicine, which he rejected, but with the supernatural support of his masculine and paternal deity, the God who had made García in his image and who was transforming him into an eternal being.

An astute social observer and a resourceful man who looked at his world through the lens of deeply held religious beliefs, Marino García captured the attention of concerned doctors at the state asylum. He, in turn, offered them snippets of his life. More than pieces of information, they were pieces of interpretation. Pieces of a life lived.

Limited and precisely located, these pieces of interpretation do not unfold; they do not develop in the temporal sequence we associate with narrative. They do not *explain*. They do not stand for or in place of modernity—if we define it as the elusive pot of gold at the end of the rainbow of the Mexican political and managerial imagination. They *are* modernity—if we define it simply as that constructed reality lived and suffered by the likes of Marino García; plagued by voids, interrupted by silence (either chosen or imposed), broken into fragments, Marino García's story is traversed by violence, both syntactical and historical. This we know for certain. This I would like to keep as it is: open, broken, interrupted. For only more violence, the kind of violence inherent in the reordering of linear narrative, could smooth the jagged surfaces of the text and turn what is disordered and broken into the smooth, unfolding narrative of academic discourse. As Kathy Acker, the experimental narrativist from San Francisco, once said, "The writer is playing—when structuring narrative or when narrative is structuring itself—with life and death."[30] These fragments are the life of Marino García. His death.

A Sense of the Tragic in Life

Much in the manner of postmodern novels, which often include multiple points of view in fluid structures with open endings, the dossier of Marino García provokes awe and confusion. There is no single truth here that develops linearly over time, a straight-forward journey toward health or toward death. No one at the asylum, not even the most conscientious and professional of the doctors, was in the position to decide which version of Marino García's life with illness best rendered its meaning, let alone its truth. Each document in the file aspires to tell the true story of Marino García. Each document revises, sometimes quite radically, its predecessor. But, in the final analysis, each document succeeds only in superimposing a new meaning of the past not necessarily logically related to previous understandings, thus transforming each successive foundational text into its own other over and over again. I am convinced that if we cannot find the one authentic version of this life it is because it never existed. Will never exist. What does exist is a dossier of paradoxical material that, by its very nature, refuses linear narrative. A "true" rendering of Marino García's life ought to preserve, by necessity, this paradoxical dis/position—the contradictions, breaks, silences, voids, revisions, versions—both on the page and in the interpretation of the page.[31] It is, after all, a matter of life and death, of life over death.

Every so often, marginal or "subaltern" subjects manage to enter the halls of academia dressed with the narrative attire of the cultural hero, saved from anonymity by the grace of our words.[32] Based on what I call a positivist interpretation of agency, historians, for the most part, pay attention to social actors who did something or contributed to something of significance—a significant and graspable something that speaks, in turn, for something larger than itself. Such a state of affairs calls for a broader understanding of the concept of agency—a concept of agency that recognizes alternative narrative forms; narratives that are broken, stammered, or uncertain; and narratives that embody the experience of those of us who fail or who reject the orderly linearity of late capitalism and its academic discourses. This broader concept of agency I call "tragic."

The term necessarily takes us back to Aristotle's *Poetics* and often signifies fatalism in common speech, for in classical tragedy the hero is destroyed. Tragedy stages "the relationship between suffering and joy in a universe which is often perceived as at best inimical or at worst radical in its hostility to human life."[33] Whether celebrated as a Dionysiac delight (after Nietzsche) or mourned as a force that strives against human will, tragedy importantly includes the concept of purgation "by pity and fear" (in Aristotelian terms), the process through which human limitations become acknowledged and accepted. Yet, as Karl Jaspers has argued, tragedy works when it reveals "some particular truth in every agent and at the same time the limitations of this truth, so [as] to reveal the injustice in everything."[34] This revelatory power has led Raymond Williams to perceive tragedy through the lenses of both suffering and affirmation: "We have to see not only that suffering is avoidable, but that it is not avoided. And not only that suffering breaks us, but that it need not break us. . . . Against the fear of a general death, and against the loss of connection, a sense of life is affirmed, learned as closely in suffering as ever in joy, once the connections are made."[35] These tragic elements—emphasis on suffering, the limits of human experience, and the encounter of antagonistic forces able to disturb the hierarchies that hold them in place—have proven particularly useful for social analyses of revolutions.[36]

In modern Mexico, where postrevolutionary generations have turned the 1910 revolution, more or less successfully, into an official and foundational epic, little serious attention has been paid to its tragic origins and its tragic subjects. The mad narratives in which, as in tragedy, "the detail of suffering is insistent, whether as violence or as the reshaping of lives by a new power in the state," provide us the opportunity to give tragedy its due.[37] As scholars in the emerging interdisciplinary study of "pain and suffering" have pointed out, these social and cultural experiences engage the most ominous aspects of modernization and globalization processes.[38] Moreover, by grounding their work in specific locales and in particular historical contexts, these scholars avoid representing sufferers as inadequate, passive, or fatalistic victims. Instead, they seek to draw long overdue attention to both the "devastating injuries that social force can inflict on human experience" and the various ways in which sufferers identify, endure, and unmask the sources of their misfortune. My understanding of tragic agency (although perhaps more an intimation than a concept) attempts to grasp what appears commonsensical in so many illness narratives from the insane asylum: that while suffering destroys, it also bestows dignity—a higher moral status—on the sufferer. As Jorge Luis Borges once said, "Men have always sought affinity with the defeated Trojans, and not with the victorious Greeks. Perhaps that is because there is a dignity in defeat that is hard to reconcile with victory."[39]

The Air That Cleanses

"Here you have me," he said. Then, rolling his shoulders up, he added, "It is the air that cleanses it all."

It could have happened that way.

Marino García, the elderly man of ascetic features, knew hope. If he was ninety-eight years old and still alive after a life spent in and out of poorly funded state institutions in early twentieth-century Mexico City, he knew hope firsthand. And, after all my readings, after all the years of academic training, after the many hours spent in comfortable offices with a view, I am not in the position to say that it was not thanks to the protection of the masculine and paternalistic divinity he called God.

Notes

1. Archivo Histórico de la Secretaría de Salubridad y Asistencia, rama del Manicomio General, sección de casos clínicos, no. 6002 (hereafter cited as AHSSA:MG:CC, 6002). While the file of Marino García includes more documents of a medical and bureaucratic nature, I am including here only the narrative sections.
2. I am referring especially to anthropologist Ruth Behar's story of how her determined informant, Esperanza, *chose* Behar to hear, record, and translate the story of her life. See Ruth Behar, *Translated Woman: Crossing the Border with Esperanza's Story* (New York: Beacon Press, 1987).
3. Historians have devoted a considerable number of pages to analyzing both the Revolution and the postrevolutionary period in Mexico. Among the best analyses are John Mason Hart, *Revolutionary Mexico: The Coming and Process of the Mexican Revolution* (Berkeley: University of California Press, 1987); Alan Knight, *The Mexican Revolution*, 2 vols. (New York: Cambridge University Press, 1986); Gilbert Joseph and Daniel Nugent, eds., *Everyday Forms of State Formation: Revolution and the Negotiation of Rule in Modern Mexico* (Durham, NC: Duke University Press, 1994); John Mason Hart, *Empire and Revolution: The Americans in Mexico since the Civil War* (Berkeley: University of California Press, 2002).
4. Walter Benjamin, "Theses on the Philosophy of History," in *Illuminations*, trans. Harry Zohn (New York: Harcourt, Brace and World Inc., 1968).
5. Jacques Lacan, *Ecrits: A Selection*, trans. Bruce Fink (New York: Norton, 2002). See especially his analysis of Edgar Allan Poe's story, "The Purloined Letter."
6. Judith Butler, *Precarious Life: The Powers of Mourning and Violence* (New York: Verso, 2004), 33–34.
7. For a good discussion of the competing theoretical and methodological views in contemporary historical writing as it relates to the history of Mexico (as practiced in the United States), see the articles in "Mexico's New Cultural History: ¿Una lucha libre?" *Hispanic American Historical Review* 79, no. 2 (May 1999).

8. Gertrude Stein, *How Writing Is Written*, ed. Robert B. Haas (Los Angeles: Black Sparrow Press, 1994).
9. I am not referring, of course, to the mythical author who, after Roland Barthes and, more emphatically, after Michel Foucault, lies dead in our hands, but to the polysemic and heteroglot convention that attributes a sense of the intimate and the uniquely personal to the "I" that lies at the core and in the corners of the "system of discursive meaning production" embedded in and by the text. See Roland Barthes, *A Barthes Reader*, ed. Susan Sontag (New York: Hill and Wang, 1981); Michel Foucault, "Orders of Discourse," in *The Archaeology of Knowledge*, trans. A. M. Sheridan Smith (New York: Pantheon Books, 1982); Mikhail Bakhtin, *The Dialogical Imagination: Four Essays*, ed. Michael Holquist, trans. Caryl Emerson and Michael Holquist (Austin: University of Texas Press, 1981); and Hayden White, *The Content of the Form: Narrative Discourse and Historical Representation* (Baltimore, MD: John Hopkins University Press, 1987), x.
10. Because of space constraints, I am not including the actual questionnaire here, opting instead to make references to it indirectly throughout this section.
11. For a history of nineteenth-century psychiatry in Europe and the United States, see William Bynum, Roy Porter, and Michael Shepherd, eds., *The Anatomy of Madness: Essays in the History of Psychiatry* (London: Tavistock Publications, 1985); Mark S. Micale and Roy Porter, eds., *Discovering the History of Psychiatry* (New York: Oxford University Press, 1994); Jan Goldstein, *Console and Classify: The French Psychiatric Profession in the Nineteenth Century* (Cambridge: Cambridge University Press, 1987); Nancy Scheper-Hughes, *Saints, Scholars, and Schizophrenics: Mental Illness in Rural Ireland* (Berkeley: University of California Press, 1979); Elizabeth Lunbeck, *The Psychiatric Persuasion: Knowledge, Gender, and Power in Modern America* (Princeton, NJ: Princeton University Press, 1994); and Ann Goldberg, *Sex, Religion, and the Making of Modern Madness: The Eberbach Asylum and German Society, 1815–1849* (New York: Oxford University Press, 1999).
12. The phrase repeats, almost verbatim, the words used by the followers of Santa Teresita de Cabora who had rebelled against the Díaz regime some twenty-five years earlier. Paul Vanderwood, *The Power of God Against the Guns of Government* (Stanford: Stanford University Press, 1998).
13. For a description of the internal structure of the General Insane Asylum, see Cristina Rivera-Garza, "Por la salud mental de la nación: vida cotidiana y estado dentro del Manicomio General La Castañeda, México 1910–1930," *Secuencia* 51 (September–December 2001): 57–90.
14. For a discussion about the character of the doctor-patient relationship at the Mexican General Insane Asylum, see Cristina Rivera-Garza, "Beyond Medicalization: Psychiatrists and Patients Produce Sexual Knowledge in Late Porfirian Mexico," in *The Famous 41: Sexuality and Social Control in Mexico, 1901*, ed. Robert McKee Irwin, Edward J. McCaughan, and Michelle Rocío Nasser (New York: Palgrave Macmillan, 2003), 267–90. Two fundamental perspectives on this issue are Arthur Kleinman, *Illness Narratives: Suffering, Healing, and the Human Condition* (New York: Basic Books, 1988); and Michael Taussig, "Reification and the Consciousness of the Patient," in *The Nervous System* (New York: Routledge, 1992), 83–110.

15. For a detailed description of the medical and architectural organization of the General Insane Asylum, see Cristina Rivera-Garza, "La vida en reclusión: cotidianidad y Estado en el Manicomio General La Castañeda," in *Entre médicos y curanderos: Historia, cultura y enfermedad en la América latina moderna*, ed. Diego Armus (Buenos Aires: Editorial Norma, 2002), 179–220.
16. A basic bibliography of this period includes Jean Meyer, *The Cristero Rebellion: The Mexican People between Church and State, 1926–1929*, trans. Richard Southern (New York: Cambridge University Press, 1976); Ramón Jrade, *Counterrevolution in Mexico: The Cristero Movement in Sociological and Historical Perspective* (Ann Arbor: University of Michigan Press, 1980); and Jennie Purnell, *Popular Movements and State Formation in Revolutionary Mexico: The Agraristas and Cristeros of Michoacán* (Durham, NC: Duke University Press, 1999).
17. Cultural analyses of postrevolutionary Mexico include Gilbert Joseph, Anne Rubenstein, and Eric Zolov, eds., *Fragments of a Golden Age: The Politics of Culture in Mexico since 1940* (Durham, NC: Duke University Press, 2001); and Gilbert Joseph, Catherine C. LeGrand, and Ricardo Salvatore, eds., *Close Encounters of Empire: Writing the Cultural History of U.S.–Latin American Relations* (Durham, NC: Duke University Press, 1998).
18. Works by Samuel Ramírez Moreno include *La asistencia psiquiátrica en México. Congreso Internacional de Psiquiatría, Paris 1950* (Mexico City: Secretaría de Salubridad y Asistencia/Artes Gráficas del Estado, 1950); and "Anexos psiquiátricos en los hospitales generales," *Revista Mexicana de Psiquiatría, Neurología y Medicina Legal* 13, nos. 75–76 (September–November 1940): 25. For a historical analysis of the emergence of the psychiatric profession in Mexico, see Cristina Rivera-Garza, "Dangerous Minds: Changing Psychiatric Views of the Mentally Ill in Porfirian Mexico," *The Journal of the History of Medicine and Allied Sciences*, 56, no. 1 (2001): 36–67.
19. See José Félix Gutiérrez del Olmo, "De la Caridad a la Asistencia," *La atención materno-infantil. Apuntes para su historia* (Mexico City: Secretaría de Salubridad y Asistencia, 1993).
20. See Mauricio Tenorio-Trillo, *Mexico at the World's Fairs: Crafting a Modern Nation* (Berkeley: University of California Press, 1996).
21. Books on Cardenismo and the post-Cárdenas era include Christopher Boyer, *Becoming Campesinos: Politics, Identity, and Agrarian Struggle in Post-Revolutionary Michoacán 1920–1935* (Stanford: Stanford University Press, 2003); Adrian Bantjes, *As if Jesus Walked on Earth: Cardenismo, Sonora, and the Mexican Revolution* (Wilmington: Scholarly Resources, 1998); and Marjorie Becker, *Setting the Virgin on Fire: Lázaro Cárdenas, Michoacán Peasants, and the Redemption of the Mexican Revolution* (Berkeley: University of California Press, 1995).
22. Edmundo Buentello's work includes "Orígenes y estado actual del Manicomio de la Castañeda," *Asistencia. Publicación Mensual de la Beneficencia Pública* 2, no. 3 (1936).
23. See Kleinman, *Illness Narratives*.
24. Cases of other peaceful inmates who became guards on their own wards confirm this view. See "Rosario E.," AHSSA:MG:CC, box 1, exp. 31.

25. Slajov Žižek, "The Seven Veils of Fantasy," in *The Plague of Fantasies* (New York: Verso, 1997), 16.
26. *Aleph* refers to the by now mythical figure coined by Jorge Luis Borges in the book of the same title, *El Aleph, Obras completas*, vol. 1 (Barcelona: Emecé, 1996). In Borges's story the aleph is the iridescent sphere in which the protagonist can glean glimpses of universal space.
27. A basic bibliography on Mexican folk Catholicism includes Gary Gossen and Miguel León-Portilla, *South and Meso-American Native Spirituality: From the Cult of the Feathered Serpent to the Theology of Liberation* (New York: Crossroad/Herder and Herder, 1993); Christian Smith and Joshua Prokopy, *Latin American Religion in Motion* (New York: Routledge, 1999); and John M. Ingham, *Mary, Michael, and Lucifer: Folk Catholicism in Central Mexico* (Austin: University of Texas Press, 1986).
28. See Mary Douglas, *Purity and Danger: An Analysis of the Concepts of Pollution and Taboo* (New York: Routledge Classics, 2002).
29. See Jorge Luis Borges's charts of fantastic animals in *Manual de zoología fantástica* (Mexico City: Fondo de Cultura Económica, 1957).
30. Kathy Acker, "The Killers," *Narrativity* 1. http://www.sfsu.edu/~poetry/narrativity/issue_one/acker.html. (Kathy Acker gave this talk on a panel called "In Extremis, Writing at Century's End" for Small Press Traffic, San Francisco, 29 April 1993.)
31. For a critical exploration of realism and its strategies, see Kathy Acker, *Bodies of Work*.
32. Behar, *Translated Woman*.
33. John Drakakis and Naomi Conn Liebler, eds., *Tragedy* (New York: Longman, 1998), 2. The definition from Aristotle reads, "Tragedy . . . is a representation of an action that is worth serious attention, complete in itself, and of some amplitude; in language enriched by a variety of artistic devices appropriate to the several parts of the play; presented in the form of action, not narration; by means of pity and fear bringing about the purgation of such emotions." Aristotle, *Poetics*, trans. T. S. Dorsch, in *Aristotle/Horace/Longinus: Classical Literary Criticism* (London: Penguin, 1965).
34. Karl Jaspers, *Tragedy Is Not Enough*, trans. Harald A. T. Reiche, Harry T. Moore, and Karl W. Deutsch (Hamden, CT: Archon, 1969), 57.
35. Raymond Williams, *Modern Tragedy* (London: Chatto and Windus, 1966), 202–3.
36. In addition to Williams, see Hannah Arendt, *On Revolution* (New York: Penguin, 1979).
37. Williams, *Modern Tragedy*, 163.
38. For examples of recent studies on suffering and pain, see Arthur Kleinman, Veena Das, and Margaret Lock, eds., *Social Suffering* (Berkeley: University of California Press, 1997); Elaine Scarry, *The Body in Pain: The Making and Unmaking of the World* (New York: Oxford University Press, 1985); Mary-Jo DelVecchio Good, Paul E. Brodwin, Byron J. Good, and Arthur Kleinman, eds., *Pain as Human Experience: An Anthropological Perspective* (Berkeley: University of California Press, 1992); Peter Morris, *The Culture of Pain* (Berkeley: University of California Press, 1991); and Roselyne Rey, *The History of Pain* (Cambridge: Harvard University Press,

1995). For contemporary Mexico, see Kaja Finkler, *Women in Pain: Gender and Morbidity in Mexico* (Philadelphia: University of Pennsylvania Press, 1994). The most striking example in the context of Latin American historiography is, without doubt, Nancy Scheper-Hughes, *Death Without Weeping: The Violence of Everyday Life in Brazil* (Berkeley: University of California Press, 1992).

39. Jorge Luis Borges, "El arte de contar historias," in *Arte Poética. Seis conferencias* (Barcelona: Crítica, 2001), 63. "Los hombres siempre han buscado la afinidad con los troyanos derrotados, y no con los griegos victoriosos. Quizá sea porque hay una dignidad en la derrota que a duras penas corresponde a la victoria."

CHAPTER FOUR

The Girl Who Killed a Senator
Femininity and the Public Sphere in Postrevolutionary Mexico

 Pablo Piccato

On July 10, 1922, when she was fourteen years old, María del Pilar Moreno murdered Francisco Tejeda Llorca in front of his house on Tonalá Street in Mexico City. Tejeda Llorca had killed her father, Jesús Moreno, two months earlier but had escaped prosecution because he was a member of congress. María del Pilar's action provoked demonstrations of popular support that led to her acquittal by a jury in April 1924. As with other causes célèbres, this case tied together several interdependent but not always consistent narratives: press accounts of her crime and trial, speeches by her famous defense lawyer, Querido Moheno, and her own autobiography. Taking place in an early post-revolutionary period characterized by sporadic rebellion, guerrilla activity, and assassination, this case exposed the problematic cultural products of violence: the masculine ferocity of politics, a widening gap between judicial institutions and justice, and uncertainty about the role that women would play in a new era expected to increase political liberties yet increasingly dominated by images of male heroism.

Recent historical literature on modern Europe has demonstrated both the importance of famous courtroom cases in the development of the public sphere and the centrality of a gendered perspective for understanding that development.[1] These analyses have noted the role of stage, melodrama, and courtroom metaphors in mounting a critique of normative discourses about privacy and sexuality. Among other things, this work has revealed the ways in which narrative self-representations and notions of honor by women accused of crimes have impacted scientific and judicial views, and have sometimes helped them to escape punishment.² In Mexico, a society marked by racialized divides and political violence, public debates about private life went beyond the metaphorical and became clearly political in their consequences. María del Pilar's case provided a point of reference around which to discuss, explain, and perform notions of femininity and masculinity. As a consequence, the case became more than a moral example and transformed the same public sphere that gave it coherence and cultural impact.³

By "public sphere," however, I do not mean a neutral space of elite sociability and rationality, or a discursive realm where individuals become metaphors with a "deeper" social and political meaning. Instead I argue that the public sphere is a realm understood by its participants as an egalitarian and rational place in which to discuss common problems. Thus, the public sphere is composed of multiple interacting elements, not all rational or egalitarian: discourses with different levels of cultural authority, media whose rules structure discussions, and whose performances are charged with emotions and addressed in public opinion through commonly held notions of honor and the body.⁴ This case exposed the tensions between the democratization and massive political participation that followed the Revolution, tensions expressed through gendered attitudes about violence in politics, the role of women in public life, and the influence of mass media. The criminal jury was the best forum for expressing those tensions because it was a dialogical yet authoritative institution with the ability to simultaneously represent public opinion, an emotional audience, and contending notions of honor.

The drama began on May 24, 1922, when Francisco Tejeda Llorca and Jesús Moreno, both congressmen and members of the postrevolutionary political elite, bumped into each other at the doors of the Secretaría de Gobernación (Ministry of the Interior). The two intended to see Interior Secretary Plutarco Elías Calles. Moreno tried to go through the door first but Tejeda Llorca, who was taller and stronger, pushed him aside, and a fight broke out. Tejeda Llorca took Moreno's gun, but Moreno's chauffeur in turn grabbed it. Tejeda Llorca shot his own gun into the air, and, freeing himself from the chauffeur's grasp, aimed at Moreno. The friends who accompanied Tejeda Llorca held Moreno and encouraged Tejeda Llorca to kill him. A single fatal bullet entered the back of the victim's right shoulder. Tejeda Llorca surrendered the gun to police and later gave a statement at the station. As a federal deputy, however, he could not be charged unless congress stripped him of his immunity, and he walked free from the station. In the following weeks, María del Pilar and her mother, Ana Díaz, met with several high-ranking politicians, asking for justice and the arrest of Tejeda Llorca. Judicial authorities could do nothing at the moment, they were told, because congress was in recess, nor would they be able to act after July because Tejeda Llorca had been elected senator for the state of Veracruz, an action that renewed his parliamentary immunity.[5]

When she finally decided to kill Francisco Tejeda Llorca, María del Pilar dressed in white and ordered her chauffeur to take her to her favorite church, the Sagrada Familia, in the Colonia Roma. Her aunt Otilia accompanied her. María del Pilar stepped down from the car and approached Tejeda Llorca, who was standing on the sidewalk on Tonalá Street with some other men. She grabbed him by his lapel and told him to "[k]ill me, like you killed my father." He grabbed her arm and tried to force her to her knees, but she was able to draw her gun and shoot Tejeda Llorca four times. Manuel Zapata, a friend of the victim who had also been involved in Moreno's death, disarmed and hit María del Pilar. Her mother arrived shortly afterward in another car and took her to the offices of *El Heraldo*, the newspaper that Jesús Moreno ran before he died. The newspaper's new director accompanied them to the police station, where María del Pilar confessed, was arrested, and spent the night in the company of her mother.

In her statements to authorities, María del Pilar gave differing accounts. At first she said she had premeditated the crime and was satisfied with having avenged her father: "[A]lready I was calmer because something told me that, if I had killed, I had done in it in self-defense and to defend the honor of my father and to defend my orphan-hood." Although she would later repeat this explanation, when questioned about the details of the crime she stated that she was not looking for her victim on Tonalá Street; she had used her gun because she believed Tejeda Llorca was going to draw his, and she did not intend to kill him but was forced to pull the trigger by the victim's painful pressure on her arm—thus implying that there was no premeditation in her actions. But residents of Tonalá Street suggested otherwise, declaring later to the police that, days before the crime, they had seen a "mysterious car" parked on their street with a man and two women inside. Other witnesses stated that on July 10 they saw a "strong man" shooting twice at Tejeda Llorca as he stumbled, already wounded, toward his house. The autopsy later revealed that Tejeda Llorca's body contained a .38-caliber bullet, along with María del Pilar's .32-caliber bullets. The ensuing investigation, however, did not lead to anyone besides the confessed shooter, and her contradictions were never resolved during the trial.[6]

The proceedings that followed María del Pilar's indictment were less about the facts of the crime than a tense negotiation involving multiple actors and an anxious public. The relatives of the victim sued María del Pilar for thirty thousand pesos, thus becoming directly involved in the trial. Their true intention was to clear Tejeda Llorca's name in the eyes of public opinion. Reputation also interested María del Pilar: when she was offered freedom on bail she refused it, against the advice of her lawyer, explaining that she felt safer at the correctional school and preferred that the jury decide her fate. She stayed eight months at the school—leaving only twice a week to place flowers at her father's grave—until it became clear that prosecutors and judges were delaying the conclusion of the trial.[7] She and her attorneys (Abel C. Salazar, later joined by "prominent lawyers" Telésforo Ocampo, Manuel Zamora, Juan B. Cervantes, José Moreno Salido, and Querido Moheno) denounced the "hatred" of the judge in charge of the investigation, but the judge did not recuse himself. Anxious for a denouement, newspapers guessed that jury deliberations would take place in August 1922. The case, however, dragged on for almost two years.[8]

The main factor in the delay—politics—trumped the power of lawyers and the desires of readers. By mid-1922, Plutarco Elías Calles had become one of the potential successors of President Álvaro Obregón. Late the following year, a military rebellion, clumsily led by Calles's rival in Obregón's cabinet, Adolfo de la Huerta, mounted a serious threat to the government that took several months to be repressed.[9] The political implications of the case against María del Pilar became obvious as these events unfolded. The press attributed Moreno's death in equal measure to "political passion" and to electoral struggles in the state of Veracruz. The Partido Nacional Cooperatista (to which both Moreno and Tejeda Llorca belonged and whose main leaders would later side with the rebels) supported Moreno as the candidate for deputy in the district of Coatepec. Tejeda Llorca, with the backing of his cousin and governor of the state, Adalberto Tejeda, promoted instead the candidacy of Francisco Reyes, one of the men who would hold Moreno on May 24. Moreno broke with party discipline and sponsored another candidate, Antonio Nava, against Tejeda Llorca's own run for the senate. Both sides claimed to have popular support but it was clear that the blessing of Calles, which both hoped to receive on May 24, 1922, was the key to electoral success.[10]

Tejeda Llorca and Moreno met twice in unsuccessful attempts to resolve their differences. The problem, however, might have been their similarities. Both were federal deputies and shared a middling status in national politics, acting as intermediaries between Mexico City leadership and regional actors. Tejeda Llorca was one of the main operatives and advisers for his cousin in the state legislature in Xalapa and Mexico City. Calles himself kept Tejeda informed of the events in May and July and extended his condolences when Tejeda Llorca was killed.[11] The list of people who attended his funeral suggests that he had strong connections with both revolutionary and Porfirian elites. After his death, however, his immediate family seemed unable to exercise much influence. They could not to prevent the autopsy and failed in their civil suit against María del Pilar.[12]

Jesús Moreno compensated for the lack of support from Governor Tejeda, whom he criticized in his newspaper and in the Chamber of Deputies, with stronger revolutionary credentials than his rival. He had been an opposition journalist since the 1900s, jailed by Nuevo León's Porfirian proconsul Bernardo Reyes, and persecuted by the *jefe político* of Atlixco, Puebla, because of his legal defense of the region's Indians. He was commander of the *rurales* in Puebla under Francisco I. Madero's government, and in 1920 had supported Obregón and Calles in the Agua Prieta rebellion against Venustiano Carranza. He had worked with another *norteño*, Salvador Alvarado, to establish and later direct *El Heraldo* in Mexico City.[13] His connection with Calles, his paisano from Sonora, was strong. He had occupied a sensitive post in the Ministry of the Interior, and Calles considered him "a person of my complete confidence and of well-known probity."[14] Again, in this case, connections in life did not seem to have helped the family after death. Before taking matters in her own hands, María del Pilar had met twice with Calles but the minister had told her he could do nothing to bring Tejeda Llorca to justice or to prevent his election as a senator.[15]

By the time the trial reached its final phase, political events pitted María del Pilar against Calles. Alvarado, her father's friend, was the leader of one of the last *focos* of the de la Huerta rebellion still fighting Obregón and Calles. Days before the trial, one of María del Pilar's lawyers, Juan B. Cervantes, resigned from his job fearing that his defense colleagues were going to attack Calles.[16] Although Calles was not the target of criticism during the trial, attorney Querido Moheno derided the regime, and, during the final sessions, requested an homage to rebel lawyer Ramón Treviño, who had been executed three weeks earlier. Everyone in the courtroom stood up in silence.[17] Yet the political implications of the case did not affect its result: despite her apparent premeditation, María del Pilar was unanimously acquitted. The rebellion was defeated and Calles continued on his path to the presidency. All these were foregone conclusions by the time of the trial, suggesting that the case's significance for its entranced audience lay beneath the political anecdote.

The trial of María del Pilar Moreno became an instantaneous focus of public interest throughout the country because it tied together multiple strands of public debate as a current affair, a theme of *actualidad*: news that circulated by word of mouth and the mass media, and momentarily defined the public's interests. Common newspaper readers, judges, lawyers, suspects, students, many women, and even writers—"all of society" according to *El Heraldo*—knew about the details of the case and spoke about them with puzzlement and feeling. From our contemporary perspective, the coming together of such a diverse public was itself an event in a country with limited literacy, yet for contemporaries the complex building of the case as a narrative was more meaningful, as variegated pieces of evidence and opinions became comments on the political situation and provided new meanings of age, gender, privacy, and justice in postrevolutionary times.[18]

The center of attention was the fourteen-year-old girl who attracted the sympathy of many interested in the case. The evening of the crime, María del Pilar began to receive flowers while at the police station. She was surrounded by flowers at the correctional school, and she departed the courtroom "walking on flowers" after she was acquitted. That day the crowd around the courthouse at the Belén jail was so large that traffic stopped for almost half an hour.[19] People from around the country wrote to her, or approached her to embrace her or kiss her hands.

Expressions of sympathy followed patterns, however. Men stressed her courage: Federico Díaz González, for example, manifested his "respect and veneration," as she had no choice but to "take justice in her own hands" and fulfill the "duty of a loving daughter."[20] Thus, he and other men emphasized the importance of her age and filial duty, the bravery of having placed her love as a "model daughter" above the law. Some offered their help to complete the manly deed: Adolfo Issasi offered forty thousand pesos to cover the girl's bail, and others offered their own bodies to take her place at the correctional school or the Islas Marías penal colony, should she be convicted and sentenced to prison.[21] In the words of these men, María del Pilar acquired masculine traits that were all the more admirable because of her sex, including a "forceful personality" and a "virile attitude."[22] After all, a group of "honest workers" from Matamoros argued with some irony, she did what neither men nor revolutionary institutions could do—she punished a politician.[23]

As visible as male admirers were, the "elegant ladies" from "the best of society" brought María del Pilar flowers and hugs, listened to her every word, cried with her at the courtroom (where they outnumbered men), visited her at the correctional school, and even offered their homes as supplemental prisons.[24] They provided a rationale for *El Heraldo* to justify its extensive coverage of the case: "We are interested in the Mexican woman, being mother, daughter, wife or sister."[25] But women's reactions went beyond curiosity. With her use of violence, María del Pilar seemed to offer an example for others to follow. *El Universal* suggested as much when a thirteen-year-old girl in Torreón shot a soldier who was accosting her mother. Men, it seemed, now felt endangered by popular reactions instigated by women: friends of Tejeda Llorca received anonymous threats and refused to attend the jury trial for fear of their own safety.[26]

María del Pilar inspired these reactions because she constructed a narrative of her life that exemplified the dilemmas of femininity vis-à-vis the new postrevolutionary notions of privacy and violence. According to her precocious memoirs, *La tragedia de mi vida* (written with the help of journalists and published in 1922), she had not shied away from intervening in defense of her father when politics threatened the family. Once, she threw herself in front of officers coming to arrest him, and on another occasion she followed her mother on a long trek to the countryside to take care of an illness her father contracted while campaigning. After his death, she enacted her filial love in tragic scenes: when she saw Jesús Moreno's corpse at the hospital (she had been told that he was sick, not dead), she tried to climb over a railing to kill herself, then embraced his body and promised to seek revenge. At the funeral, despite a heavy rain and in front of politicians and relatives, she erupted into "wrenching cries" and demanded, "Justice, sir! My father has been villainously murdered."[27] After her crime, she frankly confessed that she was now at peace. Almost two years later, press coverage of her trial still recalled these scenes.[28]

This very public tragedy was starkly projected against the background of a happy life in a prosperous and protective household. María del Pilar had studied with private tutors at the Colegio Francés and at the Escuela Normal para Profesoras (Teachers' College). Her father encouraged her to learn piano, singing, and embroidery, and hoped she would become a journalist. He instructed his wife to spare his daughter domestic chores that might hurt her hands and expected María del Pilar to dress well but without ostentation.[29] The most visible sign of respectable family life in her memoirs and other accounts was the house they inhabited in July 1922. Riding in their car around the city, María del Pilar had asked her father one day to buy her a house in the Colonia Portales, a still sparsely populated area south of downtown. He bought land and built a first house, then bought more land and built yet another, larger house named "María del Pilar," whose property titles he presented to her. In press accounts and in Moheno's concluding speech at the trial, the house was used to evoke the bliss of domesticity and the modern, self-sufficient life of American-style architecture and automobiles characteristic of Mexico City's new *colonias*.[30]

The source of the prosperity that made this happiness possible also threatened it, laying siege to the house of Colonia Portales. María del Pilar and her mother often asked Jesús to abandon politics and focus on journalism, and he promised to do so in two years. His career as a revolutionary had led to prison, persecution, exile, illnesses, and duels. In the 1920s, the job of congressman still carried considerable risks, with gunfights and even homicides taking place on the floor of the Chamber of Deputies.[31] Politics was probably the reason several masked men stalked the Colonia Portales house at night and once tried to climb onto María del Pilar's terrace.

This vulnerability of private space to public life shaped María del Pilar in ways that departed from the femininity of daughters of respectable prerevolutionary families. A friend of her father gave her a small "toy rifle," which she had fired that night to call attention to the men trying to break into the house. Since the rifle was too flimsy, her father later gave her another that proved too heavy, and then a small handgun that she kept in her nightstand and later used to kill Tejeda Llorca.[32] Women, particularly those of the upper classes, were not supposed to know how to handle arms. In his 1923 defense of another female accused of killing a man, Moheno argued that women feared guns and could not have the skill of famous revolutionary gunmen such as Pancho Villa's lieutenant Rodolfo Fierro. In his defense of María del Pilar, Moheno downplayed her aptitude with the gun, as it echoed the upsetting practices of other famous *criminelles passionnelles* and might influence the jury against her.[33] Legal considerations aside, María's male admirers could not have failed to notice her courageous use of such a highly symbolic part of her father's legacy.

Other aspects of María del Pilar's upbringing were related to her father's revolutionary ideas. For the new political elites, religion occupied an ambivalent space between the radical ideologies Calles espoused and social respectability. María del Pilar prayed and went to church, favoring a distant upper-class parish that, at times, she entered on her knees after making a promise to the Virgin in exchange for her father's good health. Her parents, however, seemed mindful of official antireligious attitudes when they told her that she could be baptized whenever she decided to become a Christian, as she did only when she was thirteen years old.[34] Jesús Moreno also brought home a concern about social equality. He instructed his daughter to respect servants and to avoid scolding them, and invited her to wear their clothes to understand that she was no different from them. "Daughter, we are all equal," he insisted.[35] When she had to travel to Veracruz to help her ailing father, María del Pilar commented on "[h]ow good are the Indians!"[36]

This egalitarianism had its obvious limits, yet it led María del Pilar to another decision that further endeared her to public opinion. When she decided to stay at the correctional school rather than leave on bail, she embraced the protection of a welfare institution that, like the poor house in the past, was intended to protect the "deserving" poor, including elite women threatened by destitution.[37] Mindful of her father's lessons, she did not want to offend her fellow inmates by bringing valuables to her cell. She offered the profits of her book's sales to the school, and gratefully acknowledged in it the warden's favors.[38]

All of this was relevant for her defense because personal stories and intimate beliefs had public resonance. María del Pilar was constantly aware of the impact of her actions and words on public opinion. After she murdered Tejeda Llorca, she explained to journalists the emotions that had moved her to commit the crime.[39] She wrote her autobiography with the help of *El Heraldo* staff and, until the final days of the trial, she was still eagerly talking to newspapers, assuring *Excélsior* that she was calm "in spite of my feminine and nervous temperament."[40] But her courtroom performance was her greatest achievement. She cried several times during the interrogations and speeches in front of the jury, yet when it was time for her to testify she delivered a clear and moving version of her story in which, besides the basic elements discussed above, she seemed to deride Calles's negative answer to her pleas for justice.[41] In contrast to the usual image of mournful and silent women in criminal trials, which she and her mother nevertheless provided for photographers, she was outspoken, almost commanding, throughout the proceedings: asking the judge not to expel the noisy public from the room, inviting the audience to show respect to her prosecutors, and thanking the victim's relatives for dropping their request to have her father's murder discussed as part of the trial. The latter intervention prompted "a storm of applause from the profoundly moved audience."[42]

María del Pilar knew that her engagement in the public sphere, even in the context of judicial proceedings, did not have to be limited to rational and objective utterances: her performance in public and her melodramatic construction of a narrative about her life and actions were the most effective tools to avoid punishment and, more importantly, to invest her deed with a clear moral meaning. She would not write again, she promised in her book, but her gestures and words before the jury audience and her picture in the press created a paradigm of filial love, private justice, and dignity that stood on the blurring threshold between the private and public spheres. Paradoxically, her defense of honor linked those values with a reversal of the gendered legitimacy of violence. We might speculate that the emotional contents of her case bridged that paradox by creating a favorable audience of men and women.

Yet María del Pilar's story was not the only interpretation of the case's lessons. Querido Moheno, her main attorney, concluded the defense with a speech that took elements from her narrative but inserted them into a powerful denunciation of postrevolutionary morality and, despite his own conservatism, a critique of Mexican manhood.

Moheno's own personal trajectory and political ideas gave the case an additional layer of political implications. He had been an opposition journalist turned loyal congressman under Porfirio Díaz. In the years leading to the 1910 revolution, and in the first legislature under Madero, he wrote a book and spoke in congress in favor of a greater role for public opinion in leading the country toward a peaceful transition out of Díaz's dictatorship. By public opinion, he meant only the voice of the most educated sectors of society. Hence, he proposed a parliamentary regime and further restrictions on voting rights as the most reliable and peaceful path to translate opinion into policy. Although informally banned from politics after he sided with Victoriano Huerta, the general who betrayed Madero in 1913, Moheno was allowed to return from exile in 1920, and remained a critic of the postrevolutionary order.[43] During the following years, he became well known for the power of his oratory, which obtained acquittals for female defendants in cases that, without being clearly political, could only be interpreted as defeats for the government.[44]

In his forensic speeches, Moheno followed the rules of classical rhetoric but added improvisation and a skillful manipulation of the crowd's emotions reflecting both the Romantic influence of Spanish orator Emilio Castelar, and the ideas about the crowd and its emotions espoused by positivist thinkers such as Gustave Le Bon.[45] In his defense of María del Pilar, he manipulated the jury members' sentiments to move them toward a quick vote for acquittal. With this in mind, he always invoked the influence and autonomy of the courtroom audience and, more generally, public opinion. The goal, however, was not to convince jurors with reason but to move them to action, as classical rhetoric dictated, through the warmth and passion of emotions. His tools were few but effective: repetition of "great ideas" and metaphors, attacks against the prosecution's witnesses, constant references to the suffering of his defendants, to religion, mythology, national history, and literature, and pathetic calls for forgiveness.[46]

The political subtext of the case was also part of its emotional appeal: Moheno began by introducing himself as the man who had successfully defended other women accused by the government, and he later reminded the audience that he was defending María del Pilar pro bono after rejecting an early retainer from Tejeda Llorca's relatives. He framed the controversy all along in terms of moral implications rather than facts. Thus, he reiterated images of the Morenos' domestic bliss and contrasted them with "the sordid two-room apartment in a horrible tenement" where the accused and her mother had to move afterward and María del Pilar now had to do domestic work.[47] Moheno's descriptions caused everyone in the courtroom to cry. Such misfortune was the product, Moheno explained, of "our lowly, bloody, and suicidal politics."[48] The interjection was intended to counter the prosecutor's claim that the accused's popularity was a symptom of social immorality, but also to set the stage for an attack on the current government calculated to please the jury, steering its reasoning toward causes that were larger than the case at hand yet just as emotionally charged. The real crime, he argued, had been the electoral fraud that gave Tejeda Llorca a seat in the senate after the murder, which afforded him continued impunity. Moheno concluded with a strong appeal to the jury to take justice in its own hands, as María del Pilar had done, and acquit her, disregarding the letter of the law. He was applauded for several long minutes, and even the judge congratulated him on the beauty of his speech. After the verdict, he was carried out of the courtroom on the shoulders of the joyous audience.[49]

The public celebrated the orator's art but also its own role as a representative of public opinion. The autonomy of the popular jury was key to Moheno's strategy and was a central argument in his attack against the regime. He and other famous lawyers in the 1920s insisted that the jury was the only institution able to provide a measure of justice in a corrupted judicial system. Juries for serious crimes functioned in Mexico City between 1869 and 1929, but they were often attacked by the judicial establishment as contrary to the inquisitorial and bureaucratic practices of Mexican and Spanish penal institutions. The dilemma—between one tradition based on the book, on written, secret proceedings, and the decisions of experts, and a newer system (a version of the English tradition interpreted through the 1789 revolution), embodied in jury trials and stressing orality, common sense, and citizens' participation—was similar to that faced by the nineteenth-century French legal system. As a transaction, a *juez de instrucción* was maintained in Mexico to compile evidence during a written and usually longer first phase of trials, while another, the *presidente de los debates*, was put in charge of public hearings. Juries were then supposed to only answer questions of fact such as "Did the accused shoot the bullet that killed the victim?" Mexican defense lawyers, however, framed their duty as one that superseded the written law and involved an assessment of the actors' morality and credibility. "Official justice" was nothing more, after all, than a delegation of everyone's right to seek justice—a mandate that could always be revoked. This belief led to specific transactions in the daily operations of Mexican juries: according to regulations, jurors were asked about their "intimate conviction" concerning the facts presented to them. In practice, they construed "intimate conviction" to mean a moral belief rather than certainty about objective truth.[50] Emotion, therefore, could be a legitimate foundation for verdicts because publicity, the vigilant eye of public opinion, guaranteed the sincerity of juries' decisions and made them, in this case, faithful representatives of the public's overwhelming support for María del Pilar. This obviously contradicted the rational logic of the investigation of the "truth," a position that jurists insisted was the only permissible rationale in judicial investigations.[51]

Some Mexican courts tried to undermine juries' autonomy by drawing them from a list of men known to judges, a pool more receptive to the prosecution. In the trial against María del Pilar, an autonomous group of jurors was central not only to the success of the defense but also to exposing the political implications of the case. Along with the accused and other members of the defense team, Moheno attended the drawing of names for the jury list and voiced his confidence that they would faithfully represent the public's overwhelming support for María del Pilar. Stressing the public responsibility of the jurors, *Excélsior* printed their names and portraits in a prominent place during the trial.[52]

In the perspective Moheno established, the authentic representation of the jury contrasted with the corruption of the justice system and the impunity of the new political class. Tejeda Llorca was the best example of the privileges enjoyed by that group of violent men, and the case became, even before the trial, an indictment of congress in general.[53] Even though President Obregón had promised to respect the legislative branch's autonomy, the two major parties in the chambers (in reality, loose coalitions of candidates allied in the preparatory sessions of each legislature to secure the approval of their electoral credentials) were soon eliminated as independent actors: the Partido Liberal Constitucionalista (Liberal Constitutionalist Party) in late 1921, after an attempt to establish a parliamentary regime, and the Partido Nacional Cooperatista (Cooperative National Party), as a consequence of the de la Huerta rebellion in 1923–1924. Thus, during María del Pilar's trial, congress was no longer seen as a potential representative of public opinion and was replaced, in the eyes of the capital's audience, by the criminal jury as the last authentic domain of autonomous public opinion.[54]

Class distinction, however, was a requisite of autonomy. Just as he had supported suffrage restrictions in 1908, in the early 1920s Moheno insisted that a truly independent jury had to be drawn from a list that represented the "intellectual level" of Mexican society: neither intellectuals nor the ignorant "sandal wearers or peasants."[55] His vindication of public opinion coexisted with an elitist view of society: the Mexican present was one characterized by anomie and the "excessive claims" of the masses mobilized by the Revolution, which he defined as "this horrible nightmare, these ten years of butchery between brothers in which a million Mexicans died."[56] Such a bleak view of the present included racist views that Moheno shared with many in the jury trial audience. The reverential view of indigenous cultures, sponsored by the Secretaría de Educación Pública (Ministry of Public Education) and minister José Vasconcelos, Moheno argued, was only an excuse to indulge the lowest appetites of the people—even though that same reverence was echoed in María del Pilar's book. The decadence of the judiciary was a result of the *mestizaje* (interracial mixing) that was "strangling the republic."[57] This racism went beyond traditional ethnic prejudice and was best portrayed by attitudes toward blacks: Tejeda Llorca had a black Cuban chauffer who, according to María del Pilar, had stalked her house. When he was interrogated during the trial, the judge made jokes about his color, and the audience laughed at his stuttering.[58] Moheno, who had lived in Cuba and the United States during his exile, alluded to the "African savagery" of blacks in Cuba who he claimed killed and ate white children; and he justified lynching in the U.S. South as a protection for white women's honor.[59]

The paradox here is that racism and conservatism coexisted with a defense of women that empowered them to use violence against abusive men. To understand this apparent contradiction we should look at Moheno's construction of gender difference. This is not a secondary issue: his popularity as a lawyer, after all, was based on his perfect record when defending female murderers.[60] María del Pilar was the paradigmatic embodiment of such causes: other women had killed men who lived with them, but she came from "the heights of her virginal bed" as "a strong and avenging virgin" in a slight body.[61] Tejeda Llorca offered an equally suitable contrast: he was muscular, wealthy, and untouchable, yet he did not threaten the asexuality of the defendant. The moral lesson of the melodrama was as strong as its characters were superficial.[62]

Using this symbolic setup, Moheno brought into play his strongest card: eliciting sentiments through the "intimate" identification of male jurors with the female suspect. He asked jurors to imagine the cadaver of their own father, and to imagine their children demanding an explanation should they happen to convict María del Pilar. He invited them to empathize with the "tempestuous disorder of [her] feelings of tenderness, hopelessness, and indignant rage."[63] The description referred to criminological ideas about women's irrational predisposition, but combined it somewhat contradictorily with a more traditional piece of criminological knowledge. María del Pilar, Moheno argued, had committed a crime of passion because she had acted with premeditation and in defense of her honor. Her behavior compared with that of "strong men deserving reverence."[64] It was common knowledge that criminals of passion were not authentic criminals—not at least in terms of the somatic classifications and hereditary causality of positivist criminology—because they committed crimes inspired by high feelings and placed honor above the law.[65] Moheno's interpretation returned to its initial political argument by joining two premises: first, that taking justice into one's hands deserved everyone's praise in these times of immorality, and, second, that the defense of Mexican women (or their acquittal, as the case might be) was a national duty, particularly as the Revolution had increased male oppression. Women, therefore, had the right to kill when they were exploited or dishonored.[66]

This thesis touched a central aspect of the construction of postrevolutionary political legitimacy. Participation in the civil war and the ability to defend one's political beliefs through the use of violence were two key assets for politicians, as proven by the trajectories and deaths of Jesús Moreno and Francisco Tejeda Llorca.[67] Yet the latter's murder by a weak young woman seemed to subvert those rules. Graphic depictions of the events and press transcriptions of his autopsy presented the politician's body as exposed and vulnerable. One of the bullets, according to the doctors, had exited through his penis.[68] This was all the more upsetting because men's right to exercise violence in the name of honor was regaining public acceptance in the 1920s, as part of the Revolution's cultural re-elaboration of violence. As if to emphasize the dilemma, while María del Pilar's trial unfolded, several other cases of men who killed in defense of their honor ended in acquittals or early dismissal of charges following the Federal District attorney general's instruction to prosecutors to facilitate the release of men accused of murder in such circumstances. Duels continued to be fought. Even Moheno, ever wily, asked the jury in a later trial to acquit a man who had killed out of jealousy.[69]

But the challenge posed by this case is only apparent if we bear in mind that the jury's operation was based on nine men's "intimate convictions." While María del Pilar's case seemed to set a dangerous example, the criminal jury (in this regard aided by the state), was itself a guarantee that men who defended their honor could appeal to reasons of the heart, to use Pascal's words, or, in those of jurist Raúl Ramos Pedrueza, to "a more human rule" above the procedural strictures of the law.[70] Courtroom melodrama validated passion, violence, and the irrational in a supposedly objective public sphere.

At the end of her trial, María del Pilar Moreno was surrounded by a multitude throwing flower petals at her feet. *Excélsior* noted that the public of this trial and the crowd outside Belén contrasted with usual jury spectators: this time there was a large number of middle-class people and many "beautiful and elegant women."[71] Those women were attracted to this trial by something more than the seedy stories, artistic oratory, and melodrama that were the standard fare of jury trials. Through their appearance in the courtroom, they entered larger debates about their place and rights in postrevolutionary society. Their large numbers in a space traditionally dominated by men was a statement about women's role in public life and an implicit challenge to the state. The press accounts examined in this chapter and the emotional elements of Moheno's rhetoric were new devices of public discourse that recognized the limits of the state's promotion of mass politics.

María del Pilar Moreno's fifteen minutes of fame built a strong narrative about femininity, honor, and the use of violence.[72] She reincarnated Greek heroines who defied male authority: Antigone, who sacrificed herself for her duty by burying the family's dead, or Electra, who openly expressed her sorrow and promised to avenge her fallen father. The latter ignored the law and thus "rejected dishonor, / to win at once two reputations / as wise and best of daughters"; Creon condemned the former because "disobedience to authority . . . destroys cities."[73] Such defiance had parallels in the process of postrevolutionary state-building. It is useful to remember that during the 1920s policy makers were increasingly interested in the possibilities of state intervention in family relations as a recipe to help Mexican society out of the demographic consequences of the Revolution. This included a greater concern about the problems of childhood and a renewed stress on women's domestic responsibilities. Even feminists embraced the eugenic program.[74] María del Pilar's story condensed these worries with an important twist: while social policies sought to modernize domesticity by rationalizing femininity, her case showed domesticity disrupted by politics and, through Moheno's rhetorical strategies, brought out affections and emotions as legitimate elements of public life, creating a massive public that included women. And, to that extent, it transformed public discourse.

Moheno, despite his apparent erudition, failed to cite Sophocles and he was certainly no feminist. In a larger context, the case's aftermath was not so positive in terms of the development of women's public voice: María del Pilar, as far as I know, never published again; the use of juries in criminal trials was abolished by a 1929 presidential decree, without great public debate; that year also saw the creation of the Partido Nacional Revolucionario (National Revolutionary Party) and the consolidation of Plutarco Elías Calles's power behind the presidency as *jefe máximo*. Observers interpreted the elimination of the jury as the final blow to the tradition of great intellectuals and orators from the heroic times of nineteenth-century liberalism, and a loss of protection for women who used violence against men.⁷⁵ We may add, following Sarah Maza's argument, that the public sphere changed from an iconic, oral, potentially feminine symbolical system, to one that was more male in its preference for textuality and rationality.⁷⁶ That was clearly the concern when the 1916–1917 constitutional congress debated voting rights: assemblies and crowds were not rational, representatives argued, but governed by "sentimentalism" and the influence of "idealists[,] dreamers," and the clergy. The feminine nature of these characteristics did not escape deputies, who did not vote on a proposal to extend voting rights to women.⁷⁷ Later, the suffragist movement failed to capitalize on their mobilization during the 1920s and 1930s or to achieve electoral reform under the sympathetic government of Lázaro Cárdenas (1934–1940).⁷⁸ To a certain extent, one might argue, the blame can be placed on María del Pilar's acquittal because it could have been read as a feminine indictment of the political class, the revolutionary regime, and, perhaps implicitly, presidential candidate Plutarco Elías Calles himself.

But this story's significance lies beyond actualidad. Mexican liberals believed and contemporary historians support the idea that the jury taught audiences how to codify, in everyday life, diverse ethical and political situations.⁷⁹ What, then, was the legacy of this case? Superficially, it seemed to justify women's use of violence in defense of honor and justice. It seemed to make of emotions a legitimate aspect of public debates. But emotion was a rhetorical tool more than a critique of gendered political exclusions. Looking with hindsight at the overwhelming male domination of Mexican politics in the following decades, women's rights may have instead suffered because of this case and others like it.⁸⁰

María del Pilar's story must be remembered as an ironic counterpoint to the masculinization of the public sphere that followed the Revolution: women could be actors in the melodramas that shaped culture and politics, yet the moral attributes that informed their roles, and their roles themselves, which were unwieldy and powerful, guaranteed the continuity of educated men's right to use violence in the defense of honor and to silence others who sought a place on the stage of public debates. "If we must accept defeat," these men may have thought, following Creon, "let it be from a man; / we must not let people say that a woman beat us."⁸¹

Notes

1. Famous cases "offer vivid illustrations of the ways in which the public discussion of private life helped to shape the culture of the new public sphere." Sarah C. Maza, *Private Lives and Public Affairs: The Causes Célèbres of Prerevolutionary France*

(Berkeley: University of California Press, 1993), 264 (also see 3, 24, 68, 320); Richard Sennett, *The Fall of Public Man* (New York: Knopf, 1977); Madeleine Hurd, *Public Spheres, Public Mores, and Democracy: Hamburg and Stockholm, 1870–1914* (Ann Arbor: University of Michigan Press, 2000); James Van Horn Melton, *The Rise of the Public in Enlightenment Europe* (New York: Cambridge University Press, 2001); Katherine Fischer Taylor, *In the Theater of Criminal Justice: The Palais de Justice in Second Empire Paris* (Princeton, NJ: Princeton University Press, 1993), xix. This chapter would not have been possible without the knowledgeable assistance of Laura Rojas, who pointed me to this story, and the advice of Gabriela Cano and Eugenia Lean, whose study of 1930s girl-killer Shi Jianqiao offers surprising parallels to this case.

2. Ruth Harris, "Melodrama, Hysteria and Feminine Crimes of Passion in the Fin-de-Siècle," *History Workshop* 25 (1988): 32, 34, 38; Mary S. Hartman, *Victorian Murderesses: A True History of Thirteen Respectable French and English Women Accused of Unspeakable Crimes* (New York: Schocken Books, 1977), especially 1, 5, 8. Also see Kristin Ruggiero, "Honor, Maternity, and the Disciplining of Women: Infanticide in Late Nineteenth-Century Buenos Aires," *Hispanic American Historical Review* 72, no. 3 (1992). On the cultural consequences of the Mexican Revolution, see Gilbert M. Joseph and Daniel Nugent, eds., *Everyday Forms of State Formation: Revolution and the Negotiation of Rule in Modern Mexico* (Durham, NC: Duke University Press, 1994); Alan Knight, "Popular Culture and the Revolutionary State in Mexico, 1910–1940," *Hispanic American Historical Review* 74, no. 3 (1994); Jeffrey Rubin, *Decentering the Regime: Ethnicity, Radicalism, and Democracy in Juchitán, Mexico* (Durham, NC: Duke University Press, 1997); and Mary Kay Vaughan, *Cultural Politics in Revolution: Teachers, Peasants, and Schools in Mexico, 1930–1940* (Tucson: University of Arizona Press, 1997).

3. For another sensational trial that resulted in acquittal—a 1929 murder of an army general by a beauty queen—see chapter 8 in this volume. My interpretation differs in that it emphasizes the rupture rather than the continuities with Porfirian values.

4. A key point of reference here is Joan B. Landes, "The Public and the Private Sphere: A Feminist Reconsideration," in *Feminism, the Public and the Private*, ed. Joan B. Landes (New York: Oxford University Press, 1998). "Habermas," she states, "overlooks the strong association of women's discourse and their interests with 'particularity,' and conversely the alignment of masculine speech with truth, objectivity, and reason." (pp. 142–43). See Jürgen Habermas, *The Structural Transformation of the Public Sphere: An Inquiry into a Category of Bourgeois Society* (Cambridge, MA: The MIT Press, 1991). A discussion of the relevant literature appears in Pablo Piccato, "Introducción: ¿Modelo para armar? Hacia un acercamiento crítico a la teoría de la esfera pública," in *Actores, espacios y debates en la historia de la esfera pública en la ciudad de México*, ed. Cristina Sacristán and Pablo Piccato (Mexico City: Instituto Mora, 2005), 9–39. For a study of the intersection of public and private spheres around violence, see Steve Stern, *The Secret History of Gender: Women, Men, and Power in Late Colonial Mexico* (Chapel Hill: University of North Carolina Press, 1995), 9.

5. This description is drawn from *El Universal*, 25 May 1922, p. 1; *El Heraldo*, 25 May 1922, p. 1; *El Heraldo*, 28 May 1922, p. 1; *El Heraldo*, 31 May 1922, p. 8; María del Pilar Moreno, *La tragedia de mi vida. Memorias escritas por la niña* (Mexico City: Phoenix, 1922), 50–54. The episode is analyzed from the point of view of parliamentary immunity in Glenn James Avent, "Representing Revolution: The Mexican Congress and the Origins of Single-Party Rule, 1916–1934" (PhD diss., University of Arizona, 2004).
6. One of these witnesses was Manuel Zapata. Moreno, *La tragedia*, 54–57; *El Universal*, 11 July 1922, p. 1; *El Universal*, 13 July 1922, sec. 2, pp. 1, 11; *El Universal*, 14 July 1922, sec. 2, p. 10; *El Universal*, 15 July 1922, p. 1; *El Universal*, 18 July 1922, sec. 2, pp. 1, 8; *El Heraldo*, 11 July 1922, p. 3; *El Heraldo*, 12 July 1922, p. 1; *El Heraldo*, 14 July 1922, pp. 1, 5.
7. Moreno, *La tragedia*, 65; *El Universal*, 23 July 1922, sec. 2, p. 1; *Excélsior*, 29 April 1924, sec. 2, p. 8.
8. One reason for the request to change the judge was an interrogation of María del Pilar conducted without the presence of her lawyers. *El Universal*, 16 July 1922, p. 9; *El Universal*, 19 July 1922, pp. 1, 8; *El Universal*, 22 July 1922, sec. 2, p. 1; *El Universal*, 4 August 1922, sec. 2, p. 1; *El Universal*, 25 August 1922, p. 5. On her defense team and the delay, see *El Universal*, 25 July 1922, sec. 2, p. 1; and *El Universal*, 26 July 1922, sec. 2, p. 7. Long delays were not unprecedented. See Aurelio de los Reyes, *Cine y sociedad en México, 1896–1930: Bajo el cielo de México (1920–1924)* (Mexico City: Universidad Nacional Autónoma de México, 1993), 79.
9. See Enrique Plasencia de la Parra, *Personajes y escenarios de la rebelión delahuertista, 1923–1924* (Mexico City: Instituto de Investigaciones Históricas UNAM: M. A. Porrúa Grupo Editorial, 1998).
10. *El Universal*, 25 May 1922, p. 1; *El Heraldo de México*, 25 May 1922, p. 1. In a May 1922 letter to Moreno, Adalberto Tejeda claimed that he had not intervened in local elections and that he had tried to discourage his cousin from running for the senate. Adalberto Tejeda to Jesús Z. Moreno, Fideicomiso Archivo Elías Calles y Fernando Torreblanca, Mexico City (hereafter cited as FAECFT), gaveta 12, exp. 26, leg. 3/15, inv. 5558, f. 139. In a February letter, the governor asked Secretary Calles to persuade Tejeda Llorca to abandon his candidacy. Adalberto Tejeda to Plutarco Elías Calles, 13 February 1922, FAECFT, gaveta 72, exp. 26, leg. 2/15, inv. 5558, f. 84. The conflict dated back to 1920, when Moreno denounced in the Chamber of Deputies Tejeda's improper influence on the composition of the state legislature, operated through Tejeda Llorca. Twenty-Ninth Legislature, *Diario de los Debates de la Cámara de Diputados* (Mexico City: N.p., 11 October 1920), pp. 30–31; Francisco Tejeda Llorca to Álvaro Obregón, 7 October [1920], FAECFT, exp. D; María Eugenia Terrones, "Veracruz: de la sedición a la sumisión: Conflicto político y legislatura estatal en la posrevolución, 1920–1932," in *El Poder Legislativo en las décadas revolucionarias, 1908–1934*, ed. Pablo Piccato (Mexico City: Instituto de Investigaciones Legislativas—Cámara de Diputados, 1997), 187. For the fluidity and violence of *veracruzano* politics, and the radicalism of Governor Tejeda, see Romana Falcon, *El agrarismo en Veracruz; la etapa radical, 1928–1935* (Mexico City:

El Colegio de México, 1977), 39; and Plasencia de la Parra, *Personajes y escenarios*, 28–34.

11. According to *El Universal*, Adalberto Tejeda owed the governorship to Tejeda Llorca's connections in Mexico City. Francisco Tejeda Llorca to Álvaro Obregón, FAECFT, exp. D; *El Universal*, 13 July 1922, 2nd sec., p. 3; Plutarco Elías Calles to Adalberto Tejeda, 24 May 1922, FAECFT, gaveta 54, exp. 96, inv. 3878; Adalberto Tejeda to Plutarco Elías Calles, 10 July 1922, FAECFT, gaveta 72, exp. 26, inv. 5558, leg. 4/15, fs. 160–210. On the meeting, see *El Heraldo*, 26 May 1922, p. 6.

12. *El Heraldo*, 14 July 1922, p. 5; *Excélsior*, 27 April 1924, sec. 2, p. 8; *Excélsior*, 29 April 1924, p. 6. Among the names at the funeral were Antonio Escandón, Remigio Noriega, and Interior Secretary Calles. President Obregón sent flowers, as did Minister of War Francisco R. Serrano, and businessman Alberto Braniff. *El Heraldo*, 14 July 1922, p. 5. At Tejeda Llorca's wedding in 1910, President Porfirio Díaz had been a witness, as well as Vice President Ramón Corral, Minister of Justice Justino Fernández, and other prominent *científicos* such as Rosendo Pineda and Fernando Pimentel y Fagoaga. *Excélsior*, 27 April 1924, sec. 2, p. 1.

13. Moreno, *La tragedia*, 6–7, 28, 74. Tejedista deputies accused him of meddling in Veracruz's politics without being from the state. Twenty-Ninth Legislature, *Diario de los Debates de la Cámara de Diputados* (Mexico City: N.p., 11 October 1920), pp. 30–31.

14. Plutarco Elías Calles to Adolfo de la Huerta, 29 April 1921, FAECFT, MFN 4755, gaveta 54, exp. 73, inv. 3855, 1920–1921. Also see Jesús Moreno to Plutarco Elías Calles, 18 December 1920, FAECFT, serie 12010400, exp. 25, leg. 2/3, inv. 70, f. 131. According to Calles, the two men had met in the early 1900s in Sonora and worked together at several newspapers. *El Heraldo*, 25 May 1922, p. 6. Calles attended Moreno's funeral.

15. *El Heraldo*, 14 July 1922, p. 5.

16. The remaining lawyers denied this. *Excélsior*, 24 April 1924, sec. 2, p. 6.

17. To avoid seeming partisan, however, Moheno noted that "the revolution that has just finished did not have ideals." *Excélsior*, 29 April 1924, p. 1.

18. Novelist Federico Gamboa noted his disapproval of the murder in his diary. Federico Gamboa, *Mi diario VII (1920–1939). Mucho de mi vida y algo de la de otros* (Mexico City: Consejo Nacional para la Cultura y las Artes, 1995), 78–79. A supreme court justice's "deep reflections" appeared in *El Heraldo*, 13 July 1922, p. 1. Also see *El Heraldo*, 11 July 1922, pp. 1, 3; and *El Heraldo*, 14 July 1922, p. 5. The case would be remembered as one of the most famous tried before a popular jury. *Excélsior*, 8 October 1929, sec. 2, p. 1.

19. "En medio de una ovación cerrada y pisando flores, la niña Ana María del Pilar Moreno quedó libre," *Excélsior*, 30 April 1924, p. 6.

20. *El Heraldo*, 12 July 1922, p. 1. Letters came from the interns of the general hospital, a mechanics union, a violinist, railroad workers, and from Guanajuato, Hidalgo, Jalisco, and Veracruz. *El Heraldo*, 12 July 1922, p. 1; *El Heraldo*, 14 July 1922, p. 1; *El Heraldo* 19 July 1922, pp. 1, 8. Even the Salvation Army offered to pay for María del Pilar's defense. Querido Moheno, *Sobre la brecha* (Mexico City: Ediciones Botas, 1925), 173.

21. *El Heraldo*, 11 July 1922, p. 1; *El Heraldo*, 14 July 1922, p. 1. From Tampico the Por la niñez (For the Children) association demanded that the trial be cut short to protect the suspect. *El Universal*, 14 July 1922, sec. 2, p. 10.
22. *El Heraldo*, 15 July 1922, p. 5; *Excélsior*, 29 May 1924, sec. 2, p. 1.
23. *El Heraldo*, 13 July 1922, p. 5.
24. *El Heraldo*, 12 July 1922, p. 5; *El Heraldo*, 13 July 1922, p. 5; Moreno, *La tragedia*, 59, 68; *El Universal*, 13 July 1922, sec. 2, p. 1.
25. *El Heraldo*, 13 July 1922, p. 5. For similar responses from women and lawyers, see de los Reyes, *Cine y sociedad* 2:87.
26. *El Universal*, 17 August 1922, sec. 2, p. 1. The fearful witnesses were Manuel Zapata and Rafael Rebollar. *El Universal*, 20 July 1922, sec. 2, p. 1; *Excélsior*, 30 April 1924, p. 1.
27. *El Universal*, 26 May 1922, p. 6; Moheno, *Sobre la brecha*; Moreno, *La tragedia*, 18, 21, 23. In the case of Magdalena Jurado, a similarly successful narrative was presented at a jury trial; see de los Reyes, *Cine y sociedad* 2:85; Querido Moheno, *Mis últimos discursos: La caravana pasa. (Preliminar) Discursos ante el Congreso Jurídico, defensa de la Sra. Jurado, Defensa de la Sra. Alicia Olvera* (Mexico City: Ediciones Botas, 1923), 88–140. Other women accused of murder wrote down their memories; see Hartman, *Victorian Murderesses*, 20. For the cultural impact of violence in revolutionary legitimacy, see Jorge Aguilar Mora, *Una muerte sencilla, justa, eterna: Cultura y guerra durante la revolución mexicana* (Mexico City: Ediciones ERA, 1990); Marjorie Becker, "Torching La Purísima, Dancing at the Altar: The Construction of Revolutionary Hegemony in Michoacán, 1934–1940," in *Everyday Forms of State Formation: Revolution and the Negotiation of Rule in Modern Mexico*, ed. Gilbert M. Joseph and Daniel Nugent (Durham, NC: Duke University Press, 1994); Daniel Nugent, *Spent Cartridges of Revolution* (Chicago: University of Chicago Press, 1994); and Frank Tannenbaum, *Mexico: The Struggle for Peace and Bread* (New York: Knopf, 1950), 83.
28. Moreno, *La tragedia*, 57; *Excélsior*, 17 April 1924, p. 1.
29. Ibid., 17, 24, 31, 35, 43. This is not a great departure here from Porfirian models. See Macías González in this volume; Carmen Ramos, et al., eds., *Presencia y transparencia: La mujer en la historia de México* (Mexico City: El Colegio de México, 1987).
30. The Morenos had one car and Jesús had just bought a second when he was murdered. Moheno, *Sobre la brecha*, 84, 178; Moreno, *La tragedia*, 28, 32–34.
31. Moreno, *La tragedia*, 4, 44. On Moreno's career, see Moreno, *La tragedia*, 7, 11, 14, 17, 21. For gunfights between partisans of de la Huerta and Obregón in the Chamber of Deputies, see *El Universal*, 3 October 1923, p. 1. An example of public perceptions of congressmen's violence is evident in the caricature by García Cabral, *Excélsior*, 28 May 1924, p. 5. On violence in the chambers, see Pablo Piccato, "El parlamentarismo y la construcción de una esfera pública posrevolucionaria," *Historias* 39, no. 2 (1998): 65–86.
32. Moreno, *La tragedia*, 41–42.
33. Moheno, *Mis últimos discursos*. For women's relatively small involvement in cases of serious violence, see Elisa Speckman Guerra, "Las flores del mal: Mujeres

criminales en el porfiriato," *Historia Mexicana* 47, no. 1 (1997): 189. But for lower-class women's participation in the Revolution, see Gabriela Cano, "Soldaderas and Coronelas," in *Encyclopedia of Mexico: History, Society and Culture*, ed. Michael S. Werner (Chicago: Fitzroy Dearborn Publishers, 1997); and Ana Lau and Carmen Ramos, *Mujeres y Revolución, 1900–1917* (Mexico City: Instituto Nacional de Estudios Históricos de la Revolución Mexicana, 1993).

34. Moreno, *La tragedia*, 21, 25–26. On the ambivalence of the revolutionary elite toward religion, see Alan Knight, "Revolutionary Project, Recalcitrant People: Mexico, 1910–1940," in *The Revolutionary Process in Mexico: Essays on Political and Social Change, 1880–1940*, ed. Jaime O. Rodríguez (Irvine: UCLA Latin American Center Publications, 1990); and Mary Kay Vaughan, "Modernizing Patriarchy: State Policies, Rural Households, and Women in Mexico, 1930–1940," in *Hidden Histories of Gender and the State in Latin America*, ed. Elizabeth Dore and Maxine Molyneux (Durham, NC: Duke University Press, 2000), 198. Calles's anticlerical policies would be a central factor in the Cristero rebellion against the regime a few years later.

35. Moreno, *La tragedia*, 31–32, 60.

36. Ibid., 18.

37. Her sympathizers worried about her exposure to "vices" at the institution, and were glad to see her placed in a special room where she could safely be with her family. *El Heraldo*, 12 julio 1922, p. 1; *El Universal*, 12 julio 1922, p. 1. All prisons had sections intended for upper-class inmates. General José Ceballos, *Memoria presentada al C. Lic Manuel Romero Rubio Secretario de Estado y del Despacho de Gobernación por el. Gobernador del Distrito Federal y que comprende los años de 1886 y 1887* (Mexico City: Eduardo Dublan, 1888); and Joaquín García Icazbalceta, *Informe sobre los establecimientos de beneficencia y corrección de esta capital; su estado actual; noticia de sus fondos; reformas que desde luego necesitan y plan general de su arreglo presentado por José María Andrade* (Mexico City: Moderna Librería Religiosa, 1907). On the poor house, see Silvia Arrom, *Containing the Poor: The Mexico City Poor House, 1774–1871* (Durham, NC: Duke University Press, 2000). On juvenile correctional facilities, see Elena Azaola Garrido, *La institución correccional en México: Una mirada extraviada* (Mexico City: Siglo Veintiuno, 1990).

38. Moreno, *La tragedia*, 1, 60.

39. *El Heraldo*, 11 July 22, p. 1.

40. Moreno, *La tragedia*, 1, 2; *Excélsior*, 27 April 1924, sec. 2, p. 1.

41. When she was told that Tejeda Llorca had been elected senator, she asked Calles, "[W]on't the people of Veracruz be ashamed of having a murderer as their representative?" *Excélsior*, 29 April 1924, p. 6.

42. *Excélsior*, 30 April 1924, p. 1; *Excélsior*, 29 April 1924, p. 6. Photographs included reconstructions of María del Pilar's shooting of Tejeda Llorca, images of her talking to the court, and the crowd outside the courthouse. Moreno, *La tragedia*; and *Excélsior*, 29 April 1924, p. 1. Avent, however, depicts María del Pilar as passive throughout the trial. Avent, "Representing Revolution," 236. On other female suspects dressed in black, who were probably advised to do so to impress the jury, see de los Reyes, *Cine y sociedad*, vol. 2, pp. 18, 80.

43. Querido Moheno was born in Pichucalco, Chiapas, in 1873, and died in Mexico City in 1933. He graduated from the Escuela Nacional de Jurisprudencia in 1896. Francois-Xavier Guerra, *México: Del Antiguo Régimen a la Revolución* (Mexico City: Fondo de Cultura Económica, 1988), 1:437, 2:13. In 1913, Moheno became a minister in Huerta's cabinet. On his ideas and political activities under Madero, see Pablo Piccato, *Congreso y Revolución: El parlamentarismo en la XXVI Legislatura* (Mexico City: Instituto Nacional de Estudios Históricos de la Revolución Mexicana, 1992). Querido Moheno's main works on politics include *¿Hacia dónde vamos? Bosquejo de un cuadro de instituciones políticas adecuadas al pueblo mexicano* (Mexico City: I. Lara, 1908); *Mi actuación política después de la Decena Trágica* (Mexico City: Ediciones Botas, 1939); and *Problemas contemporáneos* (Mexico City: Imprenta Central, 1903). For other opinions linking congressional rule, restricted political rights, and decrease of violence, see Antonio Enríquez, *Dictadura presidencial o parlamentarismo democrático. Estudio crítico de nuestro sistema federal, y proposiciones de reforma a la Constitución, mediante la creación del parlamentarismo y de la república central* (Mexico City: A. Enríquez, 1913). A project to modify the constitution by establishing a cabinet regime was close to approval by the Chamber of Deputies in late 1921 but it was defeated, and the following years saw an increase in presidential powers mainly through the abrogation of reelection for congressmen in 1924. Jeffrey A. Weldon, "El presidente como legislador, 1917–1930," in *El Poder Legislativo en las décadas revolucionarias, 1908–1934*, ed. Pablo Piccato (Mexico City: Instituto de Investigaciones Legislativas—Cámara de Diputados, 1997).
44. Moheno, *Mis últimos discursos*, 10–12, 20, 118.
45. On Castelar in Mexico, see *Velada fúnebre organizada por la Escuela N. de Jurisprudencia de Mejico, en honor de Don Emilio Castelar y verificada en la Camara de Diputados la noche del 17 de junio de 1899, bajo la presidencia del Primer Magistrado de la República* (Mexico City: Imp. J. de Elizalde, 1900); Francisco J. Hernández, "No es tan fácil ser orador," 27 October 1923, Archivo General de la Nación, Fondo Antonio Díaz Soto y Gama, rollo 1. Moheno cited Le Bon repeatedly in his speeches in the Chamber of Deputies. On Le Bon's influence on Mexican rhetoricians, see Aguilar Mora, *Una muerte sencilla*, 254; Demetrio Sodi, *El jurado en México: Estudios sobre el jurado popular* (Mexico City: Secretaría de Fomento, 1909). For Edgar Demange, a successful defender of women accused of homicide who may have offered some inspiration to Moheno, see Hartman, *Victorian Murderesses*, 155. As a speaker, Moheno was described as an "artist" because of his shrewd use of emotions. Querido Moheno, *Procesos Célebres. Rubin. Discurso en defensa de la acusada* (Mexico City: Ediciones Botas, 1925), 7–8.
46. Moheno, *Mis últimos discursos*, 18–19, 22, 23; Querido Moheno, *Procesos Célebres. Honorio Rodríguez, discurso de defensa* (Mexico City: Ediciones Botas, 1928).
47. *Excélsior*, 29 April 1924, p. 1; *Excélsior*, 30 April 1924, sec. 2, p. 6; Moheno, *Sobre la brecha*, 78, 84, 175; Moreno, *La tragedia*, 28, 32–34; *Excélsior*, 29 April 1924, p. 6.
48. Moheno, *Sobre la brecha*, 180.
49. *Excélsior*, 27 April 1924, sec. 2, p. 1; *Excélsior*, 30 April 1924, p. 1; and *Excélsior*, 30 April 1924, pp. 81–83, 91, 177. In his 1925 defense of Alicia Olvera, even the soldiers

who guarded the suspect were crying during the speech. Moheno, *Mis últimos discursos*, 23, 109. Also see Moheno, *Rubín*, 44.

50. Moheno, *Mis últimos discursos*, 26, 30; Moheno, *Sobre la brecha*, 3, 89, 186, 202; *Excélsior*, 30 April 1924, sec. 2, p. 6; Taylor, *In the Theater*, xix, 6, 8, 38, 127. On the history of the jury and its opposition in France, see James M. Donovan, "Magistrates and Juries in France, 1791–1952," *French Historical Studies* 22, no. 3 (1999); Bernard Schnapper, "Le jury français aux XIX et XXème siècles," in *The Trial Jury in England, France, Germany: 1700–1900*, ed. Antonio Padoa Schioppa (Berlin: Duncker u. Humbolt, 1987). On the jury in Mexico, see Guillermo Colín Sánchez, *Derecho Mexicano de Procedimientos Penales* (Mexico City: Porrúa, 1980), 47–49, 103, 617; *Ley de Jurados en Materia Criminal para el Distrito Federal*, (Mexico City: Boletín Judicial, 1892), 28; and Antonio Padilla Arroyo, "Los jurados populares en la administración de justicia en México en el siglo XIX," *Secuencia: Revista de historia y ciencias sociales* 47 (2000). The jury as a source of impunity for criminals was an old argument against the institution. *El Siglo Diez y Nueve*, 23 April 1882, p. 1. The institution's endurance is explained in part by the existence of popular juries for press crimes; these juries were used sporadically since the 1820s, and consistently from 1868 until their elimination in 1882. Both press and criminal juries were drawn randomly from a list of the city's residents who could read and had a minimum income. Although press juries were used across the country, criminal juries were used almost exclusively in the capital. The 1917 constitution reestablished press juries but they were not used in the postrevolutionary period.

51. Antonio Ramos Pedrueza, *Conferencias* (Mexico City: Eusebio Gómez de la Puente, 1922), 99, 116.

52. For more on the selection of juries, see *Excélsior*, 27 April 1924, sec. 2, p. 1. The jurors' names and portraits are in *Excélsior*, 29 April 1924, p. 1.

53. On the debates about *fuero*, or parliamentary immunity, and the honor of congressmen, see Avent, "Representing Revolution," chapter 5.

54. Leaders of both parties sided with de la Huerta against Obregón in 1923. Plasencia de la Parra, *Personajes y escenarios*, 45. On the struggles inside and around the Mexican Congress in the early postrevolutionary period, see Pablo Piccato, ed. *El Poder Legislativo en las décadas revolucionarias, 1908–1934* (Mexico City: Instituto de Investigaciones Legislativas—Cámara de Diputados, 1997). For a survey that expressed opinions against parliamentary immunity, see *El Heraldo*, 13 July 1922, p. 1. In an editorial, *El Universal* stated that the chambers of congress now protect "individuals without morality or culture." *El Universal*, 14 July 1922, p. 3. Also see *El Universal*, 26 May 1922, p. 3. Calles, by contrast, expressed his support of the fuero. *El Universal*, 13 July 1922, p. 1. Yet he later acknowledged that some congressmen abused it. *El Universal*, 20 July 1922, p. 1. For pro-fuero opinion, see Minister of Commerce and Industry Vito Alessio Robles in *El Universal*, 14 July 1922, p. 1. For an opinion opposed to unrestricted fueros, see Francisco Bulnes in *El Universal*, 20 July 1922, pp. 3, 6.

55. Moheno, *Mis últimos discursos*, 14–15, 17. Through income requirements, the law sought to "exclude a certain group of notorious ineptitude." *Ley de Jurados*, 82, 96. Antonio Ramos Pedrueza also saw these requirements as a way to improve an

institution that was more reliable than judges, if just as emotional. Ramos Pedrueza, *Conferencias*, 17, 107. This was in response to a period when these requirements were not established and "men of certain social position stubbornly refuse to be juries." *El Siglo Diez y Nueve*, 26 April 1880, p. 1. On "professional juries" favorable to judges, see Sodi, *El jurado en México*.

56. Moheno, *Mis últimos discursos*, 18, 26, 30, 58, 88, 105; Moheno, *Rubin*, 25, 32. See Piccato, *Congreso y Revolución*.
57. *El Universal*, 20 July 1922, pp. 1, 6. Against indigenism and federalism, another bête noire of conservatives, see Moheno, *Mis últimos discursos*, 34, 44. For similar views expressed in another jury trial, this time regarding lower-class Mexicans, see chapter 7 in this volume.
58. *Excélsior*, 29 April 1924, p. 6.
59. Moheno, *Mis últimos discursos*, 83; Moheno, *Sobre la brecha*, 191, 203.
60. Moheno, *Rubin*, 13, 19, 21.
61. Moheno, *Sobre la brecha*, 93, 179.
62. Maza, *Private Lives and Public Affairs*, 66; and Moheno, *Sobre la brecha*, 188.
63. Moheno, *Sobre la brecha*, 88–89, 185.
64. Moheno had also used criminological explanations in the defenses of Nydia Camargo and Alicia Olvera. Moheno, *Mis últimos discursos*, 81; Moheno, *Rubin*, 61. On passion, see Moheno, *Sobre la brecha*, 193, 194, 200.
65. Moheno, *Sobre la brecha*, 93, 178. For the favorable view of "passion criminals" in positivist criminology, see Cesare Lombroso, *Crime: Its Causes and Remedies*, trans. Henry P. Horton (Boston: Little, Brown, 1918), 256. Also see Cesare Lombroso, *L'uomo delinquente in rapporto all'antropologia, alla giurisprudenza ed alle discipline carcerarie*, vol. 2, *Delinquente epilettico, d'impeto, pazzo e criminaloide* (Torino, Italy: Fratelli Bocca, 1889), 238.
66. Moheno, *Sobre la brecha*, 187. The argument of Mexican women's oppression was central in the defense of Nydia Camargo, who had killed a Chilean. Moheno, *Rubin*, 23, 71. He concluded this defense with a strong call intended to move jurors: "Kill him!!" Moheno, *Rubin*, 61. Also see Moheno, *Mis últimos discursos*, 53, 147–48. For other contemporary cases supporting this right, see chapter 7 in this volume.
67. See note 27 above. Tejeda Llorca was congratulated by his friends after he shot Moreno. *El Heraldo*, 30 May 1922, sec. 2. On the use of guns, see Moheno, *Mis últimos discursos*, 82.
68. *El Heraldo*, 11 July 1922, p. 3.
69. Moheno, *Honorio Rodríguez*, 78; *Excélsior*, 11 May 1924, p. 7; *Excélsior*, 12 May 1924, p. 3; *Excélsior*, 21 May 1924, sec. 2, p. 8. On dueling, see Pablo Piccato, "Politics and the Technology of Honor: Dueling in Turn-of-the-Century Mexico," *Journal of Social History* 33, no. 2 (1999). On the memorandum and the release of a man who killed his wife and her lover, thus avenging "his insulted honor," see *Excélsior*, 31 May 1924, p. 3. Also see *Excélsior*, 1 April 1924, p. 6; *Excélsior*, 29 April 1924, p. 1; *Excélsior*, 31 May 1924, p. 3; and de los Reyes, *Cine y sociedad* 2:64. For more on the cultural consequences of the Revolution, see Aguilar Mora, *Una muerte sencilla*; Ana María Alonso, *Thread of Blood: Colonialism, Revolution, and Gender on Mexico's Northern Frontier* (Tucson: University of Arizona Press, 1995); and

Carlos Monsiváis, "La aparición del subsuelo. Sobre la cultura de la Revolución mexicana," *Historias*, 8–9, no. 1 (1985): 159–77.

70. Following this logic, "a man of good antecedents" could fight a passing "troublemaker" who looked at him offensively and be acquitted because the jury using "a more humane rule, cannot believe it possible to force a man to flee when he only wants to avoid being insulted." Ramos Pedrueza, *Conferencias*, 101. A similar argument appears in Armando Z. Ostos, *Breves Comentarios sobre el Nuevo Código de Procedimientos Penales para el Distrito y Territorios Federales* (Mexico City: N.p., 1921), 38.
71. *Excélsior*, 29 April 1924, p. 1; *Excélsior*, 30 April 1929, p. 1.
72. For similar conclusions, see chapter 7 in this volume.
73. Sophocles, *Sophocles I*, trans. David Grene (Chicago: University of Chicago Press, 1991), 167; Sophocles, *Sophocles II*, trans. John Moore, Michael Jameson, and David Grene (Chicago: University of Chicago Press, 1969), 187. The importance of Antigone in twentieth-century Mexico's national narratives is noted in Jean Franco, *Plotting Women: Gender and Representation in Mexico* (New York: Columbia University Press, 1988), chapter 6.
74. See Gabriela Cano, "Revolución, feminismo y ciudadanía en México (1915–1940)," in *Historia de las mujeres en Occidente*, ed. Georges Duby and Michelle Perrot (Madrid: Taurus, 1993), 303; Alexandra Minna Stern, "Responsible Mothers and Normal Children: Eugenics, Nationalism, and Welfare in Post-Revolutionary Mexico, 1920–1940," *The Journal of Historical Sociology* 12, no. 4 (1999): 370, 377; Vaughan, "Modernizing Patriarchy."
75. On the new regulations, see Ostos, *Breves Comentarios*, 27, 31, 40. On the last cases against women, see *Excélsior*, 8 October 1929, sec. 2, p. 1. Regarding women's rights in the face of male violence and the judiciary, it is difficult to judge whether the elimination of the jury had any long-term consequence. The evidence from statistical sources about the frequency of sexual abuse, a tentative indicator, suggests an increase in rape rates, although the available data does not allow for an observation of the impact of the 1929 decrees. Ira Beltrán and Pablo Piccato, "Crimen en el siglo XX: Fragmentos de análisis sobre la evidencia cuantitativa," in *Los últimos cien años, los próximos cien años*, ed. Ariel Rodríguez Kuri and Sergio Tamayo (Mexico City: Universidad Autónoma Metropolitana, 2004).
76. See Maza, *Private Lives and Public Affairs*, 110, 314.
77. Session of 26 January 1917, *Diario de los debates del Congreso Constituyente, 1916–1917* (Mexico City: Comisión Nacional para la celebración de Sesquicentenario de la Independencia Nacional, 1960), 86–88, 982.
78. For the limited advances of feminist causes after the Revolution despite mobilization during the 1920s, see Franco, *Plotting Women*, 102; Anna Macías, *Against All Odds: The Feminist Movement in Mexico to 1940* (Westport, CT: Greenwood Press, 1982); and Enriqueta Tuñón Pablos, "El otorgamiento del sufragio femenino en México" (PhD diss., Universidad Nacional Autónoma de México, 1997), 3–4, 62. Suffrage for all elections was extended to women in 1953. One of the last famous jury trials was that of León Toral and Madre Conchita, who were convicted for the 1928 murder of president-elect Álvaro Obregón (see chapter 7 in this volume).

Hartman states that women's presence in French and English trials was a way to voice their concerns, and suggests that public Victorian reactions be understood in the context of feminism's emergence. *Victorian Murderesses*, 84, 166, 268.
79. Padilla Arroyo, "Los jurados populares," 44, 138; and Taylor, *In the Theater*, 8.
80. On the exchange value of women in the emergence of a new political class, see Aguilar Mora, *Una muerte sencilla*, 92. On the difficulties involved in "rewriting master narratives around a heroine," see Franco, *Plotting Women*, 46, 133.
81. Sophocles, *Sophocles I*, 167; Sophocles, *Sophocles II*, 187.

CHAPTER FIVE

Who Killed Roberto González?
Murder, Radicalism, and Catholic Nationalism in Postrevolutionary Michoacán

～⊛ Christopher R. Boyer ⊛～

In early February 1923, word spread through the city of Zamora, Michoacán, that the ten-year-old son of a prominent landowner had been kidnapped. The news hit the town like lightning. True, the city of some ten thousand people in western Mexico's deeply conservative Bajío (the nation's prosperous agricultural heartland) was no stranger to controversy and violence. It had just experienced nearly two years of social unrest. Radical politicians had briefly controlled the city government, a situation that sparked a series of unruly mass protests in the city's main square. Elsewhere, a modest number of peasant communities had petitioned the state government for land reform parcels known as *ejidos*, prompting a small number of hacienda owners to hire gunmen who intimidated and often killed peasant leaders. But most of these events did not play out within the city itself, nor did they physically threaten the upper-crust families of Zamora, who had never experienced anything like the kidnapping of one of their own. So, the child's abduction brought the city into uncharted territory. According to the town's Catholic newspaper, the loss of Roberto González made the well-to-do families of Zamora feel threatened even in their own "hearths and homes."[1]

The mayor of Zamora ordered the police to spare no effort in the search for the boy. At the same time, he sent urgent telegrams to municipal authorities in the rural communities around Zamora asking them to be on the lookout for a thin, dark-skinned youth wearing a cap. Still, nearly two weeks passed without any news. The police turned up nothing. One after another, the village authorities in the surrounding townships reported that they could find no trace of the victim but vowed to continue their searches nonetheless.[2]

The disappearance of Roberto González came at a particularly tense moment for the Bajío and the town of Zamora in particular. Less than a year had passed since an uprising of rancheros (small-scale landowners) and conservative politicians had succeeded in chasing Governor Francisco J. Múgica, a left-wing and anticlerical firebrand, out of office and out of the state. Many of Zamora's most visible political families had applauded the rebellion, remembering only too well that Múgica's 1920–1922 administration had repeatedly nullified local elections that had given Catholic party candidates control of the city council (*ayuntamiento*). Múgica had also prohibited public religious processions in Michoacán and had promoted land reform in select areas of the state, including communities on the outskirts of Zamora.[3] By February 1923, when Roberto González went missing, rumors had just begun to circulate in the street and in the local press suggesting that Múgica would soon return to the state capital to retake power and reinstate what the Catholic newspaper called his policies of "plunder and swindle" (*rapiña y despojo*).[4] Nor was that all. A mere two weeks before the kidnapping, the federal government had accentuated its own anticlerical stance when Interior Secretary Plutarco Elías Calles ordered that the papal delegate to Mexico be deported. Calles said that the delegate, Monsignor Ernesto E. Filippi, had broken laws prohibiting the clergy from participating in politics or leading outdoor religious processions when he led a massive pilgrimage to inaugurate the construction of a monument to Christ the King on the Cerro del Cubilete in the state of Guanajuato.[5] The expulsion of the pope's representative in Mexico, perceived as an abuse of power by the government, had triggered a series of heated protest rallies by Catholics throughout the country, including at least two loud demonstrations in Zamora.[6]

The readers of any local newspaper—and particularly Zamora's Catholic weekly, *El Cruzado* (*The Crusade*)—would therefore have read the latest news about Roberto González's disappearance right alongside sensational articles recounting ex-governor Múgica's plans to retake power, the expulsion of the papal delegate and his eventual return to Rome, and other perceived threats to religious and political expression in Zamora and the nation as a whole. It is hardly surprising that the tempers of many townspeople had already frayed when on the morning of February 10 a pair of field hands discovered the lifeless body of Roberto González floating in the Río Duero just outside town. The child had been bound hand and foot. His assailants had stabbed him in the back and dumped his body into the current to be carried away like driftwood. News of the murder sent hundreds of people once again to the city's central square, where they protested the crime and demanded that the mayor impose "exemplary punishment on whomever had committed it."[7] The respectable classes of Zamora demonstrated their outrage in a slightly more restrained but no less emphatic fashion. They called for a period of mourning, canceled a charity ball scheduled for that evening, and saw to it that the cathedral bells remained silent in respect for the deceased. Within a matter of hours, the police arrested Luis Plancarte, a former congressman from a conservative Zamora family, and charged him with having acted as the intermediary between the kidnappers and the boy's parents. Yet it remained unclear who the actual kidnappers were. A few days later, a special police delegation dispatched by President Álvaro Obregón himself arrived from Mexico City to help investigate the crime.[8]

By this point, the murder had become a national cause célèbre as newspapers throughout the country printed increasingly sensational and inaccurate versions of events. Back in Zamora, the church-affiliated newspaper referred to the killing as one of the worst crimes in the history of the state, and predicted darkly that justice would be served.[9] The big break in the case came two weeks after the discovery of the body, when the authorities made a spectacular announcement. They reported that the man they had questioned as the intermediary between the kidnappers and the victim's family, Luis Plancarte, had identified Ramón Ascencio, the leader of Zamora's tiny but steadfast cohort of radical activists, as the man behind the crime. Ascencio, his wife, and five other suspects were arrested in short order. Ascencio was a provincial clerk-turned-shopkeeper with political aspirations, just the sort of petit-bourgeois Jacobin who would be most attracted to Governor Múgica's radical policies. He had risen through the ranks of the local Agrarian Party structure to become the most visible leader of Zamora's small contingent of self-described "revolutionary" political activists. And although Governor Múgica's fall from power dealt a severe blow to Ascencio's own political fortunes, he was not about to give up on his ambitions or his implacable opposition to the Zamora-area conservatives. Just one day before his arrest, for example, he had signed a letter from the Agrarian Party complaining to the federal government that the local authorities were turning a blind eye to the public protests against the expulsion of Monsignor Filippi.[10]

Ascencio's short but contentious political career had earned him the hatred of religious conservatives in Zamora. It is hard to define with precision just who these religious conservatives were, but people from all walks of life rejected the policies of state and federal governments that seemed to undermine the traditional values that allowed the Church to have a strong presence in public debates and that assumed that social relations were structured around strictly enforced class and gender hierarchies. In the idiom of postrevolutionary Michoacán these social conservatives were often coded as "Catholics," or sometimes by even more loaded terms such as "religious fanatics" or "counterrevolutionaries." In general, they opposed government policies that promoted unionization and land reform (and in this limited sense, class struggle). They were incensed at revolutionary policies that restricted the Church's role in education and politics and consolidated power in the hands of local politicians aligned with the revolutionary generals in Mexico City. They disliked the direction that the nation's public education system seemed to be taking—questioning the authority of the religious establishment, landowners, and in some cases even patriarchy itself.[11] In short, social conservatives despised everything that people like Ramón Ascencio stood for.

Ascencio and his associates languished in jail for half a year while the controversy over their case raged just outside their cell walls. Zamora's local newspaper published articles and townspeople wrote letters and declarations that blurred the lines between the putative motive behind the crime (i.e., the desire for ransom money) and the politics of those accused of committing it. Rather than portraying the tragedy as a kidnapping gone awry, the language of conservative Zamorans equated the murderer with revolutionary politics in general and agrarianism in particular. The local Church-affiliated press was particularly insistent on this point. In each article reporting on a new development in the case, the newspaper emphasized that Ascencio had been a leader of the Agrarian Party and therefore an enemy of religion and private property. The articles were interspersed with alarmist stories contemplating the possibility that Múgica would return to office and resuscitate his campaign of anticlericalism and land reform. As far as the newspaper was concerned, Ascencio's political leanings made him little more than a criminal—someone who attempted to break down the natural order of society. The narrative structure that *El Cruzado* and leading Catholic families devised was as seamless as it was circular: radicalism equals criminality, the most serious form of criminality is the murder of a child, therefore steadfast radicals must be to blame for the death of Roberto González.

Ascencio's friends and political allies tried to challenge the Catholics' version of events, but they found themselves at a serious disadvantage. On the one hand, the police began to collect incriminating evidence about him. On the other hand, Ascencio's supporters could not generate public support for their side. Their small numbers meant they had no newspaper to publicize their version of events, nor did they have any capacity to call public rallies on behalf of the accused. Instead, they turned to the federal government. Ascencio's friends wrote scores of letters—mostly to Plutarco Elías Calles, the powerful anti-Church Interior Secretary and likely successor to Obregón—insisting on his innocence and arguing that the local elite was making a scapegoat of him. If a scapegoat was what they were after, Ascencio's enemies were playing for keeps: this murder would probably draw the death penalty. Few if any pro-Ascencio protests made it into the public sphere, however, so no civic debate emerged about whether the police had arrested the right man.[12] Ascencio's allies probably hoped that Calles or some other public official would merely order the release of the prisoners.

The controversy over the boy's death and the arrest of Ramón Ascencio firmed up existing political identities and reconfigured local politics. Within days of Ascencio's arrest, protests fanned by *El Cruzado* and the city's elite families had established in most people's minds a version of events that portrayed Ascencio as an irreligious radical who would stoop to murder if it suited him. Before long, most people understood that anyone who believed Ascencio to be innocent was doubtlessly a supporter of the Agrarian Party's radical politics. The events of the two years preceding Roberto González's murder had shown that big changes were afoot as the revolutionary government claimed the right to redistribute land and enforce laws against the Church, but the child's death blurred the lines between the intimate world of the family and the dry terrain of revolutionary politics. Were the radicals really capable of murdering a child? Alternatively, were the Catholics really willing to frame an innocent man even if it meant he might eventually be executed for the crime? Whatever the answers, the death of Roberto González proved that politics in Zamora had gotten personal, and it was time for city dwellers to take sides.

The episode also casts into relief the limits of our historical knowledge and the inadvisability of allowing historians, who are always hungry for a good historical tale, to act as judges who would use a limited and possibly biased set of documents to pronounce the innocence or guilt of historical actors. It is worth remembering that a child really was kidnapped on January 28, 1923, and that someone brutally murdered him. We cannot know for sure whether Ramón Ascencio or someone else was to blame for the death. The available evidence was circumstantial or open to partisan interpretation—indeed it still is—and everyone personally involved in the matter has taken his or her secrets to the grave. Yet for many Zamorans at the time, and for at least one historian who has paused to consider the matter, Ascencio's guilt was a foregone conclusion.[13] We need not make such a leap of faith when considering how the people of Zamora *interpreted* Roberto González's death. Once the blame came to rest on

Ramón Ascencio, the meanings attached to Catholic mobilization in Zamora continued to expand from a relatively straightforward protest against threats to religious freedom, into a broader defense of family, community, and, by extension, Mexican nationhood itself.

Catholic Nationalism in Northwestern Michoacán

The Bajío region of western Mexico had a unique political culture, both in terms of its social makeup and its religious life. A zone of vast agricultural bounty, the Bajío had been home to profitable haciendas ever since the colonial period when mining centers such as Zacatecas and San Luis Potosí created a demand for food to sustain their workers.[14] By the nineteenth century, the Bajío was also home to large number of economically independent, small-time family farmers known as rancheros. Most of these people had arrived in the area either as field hands on the haciendas or as migrants from elsewhere in Mexico, and they had managed to purchase modest parcels from haciendas that were divided up for sale or from indigenous communities that had been forced to privatize their lands during the late 1800s. Regardless of how they had acquired their property, most rancheros regarded their land as their patrimony and a badge of their hard work and thrift.[15] Unsurprisingly, many of these people vehemently opposed the land reform through which the government nationalized portions of haciendas and turned them over to peasant communities beginning in 1917. Though some rancheros may have worried that they would lose their land to peasant communities, that does not seem to have been their chief concern (theoretically, small-holders' property was not subject to expropriation and redistribution). Rather, many rancheros felt it was morally reprehensible for the government to redistribute land—the very thing they had worked so hard to purchase and in which they took so much pride—free of cost to people of markedly indigenous descent. To them, the reallocation of hacienda lands to peasant communities was less an economic question than an affront to the honor they associated with landholding.[16]

The political culture of the Bajío was also based on a deep and well-established form of Catholic observance that had evolved in the area during the late colonial period and nineteenth century and involved a strong role for the Church. Rancheros typically supported this highly institutionalized form of Catholicism and had enough money to fund services and parishes in their own communities. Wealthy families often built chapels adjacent to the hacienda main house (*casco*) and employed priests to give sacraments to their households and fieldworkers. This situation encouraged a quasi-religious bond of dependency between landowners and the laborers who depended on them not only for wages, but for religious ministrations as well. The religious patronage of the wealthy allowed the Church to establish other religious institutions as well, including convents and, especially, seminaries and bishoprics.[17] By the 1920s, Michoacán boasted three sees: the archbishopric in Morelia, a newly established bishopric in Apatzingán, and a bishopric in Zamora that had been founded in 1864. Unlike most other parts of Mexico, the density of these religious institutions meant that the majority of priests posted in Michoacán and the Bajío were native sons (often members of wealthy families) who knew local customs and had relatives and friends nearby. Together, the Church's highly institutionalized character and close relations with the landed elite led it by the late nineteenth century to promote a strict religious observance and a peculiarly conservative social agenda that historian Jesús Tapia Santamaría has labeled "intransigent Catholicism": a strict and hierarchal form of religiosity that was antimodern, antirevolutionary, antiliberal, and antisocialist.[18]

A number of events in the early twentieth century underscored Zamora's distinctive ranchero society and Catholic political culture. In 1913, Zamora was selected to host the second national conference of Catholic leaders concerned with what was then called "the social question," that is, the growing presence (and, in some cases, the growing militancy) of the working class in the cities and the fields. Rather than proposing specific means to improve workers' material conditions, however, the participants recommended in characteristic form that workers and employers learn how to "harmonize" their class interests. Lay leaders eventually succeeded in founding a few dozen Catholic workers' cooperatives and peasants' credit unions throughout the region, though these institutions existed alongside more vocal and politically militant labor organizations.[19]

The city's singularly Catholic political culture once again manifested about seven years later, in 1921, during what proved to be controversial celebrations of the nation's independence. Whereas most parts of the nation had celebrated the national centennial in 1910 (the year Father Miguel Hidalgo made his call for independence from Spain), a number of upper-class youths who belonged to Zamora's chapter of the Association of Mexican Catholic Youth (Asociación Católica de la Juventud Mexicana, better known by its acronym, ACJM) built a modest monument to Agustín de Iturbide. While Iturbide was indeed responsible for consummating Mexican independence in 1821, he left behind a legacy of controversy and bitterness. After winning independence, he ruled Mexico for a year and a half and eventually agreed to take the title of emperor during a short and ill-fated experiment in constitutional monarchy. A rebellion forced him to abdicate and flee Mexico a mere eight months into his controversial reign. He was later declared a traitor and executed as he tried to reenter the country. The Catholic youths were nonetheless inspired by Iturbide's reputation as a staunch defender of the Church. They recognized that Iturbide's memory was "mocked and ignored" (*escarnecida*) in the rest of Mexico, but they nevertheless referred to him as the nation's true "liberator," regardless of what the rest of their countrymen thought.[20]

In such an atmosphere, the land reform that haltingly began in Michoacán in 1917 was bound to be controversial, bringing together as it did secular and religious opposition. In Michoacán, like most of central Mexico, the government carried out land reform by nationalizing private property—usually hacienda land—paying former owners some sort of indemnity, and turning their property over to rural communities. The Church in Zamora (like elsewhere) denounced this redistribution of land and labeled it theft. Bishops ordered their clergy to instruct rural folk not to receive property that the government had expropriated. Rancheros and large landowners often took a more direct approach to the challenge of land reform.[21] In the early 1920s, a number of Zamora-area landowners attempted to intimidate peasant communities that had written to Governor Múgica to solicit lands.

To discourage landless peasants from requesting land reform parcels, many Zamora-area landowners turned to one man in particular: Rafael Cuadra, a small-time landowner and self-declared paramilitary leader. Cuadra had commanded a community-organized civil guard (*defensa civil*) during the revolutionary decade of the 1910s, when bandits roamed throughout Michoacán. In the following decade, he developed a new specialty, strong-arming militant peasants who considered requesting a land reform parcel for their communities. Between 1921 and early 1923, Cuadra and his fifty-man militia assassinated no fewer than nine community leaders, and probably many more. He was accused of wanton displays of violence and raping the daughters and wives of peasant leaders. Most of his victims had spearheaded efforts to solicit land reform parcels carved from the holdings of nearby haciendas, but one victim was a left-leaning state legislator from a prominent family in the town of Sahuayo. His actions provoked the leaders of one peasant community to write to President Obregón and complain that they felt as if villages were "suffering abuses as bad as during the nefarious dictatorship" of Porfirio Díaz—the very man whose twenty-five-year rule had sparked the Revolution in the first place.[22]

Here, perhaps, we learn something about the origins of the firestorm that Roberto González's death provoked. For while no one in Zamora missed the Díaz dictatorship, a number of social groups had ambiguous attitudes toward the Revolution that removed him from power. Popular radicalism and rural militancy was relatively rare in Zamora before the land reform's glory days in the 1920s and 1930s, and most people in the area regarded "revolutionary" politics such as secular public education and the politics of class struggle with deep suspicion. Since land reform entailed breaking up hacienda lands and turning them over to peasant communities, it not only tarnished the pride that many Zamorans felt for having acquired private property, but it also hit them in the pocketbook as well. It is hardly surprising, then, that the city's Catholic newspaper denounced the sort of revolutionary radicalism favored by the new generation of national leaders that had taken power in Mexico City in 1920. For example, the newspaper published a response to a fiery 1921 congressional speech by the pro–land reform politician Antonio Díaz Soto y Gama denouncing "reactionaries," i.e., people like the Catholic political elite of Zamora. *El Cruzado* opined that attitudes such as Soto y Gama's

> constitute an insult and mockery [*escarnio*] of the Mexican people. After eleven years of tasting all the bitterness and suffering all the agonies, after a decade in which many women lost their honor; many men [lost] their property, sense of shame, dignity, and lives; in which the nation lost its domestic tranquility and international stature . . . in which the law [lost] its ability to provide remedy, and political leaders any sense of prestige . . . is there anyone in Mexico who will shout vivas for the Revolution?

Instead of exclaiming vivas for revolutionary change, the paper concluded that it would be better to cry, "Death to the Revolution!"[23]

By the early 1920s, then, Catholic nationalism was a fully formed worldview, or, more specifically, a form of political culture that understood religion as the central and defining characteristic of Mexican society. Rather than hew to the revolutionary line, the Catholics promoted the more "traditional" values of private property, individual and family honor, patriarchy, and the acceptance of the existing social structure as reflective of God's will. It rejected the materialism of liberalism *and* socialism and instead insisted on the primacy of religious faith. Catholic nationalists therefore felt little more than contempt for revolutionaries who understood the basis of Mexican nationhood in terms of a shared reverence for the Revolution and the social reforms enshrined in the 1917 constitution. Catholic nationalists likewise scoffed at revolutionary politicians' promises to "redeem" the poor and disenfranchised by using government programs. And Catholics found the revolutionaries' rhetorical support for class struggle particularly objectionable.²⁴ In short, there was little if any common ground between Zamora's tradition of Catholic nationalism and the newly forming ideology of postrevolutionary secularism propounded by revolutionary progressives such as Governor Múgica and his faithful supporter in Zamora, Ramón Ascencio.

Yet Zamorans got a taste of revolution whether they wanted it or not thanks to events such as land reform, the revolutionary generals' consolidation of power in Mexico City in 1920, and Múgica's arrival in Michoacán soon afterward. Indeed, the sort of postrevolutionary politics that emerged in Michoacán were a direct response to Catholic nationalism. Governor Múgica had grown up the son of a liberal schoolteacher who plied his trade in the conservative small towns of the Michoacán bajío. He had even attended the Catholic seminary in Zamora, which was the best secondary school in the region, though he was nearly expelled for refusing to attend theology classes. Múgica later said that his childhood, which was governed by the tolling of church bells, had inspired him to write some of the anticlerical provisions of Mexico's 1917 constitution.²⁵ Once in office, he wasted no time forging links with agrarian groups, speeding up the plodding agrarian reform, and arming peasant home guards. He also closed Catholic schools and dusted off reform-era laws banning religious processions in public. Invoking executive privilege, he replaced any municipal government whose politics he deemed "counterrevolutionary." Zamora's was among the first he dissolved.²⁶

Postrevolutionary Radicalism and the Politicization of Religion in Zamora

Múgica's supporters in the Zamora area were limited to a handful of peasant leaders, leftist politicians, and progressive journalists. Perhaps the largest single contingent was composed of white-collar professionals such as teachers, clerks, and shopkeepers inspired by the promises of social equality that began to circulate during the Revolution and, especially in Michoacán, in the 1920s.²⁷ Zamora's collection of "revolutionary" activists, as they called themselves, periodically joined together in short-lived political parties that rarely lasted more than a single electoral cycle. These parties' main function was to mobilize their followers to vote in elections whose turnout rarely broke a few hundred votes.²⁸ But while the number of people who actually voted in municipal elections was rather small, the outcomes mattered. Elections decided who would hold power in the township, of course, but more importantly they were an opportunity for local politicos to impress power holders at the state and federal levels with their organizational capacity, ability to turn out followers, and (if necessary) to influence the ballot counting. In the early 1920s, it looked as if the new generation of progressive, lower-middle-class professionals and their peasant allies might have gathered enough supporters to break the political monopoly that hacienda owners and conservative elite families had held in Zamora for decades.

Ramón Ascencio typified the petit bourgeois radicals who tended to support revolutionary politicians such as Múgica. The son of shopkeepers, he was a founding member of the Melchor Ocampo Liberal Club of Zamora, which was a part social club, part political party that promoted progressive political candidates in the area beginning in 1917. Soon afterward, he was tapped to administer a newly opened public hospital in the town of La Piedad.[29] He probably received this position as a reward for his services to the party, but a lack of funding soon forced the hospital to close. At that point, Ascencio followed the family tradition and opened a small grocery store in Zamora. Then, around the time Múgica was running for governor in 1920, he joined with the other leaders of the Melchor Ocampo Party who decided that a more fitting name for their organization would be the Agrarian (Agrarista) Party of Zamora. The Agrarian Party quickly emerged as the strongest core of organized Múgica partisans in Zamora, and Ascencio once again found that his political activism paid tangible benefits: in the early 1920s, when he was vice president of the party, he received the coveted post of police chief of Zamora. He also ran for election to the city council in 1922.[30]

It is not clear whether Ascencio won that election, but even if he did Múgica's resignation meant that he had no hope of actually occupying the office. Nevertheless, he and his associates in the Agrarian Party certainly kept a high political profile in Zamora. When hundreds of people packed the town's central square a few months later to protest President Obregón's expulsion of papal delegate Ernesto Filippi, it was the Agrarian Party that alerted the federal authorities of this breach of revolutionary orthodoxy. The protest against Filippi's expulsion took place on January 15, 1923, and had been organized by a quartet of lay Catholic organizations with the implicit approval of the town's mayor. Soon the square overflowed with representatives of the ACJM, the Knights of Columbus, and various Catholic women's and workers' groups. Chants of "Death to Obregón and to bad government!" filled the air. Church bells pealed as the various groups marched with banners and placards through nearby streets.[31] According to the letter that Agrarian Party leaders wrote to the federal attorney general, the church bells had pealed as Church leaders chanted their support for Christ the King and booed agrarianism and the federal government.[32] Army troops eventually arrived to break up the rally, though it is unclear whether they acted on the orders of their general or were contacted by the leaders of the Agrarian Party. Both the radicals and the Catholics claimed that there had been unprovoked acts of violence: according to the Agrarian Party, the protestors assaulted a policeman; according to the Catholic *El Cruzado*, the troops beat a group of "defenseless ladies," and it is hard to know what to believe. Regardless, the troops quickly forced the crowd to disperse. A few prominent Catholic leaders, including the editor of *El Cruzado*, were briefly detained.[33]

The rally was little more than a historical footnote, one of dozens of such protests around the nation in the wake of President Obregón's move to expel the papal delegate. But it is worth pausing to consider the language that the two opposing groups used to describe what the rally meant to them because their political discourse provides a clear window into the incommensurability of revolutionary and Catholic forms of nationalism. As we have already seen, the Catholics regarded the expulsion of Filippi and the repression of their protest against it as yet another instance in which postrevolutionary governments demonstrated an intention to curb religious expression, and they did not hesitate to recruit the discourse of liberalism to drive home their point. *El Cruzado*, for example, expressed its "indignation and protest" at the expulsion and argued that rallying against the government's move would help restore "justice, truth, and peace to our nation." The government, it said, makes laws that impinge on Mexicans' "just and legitimate rights . . . attacking the family (which is the touchstone of society), violating every liberty" from religious freedom to the right to assemble.[34] The Catholic press was clearly outraged by the expulsion, but the nature of the complaint ran deeper still. The expulsion of the papal delegate epitomized what the Catholics believed had gone wrong in Mexico since the Revolution: the growth of government power, the undermining of fundamental rights, and a seeming lack of respect for the traditional institutions of society such as the Church.

To local revolutionaries such as the petit-bourgeois members of the Agrarian Party, these Catholic attitudes smacked of religious fanaticism and subversion. Ramón Ascencio and his wife María Teresa Alvarado de Ascencio had apparently tried to stop the rally even before the soldiers arrived to disperse the crowd. Having failed, the leaders of the Agrarian Party decided to seek support from powerful allies outside Zamora. A few days after the rally, the leaders of the Agrarian Party wrote to Obregón to praise his decision to remove Filippi, "who blatantly defied the Constitution of the Country and used his apostolic appearance as a cover while he continually worked to undercut our laws." But the letter soon made clear that the radicals' ire was not aimed so much at Filippi as it was at the organizers of the antigovernment rally and the writers of

El Cruzado. "In light of all this," the Agrarian Party leaders wrote, "one need not be shrewd to understand that we are dealing with an organized campaign—or worse, a party—that is used to [receiving] blind obedience" from the faithful. It was bad enough, from the revolutionaries' perspective, that the conservatives had become politically organized, but, worse still, they subscribed "to the ridiculous [doctrine of] Papal infallibility."[35] Thus the radicals' anger was directed not only at the illegality of the Catholic's protest rally, but also at the ideals that that produced the rally in the first place—ideals that stood in opposition to the Revolution and its core values.

The rally in the town square and the two political groups' diametric responses to it showed just how deep the divide between Catholics and radicals had become in Zamora. This was not merely a disagreement about the specific question of whether the papal delegate should be deported; it was a clear demonstration that the two groups had fundamentally different understandings of Mexican nationhood. One envisioned a nation that was traditional, family-centric, Thomistic, and pious; the other, a nation of enlightened, class-conscious, revolutionary citizens. The first group included the town's clergy, most of its elite families, and a sizeable proportion of the populace. The second was composed of a modest number of individuals fed up with the status quo, many of whom had their own political aspirations. Conditions were ripe for a confrontation of some sort, though it seems unlikely that anyone could have predicted what form it would take. Two weeks after the protest rally, Roberto González went missing. His lifeless body was found in the river a few days later, and Ramón Ascencio was charged with his murder shortly thereafter. Clearly, the stakes had gone up.

The Case against Ramón Ascencio

The local authorities had only one firm lead in the case. The kidnappers had allegedly recruited Luis Plancarte, the former congressman who was the first to be arrested, as an intermediary to pass on their demands for cash to the boy's father. Plancarte was by no means an unknown quantity in Zamora. He was one of the founders of the town's thinly disguised Catholic political party, the Partido Independiente de Zamora, which was the most influential organization in local politics. It not only represented the political will of most Zamorans but also had led the local opposition to Múgica's government as well.[36] Several people recognized Plancarte as one of the organizers of the rally protesting Filippi's expulsion. Plancarte came forward soon after the boy's body was discovered and within a matter of days identified Ramón Ascencio as the leader of a ring of kidnappers. The police briefly detained him for questioning, at which point Plancarte claimed that he had reluctantly acted as the intermediary between Ascencio and the boy's father in hope of avoiding any bloodshed. He said that he had arranged for the payment of a fifty-thousand-peso ransom but that the deal fell through for reasons that were never specified. Ascencio, he said, must have murdered the child in a rage.[37]

A picket of soldiers arrested Ascencio and his wife María Teresa at their home on January 28. The two were blindfolded and taken to the army headquarters the following day. They were met there by the mayor of Zamora, an army corporal, and General Francisco Belmar, the commandant of the federal army in the area. According to one of the Ascencios' supporters, the general began his interrogation by taunting the suspects, saying, "You have ignored the law, now let's see if you ignore me . . . Tell me the truth, you bandits, or I'll bury you alive." Both prisoners denied any involvement in the kidnapping, at which point the general allegedly ordered Ramón Ascencio tortured. Ascencio lost consciousness without confessing and later awoke in jail.[38] Arrests of other alleged accomplices came within the next few days; all those arrested were friends and family of the accused. Charges were filed against Miguel Cervantes (Ascencio's nephew), Ladislao Alvarado (María Teresa Alvarado de Ascencio's brother), and three other associates. At one point the police also detained the president of the Agrarian Party on the grounds that he could have been an accessory to the crime as well.[39]

Evidence quickly mounted against Ramón Ascencio and his alleged accomplices. We have already seen that Plancarte, who said he had served as the courier between the dead boy's father and the kidnappers, made the first and most damning accusation against Ascencio. Prosecutors soon reported that Plancarte had produced a ransom note that he said Ascencio had given him. "Eudoro [the boy's father]," the note read, "send fifty thousand pesos in gold, which is the price of your son. Send it with the ex-congressman Luis Plancarte, whom we need to see, and tell the courier not to worry about watching his back if he knows what's good for him . . . you have fifteen days to send the money to mexico city [sic]—[signed] Ascención Ramírez." Moreover, the Zamora police, along with the special team of investigators dispatched by President Obregón, searched the Ascencio residence and found one of the boy's textbooks, a sack that could have been used to take the body to the river, and evidence of blood on the house's floor tiles. The police also reported that they had learned (though it is not clear how) that Conrada Álvarez, one of the Ascencio's neighbors, had brought the boy meals while he was held captive.[40] Finally, Ramón Reyes, one of Ascencio's own relatives, testified that Ascencio had organized the kidnapping.[41]

There were a number of troubling details in this seemingly clear-cut case, and nearly every piece of evidence can be read in more than one way. The physical evidence found at the Ascencio household is a prime example. It turns out that the detachment of police who found Roberto González's schoolbook, the purported body bag, and other evidence at the Ascencio household was not the first set of officials to search the home. The first detachment of police had failed to find anything incriminating. According to a lawsuit filed by Ramón and María Teresa Ascencio's daughter (who was hardly a disinterested party in the proceedings), General Belmar and a picket of soldiers had previously searched the house in early February but did not report finding any useful evidence. Her suit alleged that a police officer named Rafael Mora was "in the pay of [her father's] political enemies" and had planted the evidence when the second detachment arrived at the home a few days after the original police search.[42]

If the police intended to frame Ascencio and his associates, why did they not simply plant the evidence the first time? The one clear thing is that the municipal authorities had replaced the lead investigator in the case between the first and second searches. Specifically, they had removed the prosecutor (*agente del ministerio público*) who ordered the first fruitless search of the house and replaced him with the man who had ordered the second search. According to Ascencio's supporters, the new prosecutor intended to see Ascencio hang whether or not he was guilty. The original prosecutor, José María Pérez, also regarded his dismissal as part of a conspiracy, and he wrote the governor to charge that the Zamora political elite had become frustrated with him because he intended to make a full and impartial examination of the facts rather than rushing to convict Ascencio. He complained that the "local bourgeoisie" and "the privileged classes" of Zamora had tried to impede his investigation by refusing to let him interrogate Ascencio or have access to the alleged witnesses to the kidnapping. He also charged that the local elite was motivated by the desire to have Plancarte, the former congressman who had served as the kidnappers' messenger, cleared of any charges and released as quickly as possible. In all, he said that the upper classes of Zamora wanted "to see Ascencio dead." He claimed that the real issue was that many of the people closest to the investigation—the judge who had jurisdiction in the case, the chief inspector and prosecutor, Plancarte, and the dead boy's father—were all members of the local elite and belonged to the local chapter of the Knights of Columbus. They intended to look out for each other, Pérez said, and Ascencio happened to present a superb scapegoat.[43] Indeed, Ascencio's supporters raised the vexing possibility that Plancarte had accused Ascencio as an act of political retribution and that the police planted evidence in the house to substantiate the ex-congressman's claims.[44]

Questions surrounded other elements of the case against Ascencio. For example, why did Plancarte wait more than a week before accusing Ascencio of the crime? Indeed, why did he not alert the police while the boy was still alive? Likewise, some of the eyewitness accounts are troubling as well. Ascencio impugned the testimony of Ramón Reyes, his kinsman who accused him of masterminding the crime. While in jail, Ascencio wrote a public protest that questioned this evidence, alleging that the police had plied Reyes with alcohol and then set him before a firing squad, threatening to shoot him unless he implicated Ascencio in the crime. The documents do not contain a transcript of Reyes's allegations, nor do they allow us to see how this potentially damning evidence played into the prosecution's case. Nevertheless, it *is* clear that the police later turned on Reyes and charged him as an accomplice to the crime.[45] Even the ransom note raises questions. The archival documents do not contain the original note; all we have is a transcription in an evidentiary file, and it states that the note was signed by someone with the last name "Ascención," not "Ascencio." Clearly, Ramón Ascencio would not have misspelled his own name, but it is hard to know what to make of the spelling error. It could be a mistaken transcription, of course, but it could also be a *faithful* transcription of a sloppily forged ransom note. We have no way of knowing for sure.

Even if it appears possible that the conservative political families of Zamora could have framed Ramón Ascencio for the kidnapping and murder, is it plausible that they would have done so? Why would they have singled him out for such a punishment? We have already seen that Ascencio had made himself quite unpopular as the town's police chief during the controversial governorship of Francisco Múgica, and that his membership in the Agrarian Party and status as one of the area's most visible anticlerical militants had earned him the wrath of townsfolk of all social classes. But there was something else. According to one of Ascencio's most ideologically motivated and unflinching advocates, a personal rift had opened between Ascencio and the dead boy's father when Ascencio had run for city council in 1922. After the Agrarian Party declared victory in the election, Eudoro González organized and armed a paramilitary band (what the agrarians called a *guardia blanca*) that dislodged Ascencio and his fellow councilmen and ran them out of town.[46] This was the same paramilitary outfit that the pistolero Rafael Cuadra commanded and that had been intimidating and killing the leaders of land reform movements in villages around Zamora since 1921. According to Ascencio's supporter, the landowners used Cuadra's militia to terrorize villagers throughout the area. "The virgin fields grew purple with the blood of those who labor in the fields [*los proletariados del campo*]" as Cuadra's men killed the agrarian leaders of village after village.⁴⁷ Thus, Ascencio and Eudoro González had had a personal rivalry even before the child went missing.

A number of Ascencio's supporters suggested that the landowner González hated the accused so much that he used his son's death as an occasion to frame him. The real culprit, according to this version of events, was González's own henchman, Rafael Cuadra. Ascencio's supporters said that the pistolero was angry because González had not paid enough for his services, so he decided to kidnap the boy and demand a ransom to recoup what he felt he was owed.⁴⁸ While this version of events does not fully explain why Cuadra would kill the child, it does appear true that González had paid Cuadra's bail when the pistolero ran afoul of federal authorities soon before the kidnapping came to light.⁴⁹ One of Ascencio's friends even said that he had spoken with a maid who allegedly saw Roberto González held prisoner at Cuadra's house—not Ascencio's.⁵⁰ Once again, however, we cannot know how seriously to take the accusation that Cuadra killed the boy because the police never followed up on it. On the other hand, it is clear that at least some people in Zamora found the allegations of Cuadra's involvement plausible, so much so that *El Cruzado* elected to publish an article dismissing them and pointing out that, despite these allegations, "everyone knows" that Cuadra was in the United States at the time of the murders.⁵¹

While the debate over Ascencio's guilt played out in handbills, newspapers, and letters to national leaders, the accused kidnappers languished in jail under unusually harsh conditions. The authorities held each of the accused in solitary confinement and refused to allow them contact with the outside world, supposedly to contain the outbreak of a contagious illness in the prison.⁵² At one point, Lázaro Cárdenas, the chief of military operations in Michoacán and young future president, complained that drunken soldiers had entered the jail without his permission and threatened to kill the agrarian leaders imprisoned there.⁵³ And according to a handbill published by friends of the Ascencio family, authorities allowed the dead boy's father to torture Ascencio by binding his wrists and beating him in an attempt to wring out a confession.⁵⁴ If he made one, it does not survive in the archives.

During the summer of 1923, Judge Ramón Duarte sentenced Ascencio and two of his fellows (Hector Duarte and Miguel Cervantes) to death. María Teresa Ascencio and two others received jail terms of between ten and twenty years. Once again, Ascencio's colleagues in the local and national agrarian parties sprang into action, filing requests for restraining orders (*amparos*) that would keep the government from carrying out the sentence.⁵⁵ Ascencio and his companions were still in jail in early 1924, when national events once again impinged on their lives, bringing the entire episode to an unanticipated end.

In December 1923, Adolfo de la Huerta and more than half the nation's army revolted against the federal government. The rebellion was far from an ideological movement, but its leader in western Mexico had a very clear political agenda. General Enrique Estrada was a dogmatic and conservative general known for his dislike of the agrarian movement and especially the middle-class politicians who supported it. In January 1924 General Estrada's troops entered Zamora, where Ramón Ascencio and his associates remained in the municipal jail waiting for a response to their appeals. A picket of Estrada's men commanded by none other than the former pistolero Rafael Cuadra—who now claimed the rank of captain—decided to hurry the punishment along, apparently after having received a payment from Eudoro González and the go-ahead from municipal authorities. The rebel soldiers hauled Ramón and María Teresa Ascencio and three of their alleged coconspirators out of the jailhouse and executed them. They then dragged their corpses to the Zamora-Jacona roadway and hung them in the trees along the boulevard. The bodies remained in public view for a full week.[56]

Conclusion: Memory and the Indeterminacy of History

Carlo Ginzburg, the renowned Italian intellectual, has observed that both judges and historians rely on historical evidence to reach a determination about events that took place in the past, but whereas historians seek to reconstruct historical context in great complexity, judges would be ill-advised to do so. If a judge were to take the broadest historical view of the social and political context in which a particular crime occurred, this approach could easily lead to the conclusion that specific individuals were not ultimately accountable for the way any particular event transpired. Therefore, judges shy away from the broad context and focus instead on the specific facts related to particular cases.[57] By the same token, we would be ill-advised to act as judges in the case of Roberto González because we simply cannot know who killed him. The historical evidence is ambiguous, and no one alive today has the firsthand knowledge that would allow us to reach a definitive conclusion.

On the other hand, two facts about Roberto González's death are beyond dispute and tell us volumes about the context of postrevolutionary Zamora. First, the boy's tragic death and the deaths that followed it demonstrate the high stakes involved in postrevolutionary politics, particularly where agrarianism and anticlericalism intersected. Clearly, western Mexican society had become so fully polarized by the mid-1920s that it was at least plausible (and perhaps justified) to believe that one political leader would kill the son of another, or that one leader would frame the other for a crime whose penalty was death. Massive social upheaval could not be far off at such a juncture, and indeed it was just around the corner. Second, the deaths quickly took on immense significance for both Catholics and revolutionaries. Each side of the dispute soon memorialized their dead—whether Roberto González or the slain proagrarian politicians led by Ramón Ascencio—and depicted them as martyrs of their respective causes. In other words, while we cannot assign responsibility for the kidnapping that set these events in motion, we can be certain that they became highly freighted with political meaning.

Within a few weeks of Roberto González's kidnapping and death, the social and historical context seemed to outweigh the actual facts of the case in the minds of just about everyone involved. The socially conservative populace of Zamora and the city's Catholic newspaper apparently had no doubt that Ramón Ascencio had kidnapped and killed the child in a cowardly act of retribution against the boy's father. Amid the controversy, a group of three hundred Zamoran townspeople decided to write to the president of Mexico arguing that the facts in the case were clear, that Ascencio had killed the boy and that his supporters only wanted to paint Zamora as a community of religious zealots. "For some time now," the letter stated,

> Zamora has been vilified and ridiculed, though it is a city that has always respected the law and government authority, regardless of what those politically motivated individuals say when they insult Zamorans, trying to make [us] appear as rebels, enemies of order, and hoards of criminals ready to commit a crime at any moment. It's time to put an end to the revolting actions born out of the perfidy and hatred of those, like Ascencio, who have used political principles as pretexts for the commission of crimes that alarm and horrify people throughout the Republic. Ascencio only participated in politics so that he could avoid punishment for his crimes.[58]

In other words, the letter writers identified Ascencio's alleged murder of the boy as a logical extension of his politics. The meaning of the child's death was in this sense made interchangeable with Ascencio's radical ideology. Ascencio and people like him posed a threat to "Mexicans throughout the Republic" not only because of their criminality, but also because of their political ideology.

Ascencio's supporters were equally adamant in arguing that Ascencio was the victim of a political witch hunt that Zamora's conservative political elite had mounted against agrarian leaders and anyone who had supported Governor

Múgica's administration. These claims gained even more strength once Ascencio and his family had perished at the hands of troops commanded by the most reactionary general of the de la Huerta revolt. Like the townspeople who gathered to denounce Ascencio, a group of pro–land reform peasants who called themselves "members of the working class" sent a collective letter expressing what they regarded as the incontrovertible facts surrounding the affair. They wrote that the deaths of Ascencio and his associates were only the latest actions by Zamoran conservatives. "For some time," the villagers wrote, they had

> suffered the injustices and cruel whims of the great landowners, the Knights of Columbus, and members of the ACJM, or to put it another way the religious fanatics of this place, even though we have never committed any crime other than belonging to the Agrarian Party of Zamora. For this, they (our victimizers) call us Bolsheviks, meaning to say that we are a bunch of heretics and excommunicates. The reactionaries win nearly every election thanks to the shameful tools they have at their disposal, such as the use of money, threats that hacienda owners make to their sharecroppers and employees, the collusion of municipal authorities, and the refusal to give voting credentials to campesinos and small farmers.[59]

This letter differed from the one the townspeople sent in nearly every way but one: it insisted that the murder of specific individuals (in this case, Ascencio and others) was merely one more manifestation of a larger dynamic of political repression and physical intimidation. To the writers of this letter, the deaths of the agrarian leaders merely confirmed that conservative Catholic elites would wage their political war by any means at their disposal; like the townspeople's letter, this one equated their enemies' politics with murder.

If we want to understand the meaning of the Roberto González affair—for this is the best we can do given that we cannot know for certain who was responsible for the boy's death—we must understand it in the historical context of a region divided between social conservatives and self-declared revolutionaries. But as these groups' own letters demonstrate, the death of Roberto González does more than merely reflect these social cleavages; it helped *define* the political context of postrevolutionary Zamora. To the majority of Zamorans, the boy's tragic death heightened the sense that political leaders such as Ascencio (and Múgica) were trying to install a murderous government that literally destroyed respectable families. This sense of besiegement seems to have helped the conservatives of Zamora think of themselves as a well-defined social group distinguished by both a history of oppression and an increasingly clear collective political identity. By the same token, agrarians and others sympathetic to Ascencio's cause saw the charges against their leader as politically motivated and yet another reason to believe they lived in the shadow of an unreformed Catholic Church working in league with ferocious landowners. In light of the intense public debate the murders of Roberto González and Ramón Ascencio provoked, it appears that the controversy not only reflected the existing political rift between these groups but also provided a particularly haunting metaphor for the nature of their differences.

Not quite three years after the death of Roberto González, western Mexico became engulfed in the Cristero rebellion, one of the most violent and intractable popular uprisings in the nation's history. The rebellion pitted the federal government and the agrarians against conservative middle-class groups and Catholic peasants.[60] It is no coincidence that the rebellion burned brightest in the Bajío, where Zamora is located, nor that it involved the same social groups that squared off over the murder of Roberto González. After all, responses to the deaths had shaped how the social groups involved defined themselves and their enemies, and each side believed that innocent blood had already been spilled in the contest between revolution and religion.

Notes

1. *El Cruzado*, 1 February 1923.
2. Report of Presidente Municipal de Tangancícuaro, 30 January 1923, and of Serafín Hernández, 13 February 1923, both in Archivo Municipal de Zamora, Ramo de Justicia (hereafter cited as AMZ-J), 1923, exp. 15.
3. For discussions see, Christopher R. Boyer, *Becoming Campesinos: Politics, Identity, and Agrarian Struggle in Postrevolutionary Michoacán, 1920–1935* (Stanford: Stanford University Press, 2003), 80–113; and Martín Sánchez Rodríguez, *Grupos de poder y centralización política en México. El Caso Michoacán 1920–1924* (Mexico City: Instituto Nacional de Estudios Históricos de la Revolución Mexicana, 1994).
4. *El Cruzado*, 15 January 1923 (extra edition).
5. Jean Meyer, *La Cristiada*, 3 vols. (Mexico City: Siglo Veintiuno, 1973–1974), 2:123–28; 2:143–66.
6. Ministro de Gobernación Morelia to Presidente Municipal de Zamora, 16 January 1923, Archivo Municipal de Zamora, Ramo de Gobierno (hereafter cited as AMZ-G), 1923, exp. 11.
7. Transcript of message of 10 February 1923, contained in Sánchez Pineda to Secreatría de Gobernación Morelia, Archivo General de la Nación, Ramo Dirección General de Gobierno (hereafter cited as AGN-DGG) D.2.71–143.

8. Report of Presidente Municipal de Zamora, 2 February 1923 [*sic*: should read 20 February] AMZ-J, 1923, exp. 15.
9. *El Cruzado*, 18 February 1923.
10. José Gutiérrez Zamora, et al. to Secretario de Gobernación, 27 January 1923, AGN-DGG D.2.51–20.
11. For more on the Sonoran Dynasty, see Jean Meyer, et al., eds., *Estado y sociedad con Calles*, 2nd ed., vol. 11, *Historia de la revolución mexicana* (Mexico City: El Colegio de México, 1977); and Lorenzo Meyer, et al., eds., *Los inicios de la institucionalización. La política del maximato*, vol. 12, *Historia de la revolución mexicana* (Mexico City: El Colegio de México, 1978).
12. On the public sphere, see Jürgen Habermas, *The Structural Transformation of the Public Sphere: An Inquiry into a Category of Bourgeois Society*, trans. Thomas Burger (Cambridge, MA: The MIT Press, 1989).
13. Marjorie Becker, "When I Was a Child, I Danced as a Child, but Now That I Am Old, I Think about Salvation: Concepción González and a Past That Would Not Stay Put," *Rethinking History* 1, no. 3 (Winter 1997): 349.
14. On the economic history of the Bajío, see D. A. Brading, *Haciendas and Ranchos in the Mexican Bajío: León, 1700–1860* (Cambridge: Cambridge University Press, 1978); and Eric Van Young, *Hacienda and Market in Eighteenth-Century Mexico: The Rural Economy of the Guadalajara Region, 1675–1820* (Berkeley: University of California Press, 1981).
15. The history of ranchero landholding is complex, so my description here is necessarily attenuated. For extended discussions, see Héctor Díaz Polanco, *La burguesía agraria de México: Un estudio de caso en El Bajío* (Mexico City: El Colegio de México, 1977); Luis González y González, *Pueblo en vilo* (Mexico City: El Colegio de México, 1968); and Frans J. Schryer, *The Rancheros of Pisaflores: The History of a Peasant Bourgeoisie in Twentieth-Century Mexico* (Toronto: University of Toronto Press, 1980).
16. For an analogous case in Chihuahua, see Ana María Alonso, *Thread of Blood: Colonialism, Revolution, and Gender on Mexico's Northern Frontier* (Tucson: University of Arizona Press, 1995).
17. Jesús Tapia Santamaría, *Campo religioso y evolución política en el Bajío zamorano* (Zamora: El Colegio de Michoacán, 1986), especially chapter 2. Also see Jennie Purnell, *Popular Movements and State Formation in Revolutionary Mexico: The Agraristas and Cristeros of Michoacán* (Durham, NC: Duke University Press, 1999), 19–24.
18. Tapia Santamaría, *Campo religioso*, 137–40. Also see Marjorie Becker, *Setting the Virgin on Fire: Lázaro Cárdenas, Michoacán Peasants, and the Redemption of the Mexican Revolution* (Berkeley: University of California Press, 1995), 10–38. For a discussion of religiosity in eastern Michoacán, see Matthew Butler, *Popular Piety and Political Identity in Mexico's Cristero Rebellion: Michoacán, 1927–1929* (London: The British Academy, 2004), 105–45.
19. *Memoria de la Segunda Gran Dieta de la Confederación Nacional de los Círculos Católicos De Obreros, Reunido en Zamora 19–23 enero de 1913* (Zamora: Tipografía

de la Escuela de Artes, 1913), 10. For a fuller discussion of these Catholic unions in Michoacán, see Boyer, *Becoming Campesinos*, 164–65.

20. Rafael Ruiz to Miguel Palomar y Vizcarra, 1 October 1920, Fondo Miguel Palomar y Vizcarra of the Archivo Histórico de la Universidad Nacional Autónoma de México—Centro de Estudios Sobre la Universidad (Mexico City), caja 3, exp. 20, doc. 1482.
21. On the attitude of the Zamora dioceses, see José Othón Núñez y Zárate, "Instrucción Pastoral," *Revista Eclesiástica de la Diócesis de Zamora* (November 1921): 17–28.
22. Comunidad Agraria de Tanaquillo to Álvaro Obregón, 21 April 1922, by way of the Casa del Obrero Mundial in Zamora, AGN-DGG C.2.71-88. For information on Cuadra's actions generally, see several other documents in that file as well as Francisco Tamayo to Plutarco Elías Calles, 21 May 1922, AGN-DGG B.2.73-38.
23. *El Cruzado*, 31 July 1921.
24. See Héctor Aguilar Camín, "La invención de México: Notas sobre nacionalismo e identidad nacional," in *Subversiones Silenciosas: Ensayos sobre historia y política de México*, ed. Aguilar Camín (Mexico City: Siglo Veintiuno, 1993); Alan Knight, "Revolutionary Project, Recalcitrant People: Mexico, 1910–1940," in *The Revolutionary Process in Mexico: Essays on Political and Social Change*, ed. Jaime E. Rodríguez O. (Los Angeles: UCLA Latin American Center Publications, 1990); Mary Kay Vaughan, *Cultural Politics in Revolution: Teachers, Peasants, and Schools in Mexico, 1930–1940* (Tucson: University of Arizona Press, 1997), chapter 1; and Gloria Villegas Moreno, "La militancia de la 'Clase Media Intelectual' en la Revolución Mexicana," in *Los intelectuales y el poder en México*, ed. Roderic A. Camp, Charles A. Hale, and Josefina Zoraida Vázquez (Los Angeles: UCLA Latin American Center Publications, 1991).
25. On Múgica's youth, see Armando de María y Campos, *Múgica, crónica biográfica* (Mexico City: Compañía de Ediciones Populares, 1939), 12–16.
26. On the removal of the Catholic council in 1920, see various documents in AMZ-G, 1920, caja 3, exp. 1.
27. On Múgica's supporters, see Martín Sánchez Rodríguez, *Grupos de Poder*, chapter 2.
28. See, for example, the discussion of parties and voting in the file on Múgica's government in Fideicomiso Archivos Plutarco Elías Calles y Fernando Torreblanca, Ramo Calles (Mexico City), gaveta 46, exp. 119. Also see Martín Sánchez Rodríguez, "Los Partidos de la Revolución en Michoacán" (unpublished paper, El Colegio de Michoacán, 1992).
29. Francisco Campos to Miguel Calderón, 8 March 1923, AGN-DGG D.2.71-143.
30. See various documents in AMZ-G, 1922, caja 5, exp. 17.
31. A handbill titled "Iniciativa" dated 15 January 1923 states that the Catholic institutions included the Asociación de Damas Católicas, Caballeros Colón, ACJM, and Unión Católica Obrera; see AMZ-G, 1923, caja 6, exp. 11; report from Procurador General de la República, 26 January 1923, transcribing a message from the Agente del Ministerio Público Federal en Zamora, AGN-DGG D.2.51-20.

32. Letter from Partido Agrarista Zamorano (signed pres. Felipe Campos and Srio Daniel Suárez), 19 January 1923, AGN-DGG D.2.51–20.
33. Telegram from Presidente Municipal de Zamora, 23 January 1923, AMZ-G, 1923, caja 6, exp. 11; *El Cruzado*, 15 January 1923 (extra edition).
34. *El Cruzado*, 15 January 1923 (extra edition). For another example Catholics borrowing the discourse of liberalism, see Matthew Butler, "The 'Liberal' *Cristero*: Ladislao Molina and the *Cristero* Rebellion in Michoacán, 1927–1929," *Journal of Latin American Studies* 31 (December 1999): 645–71.
35. Report of Partido Agrarista Zamorano, 19 January 1923, AGN-DGG D.2.51–20.
36. See the registration documents of the Partido Electoral Independiente in AMZ-G, 1922, exp. 28.
37. Report of Sidronio Sánchez Pineda, 13 April 1923, AGN-DGG D.2.71–143.
38. Francisco Campos to Miguel Calderón, 8 March 1923, AGN-DGG D.2.71–143.
39. Information on relationships among the accused is found in a letter from Ramón Ascencio, Daniel Suárez, Francisco Herrera (written by Suárez) for the following, who could not sign their names: Ladislao Alvarado, Miguel Cervantes, María Teresa Alvarado de Ascencio, and Conrada Álvarez, (Zamora) 16 April 1923, AGN-DGG D.2.51–20; and "Protesta" from Ramón Ascencio and Francisco Herrera, 20 March 1923, AGN-DGG D.2.71–143. This *protesta* (protest) may have been published and circulated.
40. Report of Presidente Municipal de Zamora, 2 March 1923, AMZ-J, 1923, caja 15.
41. "Protesta" from Ramón Ascencio and Francisco Herrera, 20 March 1923, AGN-DGG D.2.71–143.
42. Letter from Juez A. Vinancal to Presidente Municipal de Zamora, 26 February 1923, AMZ-J, 1923, exp. 15.
43. Report of Licenciado José M. Pérez, 28 February 1923, AGN-DGG D.2.71–143.
44. Francisco Campos to Miguel Calderón, 8 March 1923, AGN-DGG D.2.71–143.
45. "Protesta" from Ramón Ascencio and Francisco Herrera, 20 March 1923, AGN-DGG D.2.71–143.
46. The label *guardia blanca* or "white guard" was and still is tendentious. The term was understood to refer to squads of armed hacienda or industrial employees whose main job was to intimidate or kill agrarians, union leaders, and all other enemies of landowners and business interests.
47. Vicente Cano to Plutarco Elías Calles, 5 May 1923, AGN-DGG D.2.71–143.
48. Ibid.
49. Collective letter from approximately three hundred people in Zamora signed by Ramón Chávez, et al., 18 May 1923, AGN-DGG D.2.71–143.
50. Francisco Campos to Miguel Calderón, 8 March 1923, AGN-DGG D.2.71–143.
51. *El Cruzado*, 20 May 1923.
52. Undated writ filed by José Trinidad Carrión, ca. April 1923, AMZ-J, caja 1923, exp. 15.
53. Letter of Jefe de Operaciones Militares de Michoacán Lázaro Cárdenas to Presidente Municipal de Zamora, 30 August 1923, AMZ-J, caja 1923, exp. 15.
54. "Protesta" from Ramón Ascencio and Francisco Herrera, 20 March 1923, AGN-DGG D.2.71–143.

55. Vicente Cano to Comité Permanente of Congreso Nacional Agrarista, 4 October 1923, AGN-DGG D.2.71–143.
56. Vicente Cano to Plutarco Elías Calles, 23 January 1924, AGN-DGG D.2.71–143.
57. Carlo Ginzburg, *The Judge and the Historian*, trans. Antony Shugaar (London: Verso, 1999), 110–19.
58. Collective letter from approximately three hundred people in Zamora signed by Ramón Chávez, et al., 18 May 1923, AGN-DGG D.2.71–143.
59. Letter from Vecinos de Zamora [perhaps written by President of the Partido Agrarista Franco Campos and/or General Secretary A. Mendizábal] to President Álvaro Obregón, 1 March 1924, AGN-DGG D.2.71–143.
60. On the *cristiada*, see Meyer, *La Cristiada*; and on Michoacán specifically, see Boyer, *Becoming Campesinos*, chapter 5; Butler, *Popular Piety*; and Purnell, *Popular Movements*.

CHAPTER SIX

Of Intersections and Parallel Lives
José de León Toral and David Alfaro Siqueiros

Renato González Mello

In memory of Lorenzo Luna

José de León Toral, the devout Catholic who assassinated president-elect Álvaro Obregón in 1928, would seem to have nothing at all in common with David Alfaro Siqueiros, the militant communist, muralist for the postrevolutionary state, and quintessential figure of the Mexican artistic vanguard, yet they led parallel lives. Both were students at the National School for the Arts: Siqueiros studied there until 1915; Toral from the mid-1920s until the assassination. Both studied with the same art professor, Germán Gedovius. Along with being a militant in the Partido Comunista Mexicano (PCM) during the 1920s, Siqueiros was a sports fanatic, and he frequently photographed himself, exhibiting what in his view must have appeared as an impressive physique. Toral, an activist in the Asociación Católica de la Juventud Mexicana (Association of Mexican Catholic Youth, ACJM), was a sportsman, perhaps a "fanatic" as well, at least judging from a drawing he made of a friend from the ACJM, also executed by the government, dressed in a soccer uniform, standing on a column and holding up the palm leaf of martyrdom.

Toral and Siqueiros also committed parallel crimes. After drawing another portrait, this time of General Obregón, Toral fatally shot him in the face with a pistol. When it came to political murders, Siqueiros was a serial offender. According to his own testimony, the painter was accused of plotting to assassinate recently "elected" president Pascual Ortiz Rubio in 1930 (the circumstances of this incident are hazy at best, and Siqueiros's participation is doubted); he joined in a failed assassination attempt on exiled Soviet leader Leon Trotsky, who was living in Mexico City; and he was involved in the summary execution of Spanish republicans who were pacifists or deserters during the Spanish Civil War.[1] (He also painted, with no apparent sense of irony, a few canvases denouncing the practice of summary execution.) And both men shared a certain delusional faith in the efficacy of political violence. Siqueiros attempted to kill Trotsky because he believed—in a counterintuitive Stalinist way—that his intended victim had instigated the betrayal of Trotskyites in Catalonia. Toral was firmly convinced that killing Obregón would alleviate the persecution of Mexican Catholics by the revolutionary state.

There were even parallels in their experiences with the criminal justice system, although the end results were quite different. Siqueiros went to jail various times because of his political actions but his fame protected him from more serious punishments. Toral, however, was convicted and executed soon after he assassinated Obregón. Both men would make important declarations during their trial proceedings. Moreover, while in prison, they both drew and painted images that dealt with the themes of incarceration and pain. Siqueiros survived the experience and went on to produce great canvases and murals that can only be understood in relation to his experience of violence and confinement.

This close study of the visual works produced by Siqueiros and Toral explores the rhetoric of violence, personal responsibility, and punishment in their parallel lives. First, I analyze the oral and written evidence, both formal and informal, that relates to their imprisonment: the allegations made in court, as well as the written records of their interrogations and daily conversations. Second, I examine the drawings and paintings of Siqueiros and Toral. This analysis aims to confront the traditional approach of humanism, which seeks to transform the human body into the codex of all harmonies, with other, simpler ideas about hygienic regeneration and fortification of personality through sport. In particular, I pay special attention to the practice of sport that both men learned in school as pupils of *los maristas*, priests from the Society of Mary.

This chapter does not attempt to reveal hidden truths about the facts, nor does it ignore the irreducible differences between Toral and Siqueiros. Quite the contrary. Although both men were zealots, as Communists and Catholics they were on opposite sides of the important political struggles of the day. For Toral in particular, the most significant of those struggles was religious. Between 1926 and 1929, various regions of Mexico participated in a series of Catholic insurrections against the postrevolutionary governments of President Plutarco Elías Calles and his successors, insurrections known collectively as the Cristero rebellion or *cristiada*. The cristiada was an undeniably important political and social movement, but its cultural relevance has barely been studied even though its best known historian, Jean Meyer, has noted that without the cristiada "there would be no socialist education, with its civil, pantheistic, and archaeological liturgies."[2] Like most religious confrontations of the modern era, this one had long-lasting consequences: it reinvigorated the notion of the liberal elite that had been undermined by the Revolution, renovated the symbolic role of the state, obligated the professionalization of the army, and forced the government to develop a subtle blend of repression and cooptation as its principal mechanism of social control. Each consequence was equally important. The agents of the state realized they could not buy out or repress all intellectuals but instead needed to bring them into a symbolic regime that incorporated, for the benefit of hegemonic consensus, all symbolic constructions that might question the state's legitimacy. For example, in the two cases analyzed here, there is a dialogue about the penal system as articulated through visual representations.[3] These representations appear at first glance to be residuals of a bygone era, yet they are strangely familiar to our own symbolic world in which images documenting the systematic practice of torture circulate freely. As we will see, judicial officials were extremely interested in these images and in detailed descriptions of these practices despite the fact that those same officials did not condemn torture.

Siqueiros went to jail three times: first in 1930, accused of participating in the attempted assassination of Pascual Ortiz Rubio; again in 1940 for his participation in the failed attempt against Leon Trotsky; and from 1960 to 1964 for his public criticisms of President Adolfo López Mateos. Toral was jailed, convicted, and shot for the assassination of Obregón in 1929. During their incarcerations and afterward, both men articulated three things. First, they tried to explain their actions. These explanations were almost always verbal or written, although in both cases we also find images that would also seem to offer motives for their actions. Second, Siqueiros and Toral narrated their prison experiences. In this way, the authors defined themselves as individuals, although each believed in doctrines critical of liberal individualism (Catholicism and Communism), and they did so using similar terminology. In some cases these prison narratives included images Siqueiros and Toral produced. Third, both men used their artistic skill (which, in Toral's case, was somewhat limited) to express something that can only be described as mysticism: many of these works are apparently irrational or suprarational visions, absurd or crazed images that defy explanation. The historians of the cristiada, who took charge of Toral's memory, decided not to reproduce these visions. In contrast, Julio Scherer García, whose extensive interviews with Siqueiros are important sources of information on his life, gave great importance to the visual representation of mysticism in the artist's work.

I have examined what I believe are all the relevant visual images and transcripts from Toral's trial as well as his mother's memoirs.[4] Regarding Siqueiros, I rely heavily on a book of prison interviews recorded during his 1960s incarceration and published by Julio Scherer García as *La piel y la entraña* (*Skin and Guts*).[5] The editor's style mars the book because he never hides his own voice, a voice he often superimposes over the painter's. Because it is impossible to distinguish between the respective contributions of editor and artist, *La piel y la entraña* is both "the book of Scherer" and "the memories of Siqueiros."[6]

The second clarification involves the time frame used in this chapter. For Toral, whose artistic production was cut short by his February 9, 1929, execution, this presents no particular problem. In the case of Siqueiros, however, I analyze artworks and statements from 1930 through the 1960s. During this period the political regime changed dramatically, as did the artist. Since Siqueiros's autobiographical musings were not written until the 1960s (even though they refer to events in 1930), the entire period is important for understanding the artist's early years. Most biographies, especially those that involve political figures, are based on philosophical concepts that I do not share.[7] Instead, I am interested in geometric biographies in which "parallel lives" cross; in other words, biographies in which the central characters are *not* considered in and of themselves as though they acted solely according to their own intentions.[8] Thus, rather than accepting the strict chronological causality of standard biography, I draw from a broad range of sources to reveal the implicit commonalities in both men's construction of their own biographical narratives and their individual "truths." Moreover, this three-decade frame allows us to identify iconographic parallels that would be imperceptible if we were to look at a shorter period. This extended frame, which deliberately includes the time of memory, encompasses the mystical images that Siqueiros painted not during his first incarceration in 1930 but during his last imprisonment in 1960. These images, although produced much later than Toral's drawings, cast important light on Siqueiros's incarceration experience.

In Prison and on Trial

Siqueiros's first incarceration in 1930 was part of the Mexican state's first large-scale campaign against the Communist Party, a campaign sparked in part by the party's increasingly "suicidal" intransigence.[9] Intransigent or not, Siqueiros had been an officer in Manuel M. Diéguez's revolutionary army, and many of his old friends were in power at the time. As a result, he often received preferential treatment. This treatment included, by his own admission, an occasion in which he was allowed out of prison one evening to enjoy Mexico City's nightlife and returned to his cell in the morning.[10] Although conditions were undoubtedly poor, prison in the 1930s was, for the most part, a collective experience that often reinforced family bonds. Among other examples of preferential treatment, Siqueiros was permitted frequent visits from his father and from his wife, Blanca Luz Brum. His father, even though he considered his son's beliefs ludicrous, visited him to ensure that his offspring remained loyal to those same beliefs:

> These people do not know who you are, they do not know that despite your mistaken ideas you are still willing to die in this jail rather than to deny your thoughts. They do not know that you are a man, and a man loyal to his convictions.[11]

Reliance on family ties could sometimes backfire on the prisoner. Siqueiros's interrogator, for example, was well aware of these strong family bonds and their importance to his prisoner, and did his best to exploit them. During Siqueiros's interrogations, he even mentioned conversations he had had with his wife, Blanca Luz Brum, about the artist in order to win him over:

> I told Blanca Luz: "I think that if Mr. Siqueiros were to reconsider a few things it would be the best for the country and for him." To reiterate: I believe you [Siqueiros] have had a great effect on culture and art, but, I must repeat, I think it is a shame that someone such as you would abandon his nation over ideology.[12]

In Siqueiros's early incarceration he may have made many grand pronouncements, but they stayed within the familial sphere and reinforced his loyalties, affections, and family ties. If the accused received famous visitors, he did not discuss them. The 1960–1964 incarceration was a different story. In that instance, a great procession of celebrities began to assemble at the time of his arrest in the house of prominent art collector Alvar Carillo Gil. Allegedly worried that the painter would be murdered on his way to prison, Carillo Gil assumed the responsibility of bringing Siqueiros to jail. The journey to prison turned into something of a triumphal procession. Nobel Prize–winning Chilean poet Pablo Neruda, a fellow Communist, visited Siqueiros and then composed a poem in his honor. Mexico's most prominent photojournalist, Héctor García, took photos of him through the bars of Lecumberri. Julio Scherer García conducted the extensive interview that was the basis for two autobiographical pieces. Young artists came to show their solidarity and ask for advice. José de León Toral would not achieve such fame until the chaotic funeral that followed his execution.

Over the course of three imprisonments, Siqueiros was subjected to several interrogations, sometimes formal and other times informal. At no time did he try to demonstrate his innocence; instead, he downplayed his role in the crimes and maintained that the Mexican state was the real criminal. For example, while he admitted to participating in the attempted assassination on Trotsky, he insisted that he was not the one who entered the former Soviet leader's room with a machine gun in hand. In the 1960s, he defended himself against a charge of "social dissolution" by offering a detailed critique of President Adolfo López Mateos and his administration. Neither did José de León Toral attempt to deny assassinating Obregón. During his trial, he took sole responsibility—as Siqueiros did not—in a belated effort to exonerate Concepción Acevedo, more commonly known as Madre Conchita, a nun and spiritual counselor whom he had previously implicated in the assassination so she could share in his martyrdom.

Both Toral and Siqueiros made every effort to ensure that their stories were written down, and in Siqueiros's case, published. Toral spoke at length at his trial. On two occasions Siqueiros published his allegations against the government (alongside Scherer's book, these allegations provide great sources of information, especially about his imprisonment).[13]

In both cases the men expressed their fear of being summarily executed. Many times during his trial Toral made statements such as, "I have had the opportunity to think: This will be the last thing I will ever do, soon I shall be dead."[14] And he whispered, "Soon we shall see one another" (in heaven, we might suppose).[15] Despite his desire for martyrdom, Toral dreaded the moment of death, and his jailors played on that dread. He reported the guards telling him, "'Do not worry, we will not shoot you'—[because] they knew it was my greatest hope."[16] Siqueiros would also imagine many times that he was about to be shot. In 1930, when his companions took him out of jail for an evening, he confessed that "I was scared: I felt it in my stomach, a mass without muscles."[17] In 1940, when he was a fugitive in the mountains of Jalisco because of his attempt against Trotsky, he was apprehended by a military battalion. He described the event in vivid detail:

> I walked like a machine, but inside of me a light drew splendid pictures. Everything sparkled around me: the rocks, the path, the flowers, the

ground, the trees, and the weeds. I saw some women and I imagined them in aphrodisiac dances and long erotic pauses.

My head was filled with sounds, colors, forms and textures. I was grabbed by the most subtle and strong sensations. But at the same time I wanted to scream and run, I wanted to fall to the ground, kiss the boots of the soldiers, raise my head up to them, put my hands together as if I were praying and ask for forgiveness.[18]

Giving one's own side of the story has a distinct purpose: it assures that the person will not die in silence. The narrator's version of events may differ from that of the prosecutors, journalists, or historians, but it does not necessarily reflect a purely factual account that supersedes these other sources. Instead, the purpose of personal testimony is to bring to the public a different side of the story. For this reason, Demetrio Sodi, Toral's attorney, did not try to demonstrate Toral's innocence, but rather he praised the cultural importance of Toral's testimony (in which, of course, the accused narrated the assassination in full detail):

Yesterday's declaration by Toral is of great importance, the crime for which he is accused, is much bigger than a common crime, indeed it is part of a bigger problem that implicates the entire national character.[19]

Toral's crime, according to Sodi, should not be judged in a tribunal: "All the aspects of this process are cold, they do not have life."[20] It was the lawyer's desire to demonstrate that the assassination was not just a murder but a form of regicide—the killing of a king—that had important implications for the Revolution and the country.

The facts in the Siqueiros case were of course different, but the result was similar. Although at times he denied his participation in the alleged events (the assassination attempt against Ortiz Rubio, for example), his principal purpose was not to demonstrate his innocence. Accused in 1960 with the crime of social dissolution, Siqueiros claimed he was a political prisoner. Moreover, he affirmed many times that the actions of which he was accused were not criminal, and that he believed the crime of social dissolution to be unconstitutional.[21] He went even further, arguing that "[n]ot even the most counterrevolutionary and pro-Nazi regimes in Latin America could have created a more barbarian law; more appropriate for the worst periods of inquisitions of the Middle Ages and Colonial Mexico."[22] This was simply a political argument that challenged the law's legitimacy. But, in contrast to Toral, Siqueiros also allowed his lawyers to try to demonstrate his innocence using legal arguments.

The Martyr and the Governor

During his testimony, Toral recounted the time he was taken before President Plutarco Elías Calles. He assured the president that he alone had committed the crime, explaining that

> "I did it so that Christ could reign in Mexico." The President, after thinking for a moment about his second question, asked me: "What kind of reign is that?" I told him it was the complete and absolute reign over the souls.[23]

The model for this conversation, which very well may have taken place, is the well-known debate between Pontius Pilate and Jesus in the Gospel of John:

> My kingship is not of this world; if my kingship were of this world, my servants would fight, that I might not be handed over to the Jews. [. . .] For this was I born, and for this I have come into the world, to bear witness to the truth.[24]

Consequently, Toral addressed the president in the same thoughtful tone that Jesus used with the Roman governor. In response, Calles interrogated him "with a calm voice, thinking about what he was saying and with a kind demeanor" even though "he spent the entire time thinking about other matters."[25]

Despite his association with the PCM, Siqueiros was part of the political ruling class. As an officer in the revolutionary army, he met several future presidents, becoming drinking buddies with Adolfo Ruiz Cortínes and comrade in arms with Lázaro Cárdenas.[26] He believed that his freedom or imprisonment hinged on his personal relationship with the sitting president. In 1930 he was sent to jail by then president Emilio Portes Gil, who reportedly snapped, "The order is: 'Detain him until I say otherwise.'"[27] Siqueiros responded that Mexican public officials acted as if they were "absolute political bosses."[28] In 1939, an incident during a public demonstration provoked a new attempt to incarcerate him, even though Siqueiros had defended himself with the "gold handled, semi-automatic pistol given him by President Lázaro Cárdenas." He was shocked when the chief of police attributed the order to incarcerate him to the same President Cárdenas.[29] During his imprisonment in 1960, again on presidential authority, Siqueiros further developed his absolutist theory of the Mexican political system in which "a government of political functionaries that form part of the Executive, or more specifically the President of the Republic, has absolute authority."[30] And he attributed the failure of his legal defense to a simple phone call made by President López Mateos's personal secretary.[31]

Public Histories

The devout Catholic and the militant Communist both paid considerable attention to establishing and publicizing the motives for their crimes. Before analyzing these motives, however, it is worth noting that because of its public character, history continually repeats itself; it leaves the hands of the testifiers; and it becomes a form of exchange as other voices join in with their testimonies. Toral's biography was written by his mother and there was also a history of his trial.[32] For other historical documents relating to Toral, we can thank Antonio Rius Facius, one of the principal historians of the cristiada. Rius Facius collected the drawings by Toral reproduced here from photographs, although he barely used them in his own historical works.[33]

In *La piel y la entraña*, Scherer García does not hide his desire to recontextualize Siqueiros's testimony using the literary tools of a journalist. He places at the centerpiece of his account an intimate knowledge of the artist's persona derived from direct oral communication with Siqueiros: Scherer goes to the jail so he can hear firsthand the painter's words. He then presents his subject as a sweet old man telling bitter stories of the Revolution, a world-weary man locked away and caught up in melancholy solitude.

Despite their differences, the public histories of Siqueiros and Toral share an obsession with truth. The truth, for them and their contemporaries, resides in stories that emanate from a person's innermost self. Thus Demetrio Sodi said in the trial that "through Toral's declaration, we penetrate the deepest parts of his spirit, and put our hands on his conscience."[34] If that was true, then Toral's spirit was troubled. Even after Sodi's declaration, the accused repeatedly complained about his poor memory; at one point he asked for permission to use notes to help jog his memory, and afterward he said that the words spoken were not in reality his:

> It is like what Jesus said to his Apostles, his disciples, when they stood before their judges, and he told them: "Do not worry about how you respond, do not ponder, I will give you the words that you should say."[35]

Siqueiros also commented on a sudden loss of memory. For Siqueiros, influenced by surrealist psychological theory, any spontaneous action had significance. Amnesia was the prelude to creative outbursts. During his judicial interrogation and his journalistic interview, Siqueiros worried considerably about what he was saying because, for him, there was meaning and purpose even in the spaces between words:

> You describe me, but you do not show what I say. I am not a crazy man who screams "aah, oooh, uuuh!" I am not a trumpet between violins, as you have called me. If I talk, if I scream, if I mumble it is with a reason. Say that I protest against the jailing of the railroad workers, who after four and a half years, in violation of the constitution, still await sentencing; say that I cry out against the crime of social dissolution.[36]

The metaphor of a trumpet between violins is quite apt: the widespread introduction of brass instruments to mariachi music had just happened, and many thought that their addition had ruined the genre.

The Truth

"The truth." These are the final words in Rodolfo Usigli's famous play, *El gesticulador* (*The Gesticulator*), which is about political assassination, deceit, and the complex relationship between historical evidence, rhetorical verisimilitude, and the nature of political legitimacy in postrevolutionary years. In this play the characters do only one thing: talk. In many ways Usigli's vision resonates with the cases of Siqueiros and Toral, which stress the spoken word. Unlike the word-driven *El gesticulador*, however, these two cases also have a strong emphasis on art. In both cases, artistic production resulted in visual images, plastic representations of the experience of incarceration.

Among art historians, it is often debated whether images express the unilateral intentions of their authors. For example, Griselda Pollock critiques those who believe art can function as a metaphor for an individual conscience. The painter Artemisia Gentileschi, years after being raped, may have painted a depiction of Judith decapitating Holofernes but, according to Pollock, it would be an arbitrary assumption to insist that the painting definitively represents Artemisia's vengeance. Moreover, the simplest images are still quite complex because they are more than just sets of formal characteristics; they also participate in a social dialogue structured around differences of gender and class, among others. For this reason images produced a posteriori (after the fact) do not express the hidden desires of artists but represent facts whose truthfulness has a certain social significance. Likewise, the coherence of individual intentions is not demonstrated when a group of revolutionaries reads *The Conspiracy of Catilina* or produces its own images, whether literary or visual. On the contrary, these a posteriori constructions highlight the importance of ideology in the subsequent articulation of intentions.

Did Toral, for example, know what he was going to do in advance? Toral said that he had read the biblical story of Judith before he assassinated Obregón, noting that "What impressed me the most was that Judith worked alone."[37] Before the assassination, Toral had drawn a picture of the Cerro del Cubilete, a peasant, and a man exposing his back (see fig. 6.1). The Cerro de Cubilete shrine on a Guanajuato mountaintop had become an important pilgrimage site for members of the Catholic resistance during the cristiada. In 1928, progovernment forces destroyed the shrine's monument to the Sacred Heart of Jesus. The efforts of the bishop of León, Emeterio Valverde Téllez, to build an even bigger monument would not be completed until the 1940s. Moreover, the Vatican's ambassador to Mexico, Ernesto Filippi, had been expelled in 1923 because of his participation in political activities related to the construction of the earlier monument.[38] This particular drawing appears without explanation in an auction catalogue. And it is not included in Antonio Rius Facius's collection. Does the drawing foresee the assassination? Does it articulate Toral's intentions? This image is of particular interest because the man with his back turned bears a striking resemblance to Álvaro Obregón. Moreover, the drawing is dated 1924 from El Oro in the state of Mexico and likely resulted from a trip Toral took to the Cubilete shrine. During this time,

6.1. ~ José de León Toral, *El Oro, Mex, 1924*. Ink on paper, 12.4 × 19.9 cm.

Toral had commenced drawing classes. Although the outline of the drawing is rigid, it evokes a certain artistic ambition that goes beyond the simple practice exercises Toral would have been doing in class, which we will discuss later.

During his trial, Toral explained his motives for the assassination. In November 1927, a group of men led by Luís Segura Vilchis had thrown a bomb at Obregón's car. Although Toral was at first opposed to the idea of assassination, he began to understand the reasons that impelled the attackers. Following the failed attempt, Segura Vilchis was executed alongside three other people. One was the Jesuit priest Miguel Agustín Pro and the other his brother, Humberto Pro. Humberto had been a good friend of Toral: they had played soccer together. "Because of the murder of Humberto Pro," Toral confessed, he completely changed "his persona from a timid to an active man."[39]

At its core, Toral's assassination of Obregón was motivated by his antagonism toward a government he saw as increasingly anti-Catholic: "the persecutions are each time more atrocious, these persecutions against the Catholic Church."[40] He made the decision to kill Obregón, Toral said, when he was in the house of Madre Conchita, a nun from whom he often sought spiritual advice:

> I just heard the story on a tramway, saying that the Aviator Carranza was killed by a thunderbolt, and that it was punishment from above [. . .] God should send down a bolt to kill Obregón or Calles! And she [. . .] said: "Only God knows that. What I do know is that for things to be fixed it is necessary that Obregón, Calles and the Patriarch Pérez must die."[41]

The drawing offers another argument. Between 1924 and 1928, the Cerro del Cubilete was a symbol of the sovereignty problem that Toral, in his testimony, associated with the assassination. The Sacred Heart was the representation of God's reign on earth: his ultimate authority over the public sphere, the workplace, and over all private property. The symbol of the Sacred Heart had been revalidated in Pope Leo XIII's 1891 encyclical, *Rerum Novarum*.[42] Long-standing Church doctrine held that God gave the world a natural law that superseded any secular laws, governments, or constitutions. With *Rerum Novarum*, the Church put forth the Sacred Heart as a symbol of Catholic individualism that would offer an alternative to the self-centered individualism it associated with secular modernity. Leo XIII argued that although Jesus's power was universal, there was room for each person to consecrate him or herself with Jesus in their own way:

> For by consecrating ourselves to Him we not only declare our open and free acknowledgment and acceptance of His authority over us, but we

also testify that if what we offer as a gift were really our own, we would still offer it with our whole heart. We also beg of Him that He would vouchsafe to receive it from us, though clearly His own.⁴³

Emeterio Valverde Téllez, the bishop of León, knew this document well because it had been the impetus for the construction of the first monument on Cerro del Cubilete.⁴⁴ Toral was familiar with it too.

José de León Toral was devoted to the Sacred Heart of Jesus. He had a wedding photograph taken in front of an image of that invocation (see fig. 6.2). We

6.2. ⁂ Anonymous, *Matrimonio de José de León Toral*, s.f. Photograph, 11.3 × 6.7 cm. Centro de Estudios de Historia de México CONDUMEX, fondo CCL/1 José de León Toral fotografías 1/247, carpeta 1/1 1913/1929, inventario 103.

are also aware, thanks to the memoirs left by his mother, of a letter he sent to his co-accused, Carlos Castro Balda:

> Your gratefulness [. . .] gained the favor of the Sacred Heart: let us save a place for him, let us be delicate with Him as we are with our friends; with care let us remember his hand and let us be grateful [. . .] The best conception of Jesus, in my opinion, is as a FRIEND. What other thing can bring grace to our homes besides the acceptance of Jesus as our friend: "[. . .] I want to live your pains and joys," Jesus has said. And what is better than a loyal friend for these occasions?[45]

Pata Bendita

During his imprisonment Toral produced a series of drawings that showcased his devotion to Jesus. Judging from their characteristics, they could best be called "visions." In some of the drawings, Toral appears kneeling or sitting inside his cell receiving consolation from Jesus or the Virgin of Dolores. Others show him with Church martyrs, Saint Philip of Jesus and Saint Tarcisius.[46] In still others, Toral draws groups of fellow prisoners approaching the savior and a rider with a military uniform and a pendant dedicated to Christ the King. It is impossible to analyze all the drawings in detail; therefore, I will concentrate on three—those with well-developed allegories. These three drawings offer fresh insights into Toral's motivations, which are distinct from the motives the accused gave at his trial.

The first drawing in the series, which we can call without hyperbole "The Revelations of Toral," shows two human figures that act as columns holding up either end of a beam (see fig. 6.3). One of the figures is wearing religious attire; the other, a soccer uniform. The first figure is bowing his head slightly, but the various books on his back help him bear the weight; the soccer player is also leaning, but a ball balanced at the nape of his neck helps him support the beam. The religious figure is standing on a post; the soccer player, over a cross. Between the two is an image that appears to be the diagram of a church. The beam that the figures hold up is broken, and the crack divides the beam into two words: "Church" and "Mexico."

The second drawing is a portrait. Humberto Pro wears a soccer jersey from the team Santa María la Ribera, for which Toral also played (see fig. 6.4). Pro is standing atop a pillar like Saint Simeon Stylites.[47] In one hand, he carries the palm leaf of martyrdom. In the other, he holds a globe with Mexico at its center. Above the figure Toral wrote "Saint Humberto." The soccer jersey was an

6.3. José de León Toral, *IGLES/XICO*, 1928. Line drawing, 11.5 × 8.5 cm. Centro de Estudios de Historia de México CONDUMEX, fondo CCL/1 José de León Toral fotografías 1/247, carpeta 1/1 1913/1929, inventario 219.

important symbol to Toral. He began playing soccer at his mother's suggestion. In her autobiography, María Toral de León recounts a time when her pious son was being seduced by an old man from church who "began to make passes and become infatuated with [Toral]; he could not leave him alone for even a moment." A contrarian, although very progressive, Mrs. de León suggested the remedy: "Would you like to join an adolescent sports team, for example in Alvarado where there are Marists?"[48] Toral's mother, as this interaction shows, was a good Catholic mother with modern ideas. Instead of recommending

6.4. José de León Toral, *San Humberto*, ca. 1928. Line drawing, 11.2 × 8 cm. Centro de Estudios de Historia de México CONDUMEX, fondo CCL/1 José de León Toral fotografías 1/247, carpeta 1/1 1913/1929, inventario 203.

prayer or penitence as a way to resist the old man's temptation, she advised young José to take up a sport and divert his attention away from church; she even suggested that he attend Mass less often.

Episodes such as this were common in early twentieth-century Catholic biographies and autobiographies. This is partially due to the Marist order's belief that sports promoted the good constitution of adolescent boys. Siqueiros often boasted about playing baseball as a kid. This experience most likely occurred during the time he attended a Marist school for his elementary

6.5. ✑ Anonymous, *José de León Toral haciendo ejercicio*, 1923. Photograph, 7 × 4.8 cm. Centro de Estudios de Historia de México CONDUMEX, fondo CCL/1 José de León Toral fotografías 1/247, carpeta 1/1 1913/1929, inventario 75.

education. The emphasis on sports would continue into adulthood. Siqueiros said his art teacher (and also Toral's), Germán Gedovius, used to tell him that "'to paint well one does not only need good eyes, but also good muscles.' And he would tell me this and each time he would squeeze the impeccable biceps of my pitching arm."

Siqueiros and Toral liked to take pictures that displayed their biceps (see fig. 6.5). Vanity aside, Siqueiros did it so that his photographs could serve as models for his most famous paintings. In the photo album of Toral given to

CONDUMEX by Rius Facius, various photographs depict Toral on the parallel bars, wearing soccer and basketball uniforms, or, like Siqueiros, showing off his muscles. Referring to the introduction of modern sports during the Porfiriato, William Beezley has argued that Mexicans demonstrated little interest in physical fitness for its own sake:

> The Anglo-American tradition in the nineteenth century centered upon the Protestant Muscular Christian ideal in which the individual could testify for God by developing his body and display divine inspiration by accepting the challenges of the environment by mountaineering and hiking. [. . .] The idea of physical fitness for itself had no appeal.[49]

This is a plausible explanation for some Mexican Catholics, but not for all, at least not for the postrevolutionary era. The Marist emphasis on sports, like the Protestant Muscular Christianity noted by Beezley, was seen as a way to promote virtuous, healthy Christian citizens. The *Guía marista* thus sought to establish "a clear relationship between the body and moral virtues, where sport and activity mediate between the two" in a "somatization [embodiment] of morality."[50]

Siqueiros's life also included a story of homosexual seduction told in his own words. One night after a fight with his father, he found himself with an older man who invited Siqueiros to his home and began kissing him: "I panicked. But above all I was filled with revulsion. I felt a vicious animal on my lips and then in my mouth, and I could not spit it out or swallow it."[51] Recall that Siqueiros, when he was convinced he was going to be executed, was visited by visions of women "in aphrodisiac dances and long erotic pauses [. . . and] grabbed by the most subtle and the strong sensations." In his encounter with this older man, however, he was terrified.

In this context, sport becomes a kind of armor. The individual uses it for protection from an external world—represented in both cases by lecherous older men—that threatens to violate him without remedy and to dissolve the boundary between inside and outside. Boundaries of this kind are fundamental to the establishment of truth in judicial discourse. Art puts this truth in doubt.

The Display Case and the Heart

The drawing of San Humberto Pro shows why Antonio Rius Facius never released the drawings. The Catholic Church has very strict procedures for the determination and veneration of saints, and in the 1920s none was a football

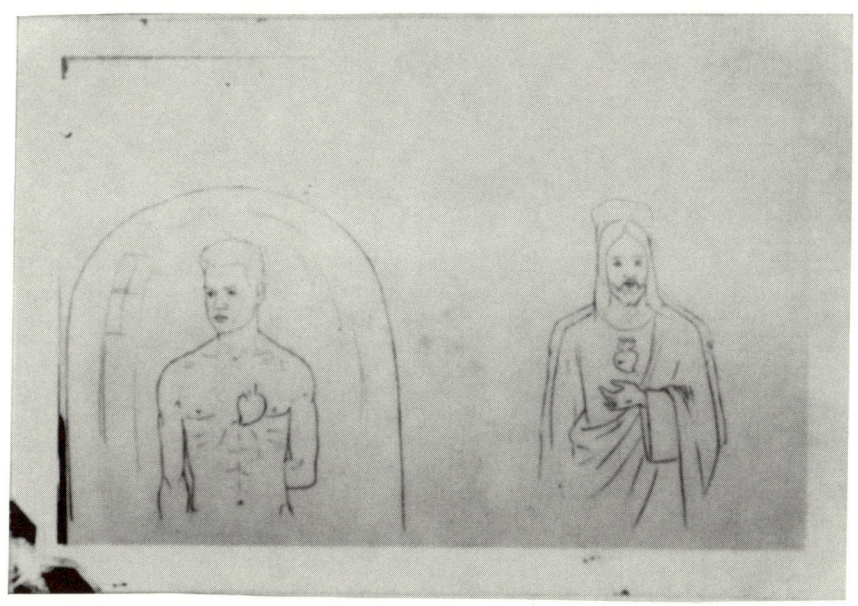

6.6. José de León Toral, *Toral y el Sagrado Corazón de Jesús*, 1928. Line drawing, dimensions unknown. Centro de Estudios de Historia de México CONDUMEX, fondo CCL/1 José de León Toral fotografías 1/247, carpeta 1/1 1913/1929, inventario 202.

player. Toral's pantheon was clearly unorthodox.[52] The last drawing in the Toral series is of the Sacred Heart of Jesus (see fig. 6.6). The image is complex and worth examining in detail. It is divided into two parts. On the left is Toral with a naked torso. His right arm is behind his back. The left hand is not visible. On his chest is a flaming heart. The strange part of the drawing is that Toral seems to be inside a bell jar, the glass covers used in museums to protect valuable pieces, in jewelry stores to protect merchandise, and in houses to protect the figures of saints. Perhaps Toral used the bell jar to express his confinement visually and relate it to his restricted access to altars, even domestic ones.

On the right appears a figure of Jesus dressed in a tunic with his right arm flexed against his chest; over him is also a flaming heart. Beyond Jesus a silhouette of Toral's body (with the naked torso) is visible. This represents a degree of transposition with the Beloved Christ. It is the construction, albeit failed, of an identification: Toral can only imagine himself inside a display case; union with the Messiah lies outside. The incarcerated Toral finds it impossible to imagine himself free or alone. Toral sees in "his friend" Jesus an anchor for an otherwise roving imagination. Jesus is the longed-for Beloved, as he is for the sixteenth-century Spanish poet-mystics Saint John of the Cross in his "dark night of the soul" and Saint Teresa of Ávila who wrote

> I live without being in me
> And in such a state I wait,
> For I die because I do not die.[53]

Like Saint Teresa, Toral dies in a spiritual sense because he is not yet united with Christ in physical death. General Obregón, although he knew nothing about it, was connected to Toral's desire to find himself, to reach the truth, to be united with Christ. During the interrogation, Toral announced that "my primary petition was, or is, that they kill me, that they open my chest, that they see my heart and that they see imprinted there, as I said they would, the truth."[54] Perhaps God, he thought, had infused the truth into his tortured heart as well as the heart of his victim:[55]

> In such a way I asked God this: "That he save himself, move his heart," and I asked for a sign. I told God [. . .] "May one of my bullets hit his heart, and may this be the sign that he has been forgiven, that you have touched him and forgiven him."
> When I discovered that two of my bullets hit his heart, it was a wonderful feeling; a tremendous consolation.[56]

The mystical delirium that Toral expresses lasted well after his death. Photographs of Toral's bullet-ridden heart held by surgical clamps began to circulate like postcards.[57]

While in jail, Siqueiros received numerous notices of public affection, especially during the 1960s. He did not, however, develop the theme of friendship in his painting during this period, with the exception of one painting that depicts him hugging a Dr. Sepúlveda.[58] Because of his frequent imprisonments, Siqueiros's prison self-portraits reflect a man who is aging progressively and, in one instance, half his face is converted into a skeleton. His reflections were pessimistic and at times pathetic: "I believe that conscience is the stripping away of the dream, as if dreams were a threat to reality."[59] During his 1960–1964 incarceration he painted a pair of bloody and painful images of Christ (see fig. 6.7). One, *Ecce Homo*, includes a saying that leaves little room for further interpretation: "He who believes in Christ, paints Christ." The saying is followed by a long justification, dogmatic and confusing, much like the arguments he

6.7. David Alfaro Siqueiros, *Cristo de Pueblo*, 1963. Enamel on wood, 81 × 61 cm. Sala de Arte Público Siqueiros, INBA. D.R. © David Alfaro Siqueiros/SOMAAP/México/2008.

made in court. The identification is clear: Jesus, with his arms tied and bloody, "Is He not also passing through a judicial proceeding?"

The Queen of Tests

The last thing the president-elect saw was his own likeness. Toral approached Obregón to show the president a just-completed pencil portrait and then shot him. Toral at first refused to state his name. He was immediately taken to the

6.8. José de León Toral, *Mi martirio*, 1928. Pencil on paper, 16.5 × 24 cm. Centro de Estudios de Historia de México CONDUMEX, fondo CDXIX Dibujos de José de León Toral, inventario 92.

jail at San Ángel where he was tortured until he revealed his identity. Regarding his torture, Toral made three drawings to show to the jury "so that the members of the jury can see and understand more or less how I was. Could you do me the favor of passing it around? The prosecutor can see it first."[60] Rather than oppose this exhibition, the prosecutor encouraged Toral to recount the details of his torment. "We are in no hurry to bring justice to an end," he told Toral with surprising magnanimity.[61]

Toral was tortured while hung from his hands, feet, thumbs, and armpits (see fig. 6.8). His martyrdom came with physical blows and verbal threats. Toral's drawings emphasize the human body. They are a bit stiff, which is probably why they have failed to attract the attention of art historians. The images talk about anatomy as much as they talk about pain: they show how the belly shrinks when an individual is suspended by his feet or arms; they show the oscillation of a body hung by its armpits. The mouth and eyes appear open, and one leg is flexed; Toral tries to show the mechanical reactions of a mechanized body. In one case, it should be noted, the pole to which Toral is tied is suspended between two springs. In his drawings, Toral is a pendulum, a ticking clock of punishment.

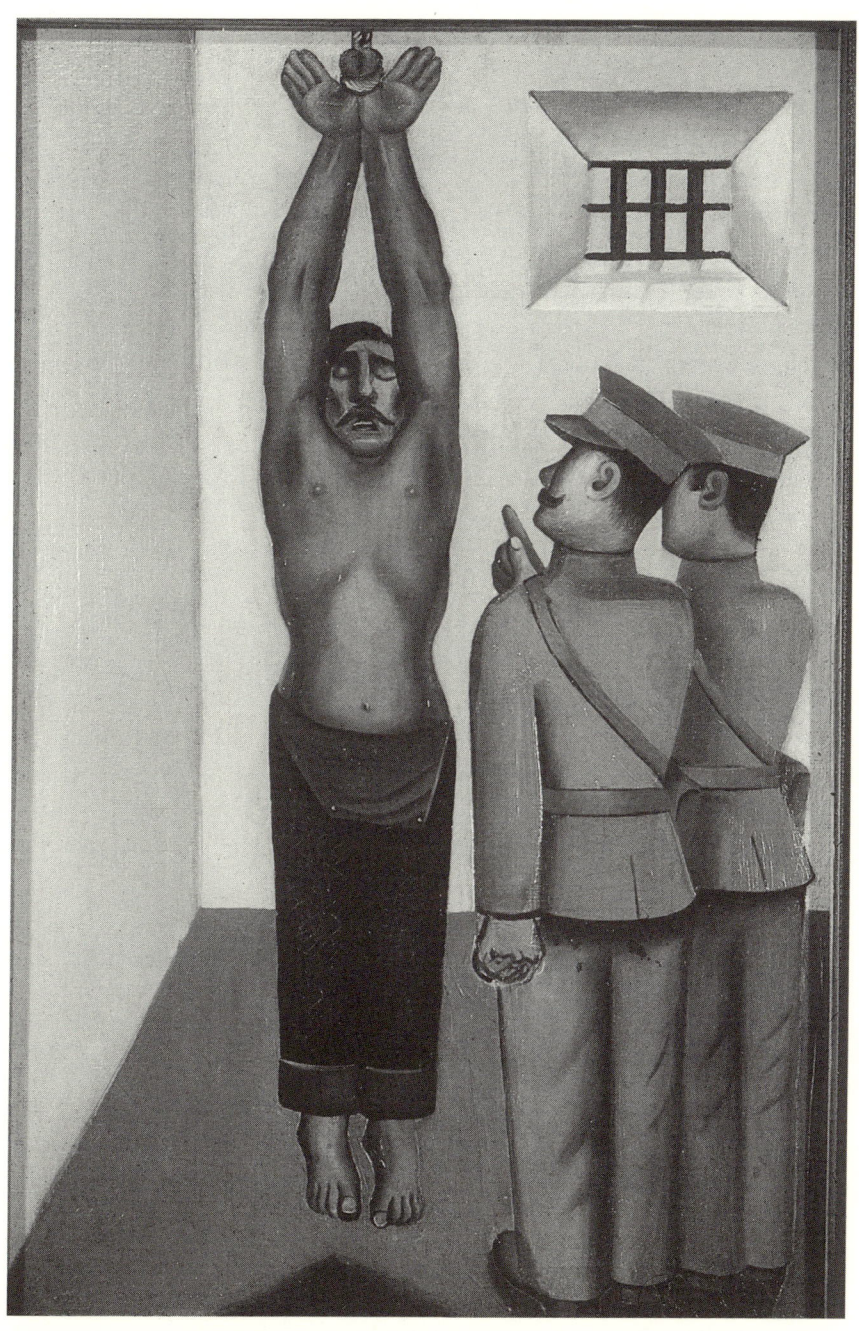

6.9. David Alfaro Siqueiros, *El tormento (El castigo del preso)*, 1930. Oil on canvas, 60 x 40 cm, private collection. D.R. © David Alfaro Siqueiros/SOMAAP/México/2008.

David Alfaro Siqueiros also refers to physical torture in his paintings (see fig. 6.9). In one of the few paintings from his imprisonment in 1930, he shows a prisoner wearing jeans hanging by his thumbs. His eyes are closed and he is being interrogated by two military men.[62] This is very different from his other works from the period in which the human figure appears as a geometric abstraction with little detail. In this case Siqueiros is interested in the victim's anatomy and face, which look vaguely like his own. He is also concerned with his victim's identity: the jeans lead us to believe the victim is a laborer or worker, whose clothing sets him apart from the military men's uniforms. The threatening attitude of these men is also important. As we have already seen, Siqueiros was being urged to renounce his ideology.

The prisoner's abdomen is stretched and smooth; the hands are open and symmetrical, as if the body were a paper airplane; the feeble legs hang loose like old socks. Torture is used to show the mechanization of the individual. The body no longer listens to the will. It flexes, double-flexes, contracts, expands, moves up and down, and opens or closes as a result of a purely mechanical system of cords, counterweights, and pulleys.

Toral and Siqueiros articulate this experience of torture—lived by one and witnessed by the other—using the drawing techniques they learned at the National School for the Arts. Germán Gedovius was the principal art professor there in the early decades of the twentieth century after Antonio Fabrés abandoned the academy and returned to Europe. Fabrés had developed a system of platforms and reflectors that, complemented by photography, allowed a model to maintain the same position day after day. To stay in one position requires dexterity and resistance, which is the same ability Toral associated with enduring punishment: "they made me stand up. [. . .] If I made any movement, I would be poked with pins."[63] When Gedovius came to the academy, photographs were discarded and models were put in motion and encouraged to adopt very strained positions. According to Siqueiros's testimony, the students supported these changes.

This kind of art education reflects a form of eighteenth-century art pedagogy in which students were first taught to copy figures of bone fragments, engravings, or even drawings by the professor. Drawing the whole human body was prohibited until the student had passed through years of training. Although Toral and Siqueiros both had the same teacher, their work reflects certain differences in their training. Siqueiros's paintings, particularly those from his imprisonment in 1930, demonstrate an anatomical synthesis; Toral's drawings do not. Toral's family kept many drawings he copied from photographs in magazines. The topics vary from famous paintings to wrestling. Nevertheless, Toral made a series of anatomical studies, possibly from a medical manual; they are écorchés, drawings of muscles without skin. Toral spent a great deal of time creating fragmented anatomical drawings, a practice ended by Fabrés but in some instances resurrected by Gedovius. He used this drawing practice to represent his torture: his images emphasize anatomical sinuosity and are a bit like clothed écorchés; at the same time, the bodies appear fragmented and the figures look like stick dolls hung together by links.

Siqueiros's painting is different: the prisoner's body is clearly unified from top to bottom. His model, as James Oles argues, is the crucified Christ.[64] The jeans suggest a working-class identity. His punishment, then, represents a form of social conflict. During this period, space, context, and landscape were more important in Siqueiros's work than the human figure, but in this painting the figure is central: it is appears as a system of proportions associated with human rationality after the manner of Leonardo da Vinci's famous sketches. Toral uses the body to represent pieces of machinery; the body in Siqueiros's painting introduces mechanism into the context and gives the image composition. There is another difference: in Toral's drawing the mouth is open as if it were a horn; Siqueiros's face has the calm dignity that artistic convention mandated for the crucified Christ. Toral's body exists in an almost indeterminate space; the places where the prisoner's hands are tied are the only points of spatial reference. Siqueiros places his prisoner inside a cell and uses the altarpiece as a referent for the spatial construction surrounding the victim.[65]

Siqueiros did not use his artwork as part of his defense in court. Nor did he use it in his written works to describe his personal experience during his 1930 incarceration (although he would use paintings that way in 1960). Toral drew so he could show the drawings to the jury, and it came as a surprise to him when the prosecutor invited him to describe the torture verbally. Shocked by the prosecutor's invitation, defense attorney Demetrio Sodi alleged that the tale of martyrdom "has made me sick, it has caused me physical harm." It did not damage Sodi enough, however, to cause him to omit any erudite references:

> I feel my hands cold because when I heard you describe your torture which you had drawn with a pencil, I did not see your painting, but rather I saw Dürer's drawing of Dante's circles of Hell. I do not understand, sir, how for the tempered spirit of the prosecutor these words are not reverberating deeply in his soul. . . .[66]

Sodi believed the prosecutor felt obliged to verify the story's truth, and, if necessary, punish the torturers. But it seems the prosecutor had another intention:

that Toral narrate the details of the torture he had received. The courtroom was full of journalists, and the prosecutor did not ignore them.

It was a confrontation between two strategies. Months before, those accused of a previous attempt on Obregón had been executed. One of the accused, a Jesuit priest, Miguel Agustín Pro, had opened his arms like the cross the moment he was shot and photographs were taken showing this occurrence. Many more photographs were taken; in fact, the government even invited journalists to visit the morgue and photograph the cadavers.[67] Did the prosecutor want to make a similar example of Toral's punishment? For his part, Toral maintained that he was inspired by the executions of the other two men: Luis Segura Vilchis and Humberto Pro. Regardless, both prosecutor and defendant followed their own strategy. Toral drew profusely because he knew his drawings had value. The prosecutor tried to relate a message through the publicizing of punishment, although he did not state his purpose explicitly.[68]

The Masses and the Cell

Siqueiros's imaginary had changed by the 1960s but in many ways had the same result. At the end of his book, Julio Scherer García mentions an easel that frustrates the painter because it reveals the intersection of the artist at work and his fantasies:

> I want to paint in front of a great wall, reach the horizon, be born multiple times, and make my mark on different planes of space, work with modern instruments, [. . .] surround myself with a team of humans that go up and down the scaffolds with mechanical precision.[69]

During art school, it was the models who went up and down the scaffolds. In Siqueiros's theory of painting, movement is also a character: the production of the image is part of its history.

Siqueiros's hallucinatory words refer specifically to a small painting, *Confinamiento solitario* (*Solitary Confinement*), which depicts a small figure sitting in a cell on the walls of which appear a multitude of tormented souls (see fig. 6.10). His imagination is programmatic: he erases the limits between things, molds figures into other figures, and paints with a certain delirium that had become his trademark since the 1930s. There is a dialogue between the body of the artist and that of the spectator. Siqueiros's work is a metaphor for the spectator in motion and also for the motion of the artist: "It is the normal movement of the spectator across the painting's topography which gives

6.10. David Alfaro Siqueiros, *Confinamiento solitario*, s.f. Enamel on wood, 81.28 × 60.96 cm. D.R. © David Alfaro Siqueiros/SOMAAP/México/2008.

pictorial composition to the painting."⁷⁰ Painting is thus a mechanism by which the individual is constituted through movement; each time the path of the dynamic spectator redefines the limits of perceivable space: "It is here that we see the street, a foot, or an automobile, the cubicles of a house, the intersection between the forms of trees, people, and objects in general as they shrink and stretch according to the rhythm of our march."⁷¹ The individual, moreover, is in constant danger:

> I could at this time, for example, describe the cuts and the blood that would run across my body, but in the case that all of this fails, the torture of pain, the anguish before death, the desperation for the end, the cries, the howls and the animal roars, I will try to hold onto life even though everything is already lost.⁷²

At the same time, Siqueiros explained to the interviewer that, during the Spanish Civil War, he had participated in the execution of a supposedly pacifist militant, even delivering the last blow.⁷³

Siqueiros often painted victims of violence (although he never painted victims of his violence, like Trotsky). In Uruguay in 1932, he painted *Víctima proletaria* (*Proletarian Victim*)—a woman tied to a wooden fence, on her knees, with her head bowed and a bullet in her head (see fig. 6.11). In 1939, upon his return from Spain, he painted *Postrado pero no vencido* (*Prostrate but Not Conquered*)—a man facedown with his arms crossed over his chest and fists clenched. This work can be interpreted in two ways. First, it might be an allegory of the resistance against Franco. Second, it might be autobiographical because Siqueiros had returned from Spain defeated by the fascists.⁷⁴ Between 1944 and 1945, he painted the mural *Nueva Democracia* (*New Democracy*), which depicts a man in a similar position: facedown, wrists tied, and his back lashed by a whip. He called this section of the mural *Víctima del fascismo* (*Victim of Fascism*). He also painted a dead soldier in that same mural. Siqueiros—ever proud of his physique—posed in various photographs for some of the figures in the mural, including those of the victims.⁷⁵

Conclusion

Toral and Siqueiros entered into judicial proceedings in which the law itself was only moderately important. One of them was tortured; the other was jailed without due process. Both, however, made public arguments through verbal discourse as well as through drawings and paintings. Their arguments, figures,

6.11. David Alfaro Siqueiros, *Víctima proletaria (también en la China contemporánea)*, 1933. Enamel and oil on wood, 205.8 × 120.6 cm. D.R. © David Alfaro Siqueiros/SOMAAP/México/2008.

compositions, and the nature of their discourse developed around the notion of truth. But, when closely examined, Toral and Siqueiros have only developed "their truth," "their response" as a form of reflexive speech. Both of the accused men highlighted the corruption of the state, political persecution, and authoritarianism, but they made these claims only in the first person: I did it, I pulled the trigger, and I hallucinated. Above all, they hallucinated. Toral did it through his drawings and Siqueiros experienced it directly. They both left behind what could be considered "visions."

Toral drew various images about the revelations the Sacred Heart of Jesus gave him. Although he had been taken to jail, Siqueiros could imagine a choir of bacchantes that desired him while at the same time he feared his imminent execution. Siqueiros may not have been a devout follower of the Sacred Heart, but he did paint and identify with Jesus. Moreover, he told Scherer García about his vision of an immense mural of the masses in rebellion, a vision that confused fantasy with reality. It is possible that this modern mysticism was a product of Siqueiros's and Toral's Catholic education.

The "truth" was for both men a tool for the construction of the individual: for its fortification, and for its representation—a way of distinguishing the "I" from a surrounding universe that threatened and controlled. When Siqueiros feared being executed, he imagined that the boundary that separates the individual from the world would be dissolved, converting the individual into a machine purely for the registration of perceptions: "My head was filled with sounds, colors, forms and textures. I was grabbed by the most subtle and strong sensations."[76] For Toral there was no doubt that his fear was related to his identity. Accordingly, his torturers asked him for his name.

But, in both cases and in a similar way, visual imagery played a part in building a rhetoric of the self. Toral interchanged himself with Jesus; he drew his friend Humberto like a stylite saint, a "pillar" of strength, a metaphor for resistance and strength. Between the testimony and paintings of Siqueiros there are sharp differences: at one point during his interviews he described himself as an executioner. This admission is difficult to correlate with his paintings, in which the executioners are always other people.

Their own bodies were prominent in this imagery. The "somatization of morality," the embodiment of virtue, turns the human body into a metaphor. This is not new: in the humanistic imagination and in the academic tradition, the body appears as the mediator between all things. Bodily proportions reflect the perfection of the world and vice versa. Bourgeois modernity invokes all these traditions to develop a distinct claim that the body is the home of the individual. But something develops when the "home" becomes more important than the inhabitant: a surface where only sensations occur—a shell, a display case, an armor that needs to be fortified.

Toral wanted to identify himself with the image of Jesus, and in many ways he could not imagine himself outside this identification. In his drawings there is no clear distinction between himself and Jesus, nothing more than the transparent glass of the bell jar. Siqueiros also painted an idealized, even religious figure: the tortured prisoner who represented the working classes, or the *Ecce Homo* he painted in jail. Siqueiros derived these figures from his own self-conception. His actions, Siqueiros believed, were dominated by the forces of history in the same way that Toral attributed his actions to divine intervention. The "I" that Siqueiros inhabited could only carry out the projects that the Communist Party supported. For this reason he denied the accusation that he participated in a simple assassination attempt:

> Any person could attempt a personal attack, and they could happen at any time, but taking into consideration orthodox criteria, the person who would have done this would be expelled from the party. All too often the Communist is confused with the anarcho-terrorist; the latter, however, is the opposite of the former.[77]

In the 1960s he stuck to the party line. After participating in a hearing in 1960 as a witness in favor of the Communist militant Encarnación Pérez Gaytán, he was asked if the other Communist had "lived honestly":

> He responded: Mr. Pérez Gaytán is a Communist, and a dishonest Communist would not stay long in the party. The Communist Party is the party of honest people. As such he has, undoubtedly, lived honestly.[78]

Toral's strategy was one of emulating Humberto Pro, Luis Segura Vilchis, Judith, and Jesus. Like Judith, he acted alone for the good of all true believers and the glory of God. Siqueiros, however, believed the opposite: his actions were not his alone but rather they were of the party; his virtues could not be attributed to him personally, but rather to the party; he could not be dishonest because the party was not dishonest. Still, Siqueiros's paintings are of himself, and it was not the party—not even Jesus—who rambled, hallucinated, or drew. It was Siqueiros. He was the one who went up and down scaffolds, flexed for photographs, and collected anecdotes from prison only to paint about them afterward.

There is, at least, consistency between Toral's statements and drawings. There is no consistency between Siqueiros's words and paintings. Of course the great muralist tried to identify himself with the working class through his paintings, but in his art there was no articulation of truth, which he had offered in his statements. His words in actuality were not symbolic representations of the party (as he says they were), but rather the narrated experiences of the painter: spatial, political, penal, and always personal.

The spoken word and the visual image exist in dialectic relation. The judicial discourse might allow for an analysis of both word and image, but this discourse highlights a larger issue relating to the history of art: the problem of truth. The truth preoccupies prisoners, their jailors and torturers, judges, and even journalists. Likewise, in academic art no problem is more important than that of the truth.[79] The academy has developed rules to govern the representation of the truth, including anatomical proportions, systems, and hierarchies. This system of artistic truth sometimes acts—as it does in this case—as a form of resistance against a legal system that involves, in theory if not always in practice, the truths of judges, police officers, and tribunal reporters (whose contributions merit greater study). At the heart of this relationship as articulated in the cases of Siqueiros and Toral is a division between an academic system of decorum (the rules of artistic truth) and the legal system of punishment (the rules of juridical truth).

Translated by Keith Hernández

Notes

1. The Historical Archive of Mexico City contains the archives related to prisoners in the Belén jail and Lecumberri Penitentiary, including Toral's file. There are no files for the imprisonments of Siqueiros before 1960. One explanation for this is the possibility that Siqueiros was not formally charged in 1930.
2. Jean Meyer, *La Cristiada*, 18th ed., vol. 1 (Mexico City: Siglo Veintiuno, 1974), 362.
3. See, for example, Wendy Lesser, *Pictures at an Execution: An Inquiry into the Subject of Murder* (Cambridge: Harvard University Press, 1993).
4. *El jurado de Toral y la Madre Conchita (lo que se dijo y lo que no se dijo en el sensacional jucio)*, stenographic version (Mexico City: N.p., 1929[?]); Antonio Rius Facius, notes to *Memorias de María Toral de León, madre de José de León Toral* by María Toral de León (Mexico City: Tradición, 1972). Rius Facius was a historian interested in the subject of oppositional Catholicism.
5. Dean of independent Mexican journalism, Scherer García was director of *Excélsior* in the 1960s, when the newspaper became a strong critic of the regime. Between 1976 and 1996 he directed the magazine *Proceso*, the most important voice of the final decades of the twentieth century.
6. All citations are from Julio Scherer García, *Siqueiros, la piel y la entraña*, 2nd ed. (Mexico City: Consejo Nacional para la Cultura y las Artes, 1996). I compared this

edition with the first (Mexico City: Era, 1965) to verify that there were no major changes in meaning (although there are changes of style). Recently a new edition was published and it too seems to have stylistic modifications. After Siqueiros's death, an extensive collection of interviews was published in David Alfaro Siqueiros, *Me llamaban El Coronelazo (memorias)* (Mexico City: Grijalbo, 1977). This text included the interviews previously published by Scherer García and other testimonies that were apparently collected by Scherer García but edited by others.

7. Mexican history is especially prone to "cult of personality" biographies. For a particularly egregious example of the genre, see Enrique Krauze, *Mexico, Biography of Power: A History of Modern Mexico: 1810–1996*, trans. Hank Heifetz (New York: HarperCollins, 1997).

8. The notion of parallel lives is developed most famously by Greek historian and philosopher Plutarch (46–120 AD) in *Lives of the Greeks and Romans* (more commonly known simply as *Lives*), a classic text in the Western literary canon that pairs the biographies of forty-six "exemplary" Greeks and Romans in order to explore common themes (usually moral) in their "parallel" lives.

9. On Siqueiros's first imprisonment, see Olivier Debroise, "Arte Acción," in *Retrato de una década: David Alfaro Siqueiros* (exhibition catalogue) (Mexico City: Instituto Nacional de Belles Artes—Museo Nacional de Arte, 1996), 36.

10. Scherer García, *Siqueiros, la piel y la entraña*, 27–28.

11. Siqueiros, *Me llamaban El Coronelazo*, 40–41.

12. Antonio Saborit, "El atentado personal: marzo de 1930. Siqueiros responde," *Curare: Espacio crítico para las Artes* 2, no. 10 (1997): 77. This is a transcript of a report Siqueiros gave to the secret police. It was discovered by Saborit in the National Archives.

13. David Alfaro Siqueiros, *La historia de una insidia: ¿Quiénes son los traidores a la patria? Mi respuesta* (Mexico City: Arte Público, 1960); David Alfaro Siqueiros, *La trácala* (Mexico City: Author's Edition, 1962).

14. *El jurado de Toral y la Madre Conchita*, 23.

15. Ibid., 24.

16. Ibid., 61.

17. Scherer García, *Siqueiros, la piel y la entraña*, 27.

18. Ibid., 44.

19. *El jurado de Toral y la Madre Conchita*, 40.

20. Ibid.

21. The crime of social dissolution was included as Article 145 of the federal penal code in 1941. All Mexican legislation can be found on the Mexican Supreme Court's Web site, http://www.scjn.gob.mx.

22. Siqueiros, *La trácala*, 57.

23. *El jurado de Toral y la Madre Conchita*, 56.

24. *The Holy Bible*, Revised Standard Version (New York: Penguin Group, 1974), John 18:36–37.

25. *El jurado de Toral y la Madre Conchita*, 56.

26. Siqueiros, *Me llamaban El Coronelazo*, 63.

27. Siqueiros, *La trácala*, 17.

28. Ibid.
29. Siqueiros, *Me llamaban El Coronelazo*, 353.
30. Ibid., 67.
31. Bowing to international pressure, López Mateos pardoned Siqueiros before he left office in 1964.
32. Toral de León, *Memorias de María Toral de León*, 144; Ramón Ruiz Rueda, *José de León Toral* (Mexico City: Tradición, 1975), 220.
33. Antonio Rius Facius, "Méjico cristero," in Toral de León, *Memorias de María Toral de León*, 361–78. Rius Facius included some photographs, some of which are included here. Rius Facius's documents are held in the Centro de Estudios Históricos CONDUMEX.
34. *El jurado de Toral y la Madre Conchita*, 40.
35. Ibid., 51.
36. Scherer García, *Siqueiros, la piel y la entraña*, 10.
37. *El jurado de Toral y la Madre Conchita*, 12.
38. See Citlali Salazar Torres, "El Monumento a Cristo Rey, de Nicolás Marisacal," in *Los pinceles de la historia, la arqueología del régimen, 1910–1955* (Mexico City: Instituto de Bellas Artes, Museo Nacional de Arte, 2003), 82–86.
39. *El jurado de Toral y la Madre Conchita*, 9–10.
40. Ibid.
41. Ibid., 11. The Patriarch Pérez was the leading Catholic official to support the government during the Cristero rebellion. Emilio Carranza was a popular aviator whose feats were celebrated in the press, but he was a military fighter pilot and this may be the reason Toral saw him as an enemy. Madre Conchita was eventually sent to the penal colony on Islas Marías. Throughout the trial, Toral tried to prove that her words had not motivated him to commit the assassination.
42. Gioacchino Pecci, Leo XIII, *Rerum Novarum* (Vatican: The Holy See, 1891). *Rerum Novarum* and other Catholic Church documents cited in this chapter can be found on the Vatican's Web site, http://www.vatican.va. English translations of these documents are from that site.
43. Gioacchino Pecci, Leo XIII, *Annum Sacrum* (Vatican: The Holy See, 1899).
44. Salazar Torres, "El Monumento a Cristo Rey," 84–85.
45. Toral de León, *Memorias de María Toral de León*, 55–56.
46. Saint Philip of Jesus, the patron saint of Mexico City, met his martyrdom in Nagasaki, Japan, in 1597. Saint Tarcisius was martyred in the third or fourth century AD for refusing to surrender the Eucharist he was carrying to Christian prisoners of the Roman state. Toral was surely alluding to the clergy's efforts to bring him Communion in prison.
47. Fifth-century saint Simeon Stylites spent thirty-seven years preaching from atop pillars in the Syrian desert. Saint Simeon was well known in Mexico, even becoming the subject of a satiric film, *Simon of the Desert* (1965), made by surrealist Spanish director Luis Buñuel who spent much of his creative life in exile in Mexico.
48. Toral de León, *Memorias de María Toral de León*, 22–24.
49. William H. Beezley, *Judas at the Jockey Club and Other Episodes of Porfirian Mexico* (Lincoln: University of Nebraska Press, 1987), 17–26.

50. Guacira López Louro, "Produciendo sujetos masculinos y cristianos," in *Crítica post-estructuralista y educación*, ed. Alfredo Veiga-Neto (Barcelona: Laertes, 1997), 91–118.
51. Scherer García, *Siqueiros, la piel y la entraña*, 35.
52. Or perhaps he was just ahead of his time. Humberto's martyred brother, Father Miguel Agustín Pro, was beatified by Pope John Paul II in 1988 and awaits canonization as a saint.
53. San Juan de la Cruz, "Noche oscura del alma" and Santa Teresa de Ávila, "Vivo sin vivir en mí." These poems are widely available in Spanish and English translation on the Internet.
54. *El jurado de Toral y la Madre Conchita*, 64.
55. Ibid., 62.
56. Ibid., 95.
57. Ruiz Rueda, *José de León Toral*, 204. Toral's heart was extracted and given to his family by Miguel M. Dominguez, a doctor who was later exiled from Mexico in San Antonio. "This fact was preserved in secret for many years." Copies and negatives of the photographs can be found in various archives.
58. Leonard Folgarait, *So Far from Heaven* (Cambridge: Cambridge University Press, 1987), sheet 11.
59. Scherer García, *Siqueiros, la piel y la entraña*, 62.
60. *El jurado de Toral y la Madre Conchita*, 54. A drawing on a single sheet of paper shows three ways in which Toral was martyred: he was hung by his feet, his arms, and his armpits. On the paper he clearly wrote "my martyrdom." This drawing has since been photocopied at CONDUMEX with others by Toral alongside some commercial illustrations and those that were in his family. His authorship is, of course, plausible. It is possible, although not likely, that two more drawings reproduced on postcards with a superimposed photograph of Obregón were also by Toral. These are similar to the others but pay little attention to the musculature of the figure as he appears wearing a shirt. Moreover, in one of the drawings, the face has a certain expressiveness that was far beyond the abilities of the young art student, even though Toral had grown as an artist through adversity. In one of the postcards, the drawing does not say "my martyrdom" but rather "Toral's torture." I believe that it is difficult but not impossible to attribute this second series to him.
61. *El jurado de Toral y la Madre Conchita*, 55.
62. See James Oles, "Catálogo de obra," in *Retrato de una década*, 109.
63. *El jurado de Toral y la Madre Conchita*, 60.
64. See Oles, "Catálogo de obra," in *Retrato de una década*, 109.
65. Ibid.
66. *El jurado de Toral y la Madre Conchita*, 83.
67. Nasheli Jiménez del Val, "El martirio de Padre Pro," in *Los pinceles de la historia, la arqueología del régimen, 1910–1955* (Mexico City: Instituto de Bellas Artes, Museo Nacional de Arte, 2003), 107–14.
68. It is possible that the prosecutor's actions can be explained by the politics of the time: in the sea of conspiracy theories that surrounded Obregón's assassination, one pointed at outgoing president Plutarco Elías Calles. To discredit this rumor,

the Callista government may have wanted to release the information about the torture to clarify that there was no relationship between the government and the assassination. This is a possible explanation given twentieth-century Mexican politics. But it still does not resolve one problem: the torture drawings accused the state and not just General Calles's government.

69. Scherer García, *Siqueiros, la piel y la entraña*, 133.
70. David Alfaro Siqueiros, *Cómo se pinta un mural* (Mexico City: Ediciones Taller, 1979), 96.
71. Siqueiros, *Cómo se pinta un mural*, 97.
72. Scherer García, *Siqueiros, la piel y la entraña*, 137.
73. Ibid., 88.
74. See Oles, "Catálogo de obra," in *Retrato de una década*, 155–57, 194.
75. Maricela González Cruz Manjarrez, *Siqueiros en la mira* (Mexico City: Instituto Nacional de Bellas Artes, Museo de Arte Moderno, 1996), cat. 21–24.
76. Scherer García, *Siqueiros, la piel y la entraña*.
77. Antonio Saborit, "El atentado personal: marzo de 1930. Siqueiros responde," *Curare: Espacio crítico para las Artes* 2, no. 10 (1997): 66–78.
78. Siqueiros, *La historia de una insidia*, 113.
79. This is the essence of academic decorum, whose residuals are still visible in the techniques of the muralists (although they are not utilized by more recent artistic traditions, such as the avant-garde). See Rensselaer Wright Lee, *Ut pictura poesis: La teoría humanística de la pintura* (Madrid: Cátedra, 1982). This is also evident in the conclusion of Carlo Ginzburg's *The Judge and the Historian*, trans. Antony Shugaar (London: Verso, 1999).

CHAPTER SEVEN

The Case of the Murdering Beauty
Narrative Construction, Beauty Pageants, and the Postrevolutionary Mexican National Myth, 1921–1931

Víctor M. Macías-González

Shortly before noon on Sunday, August 25, 1929, María Teresa de Landa—Miss Mexico 1928—awoke to bad news. Newspapers accused her and her husband, Brigadier General Moisés Vidal Corro, of bigamy. Vidal, it turns out, had not divorced his first wife before wedding de Landa. His new wife demanded to know why he had deceived her. Vidal's nonchalant attitude, combined with the realization that their marriage was over, momentarily blinded her judgment. She grabbed his pistol and pumped him full of lead.

In the weeks leading up to de Landa's trial in the fall of 1929, the newspapers of Mexico City wrote volumes about this sensational crime, creating different narratives about the event. Journalists at *Excélsior*, the capital's leading daily, were among de Landa's most ardent supporters, elaborating a coverage that discredited Vidal and his associates as Miss Mexico's social and moral inferiors. Despite forensic evidence corroborating her confession to the crime, the center-right newspaper—otherwise tough on crime—seemed intent on mobilizing public opinion in her favor. During the trial, her lawyer, the renowned José María Lozano, deployed these narratives, as well as de Landa's feminine image, to make emotional appeals to the jury members' sense of chivalry, duty, honor, and justice, asking them to overlook the evidence and pardon her. She embodied proper Mexican femininity, he argued, and was, after all, the only real victim in the affair. Not surprisingly, after a six-hour-long deliberation, at 2:45 AM on December 1, 1929, the court announced María Teresa de Landa's acquittal to the delight of her many supporters, and the approximately four hundred thousand people listening to the live radio broadcast.[1]

The details of this private affair entered the public sphere through the narratives that the state, journalists, lawyers, witnesses, participants in the case, and members of the public, created to explicate or make sense of the crime. Whether they created these explanations of the case to elicit a guilty or innocent verdict from the court is irrelevant. It is how they construed or gave meaning to the crime that makes this cause célèbre especially interesting. Like other such sensational cases, it allowed Mexicans to publicly discuss matters of great social concern and to explore how economic and social transformations impacted society; they made sense of it by creating narratives that reflected some of their own preoccupations, struggles, and circumstances. Elements of the narratives that circulated in and around the scandal thus intersected with other issues that people dealt with or debated every day. Most significantly, these narratives allowed Mexicans to debate the postrevolutionary government's national project; society's different views on gender, ethnicity, and class; and the limited confidence of some societal sectors in the judicial system and the state that it sought to uphold.

Gente decente—the literate, God-fearing, propertied, professional classes—as well as members of the military crafted some of these narratives. In explaining de Landa's anger toward her bigamous husband, they may have expressed the vicarious vindication of their own victimization under the rule of the violent, despotic, anticlerical, corporatist Sonoran generals who dominated Mexican politics in the 1920s.[2] Conservatives and others would subsequently mirror Miss Mexico's violent response to her husband's outrageous behavior and carry out protracted, often violent campaigns against the state, such as the Cristero rebellion, military revolts such as the Escobarista Revolt, and numerous agrarian, labor, and student uprisings.[3] Thus the violence and celebrity of this widely discussed private family affair reflected broader issues.

Cultural historians' recent work on issues of representation and narrative construction have greatly influenced this deconstruction of the case of the murdering beauty. Natalie Zemon Davis demonstrates how women in Early Modern France employed creative narrative strategies to appeal to authorities.[4] Sarah Maza's study of prerevolutionary French judges and lawyers features judicial briefs encoded with statements of gender and class that appealed to jurists' notions of hierarchy and helped to predetermine the outcome.[5] Similarly, Joan Wallach Scott's seminal essay on gender as an analytical category suggests ways to examine questions of power and justice through the lenses of gender, class, and ethnicity.[6] The case of the murdering beauty in 1920s Mexico allows us to fathom how a society accommodated itself to a postrevolutionary regime, engaging—if at times in a selective and doubtful manner—those elements of the new culture that they found convenient and expedient.

Some of Miss Mexico's contemporaries may have understood the violent murder of her husband as an allegory of traditional society's backlash against the emerging state. When de Landa's advocates discussed her case in the press, they tended to construct a narrative that painted her as the embodiment of the traditional, honorable, ideal wife and as a model of modern womanhood that the Revolution made possible. The media and her lawyer's narratives overpowered the damning evidence in the case. Weeks before the verdict, newspapers preached María Teresa's innocence. They noted that she had performed meritorious services for the country as Miss Mexico, underlining her physical beauty, her fair skin, blue eyes, and family background. Conversely, they presented her accusers, her husband, and his accomplices in negative terms, underlining their disreputable morals, questionable social origins, and "coarse," racialized phenotypes. Her lawyer constructed a narrative of her actions revolving around the role that her sense of honor and gender propriety had played in her decision to first attempt suicide and then, after struggling with Vidal over the gun, to shoot him. The jury's verdict, ruling de Landa's murder of Vidal a crime of passion—that is to say guided by noble feelings and worthy of mercy—suggests the degree to which fame, fortune, and physical appearance secured impunity from the law.

How can a story about a beauty queen illuminate conflicting views of the national project in 1920s Mexico? Beauty pageants provide a window on a relatively unexplored space where various sectors of society negotiate and elaborate identity. Beauty queens, in serving as the symbolic vessels of the national community's values, function as sites for the elaboration, negotiation, and reproduction of the nation.[7] While feminists castigate beauty pageants for their reinforcement of a passive, commodified feminine stereotype—i.e., pageants impose "dangerous body images of women promoting self-hatred"—they concur with other cultural theorists in observing that beauty contests provide a rich site of ethnographic study.[8] Beauty contests are not just about feminine identity, aesthetic codes, or competitive desire; they also allow for a public refashioning of community identity:

> They evoke passionate interest and engagement with political issues central to the lives of contestants, sponsors, organizers and audiences ... [B]y choosing an individual whose deportment, appearance and style embodies the values and goals of a nation, locality, or group, beauty contests expose these same values and goals to interpretation and challenge; they provide opportunities for public expression and negotiation of standards and values.[9]

Thus, the de Landa case adds to our understanding of the dynamics involved in the emergence of a postrevolutionary kulturkampf (culture war) by allowing us to analyze the images and rituals of beauty pageants in Mexico and to see how de Landa's identity as a celebrity beauty queen came to be interpreted when woven into the many narratives surrounding her husband's death.

Each of the four stages of the murdering beauty's cause célèbre reveal important components of the narratives that subsequently circulated through Mexican society. The first part of the tale—María Teresa's life up to the moment of her crowning in the 1928 Miss Mexico contest—involved a broad spectrum of views, including her own ideas about modernity and womanhood, ideas that would be discussed subsequently in the trial in particular. The pageant itself allows for an exploration of societal representations of gender and national identity, as well as propriety, which would lead to a public debate about femininity, honor, class, and ethnicity. These societal representations (also examined in part two through the particulars of de Landa's marriage to Vidal) were mobilized in the narratives of *Excélsior* and defense attorney Lozano and their efforts to give a larger meaning to de Landa's subsequent actions. After the second section examines her difficult marriage, the third part discusses the circumstances surrounding María Teresa's murder of her husband and authorities' investigations of the crime. The fourth part interprets the narratives present in the case, particularly those that stem from de Landa's strategies of self-fashioning and self-representation as they developed during her trial.

Part I: A Queen is Born

Born in 1910, the final year of the Porfirian era, María Teresa de Landa came of age in a postrevolutionary society in which attitudes about class, gender, race, and ethnicity showed more continuities with past attitudes than widespread acceptance of new ideas. Foreign travelers noted that women's educational opportunities and legal status in Mexico had changed relatively little in the first quarter of the twentieth century.[10] Most young women of the upper and middle classes had to content themselves with an elementary, convent-school education that prepared them for matrimony and motherhood with lessons in home economics, moralizing Catholic literature, portraiture, voice training, sewing, and French.[11] Few women obtained university educations, and those who did pursued careers in teaching, nursing, or gynecology. A common saying or *dicho* illustrates societal attitudes toward educated women: *Mujer que sabe latín no tiene marido ni buen fín*—"Men don't make passes at girls who wear glasses."[12]

María Teresa de Landa's experience transcended the limits that privileged family backgrounds like hers imposed on women. Her parents probably expected a life of bourgeois comfort for this blue-eyed, rosy-cheeked beauty. Her father, Rafael de Landa y Tamayo, was the enterprising son of a cadet branch of the de Landa family, which had figured prominently in Mexican high society since the days of the first empire. Her mother, Dolores de los Ríos de Landa, was a pious Catholic woman from a respectable family of professionals and magistrates.[13] From age six to age twelve, María Teresa traveled daily from her family's massive balconied colonial mansion in downtown Mexico City to a convent school in Santa María de la Ribera. On the weekends and in the summer, her family traveled to a two-story villa her mother's family owned in the Mexico City suburbs. After completing elementary school in 1923, María Teresa enrolled for a year at the Escuela Central to finish her secondary education before moving on to the Teachers' College at the Escuela Normal de Maestras in 1924. There she completed her high school education and prepared for a career as an educator.[14] An intelligent student, María Teresa graduated in three years (not the usual four), earning a medal for her literary skills. She avidly read English, French, and Hispanic authors such as Anatole France, Paul Bourget, Romain Rolland, George Bernard Shaw, H. G. Wells, Arnold Bennett, Oscar Wilde, Amado Nervo, and Juan José Soiza Reilly. In the fall of 1926, at age sixteen, she enrolled in the dentistry program of the Escuela Odontológica Nacional. Unlike women of her mother's generation, María Teresa sought a life beyond the confines of the Church and home, hoping to join the growing ranks of Mexico's fifty women lawyers, doctors, and dentists.[15] At the university, she especially enjoyed psychology and philosophy. María Teresa complemented her intellectual development with an active sporting life that included dancing, swimming, boxing, and automobile racing. Her sense of adventure was evident in her desire to live in Los Angeles and travel in France.[16] María Teresa became a social hit at school, making many friends among the students and teachers. This supported her belief that class did not limit one's opportunities, particularly if people had access to education. When people of different classes interacted civilly, she later declared, they could learn from one another to the benefit of all society.

Changes in social attitudes, especially those regarding class, gender, and ethnicity were discussed openly in Mexican institutions of higher learning at the time.[17] María Teresa partook of this ambience and came to believe that education would provide the key to Mexico's social transformation. She felt that educated, modern women would especially benefit from the opportunity to advance in life. "After all," she noted in an interview, "ever since the end of the

World War, societies have been abandoning old ways and now recognize that women have an energetic spirit and no longer consider us weak."[18]

The beauty queen's call for the empowerment of women through education was not as aggressive as the protests that some of her contemporaries launched. In 1924, female university students took up arms against a group of male medical students who had shown their disapproval of women's bobbed hair by shaving a young girl's head as a warning to her female classmates who favored short hair and skirts. The young women fought fire with fire and reportedly bought out the local gun merchants' stock of .22-caliber pistolettes. Male students from the National University and cadets of the Military College and the School of Aviation challenged the offenders of feminine honor to a duel. Authorities interceded to keep the confrontation from exploding into a citywide conflagration, but it nevertheless elicited incisive commentary from political cartoonists who remarked on the episode's symbolic subversion of gender roles.[19]

Perhaps it was María Teresa's progressive ideas about gender that prompted her classmates to think about entering her in the Miss Mexico Pageant that *Excélsior*, Mexico City's most popular daily newspaper, announced in the spring of 1928. Founded by the conservative Puebla businessman Rafael Alducín Bedolla in 1917, *Excélsior* soon became known as the mouthpiece of business and center-right elements in Mexico. Like its forerunners *El Imparcial* and *El Universal* (both edited by Félix F. Palavicini), *Excélsior* frequently eschewed political reporting in favor of "modern news," covering sensational events, crime, and short pieces from the wire services interspersed with films, sports reviews, and photographic essays. Ample space was dedicated to advertising, and glossy inserts increased the newspaper's circulation numbers and profitability.[20] Its liberal use of illustrations suggests that *Excélsior* editors recognized the importance of providing narratives understandable even to semiliterate readers.[21]

Alducín Bedolla often used his newspaper to advance conservative causes through campaigns that, on the surface, appeared free of any clear ideological content, such as the orchestration of holidays, festivals, and contests. In 1922, for example, *Excélsior* initiated a celebration of motherhood in order to combat Yucatecan governor Felipe Carrillo Puerto's polemical efforts to institute divorce, family planning, and birth control methods.[22] Archbishops and lay Catholic leaders supported the campaign with guest editorials. The date chosen, May 10, betrayed his conservative views and business savvy: the Church had dedicated May to the Virgin Mary, and paydays fell on the tenth, twentieth, and thirtieth days of the month.[23] Alducín Bedolla's death in the spring of 1924 did not keep *Excélsior* from promoting conservative causes under the new editor, Rodrigo del Llano. *Excélsior*'s sponsorship of the Miss Mexico Pageant was probably intended to undercut feminists' growing presence in Mexican society by reinscribing women as objects of display. *Excélsior* reporters, as purveyors of feminine fantasies, played an important role in the contest with eloquent discourses on beauty and matrimony. They not only referred to contestants' physical beauty, but also wrote about the prizes contestants would receive in terms of a bridal trousseau or a dowry. Most prizes were household goods, particularly "modern" kitchen appliances, furnishings, and linens. Symbolically, literally, in some accounts, Miss Mexico would become "the bride of commerce."[24]

A group of María Teresa de Landa's classmates at the dental school urged her to sign up as their representative in *Excélsior*'s beauty pageant. She accepted their nomination—once she secured parental permission.[25] A committee of students visited her family's home and assured don Rafael of the contest's propriety, especially given the requirement that contestants wear bathing suits to the weekly publicity events held at a popular swimming club, the Alberca Esther, in the swanky San Ángel neighborhood. The aim of such antics, they explained, was to incite popular participation in an event that would ultimately select a Mexican representative to vie against women from other countries in the aptly named Galveston International Pageant of Pulchritude Miss World Bathing Beauty Contest. His daughter would not be exhibiting herself to indecent, lustful *pelado* (lower-class, mixed-race) male crowds, but to the proper middle-class families that frequented the pool. Contest organizers went to great lengths to assure the community of the contest's legitimacy by providing female chaperones to escort and transport contestants to events. They called attention to the "reputable" business firms donating prizes and emphasized the modernity of an event "so common in the United States and Europe."[26]

The contest, which was limited to single young women sixteen to twenty-five years of age "of good moral reputation and not involved in film, theater, or vaudeville" seemed to suit María Teresa.[27] These requirements concur with historians' observations that turn-of-the-century beauty pageants reinforced bourgeois notions of feminine respectability and explains not only de Landa's participation, but also that of other "daughters of respectable families" such as Eva Frías, daughter of famed novelist and journalist Heriberto Frías.[28] On the other hand, the participation of representatives of labor organizations, such as Raquel del Castillo from the union of electricians and railroad workers, speaks to how the Revolution included the proletariat in the elaboration of shared values—supporting cultural critics' observation that beauty pageants function as crucibles of community identity. Thus, well before she met her future husband, readers of the Mexico City press had already come to associate de Landa with propriety and honor.

As part of the publicity promoting the 1928 pageant, *Excélsior* published an interview with María Teresa de Landa on April 20, making evident her thoughtful, modern, feminist views. This text introduced the newspaper's readers to de Landa as the embodiment of modern womanhood, an image to which her supporters would often refer during the trial. Interestingly, the reporter employed a narrative strategy that veiled her more extreme opinions, with a seemingly thoughtful de Landa taking back some of her most salient comments about the meaning and practice of feminism as she conversed with a female classmate present during the interview. With her friend, de Landa discussed her initial replies to the reporter's questions and often interjected, "My God! They are going to think I am some sort of raving feminist! Oh well! I hope they understand." In a portentous warning to the reporter, she urged him to be fair and accurate with the story: "Make sure you get all my comments right. Remember, I know boxing, so I will come after you if you misrepresent me!"[29]

The interview presented de Landa's comments as thoughtful and progressive, thus lending credence to social reformers' model of modern womanhood. These comments were perhaps inspired by some of the lectures that Nicaraguan poet Santiago Argüello—brought to Mexico by the National University—had given at the National Preparatory School; Argüello called for the emancipation of women through education. In a note that may have struck a chord with de Landa, Argüello proposed that women create beautiful, strong, healthy, sculpted bodies to house the cultured mind that education would make possible.[30] Since the nineteenth century social critics had seen the possibility of improving the education of Mexican women.[31] José Manuel Puig Casauranc, Secretary of Education and Secretary of Foreign Relations during the 1920s and 1930s, argued in 1922 that postrevolutionary national reconstruction required the transformation of Mexican womanhood. He wanted to dismantle the model of *la mujer bibelot*—the plaything, display-object woman—in favor of *la mujer compañera*, the companionate woman. "Practical men in times of struggle," Puig Casauranc argued, were "more inclined towards the companionate woman, the woman who in body and soul, in enthusiasm and effort, is linked to the life of the male. Less heart, possibly, but more brains, more energetic will, and much more conscious of the world around her."[32] This new woman would be more of an equal to men and in her role as mother would require a better education in order to comply with her duty as the womb of future citizens.

For María Teresa, events such as the Miss Mexico Pageant allowed the nation to demonstrate its adoption of these new notions of womanhood and to proudly display its "civilization" abroad because the winner of the pageant would subsequently represent the country at the world finals. María Teresa defended the pageant, arguing it was "a sign of culture that can only be successful where the spirit of yore cedes to that of a promising future."[33] She felt that the contest's success demonstrated that Mexican women were widening their view of the world and contemplating new roles and possibilities in the future. De Landa credited the press with this revolution in thinking, noting that it functioned as "an agent of indispensable primary force" without which such cultural transformation would not easily occur. "Women," she argued, "can expand their thinking and acquire a greater degree of freedom thanks to this development."

María Teresa credited the newspapers' coverage of gender issues, such as that arising from their treatment of beauty and femininity in the articles covering the pageant, with contributing to the public debate on issues concerning women in Mexico. She was particularly critical of those people who did not empower themselves or their family through the opportunities afforded them by press coverage and by changing societal attitudes. She felt that women who did not think of themselves as equals to men and who continued to think of themselves as somehow inferior to males were pitiful creatures "that shall remain forever waiting for Prince Charming to sweep them off their feet." Education would benefit these passive women if they would only take advantage of it: "Women students are as able as men and can often get ahead faster than men because we have much more patience, we are more diligent and can assimilate facts and knowledge faster than they can."

As the months passed, newspapers published interviews with other contestants. Many of the interviewees' replies compared unfavorably with María Teresa's, revealing them to be childish, badly educated, and with few aspirations in life. Sixteen-year-old Mercedes Ortega Ojeda, a native of Yucatán, while captivated with Mexico City's great buildings, confessed that she did not like the poverty she saw there or the degree of liberty she noticed women enjoying in the capital.[34] Enriqueta Lorda, a native of Sonora who claimed to adore modern dancer Isadora Duncan, said her favorite book was *Sleeping Beauty*, confessing that its character inspired her greatest dream: to sleep without any preoccupation.[35] Mexico City natives Maruca Morales and Micaela Canales, who enjoyed riding horses and who swooned at the sight of silver screen actors Ramón Novarro and Rudolph Valentino, noted that they did not continue their schooling past elementary school "because science is painful."[36] María Teresa's only likely competitor, Luz Guzmán, a twenty-year-old native of Mexico City who enjoyed reading and dancing Spanish flamenco, urged Mexican women to imitate American women:

Open up your eyes in awe of the power of the woman from the United States! Imitate her in all her lawful activities because she is a happy woman that is respected, loved, and protected by her man without having to abandon her occupations and ideals.[37]

Guzmán's article, published a few days after de Landa's interview, presented an openly feminist appeal and urged Mexican women to free themselves from machismo's oppression.

On May 15, 1928, after *Excélsior*'s representatives tallied the fifty thousand votes cast, they selected five finalists. María Teresa de Landa de los Ríos was the favorite, garnering 9,473 votes. The press subsequently announced festivities for the crowning of Miss Mexico, including receptions, a formal ball, and a grand parade. A group of businessmen proposed to crown Miss Mexico the "bride of commerce" and offered to shower her with gifts that the press described as a "fantasy bridal trousseau": evening gowns, hats, furs, costly imported accessories, and toiletries.[38] Tobacco products giant El Buen Tono Industries announced it would sponsor a float to carry Miss Mexico in the triumphal parade planned in the winner's honor.[39] On May 19, a jury consisting of officials from the Ministry of Education and the National Institute of Fine Arts selected de Landa as the winner. That night, her supporters at the National School of Dentistry organized an impromptu celebration in her honor.[40]

As planners worked on the celebration's final details, they learned that a luxury ocean liner had docked in Veracruz carrying most of the European contestants to the Galveston "Miss World" contest. Realizing that this presented them with an unparalleled opportunity not only to publicize Mexico internationally but also to add a cosmopolitan flair to the celebration, contest organizers invited the beauties to join Miss Mexico in her triumphal parade on May 27. Firms lined up to provide services, and automobile dealerships donated the use of their most luxurious models to transport the foreign representatives. The parade, with its many privately and publicly sponsored floats, was a memorable affair that drew more than seventy-five thousand spectators to see the many celebrities—among them Charles A. Lindbergh—who attended this great secular festival of national beauty.[41]

Part II: A Queen Falls in Love

In the weeks following her crowning as Miss Mexico, María Teresa dropped out of the spotlight. Perhaps after the weeks of coverage leading up to the contest and the arrival of the foreign beauties, the reading public had become bored with the subject. Newspapers fell silent about Miss Mexico. What we know about her during this time is surmised from evidence submitted during her 1929 trial. On May 29, 1928, with her mother as chaperone, she journeyed to Galveston and competed with other bathing beauties. There representatives of U.S. film studios contacted her and offered the possibility of employment if she cared to audition. Perhaps they did so remembering the success of other Mexican women in Hollywood such as Lupe Vélez and Dolores del Río. After the contest, Miss Mexico and her mother returned home, possibly hesitant to take up studio offers without first consulting María Teresa's father. While he had supported her participation in the beauty contest out of patriotism, having his daughter acting in movies "as a public woman" was another thing. Three years earlier, in 1925, Mexican high society had ostracized Dolores del Río (née Asúnsolo y López Negrete) and her husband Jaime Martínez del Río when she became a Hollywood starlet.[42] For all the social advances of the Revolution, society remained strongly patriarchal, restricting women's activities to the domestic sphere, the home, and school. This was the case for María Teresa.

Upon returning to Mexico City, María Teresa resumed her studies at the School of Dentistry and formalized her relationship with Brigadier General Moisés Vidal Corro. They had met on May 8, 1928, at her paternal grandmother's funeral, but in all likelihood the general had probably first glimpsed the beauty in the newspapers. A week later, after the general offered a toast in her honor at the Miss Mexico finals, the nineteen-year-old beauty pledged him her love and promised to marry him when she returned from the United States. They dated during the summer and fall, usually meeting at the university where the general could visit without her parents' knowledge. María Teresa became enamored of the tall, curly-haired, handsome general. Vidal's friend and brother-in-law General Rodolfo Martínez would later testify that he had met de Landa outside a restaurant on Calle Madero in June 1928, when Vidal presented her as his girlfriend. The happy couple knew that her family would never acquiesce to a relationship as disparate as theirs: the daughter of a prominent family and a revolutionary of humble origins.[43] Consequently, they eloped and married in a civil ceremony on September 24.[44]

Unbeknownst to Miss Mexico, the general made arrangements with friends to forge the marriage license. To circumvent his previous marriage, he entered a cousin's name as his own on the document. It seemed legal because the general's middle name was his cousin's first name. In this manner, Vidal would avoid any complications with his first wife, María Teresa Herrejón de Vidal, whom he had married in a similar civil ceremony on April 27, 1924. Herrejón and Vidal had had two daughters and had lived in Mexico City until the spring of 1928, when the family had returned to Veracruz. After the government offered to recommission Vidal, he returned to Mexico City, leaving his wife and children with his family in Cosamaloapan, Veracruz.

De Landa, who knew nothing of her husband's double life, announced her marriage to Vidal to her shocked family a few days after the event. After an emotional scene, her father stormed out of the house and went to the courthouse to demand to see his daughter's marriage license. He returned and angrily confronted her, asking why she had given her age as twenty-two and not nineteen.[45] María Teresa's parents finally and bitterly accepted the events but insisted on sanctifying the union with a religious wedding.[46] As the country's churches remained closed because of the Catholic hierarchy's standoff with the government, a priest had to be found who would perform the ritual in the family's home.[47] On October 1, the general's half brother Father Buenaventura Corro performed the ceremony.[48] During the trial it was revealed that the priest had known of Vidal's liaison with Herrejón. This did not seem relevant to either the public or to de Landa, her family, or the press, probably because all parties assumed the earlier marriage had no legitimacy because it involved only a civil ceremony rather than religious rites. Consequently, the conservative press described María Teresa de Landa as "the Widow Vidal" and María Teresa Herrejón simply as "la señora Herrejón." And, while some conservative readers might have been willing to overlook the role that a priest had played in de Landa's predicament, moderates and radicals must have seen in this evidence for their belief in the prevalence of corruption within the Church.

After the wedding, the happy couple toured the Isthmus of Tehuantepec and visited the groom's hometown of Cosamaloapan, Veracruz. His family did not mention Vidal's first wife to de Landa. Herrejón eventually learned of Vidal's marriage to Miss Mexico from her friends and relatives in Mexico City. Herrejón subsequently wrote anonymous letters to de Landa's family informing them of the general's deceit, but don Rafael and doña Dolores dismissed these charges and kept the details from their daughter. When the couple returned from their honeymoon, they moved into a suite in her family's spacious home, as Mr. and Mrs. de Landa were not pleased by the general's living quarters. Don Rafael objected to the small apartment Vidal wanted to rent in the Colonia Roma and told him that if he actually loved María Teresa, he should save up to buy her a proper home.[49] María Teresa, seemingly caught up in connubial bliss, dropped out of school, forgot her feminist ideas, and dedicated herself to her wifely duties. In actuality, Vidal had beaten and verbally abused her into submission, restricting her to the home and cutting her off from the outside world.[50] Vidal allowed her to read novels and pious literature but prohibited newspapers because his first wife, with whose lawyer Vidal was then negotiating a divorce settlement, had threatened to expose Vidal to the press if he did not meet her demands. Oblivious to this, María Teresa did not question her husband's censorship. She stayed at home with her mother, sister, and nanny while the men of the house went off to work. Her only amusement over the winter of 1928 and spring of 1929 was traveling with Vidal on political investigations to the countryside. These often led to thrilling, dangerous episodes such as when Vidal trailed and captured the outlaw Cardona.[51]

One week before the general's tragic death on August 25, 1929, the couple quarreled bitterly because Vidal had flirted with another woman at a theater performance. María Teresa suspected that her husband and the woman were acquainted because their body language denoted a certain familiarity. Both had appeared transfixed and had stared into each other's eyes. María Teresa wondered about the incident's meaning and began to fear that something was happening behind her back when her husband arrived late from work all that week. When she confronted him and demanded to know his whereabouts, he replied that he was busy attending to his affairs with a lawyer because "some people are threatening to take away my properties."[52]

This was partially true because the general's first wife had initiated legal proceedings against Vidal for abandonment after he had ceased to support her and his daughters in November 1928. Her attorney (and brother-in-law), *licenciado* Victoriano Morales, had met with Vidal repeatedly over the spring of 1929 to negotiate a divorce. Finally, in the summer, they agreed that the general would cede his real estate in Mexico City and Veracruz to his daughters and provide them with cattle and a monthly pension of one hundred fifty pesos, about seventy U.S. dollars. It soon became apparent that Vidal had mismanaged his Veracruz properties, so Herrejón and her lawyer pressured the general to renegotiate on August 23, threatening to publicize his bigamy if he did not meet their terms. When that meeting proved unproductive, Herrejón pressed charges against Vidal and de Landa in a Mexico City court. The news of de Landa's imminent arrest quickly leaked to the media. On August 24, 1929, *Excélsior* reported the charges against Miss Mexico.[53] Later, during de Landa's trial, Herrejón claimed that Vidal had contacted her that same evening after reading the news, agreeing to new terms, which included paying Herrejón a $1,900-peso annuity. They had made plans to meet on the afternoon of August 26 to sign the documents that her lawyer planned to draft on the twenty-fifth.[54] Events came to a grinding halt, however, when Miss Mexico emptied a Smith and Wesson .44-caliber pistol into the body of her double-crossing husband.

Part III: The Crime

After rising from bed at 11:30 AM on Sunday, August 25, María Teresa de Landa put on her blue silk robe and walked to the dining room to take her breakfast. No one else was in the house except for her husband and a servant. Her father had departed at 6 AM to check on his dairy. Her mother and sister had gone to the market. Her brother was out with some friends.[55] Alone in the dining room, she drank half a glass of milk and began to glance through a stack of newspapers. She was surprised at their presence on the table, as her husband had always given instructions that no periodicals were to be purchased for the home. He would often exclaim, "Those guys used you! Don't you think they have already exposed you enough?"[56] She noticed her picture in one of the journals, and as she read the caption heralding her imminent incarceration for marrying a bigamist, the events of the past week took on new meaning. She could not believe her eyes. She immediately headed for the parlor, where her husband sat reading on the large, tiger-fur-covered Viennese bentwood sofa. Standing shaking before him, she showed him the newspaper and asked, "What have you done to me? You knew I loved you, how could you have lied to me so?" Vidal laughed at her and refused to answer her question, defiantly stating, "How dare you question things?" Again she insisted, becoming angry at his deceit and the nonchalant, ironic, condescending tone in which he replied, "Don't worry about it, they don't know what they say. It is all foolishness." De Landa later testified that at that moment, despair and anger overwhelmed her and she lost control at the thought of

> knowing that I had lived a life of lies, that I would soon lose my beloved husband . . . my whole life unraveled before my eyes. I wanted to kill myself rather than face a life without him, where I would be dishonored and shamed . . . I told him so and he laughed, he did not take me seriously. I picked up his gun, seizing it from the table before him and cocked it ready to shoot myself in the chest.[57]

According to de Landa's testimony, Vidal got up from the sofa and attempted to take the gun from her, screaming, "No, Teche, you would not dare!" She then turned the gun on him, telling him to leave her alone, to let her kill herself. She threatened to kill him if he attempted to stop her, so he sat back on the sofa. She seized the opportunity and again turned the gun on herself. As he rose and again attempted to disarm her, she fired at him.[58] De Landa's first shot impacted Vidal's breastbone, its force sending him back against the sofa in time for the second shot to ricochet from the wall and lodge itself in his cheekbone. The other four bullets also bounced off the wall and entered his back, thigh, gluteus, and cranium. María Teresa screamed at the sight of her dying husband, rushed to his side, and cradled him in her arms. In her despair, she cocked the gun and attempted to kill herself yet again, but by this time the gun was out of bullets. She would later remember that she had had a brief conversation with her moribund husband during which he told her, "I forgive you."[59] Ballistic experts General Gabriel Terrés and Colonel Alejandro Peña as well as forensic experts Dr. Uzeta and Dr. Romero would later verify her version of the events with scientific evidence. They calculated the trajectory of the bullets and the speed and angle of impact, and they observed that the body did not exhibit any powder burns.[60] They would later testify in court that the general's death had been accidental. In the words of a journalist, "the General cooked his own goose."[61]

Within an hour, the house was full of policemen and magistrates taking photographs of the crime scene. De Landa's mother and sister returned from the market; someone called her father back to the house. Antonio B. Quijano, dispatched to the scene from the office of the chief of police, later testified that María Teresa had been in "an abnormal state of nerves, very excited." María Teresa was dumbstruck and clung to her husband's bloodied corpse.[62] Still in shock, she slowly dressed, and in the company of her parents, officials took her to the Second Precinct to take her statement. Unable to get her to speak, officials transferred her to the women's pavilion at the Belén jail. The following day, August 26, she was booked. Sullen and dressed in black, her body covered by a silk cape and with a translucent black shawl covering her face, she narrated the events. After she finished making her statement and her fingerprints and anthropometric measurements had been taken, officials scrambled to find a cell to hold the celebrity prisoner until the preliminary hearing. While they readied "an apartment with appropriate lodgings," she and her mother remained under custody in the jail's garden. There they received the press and her lawyer, licenciado José María Lozano, an old supporter of Díaz and Huerta whose antirevolutionary affiliations had done nothing to stall a brilliant legal career.[63] In the ensuing months, hardly a day passed that she did not receive a visitor.

The press, especially *Excélsior*, published a barrage of interviews with the *autoviuda* (self-made widow) putting her in a positive light, alluding to her beauty, charm, and status as "the daughter of an honorable family, esteemed and known by the best of our society."[64] These interviews influenced public perceptions of the confessed killer, constructed a narrative of events favorable to her cause, and turned her into her husband's victim. Photographs accompanying these stories—published worldwide by the Associated Press for a public fascinated with the scandal—always showed her attired in a widow's costume as if hinting that her appropriate grieving behavior and adherence to sartorial codes demonstrated her innocence. Her use of a veil to mitigate her beauty represented her willingness to respect and honor the memory of her dead spouse. She repeatedly stated her love for her husband, recalled their moments together, and reiterated her intention of guarding his memory. She confessed that she had forgiven his actions and claimed that she regularly prayed to the Virgin of Guadalupe for the repose of his soul. Should the jury declare her guilty, she promised readers that she would kill herself ("Life is now meaningless"); should they find her not guilty, she promised never to remarry and to become a nun.[65] The captions, especially in *Excélsior*'s coverage, contrasted her lachrymose visage with the beaming face she had exhibited after winning the 1928 beauty contest a few months previously. Shortly before her trial, readers gasped at the news that their "blue-eyed beauty" had lost more than forty pounds![66]

María Teresa's apt manipulation of public opinion through the press worried the prosecution. Under the circumstances, to get the jury to indict her despite her own damning testimony and the forensic evidence would be difficult. After lobbying by the prosecution—and perhaps by General Vidal's friends in the armed forces or by executives at *Excélsior*, who stood to profit from monopolizing the story—an order arrived from the presidential palace prohibiting the publication of de Landa's "memoirs." Perhaps attempting to capitalize on the notoriety of the case to boost their readership and increase advertising revenues, competitors of *Excélsior* gave increased coverage to the case, adding to the aura of sensationalism. A morning tabloid, *La Prensa*, secured María Teresa's permission to publish a pamphlet detailing the particulars of the case. Manuel Espejel y Álvarez, a well-known journalist who specialized in penning sensational accounts of crime, began to work on the draft. Fearful of its influence on the yet-to-be-selected jury, the prosecutor sought to suppress the so-called *Miss Mexico Memoirs* to keep it out of circulation before and during the trial. Thus, on October 30, the presiding judge ordered that the account be suppressed until after the trial, arguing that "its publicity was harmful to society."[67]

Part IV: The Queen's Trial

The wheels of the Mexican legal system creaked along until late November, when, after months of sensational preliminary hearings and her indictment, the trial of María Teresa de Landa finally arrived. On November 22, the names of thirty men were placed into a glass bowl from which de Landa selected fifteen to constitute the nine-member jury and alternates. The men selected swore they were qualified to serve on the jury charged with hearing Miss Mexico's case; they were all thirty years of age or older, knew how to read and write, and professed to be persons of reputable moral character.[68] These jurors thus fit the gentlemanly Porfirian stereotype; they were individuals whose social pride, discretion, refinement, poise, and gallantry exuded a strong sense of moral superiority traditionally associated with the urban *criollo*. As cultural critic Carlos Monsiváis has keenly observed, a strong sense of personal honor guided these men's lives, as they saw it "your prime gift . . . your shield and your fortress, your relief, your raison d'être, and your plenitude."[69] Given the importance of honor and appearance to these men, de Landa's sympathizers and her defender constructed their narrative of the murdering beauty's actions around a discourse of honor that highlighted her beauty, fame, and family background. Her lawyer sought to sway the jury with emotional appeals, while her supporters in the press sought to influence public opinion favorably. To a great degree, her status as beauty queen assisted them, for jurors already saw her as the national embodiment of ideal feminine beauty and goodness. In his concluding arguments, Lozano reminded jurors that they were in a unique position to "safeguard" the values of justice and honor society held dear. He was confident they would not act as cold judges and condemn de Landa. Instead, they would "touch their hearts." As thinking men sensitive to her cause, the jurors would act to "secure justice in the same spirit of patriotism, duty, and republicanism that inspired English and French juries across the seas."[70]

Lozano had a spectacular track record that helped ensure de Landa's acquittal. Lozano's long career, not to mention his nickname "The Prince of Words," testified to his argumentative skill and eloquence. Moreover, Lozano represented traditional morality and liberal values, having earned his reputation as a firm supporter of "order and progress" as district attorney, congressman, and cabinet member under the dictatorships of military strongmen Porfirio Díaz and Victoriano Huerta. Lozano had achieved notoriety when he successfully prosecuted the famed outlaw El Tigre de Santa Julia (see chapter 3) and the murderers of exiled Guatemalan president Manuel Lisandro Barillas. His austere, elegant style earned him the praise and admiration of many, notwithstanding his role, along with Querido Moheno, in the downfall of President Madero in 1913 as one of the most vocal members of congress to legitimize Victoriano Huerta's coup (see chapter 4).[71] Lozano's intellectual formation combined the humanist tradition he learned at a Jesuit college with the positivist cult of science that shaped his experience at the National Preparatory School and the National School of Jurisprudence. Lozano was a master of rhetoric and perhaps the best defense attorney practicing in 1920s Mexico.

Throughout the trial, Lozano and de Landa's admirers in the press attacked the prosecutor, Luis Corona. Journalists presented him as a narcissistic ignoramus bent on self-promotion and only concerned about ordering the radio broadcast technicians to adjust their equipment in the courthouse before he made any statement.[72] This "Mr. Nobody," as they called him, incurred the press's wrath because he sought to portray de Landa as a dishonorable woman. Corona maintained that de Landa could not argue that she had been moved to kill her husband out of her concern for her dishonor because, according to him, she had no honor. What kind of honorable woman, Corona claimed, could de Landa possibly be if during the Miss Mexico Pageant preliminaries she had worn a bathing suit in public? Corona described de Landa as "a lustful, frivolous animal" and called her "an insult to Mexican womanhood."[73] Moreover, he repeatedly argued that she had not hesitated in killing her husband because she knew that, as a beautiful woman, she could beguile authorities with her appearance.[74]

Lozano countered Corona's prudery in a condescending, humorous manner that made the prosecutor seem a puritanical simpleton. Simply put, Corona was out of touch with reality. Lozano explained that during his vacation in European spas, he and his family had seen European aristocratic women wearing bathing suits, noting his "provincial colleague's narrow experience" had obviously conditioned Corona's argument. "I assure you," Lozano said, addressing Corona,

> that I saw this spectacle that you label immoral with my very own eyes. Women today walk around half nude. They show off their knees and, yes, even their thighs. They bare their armpits and their low-cut décolletage shows us the alluring cup of their breasts. I saw in Deauville, Biarritz, and San Sebastián women of the oldest lineages of Europe, ladies of great quality, dressed in this manner, nude but for their bathing suit.[75]

Lozano approached the jury and admitted that Corona's statements against de Landa surprised him: "What sort of prude is he? Is he a Quaker? Is he a Trappist Monk? Today, gentlemen, we are used to this 'nudity.' It is here to stay [and] it should not shock us." Lozano reminded the jurors that de Landa's appearance was typical of a modern world where "women are freeing themselves from old ideas, from millennia of subjugation to men, from untold slavery." Pointing to de Landa, he continued, "My dear sirs, this is the modern woman. They have a right to be passionate, they have a right to think, and to do as they wish." The suave, cosmopolitan Lozano wondered why men should continue to constrain women with such antiquated ideas.

Lozano wove into his narrative the idea that de Landa was caught up in both traditional and modern social attitudes. After pointing out that she was a passionate, patriotic, modern woman, Lozano also stressed how her violent reaction to Vidal represented her observance of tradition. He claimed she had only killed her husband as a final recourse in defense of her honor. Vidal's irresponsible actions had threatened her with imminent danger, for she feared losing her husband, her honor, and her liberty if she were charged with bigamy. She feared societal opprobrium, and, fearing society's moral judgment, she had acted violently. Her emotional shock had led her to murder Vidal, not out of premeditation, but in a moment of weakness when she had been momentarily blinded by her husband's aggressive and immoral actions. Vidal had laughed at her and remorselessly dismissed her threat of suicide, almost daring her to kill herself.[76] All of these arguments presented de Landa as a modern individual who was nonetheless susceptible to tradition.

In addition to the narrative of honor she conveyed through the press and in the courtroom thanks to Lozano, de Landa gave great attention to producing a powerful visual statement of her remorse and atonement. Both the photographic images and the text accompanying them provide invaluable evidence of how some early twentieth-century Mexicans consciously fashioned their appearance to condition others' behavior toward them. Mexican culture during these years typically placed great importance on elaborating and presenting one's image, knowing that others—especially subordinates or competitors—were intent on reading visual or spatial manifestations of power and status. Carlos Monsiváis has stressed this point, noting that early twentieth-century Mexico was a "world dominated by and lived through purely external sensation, of controlled and administered happiness, [where] individual feelings do not matter very much."[77] According to Monsiváis, appearance was paramount; it externalized private fantasies of reality, announced secret desires one could not manifest, and elaborated a fiction that did not exist in reality. It allowed dreams to come alive. In de Landa's case, her appearance portrayed her innocence by making reference to her sense of honor and *vergüenza* (shame). She sought, with her attire, to elicit the jury's sympathy and thus their clemency for a grieving widow: she was "draped in elegant black, in very high heels and wearing the moving veiled coif [headgear] of a mourning widow."[78] De Landa's use of a veil to mitigate her beauty represented her willingness to respect and honor her dead spouse's memory. What is described as "a moving veiled coif" appeared to draw attention away from her beauty, indicating that she acknowledged her ability to incite masculine thoughts disrespectful of her deceased husband's honor. De Landa's high heels provided pedestals on which a proper grieving widow, attired in elegant black, awaited absolution, as alluded to in biblical verse: "Thou art clothed with honor and majesty. Who coverest thyself with light as with a garment."[79]

De Landa and Lozano strove to undermine her accusers' credibility. Lozano strengthened this argument by questioning the morality of witnesses testifying against de Landa. In turn, she and Lozano countered her accusers' testimony by employing arguments full of allusions to the class and ethnicity of the prosecution's witnesses in order to undermine their credibility. Vidal's ex-lover, Consuelo Flores Reyes, had testified in preliminary hearings that de Landa's claims to innocence were obfuscated by her immoral actions. Flores assured the jury that she had seen de Landa accompany Vidal to his bachelor's apartment on a number of occasions.[80] To counter these accusations, Lozano produced affidavits from the Ministry of Education explaining to the jury that Flores had lied about being a teacher. Her true profession—a singer and dancer in vaudeville revues—did not make her the ideal expert on matters of morality. He called on one witness, first-year law student Teodosio Montalván, to describe to the jury Flores's appearance and demeanor when he had visited her a week after the preliminary hearings on the de Landa case hoping to obtain information to write a play about the case. Montalván noted that Flores opened her door in a state of deshabille, wearing nothing but a sheer gown. She had smiled, invited him and a friend who accompanied him into her bedroom, and asked them to sit on her bed. Flores reportedly told them about her love for the deceased general, making repeated references to him "in endearing ways" and implying they had known each other carnally. She also told them that she was sure de Landa had lied about the circumstances surrounding the murder, and that although she wanted de Landa to be condemned for murdering Vidal, she had not ever actually seen Vidal and de Landa together as she had declared in court.[81] As Flores was not present for the final trial (the prosecution read her testimony from previous declarations to authorities), Lozano argued that the jury should suspect her absence. He next asked de Landa whether she wished to comment on Flores's statements. De Landa began by noting that Flores had lied about her occupation knowing that, had they been aware of it, the jurors would have dismissed her testimony because it was evident from her coarse speech and demeanor that she was neither a lady of quality or education, and as such could never have convinced anyone she was a teacher. De Landa also stated that she felt Flores had ulterior motives, and that as a person of questionable morality Flores was not qualified to speak on anyone's character. In arguing so, de Landa mobilized Mexican society's stereotyping and condemnation of vaudeville actresses. The campy performances, curved bodies, sans souci sensuality, and seductive attire of great divas such as María Conesa, Celia Montalván, and Mimí Derba were very successful among male audiences but, the accused implied, such women were hardly reliable witnesses in a court of law.[82]

Subsequent witnesses for the prosecution made arguments similar to Flores's, only to be similarly rebuffed. Jesús Ramírez and his wife Eva Serrano, friends of Flores, affirmed that as the general's neighbors, they had noticed an elegant lady enter his apartment regularly, implying that de Landa had regularly had sex with Vidal prior to their marriage. Ana María Castillo de Jordán, Vidal's landlord, testified she had almost evicted the general from her boardinghouse because she felt he had too many female guests. Ana María's freckled, red-haired son, Arturo Jordán Castillo, told jurors he had seen de Landa twice. The young boy said he had once delivered a tray to the general's room with two plates of soup and sardines, and he recognized de Landa as the woman who had answered the door. De Landa refuted their statements, arguing that their depositions were incoherent. If, as they claimed, she and Vidal had had an affair, why would she be seen in public or call attention to herself by wearing, as they claimed, a large, elegant hat and expensive clothing? Moreover, Victoria Hernández de Domínguez, who had been appointed de Landa's chaperone during the Miss Mexico Pageant finals, testified that she had always been beside her at events, and de Landa had never accompanied men anywhere. Hernández claimed that de Landa "behaved with great modesty and all the decorum appropriate to a young lady."[83] When de Landa confronted the young Jordán Castillo, she spoke to him in a haughty manner and played the role of an outraged snob, saying, "Do you honestly expect the jury to believe that *I* would ever lunch on watery soup and sardines or that a man like my husband would ever entertain a lady with such a menu?"[84] The press, siding with de Landa, noted that Ramírez was "but a quaint tailor" and described Serrano as "a fat, flat nosed, pug faced woman" as if implying that their mixed-race, lower-class backgrounds discredited their statements against the white, upper-class Miss Mexico.[85] Descriptions of Vidal's first wife carried similar implications, noting that Herrejón was "thick lipped" and had "coarse features." The comparison was most obvious during the final trial, when Herrejón sat next to Miss Mexico, as if in seeing the second wife's beauty highlighted, the jury would rule in her favor.[86]

Throughout the trial, Lozano also attacked Vidal's chaotic, immoral masculinity and contrasted it to de Landa's ability to cultivate a modern femininity while remaining observant of traditional modes of honor. Vidal was violent, deceitful, and dishonorable. He had abused his new wife, restricted her, beat her, and taken her away from her family, friends, and school. He consorted with prostitutes, chorus girls, and other individuals of ill repute. He was not a good steward of his capital: he could not provide a house for de Landa, lived in substandard quarters, and mismanaged his properties. He had also failed to provide for his children. Vidal clearly was anything but the thrifty, rational, hardworking, moral masculine ideal the Revolution had hoped to foster. In a sense, her patriotic service to the nation as Miss Mexico, her interest in education, her desire to bridge class differences for the common good, and her adherence to traditional codes of honor could be seen to have masculinized María Teresa. By picking up Vidal's gun and shooting him, de Landa had not just refused to take his abuse or forgive his scandalous conduct; she had killed a man who failed to live up to his proper gender role.

It is curious that the prosecution never referred to María Teresa's characteristic short fuse. Interviews published when she had been involved in the Miss Mexico Pageant had already hinted that below the genteel, modern, charming surface was a violent individual. As noted earlier, she had jokingly threatened to beat up a journalist if he failed to be fair and accurate in his story.[87]

Lozano sought to sway the jury in de Landa's favor during his expansive concluding statement through the use of emotional hyperbole and literary references that compared de Landa to martyred saints, mythical heroes, and historical figures. Lozano dipped deeply into his bag of tricks, peppering his remarks with poems about crimes of passion, quotations from French legal briefs, and myriad references from ancient and modern European history. He drew parallels between María Teresa's actions and those of women in the age of Pericles, the Renaissance, and Enlightened France. During these epochs, he noted, the activities and writings of women such as Eleanor of Aquitaine, doña Blanca de Castilla, and the Marquise de Rambouillet had foreshadowed de Landa's notions about an active, thinking, progressive model of womanhood. (Surprisingly, not once did Lozano mention an example from Mexican history!) Far from being an immoral person, de Landa, like her illustrious predecessors, had acted responsibly and patriotically. Modern women, he noted, educated themselves for their own good and that of their country. The jury had before it a model honorable woman. Miss Mexico had acted as "a lioness of Castile" who killed to cleanse her honor. Lozano went on to equate her actions to Othello's murder of Desdemona and so continued well into the night. He concluded his lengthy closing arguments with a lachrymose appeal to the jury and held up telegrams from every corner of Mexico and even from abroad urging him to defend de Landa to the end:

> You hold María Teresa de Landa's fate in your hands. Public opinion demands her absolution. . . . I have received many telegrams . . . in

which I have been told to defend ... this woman, who as a female has faults, but that these are faults which we could all have were we to react to the conditions in which she found herself. You must pardon her, administering justice as would an English jury, which, composed of twelve members, represents the Apostles of Jesus, because the Divine Redeemer said before His death that whenever twelve men of goodwill would meet to carry out a good deed, He would be in spirit with them. I give you then the fate of Miss Mexico, who was a symbol of the Fatherland taken by our vote to the beaches of Galveston bearing the representation of Mexican womanhood ... outside awaiting María Teresa is an anguished and stricken mother who has shed many tears in her calvary ... take into account the great weight that María Teresa has taken on, which could very well figure alongside ... the glorious St. Blandine and St. Cordelia.[88]

Applause from the public endorsed Lozano's conclusion. Within minutes, the jury retired to consider its verdict, returning at 2:45 AM to announce its exoneration of de Landa.

Widespread celebration greeted the jury's decision. During the legal process, de Landa had come to embody feminine modernity for many people. Students cheered for her, exclaiming "Long live women!" and "Long live women who know how to love."[89] The public recognized her victimization, claiming that her values were admirable: "We do not defend the murder; we defend her because she was the victim of supreme amorous passion, so rare in our times." Women especially seemed to favor the jurors' clemency. A "distinguished-looking lady" commented to reporters: "The poor dear has been a martyr already. They should let her go." Others claimed that the trial symbolized the abusive despotism of the law embodied in the prosecuting attorney's attacks on the defendant's morality. They decried "*la justicia legal y seca*" (dry, legal justice), which failed to recognize de Landa's difficult circumstances.

The public's arguments in favor of María Teresa suggest that people attached greater significance to her trial than is evident at first glance. Women and progressive elements in society, particularly her fellow students, felt she embodied a new model of womanhood that was not only inclusive of a more active vision of womanly behavior, but also one that contested male dominance. Moreover, this new feminine model incorporated traditionalists' definition of a sentimental, emotive, and nurturing woman. This is certainly implied in women's comments that referred to María Teresa's victimhood and that alluded to passion as her prime motive. Her case presents an excellent illustration of the political importance of gender in that people also understood her case as an allegory of society's struggle against the revolutionary state.

Conclusion

The death of General Moisés Vidal Corro on August 25, 1929, at the hands of his glamorous, ex-beauty-queen wife María Teresa de Landa illustrates that Mexicans' changing notions of modern womanhood and justice developed alongside longstanding views of marriage and honor. The sensationalism surrounding de Landa's exoneration speaks not only to societal changes but also to the persistence of ancien-régime attitudes of class and propriety. In addition to being a modern woman, de Landa represented the embodiment of abstract notions of racial purity and class morality that remained dear to the hearts of Eurocentric Mexican elites and essential to their legitimating ideology. In the face of the racially, intellectually, and morally inferior popular classes, de Landa's family background, feminist ideas, physical beauty, and moral conviction represented the continued viability of creoles as the class that could lead Mexico toward modernity without sacrificing traditional values and attitudes. De Landa's case also serves to demonstrate how individuals craft narratives in their own favor using the ideas and language of dominant groups to better argue their case. In Miss Mexico's retelling of the murder story, she successfully manipulated prevailing attitudes toward women to present herself as General Vidal's victim.

The balance of justice was weighed in María Teresa de Landa's favor as she, her lawyer, and the press strove to represent her as the model respectable woman. She was the intelligent, blameless, and pure daughter of a prominent family who had been victimized by a deceitful social inferior unwilling to fulfill his marital obligations. Pretrial publicity revealed that General Vidal had repeatedly beaten his wife, limited her contact with her family, restricted her movements by keeping her close to his side, and did not seem to espouse any notions of companionate matrimony. Rather, he treated de Landa like his personal property, and according to witnesses and her testimony, disregarded her opinions. He had refused to take her seriously when she attempted to commit suicide after learning she had been tricked into marrying a bigamist.[90] A proper lady—especially one whose family had figured prominently in Mexican social and political circles for nearly two hundred years—could not bear such an affront to her honor by an uncouth upstart. Further evidence for the thesis of jury solidarity with the victim emerges if one considers the widespread preference for the European racial phenotype in 1920s Mexico, for although the appearance of well-publicized events such as the India Bonita (Pretty Indian Maiden) pageant demonstrated that Mexicans did have some appreciation for indigenous beauty, they were only willing to accept Eurocentric beauty as emblematic of the nation. For all the Revolution's indigenism, the fact remained that the print media, radio, and film reinforced aesthetic values that conveyed subliminal messages of white superiority in a mixed-race country. Beautiful, educated, socially prominent, and paradoxically dressed as a grieving widow, María Teresa played into popular stereotypes of Mexican womanhood and succeeded in mesmerizing the jury into granting her liberty despite her self-confessed guilt.[91]

In murdering her husband, de Landa stepped out of recently established institutional arrangements for individual conflict resolution, chiefly the 1929 Mexico City Civil Code, which allowed for divorce on the grounds of physical abuse or marital infidelity. As she gave a personal performance that did not question (and in fact reinforced) patriarchal power, de Landa's adherence to traditional gender behavior helped her earn the jury's exoneration. De Landa put into play a serious gamble when she externalized the private and announced the secret—appearing as she did and acknowledging her crime—but she succeeded in establishing her innocence by manipulating existing gender stereotypes in her favor.[92] In presenting herself as a powerless, remorseful woman at the mercy of the jury, de Landa was one of many women who employed the age-old tactic of subverting hegemonic discourse by relying on the "weapons of the weak."[93] In this sense, the de Landa case suggests that women in early postrevolutionary Mexico exercised greater agency than historians have generally accorded them. Women had recourse to sophisticated if not always obvious "weapons" in their quotidian struggle against machismo. Women could thus negotiate the meaning and punishment of their crimes. It is important to stress, then, that in regularly addressing de Landa as "the Widow Vidal," the jury, her defender, and the press helped construct the appearance that she was remorseful for her act, that she loved her husband, and that she continued to be faithful to his memory. After all, testimony rendered by the general's family, friends, and first wife established that Vidal had regarded de Landa as his legitimate wife and had intended to divorce his first wife to safeguard de Landa's honor.

The jury's decision should not come as a surprise. Evidence suggests that popular juries regularly ruled on behalf of defendants claiming to have acted to protect their honor. De Landa's case was only the latest and perhaps the most sensational in a long line of murders in which women killed their spouses, lovers, or rivals to cleanse their reputation. Celebrated Mexican murderesses during the 1920s included Alicia Olvera de Serrano (1920), Magdalena Jurado (1922), Sara del Toro Romero (1923), and Juana Támez de Mondragón (1924).[94] These women acted out their anger at their partners' deception and betrayal of their trust. Even as the courts considered de Landa's indictment, another woman, the U.S.-trained nurse Eva Martínez, was being absolved of the murder of her superior, Dr. Narciso Cosío Aguilar, who had raped her on the outskirts of Mexico City where she had accompanied him to care for a purportedly ill patient.[95] Martínez's case, unlike that of de Landa, was tried by a judge, who concluded that a woman had "the right and the duty to kill the perpetrator of her dishonor."[96] Elsewhere in Latin America, courts and publics reached similar decisions. In the case of Ligia Parra Jahn, the Venezuelan public sympathized with her plea for justice on the grounds that she had only murdered to safeguard her honor. Like de Landa, Parra Jahn was also a beautiful woman from a respectable family.[97]

The case of the murdering beauty also safely engages within the confines of patriarchal discourse important issues relating to people's perception of the state's proper role in their everyday lives. An event charged with symbolic value, the 1929 de Landa murder underlines the importance of gender as a "useful category of historical analysis" given its recurrent use as a reference for conceiving, legitimating, and criticizing political power.[98] The dialectics of gender and politics in the 1920s reflected a widespread belief in the "natural" subjection of women to men and is in that way analogous to society's relationship to the state under the Sonoran Dynasty. De Landa's refusal to adhere to patriarchal notions of female propriety—wifely devotion and unquestioning submission—parallels the numerous challenges religious, agrarian, and labor groups posed to the revolutionary regime in the 1920s. The macho behavior of de Landa's husband, a former revolutionary general, embodied the violence and disarray for which members of Mexico's respectable classes (the bourgeois, church-attending urban inhabitants) criticized the governing elites. Thus, within the limits of a violent private family dispute, the Mexican public found an opportunity to not only discuss the renegotiation and redefinition of gender roles and marital obligations, but, more importantly, also come to imagine society's capacity to challenge the established order, for the case of the murdering beauty contained a powerful metaphor for violent attacks against the Sonoran Dynasty. Encoded in this event lurked the reminder of counterrevolutionary opposition and the centuries-old, racialized struggle between creoles, mestizos, and indios that continues to this day.

Notes

I would like to thank the University of Wisconsin–La Crosse International Faculty Development Fund for support during the completion of this project, as well as William H. Beezley (The University of Arizona), Julie Hardwick (The University of Texas), and Jane Dale Lloyd-Daley (Universidad Iberoamericana) for their comments to improve the earlier Spanish version of this chapter. My thanks as well to Rob Buffington and Pablo Piccato. All translations are my own unless otherwise noted.

1. Carlos Monsiváis, "'Red News': The Crime Pages in Mexico," in *Mexican Postcards*, ed. and trans. John Kraniauskas (London: Verso Books, 1997), 149; Isabel Fernández Tejedo, *Recuerdo de México: La tarjeta postal mexicana, 1882-1930* (Mexico City: Banobras, 1994), 134; and Eduardo Flores Clair, "Sucedió en la radio: Reseña de Bailes y Balas, Ciudad de México, 1921-1931," in *Lectura: Revista de libros de El Nacional* 154 (7 March 1992), 13.

2. Presidents of the Sonoran Dynasty were from the northern state of Sonora or had risen to prominence there. They included Álvaro Obregón, 1920-1924; Plutarco Elías Calles, 1924-1928; Emilio Portes Gil, 1928-1930; Pascual Ortíz Rubio, 1930-1932; and Abelardo L. Rodríguez, 1932-1934. As a group, they built a strong national, secular state to the detriment of the Church, local interests, and the army. They used corporatism to demobilize and disarticulate the grievances of agrarian reformers and labor activists and pacified the country by imposing the rule of law, replacing individual conflict resolution by reserving to the state a monopoly of violence to secure economic development and political stability. In seeking to transform a country perceived as "hopelessly backward and superstitious," ideologues of the Sonoran Dynasty such as José Vasconcelos tried to "regenerate" Mexico with a cultural model that infused humanism and nationalism in the schools, promoted the arts, nurtured cultural links with Spain and Latin America, assimilated the Indians, and "rediscovered" folk arts and traditions. See Alan Knight, *The Mexican Revolution*, 2 vols. (Cambridge: Cambridge University Press, 1986), 2: 498-500, 511; Arnaldo Córdova, *La Revolución en crisis: La aventura del Maximato* (Mexico City: Cal y Arena, 1995), 120-26, 187-306; Alan Knight, "Popular Culture and the Revolutionary State in Mexico, 1910-1940," *Hispanic American Historical Review* 74, no. 3 (Fall 1994): 393-444; Jean Meyer, Enrique Krauze, and Cayetano Reyes, *Historia de la revolución mexicana*, vol. 11, *Período 1924-1928: Estado y sociedad con Calles* (Mexico City: El Colegio de México, 1977); and Carlos Monsiváis, "Notas sobre la cultura nacional en el siglo XX," in *Historia general de México*, ed. Daniel Cosío Villegas (Mexico City: El Colegio de México, 1988), 2:1375-547.

3. José Manuel Puig Casauranc, *Galatea rebelde a varios pigmaliones: De Obregón a Cárdenas: Antecedentes del fenómeno mexicano actual, 1938* (Mexico City: Impresores Unidos, 1938), 271-81; and Andrae Marak, "Federalization of Education in Chihuahua," *Paedagogica Historica* 41, no. 3 (June 2005): 357-76.

4. Natalie Zemon Davis, *Fiction in the Archives: Pardon Tales and Their Tellers in Sixteenth-Century France* (Stanford: Stanford University Press, 1987).

5. Sarah C. Maza, *Private Lives and Public Affairs: The Causes Célèbres of Prerevolutionary France* (Berkeley: University of California Press, 1993).

6. Joan W. Scott, "Gender: A Useful Category of Historical Analysis," *American Historical Review* 91, no. 5 (December 1986): 1067-75.

7. For a cultural reading of beauty pageants, see Colleen Ballerino Cohen, Richard Wilk, and Beverly Stoeltje, eds., *Beauty Queens on the Global Stage: Gender, Contests, and Power* (New York: Routledge, 1996), 1-12. For a discussion of how the state used beauty pageants and other rituals to "imagine" the nation in Mexico, see

David E. Lorey, "The Revolutionary Festival in Mexico: November 20 Celebrations in the 1920s and 1930s" (paper presented at the 111th Annual Meeting of the American Historical Association, 5 January 1997); Margarita Tortajada Quiroz, *Danza y poder* (Mexico City: Instituto Nacional de Bellas Artes, 1995); Frances Toor, *A Treasury of Mexican Folkways* (New York: Crown Publishers, 1947), 312–76; and Rubén M. Campos, *El Folklore Literario de México. Investigación acerca de la producción literaria popular, 1525–1925* (Mexico City: Publicaciones de la Secretaría de Educación Pública, 1929), 69–84.

8. On modern Mexican women's writings on feminine beauty, see Rosario Castellanos, "La mujer y su imagen," in *Mujer que sabe latín*, 3rd ed. (Mexico City: Fondo de Cultura Económica, 1995), 9–21. For a recent theoretical discussion of feminine appearance, see Catherine G. Valentine, "Female Bodily Perfection and the Divided Self," in *Ideals of Feminine Beauty: Philosophical, Social, and Cultural Dimensions*, ed. Karen A. Callaghan (Westport, CT: Greenwood Press, 1994), 113–23.

9. Cohen, et al., eds., *Beauty Queens on the Global Stage*, 2–3.

10. Ernest Gruening, *Mexico and its Heritage* (New York: The Century Co., 1928), 623–31. For a well-illustrated and annotated edition of Mme. Calderón de la Barca's classic, see Frances Erskine Inglis Calderón de la Barca, *La vida en México durante una residencia de dos años en ése país*, 2 vols., trans. Felipe Teixidor (Mexico City: Porrúa, 1959).

11. Laureana Wright de Kleinhans, *Mujeres notables mexicanas* (Mexico City: Tipografía Económica, 1910); María de la Luz Parcero L., *Condiciones de la mujer en el siglo XIX* (Mexico City: Instituto Nacional de Antropología e Historia, 1982); Silvia Marina Arrom, *The Women of Mexico City, 1790–1857* (Stanford: Stanford University Press, 1985); and Carmen Ramos Escandón, "Señoritas porfirianas: Mujer e ideología en el México progresista, 1880–1910," in *Presencia y Transparencia: La mujer en la historia de México*, ed. Programa Interdisciplinario de Estudios de la Mujer (Mexico City: El Colegio de México, 1987), 143–62. For autobiographical accounts of elite Mexican women, see Piedad de Yturbe del Villar von Scholtz Hermensdorff, Marquesa de Belvís de las Navas, and Princesa Max de Hohenlohe Langenburg, *"Érase una vez . . .": Bocetos de mi juventud* (Madrid: Industrias Gráficas Seix y Barral Hnos., 1954); Carolina Escudero Luján de Múgica, *Carolina Escudero Luján: Una mujer en la historia de México. Testimonio oral* (Morelia, Mexico: Instituto Michoacano de Cultura and Centro de Estudios de la Revolución Mexicana "Lázaro Cárdenas," Archivo de Historia Oral, 1992) and Paula Amor Poniatowska, *Nomeolvides* (Mexico City: Plaza y Janés, 1996).

12. A more literal translation would be, "A woman who knows Latin lacks a husband and does not have a good end."

13. Her father owned a number of properties in and around Mexico City and derived his income by distributing products from his dairy farms in the Valley of Mexico. Her mother's father was Dr. A. de los Ríos. See "Absurda hipótesis del Sr. Lic. Corona," "Las viudas de Vidal frente a frente," and "¿Es parcial el Presidente del Jurado?" *Excélsior*, 30 November 1929, pp. 1–8. On the de Landa family, see Duque de Otranto, *Los Trescientos* (Mexico City: Editorial Stylo, 1951) and Ricardo Ortega

y Pérez Gallardo, *Historia genealógica de las familias más antiguas de México*, 3 vols., 3rd ed. (Mexico City: Imprenta de A. Carranza, 1908–1910).

14. "La Señorita México no sólo ignoraba que su esposo fuera casado sino que un sacerdote se lo ocultó," *Excélsior*, 28 August 1929, p. 1.

15. According to the 1921 census, fewer than ten thousand women were "professionals," but this figure included secretaries, executive assistants, telephone operators, and a few hundred teachers. See Anna Macías, *Against All Odds: The Feminist Movement in Mexico to 1940* (London: Greenwood Press, 1982), 105. The first native-born Mexican female general practitioner and obstetrician-gynecologist was Matilde P. Montoya y Lafragua (1859–?), who graduated from the National University's School of Medicine in 1887.

16. Rómulo Velasco Ceballos, "Demostración de cultura son los concursos como el que ahora desarrolla *Jueves de Excélsior*. Señorita María Teresa de Landa, hermosa candidata que está dispuesta a vencer en el gran torneo de la Señorita México. Formidable competidora," *Excélsior*, 20 April 1928, p. 4.

17. Monsiváis, "Notas sobre la cultura."

18. Velasco Ceballos, "Demostración de cultura."

19. An excellent analysis of this incident is Anne Rubenstein, "The War on las Pelonas: Modern Women and their Enemies, Mexico, 1924," in *Sex in Revolution: Gender, Politics, and Power in Modern Mexico*, ed. Jocelyn Olcott, Mary Kay Vaughan, and Gabriela Cano (Durham, NC: Duke University Press, 2006), 57–79. Also see "Nuestras bellas pelonas se arman para defenderse de sus agresores," *El Demócrata*, 27 July 1924, p. 5.

20. María Elena Gutiérrez Rentería, "La comunicación en América Latina. Informe de México," *Chasqui: Revista Latinoamericana de Comunicación* 74 (June 2001); and Antonio Saborit, *Como mármol recién lavado. "El Mundo Ilustrado" de Rafael Reyes Espíndola* (Mexico City: Ediciones sin nombre, Conaculta, 2006).

21. Alberto del Castillo Troncoso, "Entre la moralización y el sensacionalismo: Prensa, poder y criminalidad a fines del siglo XIX en la Ciudad de México," in *Hábitos, normas y escándalo: Prensa, criminalidad y drogas en el porfiriato tardío*, eds. Ricardo Pérez Montfort, et al. (Mexico City: Plaza y Valdés Editores, 1997), 17–73, cited in Elisa Speckman Guerra, *Crímen y castigo. Legislación penal, interpretaciones de la criminalidad y administración de justicia, Ciudad de México, 1872–1910* (Mexico City: El Colegio de México and Universidad Nacional Autnóma de México, 2002), 173; and L. Núñez Hernández, "Instantáneas cruciales de la fotografia en México: Las imágenes periodísticas constituyen su columna vertebral," *Revista mexicana de comunicación* 9, no. 46 (November 1997), 46–48.

22. Sarah A. Buck, "Control de Natalidad y el Día de la Madre: Política Feminista y Reaccionaria en México, 1922–1923," *Signos Históricos* 5 (January–June 2001): 9–53.

23. Héctor L. Zarauz López, *México: Fiestas cívicas, familares, laborales y nuevos festejos* (Mexico City: Consejo Nacional para la Cultura y las Artes, 2000), 116–21.

24. "María Teresa de Landa obtuvo el mayor número de sufragios en el concurso pro-'Señorita México' cerrado el domingo," *Excélsior*, 18 May 1928, p. 1.

25. "Absurda hipótesis del Sr. Lic. Corona; Las Viudas de Vidal Frente a Frente; ¿Es parcial el Presidente del Jurado?" *Excélsior*, 20 November 1929, pp. 1–8.
26. "Luxemburgo enviará a Gálveston en Junio a una hermosa mujer," *Excélsior*, 2 April 1928, p. 1; "Una bella fiesta de sol, de músculo y de alegría hoy en la alberca Esther. Las candidatos a 'Señorita México' se presentarán para que sus simpatizantes puedan admirarlas y votar por ella en el Gran Certámen," *Excélsior*, 12 May 1928, p. 7; "El concurso para elegir 'Señorita México,'" *Excélsior*, 13 May 1928, p. 4; and "Los cargos que hizo a Miss México fueron ya desvanecidos del todo. Rindió ayer una amplia declaración la Sra. Victoria Hernández de Domínguez," *Excélsior*, 26 Sep. 1929, pp. 1–8.
27. "Bases para el concurso de Elección de la Señorita México 1928," *Excélsior*, 15 April 1928, p. 7.
28. Frank Deford, *There She Is: The Life and Times of Miss America* (New York: Viking Books, 1971); and Flores Clair, "Sucedió en la radio," 13.
29. Velasco Ceballos, "Demostración de cultura."
30. Santiago Argüello, *Mi mensaje a la juventud y otras orientaciones* (Mexico City: Sucesores de Herrero Hermanos, 1928), 89–131.
31. Enlightened Mexican thinkers such as José Joaquín Fernández de Lizardi wrote about women's education shortly before independence in his novel *La Quijotita y su prima* (1819). Moderates such as Mariano Galván Rivera penned a number of essays on women's education that he later published in his successful ladies' journal. See Mariano Galván Rivera, *Calendario de las señoritas megicanas para el año de 1839* (Mexico City: Imprenta de Galván, 1838).
32. José Manuel Puig Casauranc, *De Nuestro México Cosas Sociales y Aspectos Políticos* (Mexico City: Editorial Cultura, 1928), 22–24, 183–93.
33. Velasco Ceballos, "Demostración de cultura." Subsequent comments come from the same citation unless otherwise noted.
34. Rómulo Velasco Ceballos, "El torneo de belleza despierta grán interés en la Ciudad de México. Bella yucateca que se halla resuelta a ser la vencedor," *Excélsior*, 12 April 1928, p. 3.
35. Rómulo Velasco Ceballos, "El sueño de la graciosa Enriqueta pronto logrará convertirse en Realidad," *Excélsior*, 14 April 1928, p. 4.
36. Rómulo Velasco Ceballos, "Un sueño maravilloso es para muchas señoritas ir a la Ciudad de Galveston," *Excélsior*, 4 May 1928, p. 2.
37. Rómulo Velasco Ceballos, "La mujer mexicana debería de seguir la corriente moderna," *Excélsior*, 26 April 1928, p. 4.
38. "María Teresa de Landa obtuvo el mayor número de sufragios en el concurso pro 'Señorita México' cerrado el domingo," *Excélsior*, 16 May 1928, p. 1.
39. "El más estupendo carro alegórico para la Señorita México 1928," *Excélsior*, 18 May 1928, p. 1.
40. "La señorita María Teresa de Landa representará a México en Gálveston," *Excélsior*, 20 May 1928, p. 1.
41. "Las bellezas europeas llegarán mañana," *Excélsior*, 25 May 1928, p. 1; and Sergio H. Peralta Sandoval and Carloslucio Ramos, *Hotel Regis: Historia de una época* (Mexico City: Editorial Diana, 1996). A complete analysis of the parade and its

symbolism is available in Víctor Manuel Macías González, "El caso de una beldad asesina: La construcción narrativa, los concursos de belleza y el mito nacional posrevolucionario (1921–1931)," *Historia y Grafía* 13 (1999): 113–54.

42. Elena Poniatowska, *Todo México* (Mexico City: Editorial Diana, 1993), 2:7–18. Del Río's cousin had been the 1921 Centennial Queen.
43. For an example of the elite's disparaging view of revolutionary bureaucrats and generals, see women's comments about "flatulent beaner ragamuffin barristers" in Guadalupe Amor, *Yo soy mi casa* (Mexico City: Fondo de Cultura Económica, 1957); and Elena Poniatowska, *La "flor de lís"* (Mexico City: Ediciones ERA, 1988).
44. "Primera declaración de la jóven uxoricida," *Excélsior*, 29 August 1929, p. 1. Also see "Absurda hipótesis." I have attempted to find information on General Vidal, but he is absent from the Mexican biographical dictionaries and encyclopedias I consulted. The only biographical information presented in the trials that the newspapers alluded to was a statement by General Rodolfo Martínez, brother-in-law of Vidal's first wife María Teresa Herrejón, who declared he had met Vidal "15 years ago" when Vidal was a lowly private. Martínez claimed Vidal had risen over the years because of his skills, which the Ministry of War recognized in recalling him to active duty in 1926 and granting him a bureaucratic post in Mexico City.
45. "Primera declaración de la jóven uxoricida," *Excélsior*, 29 August 1929, p. 1.
46. "Absurda hipótesis."
47. The Church essentially went on strike against the Sonoran Dynasty from August 1926 to June 30, 1929. See John W. Foster-Dulles, *Yesterday in Mexico: A Chronicle of the Revolution, 1919–1936* (Austin: University of Texas Press, 1961), 296–308, 459–63.
48. "Primera declaración."
49. The family lived in a four-bedroom apartment on the second story of a large colonial building. The ground floor was occupied by garages, offices, and Mr. de Landa's dairy outlet. See "Primera declaración."
50. "Primera declaración" and "Absurda hipótesis."
51. "María Teresa de Landa fue absuelta y triunfó el Príncipe de la Palabra," *Excélsior*, 1 December 1929, pp. 1, 8–9.
52. "Primera declaración."
53. "Acusan de bigamía al esposo de 'Miss México,'" *Excélsior*, 24 August 1929 (late edition), p. 1; and "Absurda hipótesis."
54. "No fue farsa la boda con María Teresa de Landa," *Excélsior*, 31 August 1929, p. 1.
55. "María Teresa de Landa fue absuelta."
56. "Saber que su marido era un bígamo la impulsó al crímen," *Excélsior*, 26 August 1929, p. 1.
57. "María Teresa relata sollozante como dió muerte al hombre que la engañó," *Excélsior*, 27 August 1929, pp. 1–3.
58. "María Teresa relata sollozante," 1–3.
59. "Primera declaración."
60. "Absurda hipótesis."
61. Flores Clair, "Sucedió en la radio," 6.
62. "Absurda hipótesis."

63. "María Teresa relata sollozante."
64. "María Teresa de Landa mató sin intención," *Excélsior*, 12 November 1929.
65. "María Teresa relata sollozante," "Atribulada refiere," and "La señorita México no sólo ignoraba que su esposo fuera casado sino que un sacerdote se lo ocultó," *Excélsior*, 28 August 1929, p. 1.
66. "María Teresa comparecerá mañana en jurado," *Excélsior*, 27 November 1929, p. 1.
67. "Suppression of Memoirs," *The Chronicle Telegram* (Elyria, Ohio), 31 October 1929, p. 1. The memoir would not appear until after the trial. It proved quite popular, prompting editors to release a second edition after the first flew off newsstands in days. See Manuel Espejel y Álvarez, *Confidencias de "Miss México"* (Mexico City: Imprenta de la Providencia, 1929).
68. "María Teresa comparece hoy ante el tribunal popular," *Excélsior*, 23 November 1929, p. 1; and William P. Tucker, *The Mexican Government Today* (Minneapolis: University of Minnesota Press, 1957), 117.
69. Monsiváis, *Mexican Postcards*, 2.
70. "María Teresa de Landa fue absuelta."
71. José María Lozano, *José María Lozano en la Tribuna Parlamentaria, 1910–1913*, (Mexico City: Editorial Jus, 1953); "María Teresa de Landa fue absuelta"; and Pablo Piccato, *Congreso y revolución: El parlamentarismo en la XXVI Legislatura* (Mexico City: Instituto Nacional de Estudios Históricos de la Revolución, 1991).
72. "María Teresa de Landa fue absuelta."
73. Ibid.
74. These observations are made in nineteenth-century Latin America's premier book of etiquette, first published in 1854 and subsequently reissued and revised. See Manuel Antonio Carreño, *Manual de urbanidad y buenas maneras para uso de la juventud de ambos sexos en el cual se encuentran las principales reglas de civilidad y etiqueta que deben observarse en las diversas situaciones sociales* (New York: D. Appleton and Co., 1880), 65–75, 77–78. Also see Condesa de Tramar, *El trato social: Costumbres de la sociedad moderna en todas las circunstancias de la vida* (Mexico City: Librería de la Viuda de Charles Bouret, 1906).
75. "María Teresa de Landa fue absuelta."
76. "María Teresa de Landa mató sin intención," *Excélsior*, 12 November 1929, p. 1. These were the arguments he presented to the court in a written statement two weeks before the case began. They were read as his opening statements on November 23.
77. Ibid., 1–2.
78. Fernández Tejedo, *Recuerdo de México*, 134.
79. Psalm 104:1–2.
80. "Absurda hipótesis."
81. "María Teresa de Landa fue absuelta."
82. Carlos Monsiváis, "María Conesa: Retrato antiguo para voyeur del pasado," in Enrique Alonso, *María Conesa* (Mexico City: Editorial Oceáno, 1987), 7–19; and Carlos Monsiváis, *Celia Montalván: Te brindas, voluptuosa e impudente* (Mexico City: Martín Casillas Editores, 1982).

83. "Los cargos que hizo a Miss Mexico fueron ya desvanecidos del todo. Rindió ayer una amplia declaración la Sra. Victoria Hernández de Domínguez," *Excélsior*, 26 September 1929, pp. 1–6.
84. "Absurda hipótesis."
85. Ibid.
86. Ibid.
87. Velasco Ceballos, "Demostración de cultura."
88. Ibid.
89. Ibid.
90. On turn-of-the-century juries ruling against social inferiors, see Mary S. Hartman, *Victorian Murderesses: A True History of Thirteen Respectable French and English Women Accused of Unspeakable Crimes* (New York: Schocken Books, 1977).
91. I say paradoxically because she really was not legally married to Vidal.
92. Women's manipulation of gender discourse in their favor is not new. See Zemon Davis's description of sixteenth-century French women's invocation of "the language and posture of humility and subjection" in the construction of their narrative strategies in *Fiction in the Archives*, 77–110. Also see "Women on Top" in Natalie Zemon Davis, *Society and Culture in Early Modern France: Eight Essays by Natalie Zemon Davis* (Stanford: Stanford University Press, 1975).
93. Steve J. Stern, *The Secret History of Gender: Women, Men, and Power in Late Colonial Mexico* (Chapel Hill: University of North Carolina Press, 1995); James C. Scott, *Domination and the Arts of Resistance: Hidden Transcripts* (New Haven, CT: Yale University Press, 1990).
94. All of these cases are discussed in de los Reyes, *Cine y sociedad en México*, 60–100. Alicia Olvera de Serrano had murdered her husband in 1920, but with her father's protection she had managed to elude authorities until 1923, when she was tried and absolved. See "Alicia Olvera quedó libre, absuelta de haber dado muerte a su marido," *El Universal*, 29 April 1923, p. 1. Magdalena Jurado's case achieved such notoriety that the proceedings were filmed for subsequent projection in movie halls in Mexico City. See de los Reyes, *Cine y sociedad en México*, 79–86. Sara del Toro Romero was absolved of killing her boyfriend, who attempted to rape her. See "Sara del Toro Romero, que para vengar su honra mató a su seductor, fue absuelta," *Excélsior*, 28 March 1923, p. 8. Támez de Mondragón killed her husband's lover. See "Mujer vengadora de su honor que hiere a su rival," *Excélsior*, 29 July 1924, p. 3.
95. "Eva Martínez de León habla de su crimen: Sostuvo ante el Juez que una mujer deshonrada puede y tiene derecho de matar al seductor," *Excélsior*, 26 September 1929, p. 1.
96. Ibid.
97. Judith Ewell, "Ligia Parra Jahn: The Blonde with the Revolver," in *The Human Tradition in Modern Latin America*, ed. William H. Beezley and Judith Ewell (Wilmington, DE: Scholarly Resources, 1997), 205–26.
98. Joan W. Scott, "Gender: A Useful Category of Historical Analysis," 1067–75.

CHAPTER EIGHT

Mothers of Invention
Narratives of Maternity, Paternity, and Modernity in Early Twentieth-Century Mexico

~~ Katherine Elaine Bliss ~~

On October 2, 1937, in the village of Tlatlilco on the outskirts of Mexico's Federal District, two male agricultural workers notified authorities that they had discovered the cadaver of a newborn baby while working in a milpa, or cornfield. The police who investigated the matter discovered that the infant was "of undetermined sex" because the left leg up to the genital area was missing, although whether that was the result of the body's exposure to the elements and disturbance by local wildlife or the consequence of a congenital deformity is unclear. However, the police quickly determined who was responsible for the child's death. Just one day later, on October 3, authorities detained twenty-three-year-old domestic servant Soledad Romero Padilla, charging the unmarried young woman with the murder of her own offspring.

Because Soledad denied having given birth and emphatically rejected the murder charge, Judge José Espinosa y López Portillo, who presided over the Federal District's Fifth Penal Court, solicited testimony from various local witnesses to piece together a narrative of her maternity and crime. Among the witnesses were Angelina Flores Martínez, who had given Soledad lodging in exchange for some light housework and who had suspected the young woman was pregnant due to her shape and large stomach; local herbalist Homero Contreras Rubio, from whom Soledad had requested a potion capable of inducing a miscarriage; and two physicians who examined Soledad's body and told the court that, based on their observation of the condition of her reproductive tract, it was likely that she had recently given birth to a full-term infant.

After reviewing this testimony, Judge Espinosa y López Portillo determined the young woman to be guilty of infanticide, a conviction that under Mexico's 1931 Penal Code carried a three-to-five-year prison sentence. The judge invoked the court's prerogative to show leniency in sentencing the convicted mother based on her sex and social status. He noted that

> using the criteria set by the law, this court deems it just to condemn Soledad Romero to three years in prison, [because she] has no education and is illiterate, she has no prior convictions, she pertains to the *clase humilde* [humble class], and she is quite poor, a factor that should be taken into consideration insofar as the accused has no other means of supporting herself but her work, which would be very difficult to keep if she were raising a child.[1]

Soledad's history and conviction raise a number of questions regarding gender, social class, and cultural expectations of young adults in early twentieth-century Mexico, including the ways in which socially marginal women might have experienced the Mexican state's often contradictory policies concerning motherhood, paternity, and modernity. Her case also raises important questions about how, when the accused does not cooperate, those in positions of power may frame narratives that reflect their normative assumptions and the influence of broadly circulated written, spoken, or visual discourses. Due to the summary nature of the trial transcripts we know very few details about Soledad's life. There is no evidence that explains the circumstances under which she became pregnant, the identity and whereabouts of the infant's father, the nature of her relationship with him, why she was on her own, or why she sought to relieve herself of the baby. Indeed, we know little about her life before the incident and nothing about where she went or what she did after she served her prison sentence. But, by considering her case within the context of larger societal tensions regarding justice and the rule of law, family formation, and the place of science in a modernizing nation, we can appreciate how her experience resonated with official concerns over the life that children born to single mothers like Soledad might enjoy in a nation freshly emerged from revolutionary conflict and embroiled in heated debates about the pace and nature of political reconstruction.[2]

In late 1930s Mexico, the seemingly contradictory identities—bad mother on the one hand, and social victim on the other—that underpinned Soledad's infanticide conviction and criminal sentencing were actually consistent with policy contradictions that challenged officials working in Mexico's public sector:

how to reconcile the government's official pronatalist position of promoting economic development through population growth and a cultural emphasis on a woman's "natural" maternal role, with the recognition that impoverished, unmarried, and uneducated women such as Soledad were often in no position to ensure the development of a healthy generation that the same officials hoped would lead Mexico to a prosperous future. The decades after the conclusion of revolutionary violence and the promulgation of the 1917 constitution were a period during which public officials sought to promote economic development and strengthen the Mexican family by emphasizing science and rationality in welfare programs dedicated to improving the "quality" of the future generation. Their policies and programmatic activities scrutinized sexual behavior, child rearing practices, and the potential of Mexican men to be good fathers. But it was also during this era that a pronatalist policy designed to compensate for the Revolution's demographic catastrophe began to emphasize the "quantity" of the future generation, criminalizing abortion and infanticide and seeking to reduce the country's high rates of infant mortality in order to secure population growth.[3] Simultaneously, a wide range of social reformers and activists, including feminists, socialists, and eugenicists sought to promote contraception availability as a critical element of modern family life.

I use the infanticide conviction of Soledad Romero Padilla as a point of entry into the legal, medical, and popular discourses related to maternity that emerged in Mexico in the 1920s and 1930s. I do so in order to analyze the distinct reformist narratives that structured discussions about population, paternity, and progress in the postrevolutionary period. In particular, I focus on three areas of narrative tension: the place of fathers within a larger discussion of pregnancy, disease, and infant death; the emphasis on science in prenatal care programs; and the early efforts to promote publicly supported birth control clinics. Considering Soledad's case within the context of narratives about maternity reveals a considerable gap between reformers' aspirations with respect to paternity and progress and the reality that, for the most part, residents of rural areas could not count on access to the programs that might have made the reformist ideal possible.

Paternal Protagonists

Accused of having murdered a defenseless infant, Soledad Romero Padilla rejected the murder charge and insisted that her visibly protruding stomach had been the result of severe constipation and not pregnancy. Her denial meant that her infanticide conviction was based on testimony provided by the men who found the baby's corpse, her former employer's statements about her body shape, the herbalist's description of her efforts to procure an abortifacient, and the statements by the two doctors who confirmed that she had given birth recently. Nowhere in the testimony did any information about the father of the baby appear. However, despite the silence surrounding his existence and his apparent disappearance from Soledad's life, the man who had fathered the deceased child, whoever he was, featured prominently—if silently—in the narrative about Soledad's actions. Indeed, Judge López Portillo's announcement that Soledad's sentence would be lenient relied in part on his assessment that the baby would have been illegitimate. Assuming there was no man available to support the mother and child, he speculated that Soledad was perhaps compelled to expose the infant because she feared the dishonor and stigma associated with an illegitimate birth or because she worried that the responsibility of being a single mother might thwart her efforts to support herself.[4]

The judge's assumptions about Soledad reflect his awareness of broadly circulating reformist perspectives on social class, masculinity, and paternity in the 1920s and 1930s. According to most social reformers, for women who were married and living in economically stable households, pregnancy represented an opportunity to enhance a positive partnership between loving spouses. Such publicly distributed booklets such as the 1933 *Libro para la madre mexicana* (*Book for the Mexican Mother*) offered a vision of a happy middle-class couple, with the father playing an important role in fostering a medically oriented pregnancy and delivery. Presented to the public by First Lady Aída Rodríguez, wife of President Abelardo Rodríguez, and with an introduction by prominent higienista Dr. Manuel Martínez Baez, the book was intended to disseminate information about pregnancy and childbirth to Mexican women of all social classes while simultaneously elevating the political profile of the state's maternal health activities. According to the text, "The husband must do his part to ensure that his wife receives the necessary attention during her pregnancy. He must insist that his wife consult a doctor as soon as possible after the pregnancy has begun and that she sees the doctor every time it is necessary. He must accompany his wife on these visits to encourage her and to carefully note any recommendations on the part of the medical staff."[5] The implication was that mothers-to-be could not be trusted to seek out high-quality prenatal care, and that it was prospective fathers who bore responsibility for ensuring a rational, science-based pregnancy.

Reformist writers who sought to guide the decisions of women of the popular classes struck a different tone, however, when depicting relations between men and women, frequently depicting Mexican men as highly irresponsible. For example, a report on the Casa Amiga de la Obrera (Home for Women

Workers), a Federal District social assistance program for working women, noted that "the Mexican woman needs help . . . Mothers are obligated to leave home and their children all day in order to earn what is necessary for their sustenance [often because they] are abandoned by their husbands, who have become alienated from the home and who set a terrible example for their children."[6] Health pamphlets warning of the perils of alcoholism featured a drawing of a drunk, angry father holding a bottle in one hand while rejecting his pregnant wife and daughter with the other to bring home the message that lower-class Mexican men might not make the best father figures.

Although these articles and other educational materials were intended for consumption by all Mexicans, it is doubtful that the illiterate and uneducated Soledad had access to any of these published opinions about the nature and parenting capacity of Mexican men. (Among other things, public officials working in settings ranging from public health and welfare institutions to the city council and judicial branches embraced the notion that men were "naturally" sexually promiscuous, while women were expected to be abstinent or monogamous.) Private groups such as the Mexican Eugenics Society also sought to warn young women of the hazards of trusting their male counterparts to be honorable or monogamous, hinting at the possibility of acquiring a sexually transmitted disease such as syphilis from irresponsible men. As one article by the Eugenics Society directed toward adolescent girls posited, "[A]t any moment you are in danger of being assaulted: on the street, at the movies, in the countryside, at the factory. Make sure your boyfriend is truthful to you, he may be sick." Encouraging sexual abstinence, the text further admonished young women: "Make sure he respects you: that way you will be worth more. Many young women have been victims of promises, but when the time for [those promises] to be fulfilled is at hand, it is often the children who are the victims."[7] In this setting, pregnancy, syphilis infection, and the spread of syphilis through birth to the infant represented twin hazards to mother and the child. Certainly many young women who came to be in the custody of the juvenile court and its educational wing, the Consejo Tutelar para Menores Infractores (Advisory Council for Delinquent Minors), did find themselves pregnant, with the child's father frequently seeking to shirk responsibility for his parental obligations.[8] Those who found themselves living and studying in the court's Casa de Corrección (House of Corrections) and Escuela Correccional (Correctional School) had the opportunity to take academic classes and vocational training even while they carried their babies to term.

Because Soledad chose not to reveal information about her life and the child's conception, we do not know if or to what extent she was aware of the publicly circulating messages about infidelity and problematic paternity. As a woman older than eighteen living outside of the metropolitan center, however, Soledad did not qualify for the court's attention and, in a rural area of the Federal District, did not have access to new institutions that endeavored to "redeem" wayward members of revolutionary society.

Science Fictions

The circumstances surrounding the 1937 discovery of an infant's corpse in the village of Tlatlilco and the subsequent accusation and infanticide conviction of young, unmarried Soledad embodied several themes that concerned Mexico's public health specialists in the years following the Revolution. The mangled state of the exposed body underscored the infant's vulnerability and pointed to several possible and worrisome explanations as to the nature of the murdering mother. Most worrisome to many would have been the possibility that Soledad was ignorant of the causes and symptoms of pregnancy, did not understand her situation, and, upon delivering the infant, abandoned it out of fear and the failure to comprehend the implications of her actions. The ignorance of the Mexican population regarding sexual behavior and its consequences in general and the importance of prenatal care in particular underpinned efforts to criticize the population's "false modesty" and to promote sexual health–seeking behavior at all levels. Official concerns regarding sexuality and family revolved principally around reproduction and sexually transmitted diseases such as syphilis and whether men and women could be trusted to produce and care for future generations. If Mexico could not deliver a "quality" population, reformers worried, how would the nation progress?

As a young, illiterate woman from a village outside the metropolitan center, Soledad did not have access to the public programs that enabled pregnant women to address the dangers of infant mortality and congenital syphilis in the 1920s and 1930s. Indeed, Soledad may have encountered the state first through the penal system, but in fact the public sector promoted a number of maternal health services for women of modest means. Reformist institutions idealized the concept of "scientific maternity" in public settings and private discussions of reproductive health. The ideology of scientific maternity drew on older tenets of sanitation and hygiene as well as the principles of eugenics, which in Mexico, as in other parts of Latin America, had achieved wide popularity among so-called progressive reformers interested less in sterilizing the "unfit" (as in Europe or North America) than in promoting population improvement through prenatal care and positive child development practices. *Higienistas* (doctors associated with public health and sanitation campaigns) and eugenicists (a group that included higienistas as well as social workers, criminologists, and psychiatrists, among others) were concerned that the high local prevalence of diseases such as syphilis, tuberculosis, and alcoholism would limit the nation's productivity through premature death and disability and could thus erode the quality of life to which Mexicans might aspire in the future.[9]

Health surveys demonstrated that maternal syphilis accounted for the majority of miscarriages between 1916 and 1920 and that the sexually transmitted infection was, along with such generally preventable maladies as diarrhea and respiratory diseases, accountable for the nation's alarming infant mortality rate, which stood at 28 percent in Mexico City alone.[10] Experts argued that state provision of prenatal care, proper instruction of mothers, and an awareness of sex education and medical attention throughout the birth process could improve these numbers.

During the period between 1921 and the 1940s, when it merged with public welfare to become the Secretaría de Salubridad y Asistencia (Ministry of Health and Social Assistance), Mexico's Departamento de Salubridad Pública (DSP; Department of Public Health) financed programs ranging from the implementation of new treatment and diagnostic services and personnel training to disease surveillance and provision of laboratories for blood and urine analysis at the various birth and venereal disease clinics established over the same years.[11] Aside from establishing new clinics, expanding federally funded health services, and promoting the circulation of visiting health educators and providers, free pamphlets and popular advice columns bombarded the rural and urban childbearing population with information regarding a variety of pregnancy complications and health dilemmas.

By 1926, taking the idea of scientific maternity a step further, health authorities began to require a prenuptial certificate of health from all couples wishing to marry. The idea behind the requirement that men and women contemplating marriage undergo a blood test to ensure that they were syphilis-free was to prevent childbearing among those infected with a disease that could cause congenital abnormalities. Dr. Bernardo Gastélum, director of the Departamento de Salubridad Pública at the time, stated that "the health certificate ... establishes the code by which it is possible to contract matrimony, and is now required. In this way the future generation is assured a life free of possible infection, to the fullest extent possible, and this is dedicated to the infant population of the Republic."[12]

For families in urban centers such as Mexico City, new Centros de Higiene Infantil (Infant Hygiene Centers), maternity clinics run by the Servicio de

Higiene Infantil (Infant Hygiene Service), endeavored to protect future generations' physical integrity. As the head of the service, Dr. Isidro Espinosa y de los Reyes wrote in a summary of Mexican initiatives for the VI Congreso Panamericano del Niño (Panamerican Conference on the Child) held in Lima, Peru, in 1930, "Our hope, our ideal, is to erase our infant mortality and morbidity statistics for infants, which are, for us, a horrible image but which at the same time stimulate us to improve our biological condition, which is the base for the social improvement that will lead to the greatness of our nation."[13] Recognizing that not all conceptions took place within the context of official marriage, the servicio's preventive approach was based on free medical attention, syphilis testing, and prenatal education for all expectant mothers, whether they were married or not. Inaugurated in the early 1920s, the clinics were recognized by President Emilio Portes Gil, who in 1929 emphasized that "it is the duty and constant preoccupation of the State to combat in the most efficient way possible infant sickness and death." The health department selected sites for clinic locations that were densely populated in order to better serve impoverished women like Soledad. As service director, Espinosa noted in 1930 that "the desire to locate these institutions in areas with high population density and in the poorer neighborhoods was taken into account, seeing as the two factors already mentioned (poverty and ignorance) create an even worse situation for the women and children in those zones."[14] The centers included the Centro Eduardo Liceaga, located in the old historic center, and the Centro Manuel Dominguez, situated a bit farther away, both of which served "working class women and maids of the comfortable families who live in those areas." The director wrote that the centers "fill a great social necessity in those populous neighborhoods where working class women and their children can receive daily medical attention."[15] These outreach efforts, however, reached mostly urban women; poor women like Soledad who lived in more rural areas usually went without services.

If public health programs directed their attention to mothers and children, public education programs targeted mothers-to-be. In the literature about motherhood, Mexican women were frequently depicted as loving and self-sacrificing but often ignorant of scientific approaches to child-rearing. To improve the situation, women's magazines sought to diffuse information, at least to a reading audience, about the advantages of hygienic marriage. *Nosotras*, the official publication of the women's arm of the Partido Nacional Revolucionario (National Revolutionary Party), for example, admonished mothers that "health is the first quality that those who are considering matrimony should think about. It is very important that people who are about to get married have a careful exam by a doctor to ensure that there is no illness that would impede such a union."[16] Health guides intended to look like popular publications also continued to emphasize the scientific aspects of maternal health.

First Lady Rodríguez's 1933 *Libro para la madre mexicana* cast doubt on "traditional" pregnancy practices in Mexico and praised "modern" approaches to childbirth instead. Señora Rodríguez, the text stated, was "shocked by the high levels of infant mortality in Mexico" and wanted to "inspire our race with vital energy by means of a future generation that is healthy and strong, free from hereditary problems caused by poor nutrition or inadequate hygiene."[17] Combating maternal ignorance was the book's principal goal. As the *Libro para la madre mexicana* noted, "disgracefully, ignorance—not to mention superstition—leads many mothers to undertake a number of practices that are prejudicial for their little ones; [and] to remedy this situation there is only one solution: fully diffuse knowledge of the principles based in truth and science to guide mothers to ensure that their children develop strong, healthy and happy." Despite this problem, the *Libro* praised Mexico's mothers, insisting that "the Mexican mother has exceptional qualities: deep affection for her children, tenacious will, indefatigable work ethic, abnegation that leads to self-sacrifice."[18] At the same time, it encouraged young mothers to view with skepticism the advice of the older generation: "Do not believe in superstitions. Perhaps they have told you that during your pregnancy you should not gaze upon deformed people, for your child, too, will be born with a deformity. But deformities are caused by illnesses. It has nothing to do with whether or not you see an eclipse, a comet, etc." The illustrations that accompanied the text presented a young, attractive, and well-informed mother-to-be looking with skeptical disdain at two older women who sought to give her "superstitious" and "inaccurate" information.[19]

Two additional publicly funded programs were available to women in urban centers, at least in Mexico City. The Junta de Beneficencia Pública (Council on Public Beneficence) renovated the maternity department at the general hospital in 1934 and made plans for a new Hospital de Maternidad e Infancia (Maternity and Infancy Hospital) to provide service for "indigent women who, pregnant and finding themselves obligated to seek public assistance," could deliver their children in a modern, medical setting free of charge.[20] And the Hospicio de Niños (Children's Hospice) continued to accept foundlings and place children for adoption during this period. Because of her refusal to acknowledge her pregnancy, of course, we do not know the circumstances surrounding Soledad's delivery of the baby, but it seems clear that in Tlatlilco she did not have access to any of the public institutions that might have affected the way in which she dealt with her condition. For women in Soledad's situation, the criminal justice system was their principal contact with state child welfare policies.

Modern Fiction

Soledad's infanticide case—particularly the unspoken assumptions about the baby's father and the judge's concerns about her unwillingness to acknowledge her condition—was consistent with broader social tensions regarding science and paternity. If women could not avoid wayward men and they could not be trusted to deliver a quality baby, then what were the options available to those who had engaged in sexual activity and were unprepared to bring a child into the world? The 1931 Penal Code held that infanticide and abortion were both criminal acts, and medical thinkers construed a woman's efforts to avoid conception and limit family size as a reflection of a deeper set of social problems. For example, in his introduction to the *Libro para la madre mexicana*, Martínez Báez condemned abortion as a symptom of a woman's problematic approach to motherhood, saying that "deliberately provoked abortion is a crime, which is committed against a defenseless creature and precisely by the person whom Nature has destined to serve as a support and custodian of that creature."[21] Eugenicist Gilberto González y Contreras similarly lambasted the deleterious effects of abortion in an article for the journal *Eugenesia*, writing that "the two most visible manifestations of the problems of feminine social maladjustment are women who kill and those who abort." However, echoing the judge's assessment of Soledad's employment prospects as an unmarried mother, González y Contreras also speculated that the economic problems associated with modern life made abortion seem like a viable option for married and unmarried women alike. He asked, "Is the problem of abortion limited to single mothers? Hardly. Many of the married couples decide that they do not want children because their income is not high enough, or stable enough to have a large family." For eugenicists such as González y Contreras,

> [f]amily planning and birth regulation . . . is equivalent to conserving and perpetuating the species in a way that is healthy, improving man physically, ethically and intellectually. This method, far from being the equivalent of abortion—as some misinformed people claim—is the most efficient of its antidotes. Based on the principles of social medicine, the regulation of fertility tends to improve the quality of the human race, and thus the quality of the family and the population overall.[22]

Since the early twentieth century, international groups had been meeting to discuss contraception, and at the Seventh International Birth Control Conference in 1930 delegates determined that "birth control must be regarded as an essential part of public health programs and of the work of preventive medicine in all countries; that the spread of knowledge of contraception is the best way of fighting against abortion; and that instruction in the techniques of birth control should be part of all medical curricula."[23]

In 1937 Hazel Moore, a representative of the New York City Birth Control Clinical Research Bureau (BCCRB), traveled to Mexico City to meet with representatives of the private and public sectors to discuss the possibilities of providing Mexican women with access to a Sanitol foaming powder that was an effective contraceptive when inserted vaginally prior to sexual intercourse.[24] Moore, who corresponded with Boston physician and ardent birth control advocate Clarence J. Gamble, reported her discussions with figures such as Dr. Enrique Villela, head of the Campaign against Venereal Diseases; Dr. Adolfo Priani, subsecretary of the Departamento de Salubridad Pública and representative of Dr. José Siurob, Lázaro Cárdenas's appointee as director. Moore, Gamble, and others who were involved in the United States birth control movement believed fertility regulation was important for several reasons, principally because birth spacing promoted maternal and child health and because fewer children lightened the economic burden for working families, thus relieving marital tension and strengthening family and, by extension, societal harmony. Moore reported on her visits with health administrators that Villela and Priani indicated interest in the contraception movement but were concerned that a populace that embraced Catholicism as the predominant religion would not tolerate the imposition of birth control after so many assaults on its faith over the previous decade—a reference to controversial efforts under presidents Calles and Cárdenas to reduce the influence of the Church through educational and cultural policies. In a report regarding her meeting with Priani and Villela, Moore wrote, "I think they tried to give the impression that they were favorable to B.C.—but the people had been given all they would take from the government—and many government officials were opposed to a decrease in population, which they absolutely knew birth control would cause. They stated that the people were still very Catholic at heart and another gesture against Catholicism would ruin public health."[25]

According to Moore, public health authorities in Mexico were unwilling to introduce contraception to mothers at the Servicio de Higiene Infantil (Infant Hygiene Service) clinics but were willing to consider experimenting with the contraceptive powder in other public sites such as the free antivenereal disease clinics under Villela's command and the rural health clinics under the direction of Dr. Angel de la Garza Brito, head of the Oficina Central de Higiene Rural y Servicios Sanitarios (Central Office for Rural Hygiene and Sanitary Services). Here, at last, was a program that might have benefited someone like Soledad, had she had access to doctors or visiting nurses in Tlatlilco. According to Moore, Garza Brito "stated he believed in Birth Control but is not in favor of Birth Control Clinics. They would upset the country and put the department under fire to such an extent that no other work could be done, according to his theory." Garza Brito, like Villela, was interested in the powder, however, and indicated he might be willing to distribute it if an outside group helped with financing and securing the materials.[26] Moore's conversations with Dr. Esperanza Oteo, head of the DSP's visiting nurses program, which included three hundred rural and two hundred urban nurses, met with similar results: Oteo, she declared to Gamble, was "favorable to Birth Control" but was unwilling to expose the nurses under her command to the potential legal ramifications of promoting it among their patients. (Contraception itself was not illegal, but promoting it was.) Oteo, Moore stated, believed it was up to doctors to pave the way by prescribing contraceptives within the confines of the clinic.

Women who worked in the government but supported feminist causes as well provided Moore and the BCCRB with the greatest hope of promoting contraception as a means of improving women's and family health in 1930s Mexico. The Frente Único Pro-Derechos de la Mujer (United Front for Women's Rights), a left-leaning umbrella organization composed of various popular women's groups and dedicated to achieving female suffrage as well as enhancing women's well-being, formed the Committee on Maternal Health and named Verna Carleton de Millán, an American married to a Mexican physician, as its liaison with the BCCRB. Moore provided members of this group such as Dr. Concha Palacios, director of the maternity hospital Primero de Mayo (First of May), with the foaming powder and suggested that the bureau might pay for a nurse to work with the doctors at the hospital to promote contraceptive services among the hospital's working and indigent patients. Finally, the Dra. Matilde Montoya clinic run by *médicas-cirujanas* (female doctor-surgeons) from the Universidad Nacional de México accepted referrals regarding the powder.[27]

It is not entirely clear what happened with the early effort to distribute contraceptives to women in late 1930s Mexico City. Moore arranged for the BCCRB to mail Villela, Oteo, Palacios, and the university doctors samples of the foaming powder, but there is little evidence regarding the powder's reception, how women responded to it, or how (or if) it was distributed. It may be that it was never used: by 1938 José Siurob, a former general and an anticlerical Cárdenas appointee, had resigned from his post at the DSP to assume the governorship of the Federal District. Some of the doctors he hired may have resigned, too.

What we do know is that Soledad's 1938 infanticide conviction led to a three-year sentence that would have kept her incarcerated until 1941. By that time the new administration of President Manuel Ávila Camacho was enjoying decidedly more cordial relations with the Catholic Church than the *cardenistas* had, and was actively promoting a variety of maternalist initiatives including state recognition of Mother's Day and the construction of a Monument to the Mother.[28] It seems unlikely that a generalized maternalist ideology, coupled with the 1947 Ley General de Población (General Law on Population) that codified pronatalist policies, would have supported contraceptive availability in any serious way. We also know that the introduction of antibiotics in the mid-1940s changed the landscape of morbidity and mortality in Mexico; penicillin rendered syphilis less of a threat to parents and their children, and antibiotic treatments made childhood respiratory and gastrointestinal illnesses less harmful than before. As a result, infant mortality declined precipitously, more children survived, and family size—and with it the Mexican population—grew rapidly.

By the early 1950s, as Soledad would have entered her late thirties, however, several groups formed to develop and provide contraceptives in Mexico. In these years experts estimated that one in every two emergency hospital admissions for women involved complications from illegal abortion, suggesting that women were desperate for some way to limit the number of children to which they gave birth. Moreover, the reports of Dr. Edris Rice-Wray, an American physician who conducted clinical trials of oral contraceptives in Mexico and who was president of the Asociación para el Bienestar de la Familia Mexicana (Association for the Well-Being of the Mexican Family) and later of the Centro para la Investigación de la Fisiología Reproductiva de la Mujer (Center for the Research on Women's Reproductive Physiology), suggest that while public officials dragged their heels and continued to worry about the political implications of contraception for church-state relations or the moral implications of fertility regulation for Mexico's people, women were arriving daily at the clinic's doors, demanding access and bringing along their sisters, mothers, daughters, and other relatives. Rice-Wray reports that sometimes entire families appeared at the clinic, stating that they could not bear to raise any more children and imploring that they have access to the medications she was testing.[29]

Publicly distributed contraceptives would not become available in Mexico until the mid-1970s, when the Mexican congress amended the national constitution to authorize family planning programs at the federal level, and Mexico's population was projected to surpass 100 million by the year 2000. Considerable research remains to be done to understand the process by which public officials and medical specialists came to endorse a narrative of maternity that embraced birth control and perhaps included new visions of parental responsibility and disease prevention. Had Soledad Romero Padilla chosen to defend herself at her infanticide trial, she might have provided insight into her relationship with the infant's father, her social situation, her health history, and why she felt she could not—or would not—care for the child to which she had given birth. After nearly seventy years, these issues are still unclear. But her conviction and the assumptions that informed Judge Espinosa y López Portillo's decision serve as reminders of the complex discursive links between individual, seemingly marginal, situations that may resonate with broader local, national, and international narrative inventions.

Notes

1. Archivo del Reclusorio del Sur del Distrito Federal, Quinta Corte Penal, Mexico. Infanticidio 1367/38. 4 October 1938. By agreement with the authorities at the Archivo del Reclusorio del Sur del Distrito Federal, the names of the accused and witnesses have been changed.
2. For Argentine judicial narratives regarding infanticide, see Kristin Ruggiero, *Modernity in the Flesh: Medicine, Law, and Society in Turn-of-the-Century Argentina* (Stanford: Stanford University Press, 2003).
3. Gustavo Cabrera, "Demographic Dynamics and Development: The Role of Population Policy in Mexico," *Population and Development Review* 20 (1994): S105–S20. Cabrera notes that Mexico's population declined from approximately 15.1 million in 1910 to 14.3 million in 1921. While the censuses of 1910 and 1921 are considered somewhat unreliable, demographers attribute the decline to "deaths directly related to the armed struggle, those caused by the Spanish influenza epidemic in 1918, Mexican emigration to the United States, and the decline in the birth rate resulting from the temporary separation of married couples and the postponement of new unions," 106–7.
4. Archivo del Reclusorio del Sur del Distrito Federal, Quinta Corte Penal, Mexico. Infanticidio 1367/38. 4 October 1938.
5. Manuel Martínez Báez, *Libro para la madre mexicana. Surgerido por la señora Aída S. De Rodríguez y preparado por el doctor Manuel Martínez Báez, con la colaboración de los señores doctores: Francisco de P. Miranda, Mario Torroella y Manuel Cárdenas de la Vega* (Mexico City: La Impresora, 1933), 23.
6. "Casa Amiga de la Obrera," *Asistencia: Organo de la Junta de Beneficencia Pública del Distrito Federal* (15 August 1934): 21.
7. "Para las jóvenes: escucha, medita," *Eugenesia* (1942), 3:9–10. Also see *Para las madres* (Mexico City: Departamento de Salubridad Pública, 1939), 51.
8. See Katherine Elaine Bliss and Ann S. Blum, "Dangerous Driving: Adolescence, Sex, and the Gendered Experience of Urban Space in Revolutionary Mexico City,"

in *Gender, Sexuality, and Power in Latin America since Independence*, ed. William E. French and Katherine Elaine Bliss (Lanham, MD: Rowman and Littlefield Publishers, 2006), 163–86.
9. See Katherine E. Bliss, "For the Health of the Nation: Gender and the Cultural Politics of Social Hygiene in Revolutionary Mexico," in *The Eagle and the Virgin: Nation and Cultural Revolution in Mexico, 1920–1940*, ed. Mary Kay Vaughan and Stephen E. Lewis (Durham, NC: Duke University Press, 2006), 197–218. For an analysis of the Mexican Eugenics Society's goals and politics, see Alexandra Minna Stern, "Responsible Mothers and Normal Children: Eugenics, Nationalism and Welfare in Post-Revolutionary Mexico, 1920–1940," *Journal of Historical Sociology* 12, no. 4 (December 1999).
10. Bernardo Gastélum, "La persecución de la sífilis desde el punto de vista de la garantía social," *Boletín de Salubridad Pública* (1926): 8.
11. Miguel E. Bustamante, Carlos Viesca Treviño, Federico Villaseñor, et al., *La Salud Pública en México, 1959–1982* (Mexico City: Secretaría de Salubridad y Asistencia, 1982), 37, 43. The Junta de Beneficencia Pública del Distrito Federal appears to have passed to the jurisdiction of the Gobierno del Distrito Federal between 1918 and 1938, after which it returned to federal jurisdiction. In 1943 Beneficencia Pública and Salubridad Pública were joined and elevated to the Secretaría de Salubridad y Asistencia Pública, which operated at the federal level.
12. *Memoria de los trabajos realizados por el Departamento de Salubridad Pública, 1925–1928*, vols. 1 and 2 (Mexico City: Departamento de Salubridad Pública, 1928), 33.
13. Departamento de Salubridad Pública, Servicio de Higiene Infantil. *Colaboración al VI Congreso Panamericano del Niño en la Ciudad de Lima, Peru* (Mexico City: Departamento de Salubridad Pública, 1930), 3.
14. Ibid., 8.
15. Ibid., 12–13.
16. "Higiene de la maternidad," *Nosotras* 1, no. 7 (January 1935): 27. The emphasis on hygienic marriages reveals a middle-class bias as many women, especially from the lower classes, were unmarried or had common-law unions.
17. Martínez Báez, *Libro para la madre mexicana*.
18. Ibid.
19. Ibid., 7.
20. "Como desarrolla la beneficencia su function social," *Asistencia: Organo de la Junta de Beneficencia Pública del Distrito Federal* (November 1934), 1:10; and "Un nuevo departamento de Maternidad en el Hospital General," *Asistencia: Organo de la Junta de Beneficencia Pública del Distrito Federal* (November 1934), 1:47–48.
21. Martínez Báez, *Libro para la madre mexicana*, 26–27.
22. Gilberto González y Contreras, "Aborto y regulación de natalidad," *Eugenesia: Revista mensual para el estudio de los problemas de la herencia* 5, no. 50 (February 29, 1944): 4–8.
23. Beryl Suitters, *Be Brave and Angry: Chronicles of the International Planned Parenthood Federation* (London: International Planned Parenthood Federation, 1973), 1–3.

24. The BCCRB was the "first permanent [birth control] clinic in America," and it opened in 1923 under the directorship of Margaret Sanger. Beryl Suitters writes that by the 1930s, groups such as the BCCRB in New York and the London-based Birth Control International Information Centre "made contact with individuals and groups all over the world" and appointed "official correspondents" in twenty-five countries. Suitters, *Be Brave and Angry*, 13.
25. Clarence J. Gamble Papers (HMSc23) Harvard Medical Library in the Francis A. Countway Library of Medicine. Box 108, file 1785. Report of Hazel Moore regarding her interview with Dr. Alfonso Priani and Dr. Enrique Villela, Mexico City, August 1937.
26. Clarence J. Gamble Papers (HMSc23) Harvard Medical Library in the Francis A. Countway Library of Medicine. Box 108, file 1785. Report of Hazel Moore regarding her interview with Dr. Angel de la Garza Brito, Mexico City, August 1937.
27. Clarence J. Gamble Papers (HMSc23) Harvard Medical Library in the Francis A. Countway Library of Medicine. Box 108, file 1785.
28. See Sarah Buck, "Mother's Day, the State, and Feminist Action: Maternalist Welfare Initiatives in 1940s Mexico" (paper presented at the Twelfth Berkshire Conference on the History of Women, Storrs, CT, 7 June 2002).
29. Clarence J. Gamble Papers (HMSc23) Harvard Medical Library in the Francis A. Countway Library of Medicine. Box 108, files 1786–89.

INDEX

Page numbers in italic text indicate illustrations.

ACJM. *See* Association of Mexican Catholic Youth
Acker, Kathy, 120–21
Acts of Meaning (Bruner), 27
Adams, Irene Pacheco de, 80, 82
agency. *See* concept of agency
Aguilar, Regino, 67, 80, 83
Agustín Pro, Miguel, 204
Albear, José, 68
Alducín, Bedolla, 220
alephs, 119, 126n26
Alvarado, Ladislao, 167
Alvarado, Salvador, 132
Álvarez, Conrada, 167
Álvarez, José, 67, 80, 83
anthropology, 110, 123n2
Argüello, Santiago, 222
Aristotle, 121–22, 126n33
Arizmendi, Daniel, 4, 22n10
army. *See* Mexican army
art: historians on images, 188; in parallel lives of Toral and Siqueiros, 180, 181, 182, 188, 195, *200*, *201*, 202–3, 206, 208, 209, *210*; truth and academic, 210, 214n79
Ascencio, María Teresa Alvarado de, 167, 168, 170, 171
Ascencio, Ramón, 18, 156, 157–58, 159, 163, 164, 166–71, 172–73, 174. *See also* González kidnapping/murder case
Association of Mexican Catholic Youth (ACJM), 179

Bajío, 154, 155, 159–60, 174
bandits, 94; Mexican Revolution and, 97; social, 62, 92, 95, 97
barrio Tepito, 20
Barthes, Roland, 60, 124n9
beauty contests: community identity and, 217, 221; de Landa, María Teresa, and, 215, 216, 217–18, 220–25, 230, 236, 238–39; postrevolutionary Mexico and, 221–22, 223–25, 238–39
Beezley, William, 196
Behar, Ruth, 123n2
Bejarano, Rafael, 80
Belina, Carlos, 76, 78
Belmar, General Francisco, 167, 168
Benjamin, Walter, 111
biography, 182, 187, 211n7
biological determinism, 72, 75
birth control, 250, 257–59, 260, 261, 263n24
Bloody Drama in Tarasquillo Square: Assassination of La Malagueña (Posada), 34, 37
Le Bon, Gustave, 137, 149n45
Bonilla, José, 68
Borges, Jorge Luis, 122, 126n26
The Bourgeois Experience: Victoria to Freud (Gay), 26–27
broadsheets (*impresos sueltos*), 58, 59–60; Negrete and, 62, 65–66, 68–70, 72, 75, 86, 88–89, 94
Bronfen, Elisabeth, 49, 50
Bruner, Jerome, 27, 33, 37, 38, 49–50
Buentello, Edmundo, 118
Buñuel, Luis, 212n47
Butler, Judith, 111

265

Cabrera, Ramona, 62, 65
Caldeira, Teresa, 3
Calles, General, 115
Calles, Plutarco Elías, 19, 115, 131, 132, 136, 143, 146n12, 146n14, 148n41, 155, 158, 180, 186, 190, 213n68, 241n2
capitalism, 121
Cárdenas, Lázaro, 118, 170, 186
Carillo Gil, Alvar, 183
Carranza, Emilio, 190, 212n41
Casasola, Agustín, 72
case studies, 11, 24n37; analysis, 9, 10, 12
La Castañeda. *See* General Insane Asylum
Castelar, Emilio, 137
Castillo, Alberto del, 71, 72
Castillo, Jordán, 235
Castro, Antonio Martínez de, 28, 51n14
Castro Balda, Carlos, 192
Catholic Church, 18, 39, 59, 63; Bajío and, 159–60; González kidnapping/murder case and, 154, 155, 156–57, 158, 159, 172, 173, 174; individualism and, 190–91; in de Landa case, 226; landowners and, 159–60; land reform and, 161; postrevolutionary Mexico and, 159–60, 161, 162, 163, 164–66, 174, 176n31, 226, 241n2, 245n47; postrevolutionary Michoacán and, 159–60, 161, 162, 163, 164–66, 174, 176n31; radicalism and, 162–63, 165–66; Sonoran Dynasty and, 226, 241n2, 245n47; sports and, 196; Toral and, 179, 180, 181, 188, 190, 191–92, 193–94, 196–97, 198, 212n46, 213n52; Zamora, Michoacán, and, 160, 161, 162, 163, 164–66, 172, 176n31
Catholic nationalism, 18, 159–63
Catholic press: González kidnapping/murder case and, 154, 155, 156, 157, 158, 170, 172; politics and, 165; radicalism *vs.*, 162, 165–66
causes célèbres: crime narratives and, 8; crime stories and, 12; González kidnapping/murder case and, 156; in de Landa case, 19, 215–16, 218, 229–30; mass media and criminal, 7–8, 12; Mexico City and, 25, 26; of Moreno case, 128, 142; public narratives as, 27; of Tarasquillo Street murder, 25–26
Cerro del Cubilete, 189, 190, 191
Cervantes, Juan B., 131, 132
Cervantes, Miguel, 167, 170
Charrasqueado, Juan, 93
Chávez, Francisco, 57–58, 71, 93
Chávez, Pancho, 85
Children of Sánchez (Lewis), 11
Christ, Jesus: in parallel lives of Toral and Siqueiros, 208, 209; Siqueiros's images of, 198, 199. *See also* Sacred Heart of Jesus

Cisneros, José y Agustín, 60, 67, 81
Cisneros, Ubelia, 62, 80
class: in de Landa case, 216, 218, 234, 236, 238; Romero Padilla case and social, 20, 249, 250, 251, 252, 253, 256–57, 261
class struggle, and textual analysis, 14
Colonia Buenos Aires, 20
communism, of Siqueiros, 179, 180, 181, 183, 186, 188, 209
Communist Party, and Mexico, 179, 180, 181, 182, 183, 186, 188, 209
concept of agency, 121
Conchita, Madre, 184, 190, 212n41
Confinamiento solitario (*Solitary Confinement*) (Siqueiros), 204, 205, 206
conscience collective, 5–6, 7, 8, 12
The Consequences of Modernity (Giddens), 33, 53n40, 54n46
context: García texts and, 112; historical, 21, 111–12, 171; illumination and, 112; texts and, 111–12
Contreras, González y, 257
Cornejo, Marciano, 60, 67
Corona, Luis, 232
corporatism, 241n2
corruption, 2, 4
crime(s): aesthetic rewriting of, 11; causes, 3, 9, 10; cultural meaning of, 11, 21; documentation, 20–21; Durkheim theory of, 5–6; fighting measures, 1; historical role of, 5; Mexican army and, 65; modernity and, 26; of Moreno case, 130; of Negrete, 65–75, 79–83, 92–93; in parallel lives of Toral and Siqueiros, 179, 180, 181, 185, 187; prevention, 2–3; public debates about, 20; of Siqueiros, 184, 185, 211n21; society and, 5–8, 26. *See also* scientific crime
crime narratives, 3–4, 8, 12. *See also* crime stories
crime rate: data, 2–3; increase, 2, 5; law enforcement and, 2; of Mexico City, 26, 51n5
crime stories: analysis, 13–14; causes célèbres and, 12; conscience collective and, 8; creating publics with, 12, 13; cultural revolutions and, 15; global processes and, 14–15; historical contexts of, 21; historical critique of, 20–21; historical perceptions and, 5; impact on Mexican history, 14; master narratives implications for, 14; media and, 20; Mexican self-perceptions and, 4; Mexico City marchers and, 5; modernity and, 33, 53n39; perceptions about criminals and, 4; public debates and deconstruction of, 20; public narratives and, 15; reflection/constitution

of social realities during change, 14; scientific, 8–9; sensationalism and, 16; social inequalities and, 15; societal perceptions and, 5. *See also* crime narratives; criminal crime stories
crime stories, by criminals. *See* criminal crime stories
crime story cases: determinate contradictions in, 14, 15; social inequalities in, 14; social realities reflected in, 14
criminal: as animal, 57; anthropology, 72, 75; common, 62, 92, 95; knowledge, 2, 3, 10; social typologies, 8–9; sociology, 75; tendency indicators, 10, 75; as unworthy of citizenship, 2
criminal crime stories: case studies and, 10, 11, 24n37; crime causes and, 9, 10; criminology and, 10, 11, 24n37; historically grounded narratives and, 9–10; literature and, 11, 24n37; objectivity and, 9; scientific crime analysis and, 10
Los criminales en México (Roumagnac), 26, 37, 38, 39–44, 54n49, 55n63, 55n65
criminality: explanations for Negrete, 72, 75; female, 44; gender and, 44; health and, 39; sexuality and, 48
criminal justice system, 7, 180. *See also* Mexican justice system
criminological narrative: of Tarasquillo Street murder, 41; on Villa by Roumagnac, 37, 38, 39–44, 54n49, 54n54, 55n63, 55n65, 55n68
criminology: criminal crime stories and, 10, 11, 24n37; as ideological narrative, 37–44; social sciences and, 11
Cristero rebellion (cristiada), 18, 174, 180–81, 187, 189, 212n41, 216
Cuadra, Rafael, 161, 169–70
cultural psychology, 27
cultural revolutions, 15
culture: hegemony and public narratives, 33; in de Landa case, 218, 233–34, 240; meaning of crime, 11, 21; narratives and, 33; of postrevolutionary Mexico, 233

Davis, Natalie Zemon, 216
debates, public, 20, 129
depravity, 5
determined informants, 110, 123n2
determinism, 72, 75
deviance, 40–41
El Diario del Hogar, 59, 94
Díaz regime. *See* Porfirio Díaz regime
Diéguez, Manual M., 182
Dijkstra, Bram, 48–49
discourses, and publics, 13
documentation, crime, 20–21, 106–10, 123n1

domesticity: in de Landa case, 19, 217; Moreno case and, 17–18, 137–38, 142; in postrevolutionary Mexico, 250; in Romero Padilla case, 20, 251
Doyle, Arthur Conan, 8–9
drug trafficking, 2
dueling, 28, 29, 51n14, 52n20, 141, 220
Dupont, Alfonse, 25
Durkheim, Emile, 5–6, 8

Ecce Homo (Siqueiros), 198–99, 209
education: de Landa, María Teresa, and, 219, 220, 221, 222, 225; in parallel lives of Toral and Siqueiros, 179, 180, 195, 202–3; in postrevolutionary Mexico, 218, 222, 244n31; women and, 218, 219, 220, 221, 222, 244n31
El Cruzado, 18
emotions: Moreno case and, 143; perceptions about crime and, 13; publics and, 12–13
Enríquez, Leonardo, 67, 80, 82
Enríquez, Rafael Zayas de, 25
estates. *See* haciendas
Estrada, Enrique, 171
ethnicity: in de Landa case, 19, 216, 217, 218, 234, 235, 238, 240; in postrevolutionary Mexico, 238–39
Excélsior, 215, 218, 220, 222, 224, 229, 230

Fabrés, Antonio, 202, 203
fear: crime narratives and, 4; immigrant/ ethnic minority discrimination and, 2; mass media and, 3; violence/corruption and public, 2
Felski, Rita, 15
female criminality, 44
femininity: death and, 49; in de Landa case, 19, 215, 217, 218, 235, 237, 240; Moreno case and, 129, 134, 135, 142, 143; and public sphere in postrevolutionary Mexico, 128, 143, 152n78
feminism, 222, 223, 224, 226, 237, 238, 240
Ferri, Enrico, 72, 75
Filippi, Ernesto E., 155, 156, 164, 165, 189
Flores Reyes, Consuelo, 234, 235
Foucault, Michel, 9–10, 16, 124n9
Fox, Vicente, 1
Frías, Lauro, 67, 80, 81, 82, 83
Fuentes, Mario, 109, 117, 118

Gaceta de Policía, 59, 68, 71, 76
Galindo, Pedro, 3
Galván, José, 60, 67
Gama, Antonio Díaz y, 162
Gamboa, Federico, 11, 26, 47, 146n18; Gutiérrez diary entry by, 44–49, 56n71

García (Marino) case: administrator in, 107–8, 111, 115, 116, 117; García as guard in, 118, 125n24; García's 1931 asylum release in, 117, 120; García's 1941 asylum reentry in, 117–18; García's words in, 114, 116, 118–19, 120; General Insane Asylum and, 106–10, 111, 113–21, 123n1; General Insane Asylum institutional dossier texts/documents of, 106–10, 123n1; General Insane Asylum texts of, 106–10, 111, 113, 114, 116, 117–18–119, 121, 123n1, 124n10; general paralysis in, 115; General Tejada and, 16, 106, 114, 116; God in, 114, 117, 120, 123, 124n12; insanity and, 106–10, 113, 114, 116; Mexican Revolution and, 115; Mexico City history and, 111; narrative and, 16–17, 115, 121; nurses in, 107, 111, 114, 116; physicians/psychiatrists in, 107, 108–9, 110, 111, 113, 114, 117, 118, 119, 120, 121; quotable past of, 110–11; superintendent in, 115, 116, 117; truth and, 121

García, Héctor, 183

García, Marino, 16; as beggar, 116; early life of, 113; on religion/nature/history/medicine/sex, 119; words of, 114, 116, 118–20

García (Marino) story: García's words and, 114, 116, 118–20; García texts and, 110–11, 119–20; General Insane Asylum and, 113–14; life and death and, 121; modernity and, 120; narrative and, 119, 120, 121; postmodern novels and, 121; truth and, 121; violence in, 120

García (Marino) texts: context and, 112; García story and, 110–11, 119–20; Mexican modernity and, 112

Garfield, James Abram, 25

Garland, David, 6–7, 8

Garmendia, Rogelio, 107, 115, 116

Gay, Peter, 26–27

Gedovius, Germán, 202, 203

gender: criminality and, 44; defending honor and, 29, 31, 52nn21–22, 141, 220; de Landa, María Teresa, and, 19, 216, 217, 220, 223, 224, 225, 236, 237–38, 239, 240, 247n92; Mexican justice system and, 32, 33; of modernity, 15–16, 26, 33, 53n39; Moreno case and, 17–18, 129, 133, 134, 135, 136, 137, 140, 142, 143; in postrevolutionary Mexico, 218, 220, 240; in Romero Padilla case, 249, 251, 252; Tarasquillo Street murder and, 15–16, 26, 31, 32, 33, 53n39. *See also* femininity; feminism; masculinity; women

General Insane Asylum: García case and, 106–10, 111, 113–21, 123n1, 124n10; institutional dossier texts/documents of García case, 106–10, 123n1; patients' vs. physicians' words in, 114; psychiatry and, 113; reform during Maximato, 115–16; texts of García case, 106–10, 111, 113, 114, 116, 117–18–119, 121, 123n1, 124n10

gente decente (proppertied professional classes), 216

El gesticulador (*The Gesticulator*) (Usigli), 188

Giddens, Anthony, 33, 37, 53nn39–40, 54n46

Ginzburg, Carlo, 9, 171

global processes, 14–15

Godínez, Vicente, 67

God, in García case, 114, 117, 120, 123, 124n12

González kidnapping/murder case: Ascencio, Ramón, and, 18, 156, 157–58, 159, 163, 164, 166–71, 172–73, 174; Catholic Church and, 154, 155, 156–57, 158, 159, 172, 173, 174; Catholic nationalism and, 18, 159–63; Catholic press and, 154, 155, 156, 157, 158, 170, 172; cause célèbre of, 156; politics of, 18, 154, 155–58, 159, 161–62, 166, 168–71, 172–74, 177n46; postrevolutionary Michoacán and, 18, 154; public and, 156, 157, 158–59, 172, 173; radicalism and, 18, 156, 157, 158, 162, 172, 173. *See also* Ascencio, Ramón

González, Roberto, 18, 154

Guadalupe Martinez, José, 60, 67

Guerrero, Julio, 11, 58

Guiteau, Charles, 25

Gutiérrez, Esperanza, 15, 25, 28–29, 30–32, 34, 35, 36, 37, 41, 48, 52n17, 54n54; diary entry by Gamboa, 44–49, 56n71. *See also* Tarasquillo Street murder

Habermas, Jürgen, 15, 144n4

haciendas (large estates), 63, 64, 154, 159, 161

health, and criminality, 39. *See also* public health

El Heraldo, 130, 132, 133, 136

hero, Negrete as popular, 93–98

Herrejón de Vidal, María Teresa, 225, 226, 227, 235, 245n44

Herrera, Engracia, 62

Herrera, Pedro, 60, 67

historians: bias and, 158; images and art, 188; as storytellers, 110–11; subject matter of, 110, 121; temporal translation of, 113

historical context, 21, 111–12, 171

historical critique, of crime stories, 20–21

historically grounded narratives, 9–10

historical perceptions, and crime stories, 5

historical research, 112, 171

historical texts, 111–12

history: crime narratives and, 4; crime's role in, 5; general *vs.* fractal, 106; memory and indeterminacy of, 171–74; psychoanalysis of, 26–27, 51n8; revision of contemporary notions of, 111; scientific crime analysis and, 10
Holmes, Sherlock, 8–9
homosexuality: in Mexican prisons, 43, 55n65; in parallel lives of Toral and Siqueiros, 193–94, 196
honor: gender and defending, 29, 31, 52nn21–22, 141, 220, 239, 240, 247n94; in de Landa case, 217, 218, 229, 231, 232, 233, 235, 236, 238, 239; Moreno case and, 129, 130, 136, 140–41, 142, 143, 152n70; penal code and defending, 29, 52n18; Tarasquillo Street murder and defending, 29, 30, 31; violence and defending, 29, 52nn20–22, 81–82, 141, 152n70, 239, 240, 247n94; women/violence and defending, 239, 240, 247n94
Huejutla lynchings, 6
de la Huerta, Adolfo, 139, 150n54, 171, 173, 231

identity: beauty contests and community, 217, 221; in de Landa case, 217, 218; media crime narratives and public's shared, 8
images, art historians on, 188
El Imparcial, 57, 58, 59, 64, 65, 67, 68, 71, 72, 75, 76, 77–78, 80, 83, 85, 86, 89, 92, 94, 97–98, 101n57, 104n105, 220
individualism, in parallel lives of Toral and Siqueiros, 181, 208
Inés Escogido, María, 62, 67, 81
infanticide, in Romero Padilla case, 19, 20, 248, 249, 250, 251, 253, 257, 260, 261
Iturbide, Agustín de, 160–61

Jameson, Fredric, 14, 15
Jann, Rosemary, 8
Jaspers, Karl, 122
Jesus Christ. *See* Christ, Jesus; Sacred Heart of Jesus
Jesús Negrete, José de. *See* Negrete, José de Jesús
Juárez, Benito, 59, 63
judge, 171; jury trial role of, 52n25, 139, 150n55; in Moreno case, 131, 145n8
judgments, murder and differing, 9
jury trial(s): judges' role in, 52n25, 139, 150n55, 213n68; in de Landa case, 215, 216, 217, 218, 222, 226, 229, 230, 231–38, 239, 246n67, 246n76; in Mexican justice system, 138–39, 142, 143, 150n50, 150n55, 152n75, 152n78; in Moreno case, 129, 130, 131, 132, 134, 135, 136, 137–39, 140–41, 142, 143, 145n6, 145n8, 146n18, 146nn16–17, 148nn41–42, 150n50, 150n55, 151n66; of Negrete, 76, 77, 78, 79, 80–83, 93, 102n70; in parallel lives of Toral and Siqueiros, 180, 184, 185, 203, 206; public and, 139, 143; of Siqueiros, 187; of Tarasquillo Street murder, 29, 30–32, 52n24, 53n36; of Toral, 200, 204, 213n60, 213n68. *See also* trial
justice: and Moreno case, 133, 143. *See also* criminal justice system; Mexican justice system

kidnappings, 3, 4, 22n9. *See also* González kidnapping/murder
knowledge, 112; criminal, 2, 3, 10

de Landa (María Teresa) case: acquittal/exoneration of, 215, 217, 237, 238, 239; appearance of, 233–34; attorney Lozano in, 215, 217, 218, 229, 231–33, 234, 235, 236–37, 246n76; beauty contests and, 215, 216, 217–18, 230, 236, 238–39; bigamy in, 215, 216, 225–26, 227, 228, 233, 247n91; as case of the murdering beauty, 215, 240; Catholic Church and, 226; cause célèbre of, 19, 215–16, 218, 229–30; class in, 216, 218, 234, 236, 238; culture in, 218, 233–34, 240; deconstruction of, 216; domesticity in, 19, 217; ethnicity/race in, 19, 216, 217, 218, 234, 235, 238, 240; femininity in, 19, 215, 217, 218, 235, 237, 240; feminism in, 237, 238, 240; gender in, 19, 216, 217, 236, 237–38, 239, 240, 247n92; honor in, 217, 218, 229, 231, 232, 233, 235, 236, 238, 239; identity in, 217, 218; jury trial in, 215, 216, 217, 218, 222, 226, 229, 230, 231–38, 239, 246n67, 246n76; media in, 19; memoirs in, 230, 246n67; Mexican justice system in, 216, 230; Miss Mexico 1928 in, 215, 216, 217–18, 230, 235, 236, 237; modernity and, 218, 237, 238; narratives in, 215, 216, 217, 218, 229, 238, 246n76; national identity in, 218; newspapers in, 215, 217, 226, 228, 229–30, 231–32, 236, 239, 246n76; politics in, 19, 216, 217, 237–38, 240, 241n2; postrevolutionary Mexico in, 19, 216, 217, 233, 237–38, 240, 241n2; public in, 215–16, 217, 222, 229–30, 231, 233, 236–37, 246n67; Sonoran Dynasty and, 216, 217, 241n2; Vidal Corro murder in, 144n3, 215–16, 217, 218, 227, 228–29, 230, 231, 232, 233, 234, 235–36, 237, 238, 239, 240; violence in, 19, 233, 235, 236, 240; women and, 222, 232–33, 234–35, 236, 237–38, 239–40, 247nn91–92

INDEX   269

de Landa, Dolores de los Ríos, 219, 226, 242n13
de Landa, María Teresa, 19; beauty contests and, 215, 216, 217–18, 220, 221, 222–25; early life of, 218–24; education and, 219, 220, 221, 222, 225; family of, 219, 222, 225, 226, 229, 242n13, 245n49; feminism and, 222, 223, 224, 226; gender and, 220, 223, 224, 225; Miss Mexico 1928 and, 215, 216, 217, 218, 220, 221, 222–25, 227, 230, 246n67; *Miss Mexico Memoirs* of, 230, 246n67; newspapers and, 222, 223, 224, 225, 227; politics and, 218–19, 220, 222–23, 224, 225; postrevolutionary Mexico and, 218–19, 220, 222–23, 224, 225; Vidal Corro and, 225–29; women and, 218–19, 220, 221, 222–23, 224, 242n12, 243n15. *See also* de Landa case
de Landa y Tamayo, Rafael, 219, 226, 242n13, 245n49
Landes, Joan B., 144n4
landowners, 159–60, 161
land reform: Catholic Church and, 161; opposition to, 161, 169; parcels (*ejidos*), 154, 161; in postrevolutionary Mexico, 159, 162, 163, 169; in postrevolutionary Michoacán, 161, 162, 163, 169
A Landscape of Events (Virilio), 106
languages, crime documentation and scientific/legal, 20–21
Lemcumberri Penitentiary, 76, 103n97, 183
León, María Toral de, 193
Leo XIII, Pope, 190
Lewis, Oscar, 11
literature, and criminal crime stories, 11, 24n37
Lives of the Greeks and Romans (Plutarch), 211n8
La llaga (Gamboa), 11
Llano, Rodrigo del, 221
Lombroso, Cesare, 72
López Mateos, Adolfo, 184, 187, 212n31, 251
López Muñoz, Simón, 107, 115, 116
López Portillo, José Espinosa y, 248, 249, 261
Lozano, José María, 76, 215, 217, 218, 229, 231–33, 234, 235, 236–37, 246n76
lynchings, 6

Madero, Francisco I., 85, 132, 231
Manilla, Manuel, 60
Marists, 193, 194, 196
Martínez, Eufemio, 81
Martínez, Rodolfo, 225, 245n44
masculinity: Moreno case and, 129, 133, 134, 137, 143; Porfirian, 45, 46, 48–49; in Romero Padilla case, 251

mass media: crime narratives and, 3–4; criminal causes célèbre and, 7–8, 12; criminal knowledge and, 3; fear and, 3; kidnappings and, 4; in de Landa case, 19; Moreno case and, 129, 133. *See also* media
master narratives: global, 14, 15; implications for crime stories, 14
Mata, Filomeno, 59
maternity: in postrevolutionary Mexico, 248–49, 250, 251–52, 253, 254, 255–56, 258, 260–61; in Romero Padilla case, 248–49, 250, 251–52, 253, 254, 256, 257, 260. *See also* motherhood
Maximato, 115
Maza, Sarah, 216
media: crime narratives and public's shared identity, 8; crime stories and, 20. *See also* mass media
Mellado, Guillermo, 85, 89, 104n100
melodrama: public narratives and, 34; Tarasquillo Street murder as, 34, 35, 36, 37, 54n44
memory: indeterminacy of history and, 171–74; in parallel lives of Toral and Siqueiros, 187–88
Mexican army: crime and, 65; Negrete in, 64–65; Siqueiros in revolutionary, 182, 186
Mexican Congress, in postrevolutionary Mexico, 139, 150n54
Mexican history: biography in, 182, 211n7; crime stories impact on, 14
Mexican justice system: gender and, 32, 33; jury trial in, 138–39, 142, 143, 150n50, 150n55, 152n75, 152n78; in de Landa case, 216, 230
el mexicano, 11
Mexican prisons, 41–42, 55nn62–63; homosexuality in, 43, 55n65; Negrete in, 67–68, 76, 83–85, 86, 103n97, 104n100; in parallel lives of Toral and Siqueiros, 180, 181; sexuality in, 42, 43; Siqueiros in, 182–83, 184, 186, 198, *201*, 202, 211n12; Toral in, 192, 200
Mexican Revolution (1910), 137, 139–40, 161–62; bandits and, 97; García case and, 115; Negrete and, 63, 97–98; tragedy and, 122
Mexico: 1821 independence of, 160–61; Communist Party and, 182; crime narratives and society of, 4; crime stories and self-perceptions of, 4; criminal types of, 11; national traits of, 11; public debates about private life in, 129; race and political violence in, 129. *See also* Porfirio Díaz regime; postrevolutionary

Mexico; postrevolutionary Michoacán; Zamora, Michoacán

Mexico City: causes célèbres and, 25, 26; crime rate, 26, 51n5; development during Tarasquillo Street murder, 33–34; history and García case, 111; march against crime (June 27, 2004), 1–2, 5, 20; murder rate of, 26, 51n5; protests against crime, 1

Mexico City's General Insane Asylum. *See* General Insane Asylum

Mexico United Against Delinquency, 3

Meyer, Jean, 181

Michoacán, 18, 154. *See also* postrevolutionary Michoacán

Miranda, Dr., 108, 109

Miss Mexico 1928 (María Teresa de Landa), 215, 216, 217–18, 220, 221, 222–25, 227, 230, 235, 236, 237, 246n67

Miss Mexico Memoirs (María Teresa de Landa), 230, 246n67

modernity, 53n40; crime and, 26; crime stories and, 33, 53n39; and female criminality in Porfirio Díaz regime, 44; García story and, 120; García texts and Mexican, 112; gender of, 15–16, 26, 33, 53n39; irruption and women in Tarasquillo Street murder, 15; in de Landa case, 218, 237, 238; in Romero Padilla case, 249, 250; Tarasquillo Street murder and, 15–16, 26, 33–34, 53n39; tragedy and, 122

Moheno, Querido, 17, 128, 131, 132, 134, 135, 136–38, 139–40, 141, 142, 146n17, 149n43, 149n45, 151n66, 231

Molina, Marcelino, 67, 80, 81, 83

Monsiváis, Carlos, 231, 233

Mora, Fortino, 60

Morales, Simona, 62

Mora, Rafael, 168

Moreno, Ana Díaz, 129

Moreno (María del Pilar) case: acquittal in, 132, 143; age and, 133; attorneys in, 128, 131, 132, 134, 135, 136–38, 139–40, 141, 142, 146nn16–17, 149n43, 149n45, 151n66; basic story of, 129–30; cause célèbre of, 128, 142; correctional school in, 131, 133, 135–36, 148n37; crime of, 130; domesticity and, 17–18, 137–38, 142; emotion and, 143; femininity and, 129, 134, 135, 142, 143; gender and, 17–18, 129, 133, 134, 135, 136, 137, 140, 142, 143; honor and, 129, 130, 136, 140–41, 142, 143, 152n70; judge in, 131, 145n8; jury trial in, 129, 130, 131, 132, 134, 135, 136, 137–39, 140–41, 142, 143, 145n6, 145n8, 146n18, 146nn16–17, 148nn41–42, 150n50, 150n55, 151n66; justice and, 133, 143; masculinity and, 129, 133, 134, 137, 143; mass media and, 129, 133; multiple actors in, 130; narratives of, 128, 133, 134; politics of, 129, 131, 132–33, 134–35, 136, 137, 138–39, 141, 142, 143, 145n10, 146nn11–14, 146nn16–17, 147n31, 150n50, 151n66, 152n70; postrevolutionary Mexico and, 129, 133, 137, 138, 140, 141, 142, 143; privacy and, 133, 134; public and, 129, 130, 132, 133, 134, 135, 136, 137, 138, 140, 141–42, 144n3, 146n18, 146n20, 147n21, 148n37, 148n42; public sphere and, 129, 136, 144n3; racism and, 140; society and, 17–18, 143; themes of, 128, 143; violence and, 129, 134, 135, 136, 140, 142, 143, 151n66; women and, 129, 133–34, 137, 140, 142, 143, 151n66; women's public roles and, 129, 143

Moreno, Jesús: murder of, 128, 129, 131, 134, 136, 141; politics and, 131, 132, 134–35, 141, 145n10, 146nn13–14, 147n31

Moreno, María del Pilar, 17, 128; family life of, 134, 135, 147nn29–30. *See also* Moreno (María del Pilar) case

Moreno Salido, José, 131

Morera, María Elena, 1, 3

motherhood: in Romero Padilla case, 19–20, 248–49, 251–52, 253, 255, 257, 261. *See also* maternity

Múgica, Francisco J., 18, 155, 156, 161, 163, 164, 169, 173

murder, 4; differing judgments about, 9; radicalism and, 157; rate of Mexico City, 26, 51n5; Toral/Siqueiros parallel lives and political, 179–80

narrative(s), 27; Bruner on, 27, 33, 37, 38, 49–50; capitalism and, 121; concept of agency and alternative forms of, 121; construals of Porfirian reality and Tarasquillo Street murder, 27, 50; criminology as ideological, 37–44; cultural function of, 33; deconstruction/critique of García case, 16–17; García case and, 16–17, 115, 121; insane asylum illness, 122; interpretation, 50; in de Landa case, 215, 216, 217, 218, 229, 238, 246n76; life and death in, 121; Moreno case and, 128, 133, 134; in parallel lives of Toral and Siqueiros, 181, 182, 208; prison, 181; psychoanalysis of, 27, 50; psychohistory, 49; public debates and, 20; in Romero Padilla case, 20, 248, 250, 261; Toral/Siqueiros parallel lives and biographical, 182, 184; violence and, 120. *See also* crime narratives; historically grounded narratives; master narratives; public narratives

INDEX   271

narrative reality, 49–50; generic particularity and, 37
Negrete, José de Jesús, 16, 57, *61*, *73*, *74*; broadsheets and, 62, 65–66, 68–70, 72, 75, 86, 88–89, 94; captures of, 67, 71; crimes of, 65–75, 79–83, 92–93; criminal band of, 60, 62, 65, 67, 68; criminal career beginnings of, 65; criminality explanations for, 72, 75; after death, 95–96; early years of, 63–65; execution of, 85–86, *87*, 88–89, *90*, *91*, 92, 94; films about, 95, 96, 97; illiteracy of, 64, 75; jury trial of, 76, *77*, 78, *79*, 80–83, 93, 102*n*70; mainstream press and, 57, 58, 59, 62, 63, 64, 65, 67, 68, 71, 72, 75, 76, 77–78, 80–81, 83, 85, 86, 89, 92, 93–94, 97–98, 101n57, 104n105; in Mexican army, 64–65; Mexican prison breaks of, 67–68; in Mexican prisons, 67–68, 76, 83–85, 86, 103n97, 104n100; Mexican revolution and, 63, 97–98; multiple histories of, 58, 60, 63, 68; myth of, 60, 62, 63, 72, 93–94, 95–98; as popular hero, 93–98; Porfirio Díaz regime and, 66, 85, 89, 93, 97; Posada and, 60, 61, 66, 72, 73, 89; public narratives and, 16; repentance of, 83–85, 86, 88–89, 92; research sources for, 58–60; social justice and, 63, 76, 92–93, 95, 96–98; as The Tiger of Santa Julia, 57, 60, 67, 71, 93, 97, 231; women and, 58, 62, 71–72, 81, 93, 95–96
Neruda, Pablo, 183
newspapers, 58; in de Landa case, 215, 217, 226, 228, 229–30, 231–32, 236, 239, 246n76; de Landa, María Teresa, and, 222, 223, 224, 225, 227; of Porfirio Díaz regime, 59; in postrevolutionary Mexico, 220–21. *See also* Catholic press; *Excélsior*; press

objectivity, and crime stories, 9
Obrador, Manuel López, 1
Obregón, Álvaro, 18, 19, 115, 131, 132, 139, 146n12, 150n54, 152n78, 158, 161, 164, 167, 241n2
Obregón assassination: by Toral, 18–19, 179, 180, 181, 185, 186, 189, 190, 198, 199–200, 204, 212n41, 213n68. *See also* parallel lives of Toral and Siqueiros; Toral, José de León
Oca, Francisco Montes de, 59
Ocampo, Telésforo A., 76, 131
Olea, Jorge Carillo, 4, 22n10
Ortigoza, Salvador, 25, 28, 29, 30, 41
Ortiz Rubio, Pascual, 179, 185
Over Her Dead Body (Bronfen), 49

el pachuco (Americanized tough guy), 11
El País, 59, 63, 64, 67, 68, 71, 72, 75, 76–77, 78, 80–81, 83, 85, 86, 89, 92, 94, 104n105
parallel lives, 182, 211n8
parallel lives of Toral and Siqueiros, 18–19, 179; art in, 180, 181, 182, 188, 195, *200*, *201*, 202–3, 206, 208, 209, 210; assassinations in, 179, 180, 181, 184, 209; biographical narratives in, 182, 184; Christ in, 208, 209; convictions in, 180; crimes in, 179, 180, 181, 185, 187; criminal justice system in, 180; differences in, 180, 203; education in, 179, 180, 195, 202–3; execution in, 179, 184, 196, 208; explanations in, 181; fame in, 184; homosexuality in, 193–94, 196; individualism in, 181, 208; jury trials in, 180, 184, 185, 203, 206; memory in, 187–88; Mexican prisons in, 180, 181, 206, 209, 210; mysticism in, 181, 182; narratives in, 181, 182, 208; paintings/drawings in, 180, 182, 195, *200*, *201*, 202–3, 206, 208–9, 210; personal responsibility in, 180; photography in, 195–96; political murders in, 179–80; politics in, 180, 185, 206, 208, 209, 210; prison narratives in, 181; public histories in, 187–88; punishment in, 180, 202, 210; sports in, 179, 180, 196; torture in, *200*, *201*, 202, 203, 208, 209, 210; truth in, 187, 208, 210; violence in, 180, 206; visual images/works in, 180, 181, 182, 188, 195, *200*, *201*, 202–3, 206, 208, 209, 210; zealousness of, 180. *See also* Siqueiros, David Alfaro; Toral, José de León
Parodi, Isidro, 9
Partido Comunista Mexicano (PCM), 179, 186
paternity, in Romero Padilla case, 249, 250, 251, 252, 253, 257
Paz, Octavio, 11
PCM. *See* Partido Comunista Mexicano
peasants/field workers (campesinos), 63
el pelado (lowly urban rascal), 11
penal code, 32, 83; defending honor and, 29, 52n18
penal signs and symbols, 7
Peña, Tranquilino, 60
pensadores (thinkers), 11
perceptions about crime, 8, 13; crime stories and, 4; and punishment in society, 7
Pérez, José María, 168
Pérez, Patriarch, 190, 212n41
physiognomic traits, and criminal tendency indicators, 10, 75
La piel y la entraña (*Skin and Guts*) (Scherer García), 182, 187
Plancarte, Luis, 156, 166–67, 168, 169
Plutarch, 211n8
Poetics (Aristotle), 121–22, 126n33

police: common sense and case studies, 10; corruption, 2, 4; magazines, 58, 59, 71, 76
The Political Unconscious: Narrative as a Socially Symbolic Act (Jameson), 14, 15
politics: academic criminal knowledge and demands of, 10; Catholic press and, 165; crime narratives and Mexican, 4; crime/punishment and, 2; González kidnapping/murder case and, 18, 154, 155–58, 159, 161–62, 166, 168–71, 172–74, 177n46; in de Landa case, 19, 216, 217, 237–38, 240, 241n2; de Landa, María Teresa, and, 218–19, 220, 222–23, 224, 225; Moreno (María del Pilar) case and, 129, 131, 132–33, 134–35, 136, 137, 138–39, 141, 142, 143, 145n10, 146nn11–14, 146nn16–17, 147n31, 150n50, 151n66, 152n70; Moreno, Jesús, and, 131, 132, 134–35, 141, 145n10, 146nn13–14, 147n31; in parallel lives of Toral and Siqueiros, 180, 185, 206, 208, 209, 210; publics and, 12–13; in Romero Padilla case, 19–20, 249–50, 253; Siqueiros and, 179, 180, 181, 183, 186, 206, *207*; of Sonoran Dynasty, 240, 241n2; Tejeda Llorca and, 131, 132, 138, 139, 141, 145n10, 146nn11–12; Toral and, 213n68; of Zamora, Michoacán, 154, 155, 156, 157, 158, 159, 160, 161–62, 163–65, 166–71, 172–74, 177n46. *See also* radicalism
Pollock, Griselda, 188
El Popular, 59, 64, 80, 93–94
Porfirian masculinity, 45, 46, 48–49
Porfirian reality, Tarasquillo Street murder and narrative construals of, 27, 50
Porfiriato, 15, 58, 196
Porfirio Díaz, José de la Cruz, 25, 33, 58, 63, 137, 146n12, 161
Porfirio Díaz regime, 137, 161; downfall of, 111; modernity/female criminality and, 44; Negrete and, 66, 85, 89, 93, 97; newspapers of, 59
Posada, José Guadalupe, 11; Negrete and, 60, 61, 66, 72, 73, 89; Tarasquillo Street murder and, 26, 29, 34–37, 54n44, 54n54
postrevolutionary Mexico: beauty contests and, 221–22, 223–25, 238–39; birth control in, 250, 257–59, 260, 261, 263n24; Catholic Church and, 159–60, 161, 162, 163, 164–66, 174, 176n31, 241n2, 245n47; culture of, 233; domesticity in, 250; education in, 218, 222, 244n31; ethnicity/race in, 238–39; femininity and public sphere in, 128, 152n78; gender in, 218, 220, 240; de Landa, María Teresa, and, 19, 216, 217, 218–19, 220, 222–23, 224, 225, 233, 237–38, 240, 241n2; land reform in, 159, 162, 163, 169; maternity in, 248–49, 250, 251–52, 253, 254, 255–56, 258, 260–61; Mexican Congress in, 139, 150n54; Moreno case and, 129, 133, 137, 138, 140, 141, 142, 143; newspapers in, 220–21; pronatalist policy of, 250, 254, 260, 261n3; public health in, 20, 252, 253–59, 260, 262n11; Romero Padilla case and, 19–20, 249–50, 253, 254–55; Sonoran Dynasty in, 240, 241n2; women in, 218, 219, 220, 221, 222, 223–25, 238, 239, 240, 242n12, 243n15, 244n31, 247n94, 250, 253–59, 260–61. *See also* Cristero rebellion; postrevolutionary Michoacán
postrevolutionary Michoacán: Catholic Church and, 159–60, 161, 162, 163, 164–66, 174, 176n31; Catholic nationalism and, 159–63; González kidnapping/murder case and, 18, 154; land reform in, 161, 162, 163, 169
postrevolutionary radicalism. *See* radicalism
press: Negrete and mainstream, 57, 58, 59, 62, 63, 64, 65, 67, 68, 71, 72, 75, 76, 77–78, 80–81, 83, 85, 86, 89, 92, 93–94, 97–98, 101n57, 104n105. *See also* Catholic press; newspapers
prison: narratives, 181. *See also* Mexican prisons
privacy, and Moreno case, 133, 134
private security, 2
Pro, Humberto, 204, 209
prostitution, 28, 29, 32, 39–40, 54n52
protests, against crime, 1, 2
psychiatry, and General Insane Asylum, 113
psychoanalysis: of history, 26–27, 51n8; of narratives, 27, 50
psychohistory, 27, 49, 51n8
psychology, cultural, 27
public: debates, 20, 129; González kidnapping/murder case and, 156, 157, 158–59, 172, 173; jury trial and, 139, 143; in de Landa case, 215–16, 217, 222, 229–30, 231, 233, 236–37, 246n67; Moreno case and, 129, 130, 132, 133, 134, 135, 136, 137, 138, 140, 141–42, 144n3, 146n18, 146n20, 147n21, 148n37, 148n42
public health: in postrevolutionary Mexico, 20, 252, 253–59, 260, 262n11; in Romero Padilla case, 20, 252, 253–56, 256–58, 260, 262n11
public narratives: causes célèbres as, 27; crime stories and, 15; cultural hegemony and, 33; melodrama and, 34; of Negrete, 16; social change and, 37; of Tarasquillo Street murder, 27–37, 50, 52n17; and truth about Tarasquillo Street murder, 27–34, 52n17. *See also* crime narratives
publics, 12, 13, 24n40

INDEX 273

public sphere: famous courtroom cases and gender in development of, 128, 143n1; and femininity in postrevolutionary Mexico, 128, 143, 152n78; meaning of, 129, 144n4; Moreno case and, 129, 136, 144n3

punishment: crime/politics and, 2; crime prevention and retributive, 2; in parallel lives of Toral and Siqueiros, 180, 202, 210; in society and perceptions about crime, 7; Toral and, 204

Punishment and Modern Society (Garland), 6–7

Quinones, Sam, 6

racism, and Moreno case, 140
radicalism: Catholic Church and, 162–63, 165–66; Catholic nationalism *vs.*, 162–63; Catholic press *vs.*, 162, 165–66; González kidnapping/murder case and, 18, 156, 157, 158, 162, 172, 173; murder and, 157; and religious politicization in Zamora, Michoacán, 163–66
Ramírez, Jesús, 235
Ramos, Samuel, 11
rancheros (small family farmers), 159, 161
rebellion: Cristero, 18, 174, 180–81, 187, 189, 212n41, 216; Huerta, 139, 150n54, 171, 173, 231
rehabilitation, 2
religion: García, Marino, on, 119; in Zamora, Michoacán, 163–66
Rerum Novarum (Leo XIII), 190–91
research, historical, 112, 171
"The Revelations of Toral" (Toral), 192, *193*
revolution: modern social organization and Mexican cultural, 15; tragedy and, 122. *See also* Mexican Revolution (1910); postrevolutionary Mexico
revolutionaries. *See* radicalism
Reyes, Francisco, 131
Reyes, Ramón, 167, 169
Reyes, Ricardo, 107, 116
Reyes Spíndola, Rafael, 59
Rius Facius, Antonio, 187, 189, 196, 212*n*33
Rivière, Pierre, 9–10, 16. *See also* criminal crime stories
Rodríguez, Fidencio, 107
Rodríguez, Heraclio, 60, 65
Romero Padilla case, 26In1; birth control and, 250, 257–59, 260, 261; conviction of, 249, 253, 260; domesticity in, 20, 251; fathers in, 251; gender in, 249, 251, 252; infanticide in, 19, 20, 248, 249, 250, 251, 253, 257, 260, 261; masculinity and, 251; maternity in, 248–49, 250, 251–52, 253,
254, 256, 257, 260; modernity in, 249, 250; motherhood in, 19–20, 248–49, 251–52, 253, 255, 257, 261; narratives in, 20, 248, 250, 261; paternity in, 249, 250, 251, 252, 253, 257; politics in, 19–20, 249–50, 253; postrevolutionary Mexico in, 19–20, 249–50, 253, 254–55; public health in, 20, 252, 253–56, 256–58, 260, 262*n*11; science in, 19–20, 249, 250, 253, 254, 257; sexuality in, 20, 252, 253; social class in, 20, 249, 250, 251, 252, 253, 256–57, 261; trial in, 19, 20, 248–49, 250–51, 261; work in, 20

Romero Padilla, Soledad, 19–20, 248. *See also* Romero Padilla case
Roto, Chucho el, 96, 249
Roumagnac, Carlos, 10–11, 26, 32, 33, 50, 51n5; Villa criminological narrative by, 37, 38, 39–44, 54n49, 54n54, 55n63, 55n65, 55n68
Ruíz, Apolunio, 60
Ruiz Cortínes, Adolfo, 186
The Rules of Sociological Method (Durkheim), 5

Sacred Heart of Jesus, 190–92, 197; drawing of Toral, *197*, 198, 208, 209
Salazar, Abel C., 131
Salazar, Dr., 108
Salem witch trials, 6
Sánchez, Arnulfo, 80, 81, 83
Sánchez Santos, Trinidad, 59
San Pedro, Justo, 76, 86
Santa (Gamboa), 11, 26, 56n71
Scherer García, Julio, 181, 182, 183–84, 187, 208, 210n5
science, in Romero Padilla case, 19–20, 249, 250, 253, 254, 257
scientific crime: analysis, 10, 12; stories, 8–9
Scott, Joan Wallach, 216
secuestros. *See* kidnappings
Segura Vilchis, Luis, 204, 209
sensationalism, and crime stories, 16
Serrano, Eva, 235
sexuality: criminality and, 48; deviance and, 40–41; in Mexican prisons, 42, 43; in Romero Padilla case, 20, 252, 253
Siqueiros, Blanca Luz Brum, 183
Siqueiros, David Alfaro: biography of, 182; Christ images of, 198, *199*; communism of, 179, 180, 181, 183, 186, 188, 209; *Confinamiento solitario* of, 204, *205*, 206; crimes of, 184, 185, 211n21; *Ecce Homo* of, 198–99, 209; family of, 183; interviews of, 181, 182, 183–84, 187; in Mexican prison, 182–83, 184, 186, 198, *201*, 202, 211n12; in Mexican revolutionary army, 182, 186; muralism of, 179, 180; paintings of, 179, 180, 182, 195, 198, *199*, *201*, 202,

204, 205, 206, 207; parallel lives of Toral and, 18–19, 179–210; pardon of, 212n31; photography of, 179; physique of, 179; politics and, 179, 180, 181, 183, 186, 206, 207; publications of, 184; Scherer García and, 181, 182, 183–84, 187, 208, 210n5; sports and, 194–95; torture and, 201, 202; trials of, 187; *Victima proletaria* of, 206, 207; violence and, 206. *See also* parallel lives of Toral and Siqueiros

social change, and public narratives, 37
social determinism, 72, 75
social dissolution, and crime rate increase, 5
social inequalities, and crime stories, 14, 15
social justice, and Negrete, 63, 76, 92–93, 95, 96–98
social realities, reflected in crime story cases, 14
social sciences, and criminology, 11
social typologies, criminal, 8–9
society: crime and, 5–8, 26; Moreno case and, 17–18, 143; perceptions about crime and punishment in, 7; perceptions and crime stories, 5
society's collective emotions about crime: criminal justice system and, 7; Durkheim crime theories and, 5
sociology, criminal, 75
Sodi, Demetrio, 185, 187, 203
Sonoran Dynasty: Catholic Church and, 226, 241n2, 245n47; in de Landa case, 216, 217, 241n2; politics of, 240, 241n2; in postrevolutionary Mexico, 240, 241n2; uprisings against, 216, 240; violence of, 216, 241n2
Soria, Pedro, 60
Spivak, Gayatri, 48
sports, and Catholic Church, 196
statistics, and crime rate data, 2–3
Stein, Gertrude, 112
storytellers, historians as, 110–11
Stylites, Simeon (saint), 192, 212n47
sufferers, 122

"talk of crime," 3
Tarasquillo Street murder: cause célèbres of, 25–26; criminological narrative of, 41; defending honor in, 29, 30, 31; gender and, 15–16, 26, 31, 32, 33; gender of modernity in, 15–16, 26, 33, 53n39; jury trial of, 29, 30–32, 52n24, 53n36; as melodrama, 34, 35, 36, 37, 54n44; Mexico City development during, 33–34; modernity and, 15–16, 26, 33–34, 53n39; narrative construals of Porfirian reality and, 27, 50; as Porfiriato causes célèbre, 15; Posada and, 26, 29, 34–37,

54n44, 54n54; public narrative and truth about, 27–34, 52n17; public narratives of, 27–37, 50, 52n17; women and modernity irruption in, 15
Tears and Sighs in Belén Jail (Posada), 35–36, 37, 54n44
Tejada, General, 16, 106, 114, 116
Tejada, Sebastián Lerdo de, 63
Tejeda, Adalberto (governor), 131, 132, 146n11
Tejeda Llorca, Francisco, 137, 140; murder of, 17, 128, 129–30, 131, 135, 136, 138, 141; politics and, 131, 132, 138, 139, 141, 145n10, 146n11–12. *See also* Moreno (María del Pilar) case
text(s): context and, 111–12; of General Insane Asylum, 106–10, 111, 113, 123n1, 124n10; historical, 111–12; "I" and, 112, 124n9; as illumination, 112. *See also* García (Marino) texts
textual analysis: class struggle and, 14; critique of, 14
"Theses on the Philosophy of History" (Benjamin), 111
The Tiger of Santa Julia. *See* Negrete, José de Jesús
Toral, José de León, 191, 195, 213n57; biography of, 187; Catholic Church and, 179, 180, 181, 188, 190, 191–92, 193–94, 196–97, 198, 212n46, 213n52; drawings of, 182, 187, 189, 190, 192, 193, 194, 196–97, 199, 200, 204, 212n33, 212n46, 213n52, 213n60; execution of, 184; jury trial of, 200, 204, 213n60, 213n68; in Mexican prison, 192, 200; mysticism and, 198; Obregón assassination by, 18–19, 179, 180, 181, 185, 186, 189, 190, 198, 199–200, 204, 212n41, 213n68; parallel lives of Siqueiros and, 18–19, 179–210; politics and, 213n68; punishment and, 204; "The Revelations of Toral" of, 192, 193; Sacred Heart of Jesus and, 190–92, 197, 208; Sacred Heart of Jesus drawing of, 197, 198, 208, 209; San Humberto Pro portrait of, 192–93, 194, 196–97, 213n52; sports and, 192–93, 194; torture of, 200, 204, 213n60, 213n68; trial of, 185, 187, 190, 192, 200, 204, 212n41, 213n60, 213n68. *See also* Obregón assassination; parallel lives of Toral and Siqueiros
Torres, Manuela, 81
Torres, Mariana, 62
torture: in lives of Toral and Siqueiros, 200, 201, 202, 203, 204, 208, 209, 210, 213n60, 213n68; visual representations and, 181
La tragedia de mi vida (María del Pilar Moreno), 134
tragedy, 121–22, 126n33

Treviño, Ramón, 132
trial: in Romero Padilla case, 19, 20, 248–49, 250–51, 261; of Toral, 185, 187, 190, 192, 200, 204, 212n41, 213n60, 213n68. *See also* jury trials
Trotsky, Leon, 19, 180, 184, 206
truth: academic art and, 210, 214n79; in parallel lives of Toral and Siqueiros, 187, 208, 210
typologies, criminal social, 8–9

El Universal, 134, 220
urban poor, marginalization of, 2
Usigli, Rodolfo, 188

Valverde Téllez, Emeterio, 191
Vanegas Arroyo, Antonio, 65–66, 71, 75, 86, 89, 92, 94
Vargas, Luis, 108, 109, 117
Vasconcelos, José, 241n2
Víctima proletaria (*Proletarian Victim*) (Siqueiros), 206, *207*
Vidal Corro, Moisés, 19, 245n44; de Landa, María Teresa, and, 225–29; de Landa murder of, 144n3, 215–16, 217, 218, 227, 228–29, 230, 231, 232, 233, 234, 235–36, 237, 238, 239, 240. *See also* de Landa case
Villalain, Julián, 86
Villa, María, 15, 25, 28–29, 30–32, *34*, 35, *36*, 48, 50, 52n17, 53n36; criminological narrative of, 37, *38*, 39–44, 54n49, 54n54, 55n63, 55n65, 55n68
violence: defending honor and, 29, 52nn20–22, 81–82, 141, 152n70; in García story, 120; in de Landa case, 19, 233, 235, 236, 240; Moreno case and, 129, 134, 135, 136, 140, 142, 143, 151n66; narrative and, 120; in parallel lives of Toral and Siqueiros, 180, 206; against protesters, 1; Siqueiros and, 206; of Sonoran Dynasty, 216, 241n2; women and, 134, 135, 140, 141, 142–43, 147n27, 151n66, 152n75, 239, 240, 247n94; women/honor and, 239, 240, 247n94
Virilio, Paul, 106
visual representations, and torture, 181

Warner, Michael, 13, 24n40
Williams, Raymond, 122
Wiltenburg, Joy, 8, 16
women: education and, 218, 219, 220, 221, 222, 244n31; honor/violence and, 239, 240, 247n94; as idols of perversity, 48; in de Landa case, 222, 232–33, 234–35, 236, 237–38, 239–40, 247nn91–92; de Landa, María Teresa, and, 218–19, 220, 221, 222–23, 224, 242n12, 243n15; and modernity irruption in Tarasquillo Street murder, 15; Moreno case and, 129, 133–34, 137, 140, 142, 143, 151n66; Negrete and, 58, 62, 71–72, 81, 93, 95–96; in postrevolutionary Mexico, 218, 219, 220, 221, 222, 223–25, 238, 239, 240, 242n12, 243n15, 244n31, 247n94, 250, 253–59, 260–61; violence and, 134, 135, 140, 141, 142–43, 147n27, 151n66, 152n75, 239, 240, 247n94

Zamora, Manuel, 131
Zamora, Michoacán: Catholic Church and, 160, 161, 162, 163, 164–66, 172, 176n31; politics of, 154, 155, 156, 157, 158, 159, 160, 161–62, 163–65, 166–71, 172–74, 177n46; postrevolutionary radicalism/religious politicization in, 163–66
Zapata, Manuel, 130, 145n6
Zola, Émile, 45